Anonymous

Asiatic Researches

Or, transactions of the Society instituted in Bengal for inquiring into the history and antiquities, the arts, sciences and literature of Asia

Anonymous

Asiatic Researches
Or, transactions of the Society instituted in Bengal for inquiring into the history and antiquities, the arts, sciences and literature of Asia

ISBN/EAN: 9783744794367

Printed in Europe, USA, Canada, Australia, Japan

Cover: Foto ©ninafisch / pixelio.de

More available books at **www.hansebooks.com**

ASIATIC RESEARCHES;

OR,

TRANSACTIONS

OF THE

SOCIETY

INSTITUTED IN BENGAL,

FOR INQUIRING INTO THE

HISTORY AND ANTIQUITIES, THE ARTS,
SCIENCES, AND LITERATURE,

OF

ASIA.

VOLUME THE FIFTH.

Printed verbatim from the Calcutta Edition.

LONDON:

PRINTED FOR J. SEWELL; VERNOR AND HOOD; J. CUTHELL;
J. WALKER; R. LEA; LACKINGTON, ALLEN, AND CO.;
OTRIDGE AND SON; R. FAULDER; AND J. SCATCHERD.

·1799·

ADVERTISEMENT.

THE deferved eftimation in which the Tranfactions of the various Societies in Great Britain, as well as upon the Continent, have hitherto been held is a circumftance fo well known that nothing in this place need be faid upon the fubject; but the lucubrations of the Afiatic Society have not been fo widely diffufed. Nearly the whole of the impreffion of the Afiatic Refearches is diftributed in the Eaft Indies, therefore very few copies reach Europe; and this among other reafons, has given rife to the prefent publication. To fuffer fo many valuable Papers, on a vaft variety of Literary, Scientific, and Antiquarian Subjects, to lie buried on the fhelves of a few perfons would have been an unpardonable offence; but to refcue from a kind of oblivion, and to prefent to their Countrymen in Europe, a regular feries of the Papers communicated to the Afiatic Society, is the intention of the Undertakers of the prefent Work. This Society, it is well known, had the late excellent and learned Sir WILLIAM JONES for its Founder, and for its Prefident many years; but fince he has favoured the world with an account of its origin in the firft volume of the work, we fhall content ourfelves with referring our Readers to that difcourfe, wherein they will find an ample difplay of its utility, and a detail of its objects of purfuit.

ADVERTISEMENT.

In the diſſertation on the Religious Ceremonies of the Hindus, p. 361, of the preſent volume, the author cites a paſſage which appears to have reference to the creation of the univerſe, and which ſeems, upon the whole, to bear ſome reſemblance to the account given by Moſes in the Pentateuch. This naturally leads us to conſider the antiquity of both the Moſaic and Hindu Scriptures, and to compare, in ſome meaſure, the accounts given in each work relative to that important fact.

The writings of Moses have generally been conſidered as more ancient than thoſe of any other perſon; but the Hindu Scriptures, ſo far as the reſearches of ſeveral learned men have extended, appear to be of very high antiquity, and are even carried by ſome beyond the time of the Hebrew Lawgiver. Sir W. Jones, in his Preface to the "Inſtitutes of Hindu Law; or the Ordinances of Menu, according to the Gloſs of Cullu'ca," carries the higheſt age of the *Yajur véda* 1580 years before the birth of Christ, which is nine years previous to the birth of Moses, and ninety before Moses departed from Egypt with the Iſraelites. This date, of 1580 years before Christ, ſeems the more probable, becauſe the Hindu ſages are ſaid to have delivered their knowledge orally. Cullu'a Bhatta produced, what may be ſaid to be very truly, the ſhorteſt, yet the moſt luminous; the leaſt oſtentatious, yet the moſt learned; the deepeſt, yet the moſt agreeable, commentary on the Hindu Scriptures, that ever

was

was compofed on any author ancient or modern, European or Afiatic: and it is this work to which the learned generally apply, on account of its clearnefs. We fhall not, however, take up your time with a differtation on the exact age of either the Hebrew or the Hindu Scriptures: both are ancient: let the learned judge: but fome extracts from the Hindu and Hebrew accounts of the creation may ferve to fhew how much they agree together: whether the Hindu Bráhmens borrowed from MOSES, or MOSES from the Hindu Bráhmens, is not our prefent enquiry.

Extracts from the Laws of MENU.

Extracts from the Writings of MOSES.

THIS *univerfe* exifted only in *the firft divine idea yet unexpanded, as if involved* in darknefs, imperceptible, undefinable, undifcoverable *by reafon, and* undifcovered *by revelation,* as if it were wholly immerfed in fleep; (chap. i. 5.)

Then the *fole* felf-exifting power, himfelf undifcerned, but making this world difcernible, with five elements and other principles *of nature,* appeared with undiminifhed glory, *expanding his idea,* or difpelling the gloom. (ib. 6.)

He, whom the mind alone can perceive, whofe effence eludes the external organs, who has no vifible parts,

IN the beginning God created the heaven and the earth. (Gen. i. 1.)

ADVERTISEMENT.

In the differtation on the Religious Ceremonies of the Hindus, p. 361, of the prefent volume, the author cites a paffage which appears to have reference to the creation of the univerfe, and which feems, upon the whole, to bear fome refemblance to the account given by Mofes in the Pentateuch. This naturally leads us to confider the antiquity of both the Mofaic and Hindu Scriptures, and to compare, in fome meafure, the accounts given in each work relative to that important fact.

The writings of Moses have generally been confidered as more ancient than thofe of any other perfon; but the Hindu Scriptures, fo far as the refearches of feveral learned men have extended, appear to be of very high antiquity, and are even carried by fome beyond the time of the Hebrew Lawgiver. Sir W. Jones, in his Preface to the "Inftitutes of Hindu Law; or the Ordinances of Menu, according to the Glofs of Cullu'ca," carries the higheft age of the *Yajur véda* 1580 years before the birth of Christ, which is nine years previous to the birth of Moses, and ninety before Moses departed from Egypt with the Ifraelites. This date, of 1580 years before Christ, feems the more probable, becaufe the Hindu fages are faid to have delivered their knowledge orally. Cullu'a Bhatta produced, what may be faid to be very truly, the fhorteft, yet the moft luminous; the leaft oftentatious, yet the moft learned; the deepeft, yet the moft agreeable, commentary on the Hindu Scriptures, that ever

was

was compofed on any author ancient or modern, European or Afiatic: and it is this work to which the learned generally apply, on account of its clearnefs. We fhall not, however, take up your time with a diflertation on the exact age of either the Hebrew or the Hindu Scriptures: both are ancient: let the learned judge: but fome extracts from the Hindu and Hebrew accounts of the creation may ferve to fhew how much they agree together: whether the Hindu Bráhmens borrowed from MOSES, or MOSES from the Hindu Bráhmens, is not our prefent enquiry.

Extracts from the Laws of MENU.

Extracts from the Writings of MOSES.

THIS *univerfe* exifted only *in the firft divine idea yet unexpanded, as if involved* in darknefs, imperceptible, undefinable, undifcoverable *by reafon, and* undifcovered *by revelation,* as if it were wholly immerfed in fleep; (chap. i. 5.)

Then the *fole* felf-exifting power, himfelf undifcerned, but making this world difcernible, with five elements and other principles *of nature,* appeared with undiminifhed glory, *expanding his idea,* or difpelling the gloom. (ib. 6.)

He, whom the mind alone can perceive, whofe effence eludes the external organs, who has no vifible

IN the beginning God created the heaven and the earth. (Gen. i. 1.)

ADVERTISEMENT.

MENU.

parts, who exists from eternity, even HE, the soul of all beings, whom no being can comprehend, shone forth in person. (ib. 7.)

He, having willed to produce various beings from his own divine substance, first with a thought created the waters, &c. (ib. 8.)

The waters are called *nárá*, because they were the production of NARA, or *the spirit of God*; and, since they were his first *ayana*, or *place of motion*, he thence is named NA'RA'YANA, or *moving on the waters* (ib. 10.)

From THAT WHICH IS, the first cause, not the object of sense, existing *every where in substance*, not existing *to our perception*, without beginning or end, was produced the divine male. (ib. 11.)

—He framed the heaven *above* and the earth *beneath*: in the midst *he placed* the subtil ether, the eight regions, and the permanent receptacle of waters. (ib. 13.)

MOSES.

And the earth was without form, and void; and darkness was upon the face of the deep: and the Spirit of God moved upon the face of the waters. (ib. 2.)

And God said, Let us make man in our image. (ib. 26.)

And God said, Let there be a firmament in the midst of the waters; —and God called the firmament Heaven. (ib. 6, 8.)

—He

ADVERTISEMENT.

MENU.	MOSES.
—He framed all creatures. (ib. 16).	And God said, Let the waters bring forth abundantly the moving creature that hath life, and fowl that may fly above the earth in the open firmament of heaven. And God created great whales, and every living creature that moveth, which the waters brought forth abundantly after their kind, and every winged fowl after his kind. And God said, Let the earth bring forth the living creature after his kind, cattle and creeping thing, and beast of the earth after his kind. (ib. 20, 21, 24.)
—He too first assigned to all creatures distinct names, distinct acts, and distinct occupations. (ib. 21.)	God brought every beast of the field unto Adam to see what he would call them. And God put the man into the garden of Eden to dress it and to keep it. Abel was a keeper of sheep, but Cain was a tiller of the ground. (ib. ii. 19, 15. iv. 2.)
—He gave being to time and the divisions of time, to the stars also, and the planets, to rivers, oceans, and mountains, to level plains, and uneven vallies. (ib. 24.)	God said, let there be lights in the firmament of heaven, to divide the day from the night; and let them be for signs and for days, and for years.— And God made two great

To

Menu.	Moses.
To devotion, speech, &c. for he willed the exist- of all created things. (ib. 25.)	lights; the greater light to rule the day, and the lesser light to rule the night. (Gen. i. 14, 16. see also chap. ii. 10, 11, 13, 14. & aliis locis.)
For the sake of distinguishing actions, He made a total difference between right and wrong. (ib. 26.)	If thou doest well, shalt thou not be accepted? and if thou doest not well, sin lieth at the door. (ib. iv. 7. see also chap. ii. 16, 17.)
—Having divided his own substance, the mighty Power became half male, half female. (ib. 32.)	God created man in his own image; in the image of God created he him; male and female created he them. (ib. i. 27.)
He, whose powers are incomprehensible, having created . . . . . . this universe, was again absorbed in the Spirit, changing *the* time *of energy* for *the* time *of repose*. (ib. 56.)	Thus the heavens and the earth were finished, and all the host of them. And on the seventh day God ended his work;— and rested on the seventh day from all his work. (ib. ii. 1, 2.)

Thus the accounts of Moses and the Hindu Scriptures concerning the creation may be easily reconciled to each other. But it is not our intention to support the Hindu writings in preference to the Hebrew Pentateuch; all we desire is, that truth may be investigated, and that error may be exploded. There are many persons, no doubt in the East better acquainted with the antiquity of the

the Sanfcrit books than we are, and by our intercourfe with the Bráhmens and learned Pundits, much may be done towards a right difcovery of this important matter. The Hindus have, for many ages, looked upon their Scriptures as a revelation from the Supreme Being of his mind and will concerning the works of his creation. They bring forward the Deity declaring his own mind, and think they have an indubitable right to follow the precepts which his word, according to their ancient lawgivers, contains. Moses too, in his Pentateuch, tells us that the Almighty ordered him to promulgate his law among the people, and to fhew them the path in which they fhould walk. The Jews, and after them the Chriftians, have generally received Moses's account as valid, and have confequently followed its dictates with a religious zeal. Enthufialm among every defcription of people muft certainly be defpifed, but zeal in contending for the truth is highly commendable in whomfoever it fhall be found. Had the Hindu writings, divefted of their fabulous paffages, been difleminated in the Weftern world with as much energy as the works of Moses have been fpread abroad, perhaps they would likewife have found many admirers and advocates.

Sir W. Jones, fpeaking of the Laws of Menu, fays, they contain abundance of curious matter extremely interefting both to fpeculative lawyers and antiquaries, with many beauties which need not be pointed out, and with many blemifhes which cannot be juftified or palliated. It is a fyftem of defpotifm and prieftcraft, both indeed limited by law, but artfully confpiring to give mutual

tual support, though with mutual checks; it is filled with strange conceits in metaphysics and natural philosophy, with idle superstition, and with a scheme of theology most obscurely figurative, and consequently liable to dangerous misconception; it abounds with minute and childish formalities, with ceremonies generally absurd and ridiculous; the punishments are partial and fanciful; for some crimes, dreadfully cruel, for other reprehensibly slight; and the very morals, though rigid enough on the whole, are in one or two instances (as in the case of light oaths and of pious perjury) unaccountably relaxed: nevertheless, a spirit of sublime devotion, of benevolence to mankind, and of amiable tenderness to all sentient creatures, pervades the whole work; the style of it has a certain austere majesty, that sounds like the language of legislation, and extorts a respectful awe; the sentiments of independence on all beings but God, and the harsh admonitions, even to kings, are truly noble; and the many panegyrics on the *Gáyatri* the *mother*, as it is called, of the *Véda*, prove the author to have *adored* (not the visible material *sun*, but) *that divine and incomparably greater light*, to use the words of the most venerable text in the Indian Scripture, *which illumines all, delights all, from which all proceed, to which all must return, and which can alone irradiate* (not our visual organs merely, but our souls and) *our intellects.*

The writings of MOSES too, are not totally exempt from passages which, to the mere reason of humanity, carry with them the appearance of fiction or of cruelty. Thus the formation of woman by throwing ADAM into a deep sleep, and taking
a rib

ADVERTISEMENT.

a rib from his side, has long been matter of ridicule for the sons of infidelity; as have many other parts of the Pentateuch. But whatever opinion may be entertained of MENU and his laws, it must be remembered that they are revered as the word of God by many millions of Hindus who compose several great nations, who are of vast importance to the political and commercial interests of Europe, whose well directed industry would add largely to the wealth of Great Britian, and who ask no greater compensation than protection for their persons and property, justice in their temporal concerns, indulgence to their old religion, and the benefit of those laws, which they hold sacred, and which alone they can understand.

I.

HISTORICAL REMARKS

ON THE

COAST OF MALABAR,

WITH

SOME DESCRIPTION OF THE MANNERS OF
ITS INHABITANTS.

By JONATHAN DUNCAN, Esquire.

SECTION.

I. IN the book called *Kerul Oodputte*, or, "The emerging of the Country of *Kerul*," (of which, during my stay at Calicut, in the year 1793, I made the best translation into English in my power, through the medium of a version first rendered into Persian, under my own inspection, from the Malabaric copy procured from one of the Rajahs of the *Zamorin's* family,) the origin of that coast is ascribed to the piety or penitence of *Pureseu Rama*, or *Puresram*, (one of the incarnations of VISHNU,) who, stung with remorse for the blood he had so profusely shed in overcoming the Rajahs of the *Khetry* tribe, applied to VARUNA, the God of the Ocean, to supply him with a tract of ground to bestow on the *Brâhmens*; and VARUNA having accordingly withdrawn his waters from the *Gowkern* (a hill in the vicinity of Mangalore) to Cape Comorin, this strip of territory has, from its situation, as lying along the foot of the *Sukhien* (by the Europeans called the *Ghaut*) range of mountains, acquired the name of *Mulyalum*, (i. e. Skirting at the Bottom of the Hills,) a term that may have been shortened into *Maleyam*, or *Maleam*; whence are also probably its common names of *Mulievar* and *Malabar*; all which *Purefram* is firmly believed, by its native Hindu inhabitants, to have parcelled out among different tribes of *Bráhmens*, and to have directed that the entire produce of the soil should be appropriated to their maintenance, and towards the edification of temples, and for the support of divine worship; whence it still continues to be distinguished in their writings by the term of *Kermbhoomy*, or, " The Land of Good Works " for the Expiation of Sin."

II. The country thus obtained from the sea*, is represented to have remained long in a marshy and scarcely habitable state; insomuch, that the first occupants, whom *Purefram* is said to have brought into it from the eastern, and even the northern, part of India, again abandoned it; being more especially scared by the multitude of serpents with which the mud and slime of this newly immerged tract is related to have then abounded; and to which numerous accidents are ascribed, until *Purefram* taught the inhabitants to propitiate these animals, by introducing the worship of them and of their images, which became from that period objects of adoration.

III. The country of *Mulyalum* was, according to the *Kerul Oodputtee*, afterwards divided into the four following Tookrees, or divisions:

1st. From Gowkern, already mentioned, to the Perumbura River, was called the *Tooroo*, or *Turu Rauje*.

2d. From

---

* In a manuscript account of Malabar that I have seen, and which is ascribed to a Bishop of Virapoli, (the seat of a famous Roman Catholic seminary near Cochin,) he observes, that, by the accounts of the learned natives of that coast, it is little more than 2300 years since the sea came up to the foot of the *Sukhien*, or Ghaut mountains; and that it once did so he thinks extremely probable from the nature of the soil, and the quantity of sand, oyster-shells, and other fragments, met with in making deep excavations.

2d. From the Perumbura to Poodumputtum was called the *Moſhek Rauje*.

3d. From Poodum, or Poodputtun, to the limits of Kunetui, was called the *Kerul* or *Keril Rauje*; and as the principal feat of the ancient government was fixed in this middle divifion of Malabar, its name prevailed over, and was in courfe of time underſtood in a general fenfe to comprehend the three others.

4th. From Kunety to Kunea Koomary, or Cape Comorin, was called the *Koop Rauje*; and thefe four grand divifions were parcelled out into a greater number of *Naadhs*, (pronounced *Naars*, and meaning diſtricts or countries,) and of *Khunds*, or fubdivifions, under the latter denomination.

IV. The proportion of the produce of their lands, that the *Bráhmens* are ſtated to have originally aſſigned for the fupport of government, amounted to only one fixth ſhare: but in the fame book of *Kerul Oodputtee* they are afterwards faid to have divided the country into three equal proportions; one of which was confecrated to fupply the expence attending religious worſhip, another for the fupport of government, and the third for their own maintenance.

V. However this may be, according to the book above quoted, the *Bráhmens* appear to have firſt fet up, and for fome time maintained, a fort of republican or ariſtocratical government, under two or three principal chiefs, elected to adminiſter the government, which was thus carried on (attended, however, with feveral intermediate modifications) till, on jealoufies arifing among themfelves, the great body of the *Bráhmen* landholders had recourfe to foreign aſſiſtance, which terminated, either by conqueſt or convention, in their receiving to rule over them a *Permal*, or chief governor, from the Prince of the neighbouring country

try of *Chaldeſh*, (a part of the Southern Carnatic,) and this ſucceſſion of Viceroys was regularly changed and relieved every twelve years; till at length one of thoſe officers, named *Sheo Ram*, or (according to the *Malabar* book) *Shermanoo Permaloo*, and by others called *Cheruma Perumal*, appears to have rendered himſelf ſo popular during his government, that, (as ſeems the moſt probable deduction from the obſcure accounts of this tranſaction in the copy obtained of the *Kerul Oodputtee*, compared with other authorities,) at the expiration of its term, he was enabled, by the encouragement of thoſe over whom his delegated ſway had extended, to confirm his own authority, and to ſet at defiance that of his late ſovereign, the Prince or King of *Chaldeſh*, who is known in their books by the name of Rajah *Kiſhen Rao*; and who having ſent an army into Malabar with a view to recover his authority, is ſtated to have been ſucceſsfully withſtood by *Shermanoo* and the Malabarians; an event which is ſuppoſed to have happened about 1000 years anterior to the preſent period; and is otherwiſe worthy of notice, as being the epoch from which all the Rajahs and chief *Nayrs*, and the other titled and principal lords and landholders of Malabar, date their anceſtors' acquiſition of ſovereignty and rule in that country; all which the greater part of their preſent repreſentatives do uniformly aſſert to have been derived from the grants thus made by *Shermanoo Permaloo*, who, becoming, after the defeat of *Kiſhen Rao's* army, either tired of his ſituation, or, from having (as is the vulgar belief) become a convert to Mahommedaniſm, and being thence deſirous to viſit Arabia, is reported to have made, before his departure, a general diviſion of Malabar among his dependents, the anceſtors of its preſent chieftains.

VI. The book entitled *Kerul Oodputtee* (which, however locally reſpected, is, at leaſt in the copy I procured of it, not a little confuſed and incoherent) mentions

mentions that, after this defeat of *Kishen Rao's* army, *Shunker*, a suppofed fon of *Mahadeo*, (the principal of the Hindu Gods,) regulated the cafts in Malabar, and reftricted the various fubdivifions of the four general tribes to their particular duties, down to the loweft orders of the fourth, confifting of the artificers, tillers of the foil, and inhabitants of the woods, whom he declared it unlawful for the other cafts to approach, infomuch, that the bare meeting with them on the road entailed pollution, for which the party of the fuperior caft is required to bathe.*

VII. It

---

* Of the feveral cafts in Malabar, and their diftinctions, I received the following fummary account from the Rajah of Cartinad. 1. *Namboory Bráhmens*. 2. *Nayrs*, each of various denominations. 3. *Teer*. 4. *Malere*. 5. *Polere*, called (he fays) *Ders* in Hindoftan. The *Teers* are cultivators of the ground, but freemen. The *Maleres* are muficians and conjurers, and alfo freemen. The *Poleres*, or *Poliars*, are bondfmen, attached to the foil in the lower part of Malabar, in like manner as are the *Puniers* above the Ghauts. The proper name of the Ghaut hills is, the Rajah adds, *Sukhien Purbut*, or hills of *Sukhien*, with the guttural *Kh* pronounced as ح

N. B. *Pouliats* and *Poulichis*, mentioned by RAYNAL, are only the one the male, and the other the female, of *Polere* aforefaid. The fyftem of obfervations in regard to diftance to be obferved by the feveral cafts in Malabar, are (according to the Rajah of Cartinad's explanation) as under fpecified.

1. A *Nayr* may approach, but muft not touch, a *Namboory Bráhmen*.
A *Teer* is to remain thirty-fix fteps off from one.
A *Malere* three or four fteps further.
A *Polere* ninety-fix fteps.

2. A *Teer* is to remain twelve fteps diftant from a *Nayr*.
A *Malere* three or four fteps further.
A *Polere* ninety-fix fteps.

3. A *Malere* may approach, but is not to touch, the *Teer*.

4. A *Polere* is not to come near even to a *Malere*, or any other caft but a *Mapilla*, the name given to the Mahommedans who are natives of Malabar. If a *Polere* wifhes to fpeak to a *Bráhmen*, or *Nayr*, or *Teer*, or *Malere*, he muft ftand at the above prefcribed diftance, and cry aloud to them.

If a *Polere* touch a *Bráhmen*, the latter muft make expiation by immediately bathing, and reading much of the divine books, and changing his *Bráhmenical* thread. If a *Polere* touch a *Nayr*, he is only to bathe; and fo of the other cafts.

VII. It is the received tradition among the Malabars, that *Shermanoo Permaloo* was, juſt at the completion of the diſtribution of the Malabar country, applied to for ſome proviſions by an *Erary*, or perſon of the cow-herd caſt; who, with his brother, had, during the preceding warfare, come from their native town of Poondra (on the banks of the Cavery, near Errode) to his aſſiſtance, and had proved the principal cauſe of his ſucceſs againſt Rajah *Kiſhen Rao's* army; upon which *Shermanoo*, having little or nothing elſe left, made a grant to him of the very narrow limits of his own place of abode at Calicut; and having further beſtowed on him his own ſword and ancle chainlet, and other inſignia of dignity, and preſented him with water and flowers, (which appears to have been uniformly the ancient ſymbol of donation and transfer of property in this part of India,) he authoriſed and inſtructed him to extend his own dominions by arms, over as much of the country as he ſhould find deſirable; a diſcretion which this adventurer (who is the anceſtor of the preſent *Samoory* or *Zamorin*) immediately began to act upon, and to endeavour to carry its object into execution, by the forcible acquiſition of the diſtricts adjoining to the preſent city of Calicut; and ever ſince his family appear to have, in the true ſpirit of their original grant, (which is the boaſt and glory of its preſent repreſentatives,) been either meditating new conqueſts, or endeavouring to maintain the acquiſitions they have thus atchieved by *Sheo Ram*, or *Shermanoo Permaloo's* ſword; which they aſſert to have ſtill preſerved as a precious relick, and to have converted into an object of domeſtic adoration, as the inſtrument of all the greatneſs of their houſe.

VIII. Anterior even to this epoch of the partition of Malabar, the *Neſtorians* had ſettled and planted *Chriſtianity* on this coaſt; and with thoſe of the Roman Catholic communion, that arrived ſeveral centuries after,

after, in consequence of *Vasco de Gama's* discovery, they continue to constitute to this day a considerable body of the lower orders of the present society in *Travancore* and *Cochin*; in which last district there live also the most considerable, or rather, perhaps, the only, colony of *Jews* in India.

IX. Of the events that took place from the partition till the above mentioned discovery of Malabar by the *Portuguese* in 1496, I am not possessed of adequate materials to afford any full or sufficiently satisfactory detail; but the principal may, as far as relates to its interior administration, be probably comprized in the wars carried on during this long period by the *Samoory* or *Zamorin* family for its aggrandizement; and in the consequent struggles kept up by the others, and especially the middle and southern principalities, to maintain their independence: for as to attacks from without, I have not been able to trace that they experienced any material ones during this long interval, or that the Prince of Chaldesh was ever able to re-establish his dominion over this southern part of the coast, within the limits assigned by the natives to Malabar Proper, or the tract by them denominated *Mulyalum*, or *Maleyam*.

X. During this period also the Mahommedan religion made great progress in Malabar, as well from the zeal of its more early proselytes in converting the natives, as in purchasing or procuring the children of the poorer classes, and bringing them up in that faith: and these Arabian traders, bringing annually sums of money to the Malabar coast, for the pepper and other spices that they carried from it for the supply of all the rest of the world, received every encouragement, and the fullest protection for their property and religion, from the successive *Samoories*, or *Zamorins*, whence they naturally grew into the habit of rendering that part of the coast the centre of their traffic and residence;

residence; and so rivetted had, through these long habits of intercourse, become the connexion between them and the *Samoory's* government, that the latter continued, after the arrival of the *Portuguese*, most pertinaciously to adhere to, and support, them against these new rivals in the gainful commerce which they had hitherto driven; a predilection that as naturally lead the Rajahs of *Cochin*, and of other petty states, that stood always in fear of the ambition and superior power of the *Samoories*, to afford to the *Portuguese* a kind reception in their ports; from which collisions of interests a very cruel warfare, by sea and land, was for many years carried on between the *Samoories*, or *Zamorins*, and their subjects, Hindus and Mahommedans, aided occasionally by the Egyptians and Turks, on the one part, and the *Portuguese*, with the *Cochin* and other Rajahs as their allies, on the other; of the various successes and reverses in which, the only *Asiatick* relation I have met with, is contained in a work, with which, during my stay in Malabar, I was obligingly favoured by my then colleague, Major (now Lieutenant-Colonel) Dow, who had traced and obtained it in the course of the extensive intercourse that, on terms the most amicable, and in views the most salutary and benign, he had long cultivated with the Mahommedan part of the Malabar community. This book, written in the Arabic language, is said to have been composed by ZEIRREDDIEN MUKHDOM, an Arab, Egyptian, or subject of the Turkish empire; who is thought to have been one of those dispatched to assist the Mahommedan Princes of India, and the *Zamorin*, against the Portuguese; and to have, during his stay in India, composed this historical account (which I have translated into *English*) of the warfare in which he bore a part, preceded by (what by many will be considered as the most interesting part of his work) a description of the manners and customs of the natives of *Malabar* at the period of his visit to it more than two centuries ago; relative to both which articles, I shall here insert some

of

of the information acquired by this Mahommedan author, whose relation terminates with the year 987 of the Hejira, answering to the year of our Lord 1579-80.

XI. This author begins with nearly the same account of the conversion of *Shermanco Permaloo* (whose real or proper name, or rather the epithet bestowed on his station, this Mussulman mentions to have been *Shukerwutty*, or *Chuckerwutty*) as has been already noticed from the *Kerul Oodputtee*, with this addition, that it was effected by a company of Dervises from Arabia, who, touching at Crungloor, or Cranganore, (then the seat of government in Malabar,) on their voyage to visit the *Footstep of Adam*,* on that mountain in *Ceylon* which mariners distinguish by the name of *Adam's Peak*; and these pilgrims imparting, on that occasion, to the *Permal*, or *Permaloo*, the then recent miracle of *Mahommed's* having *divided the Moon*, the Viceroy was so affected by this instance of supernatural power, and so captivated by the fervid representation of these enthusiasts, that he determined to abandon all for the sake of proceeding with them into Arabia, to have an opportunity of conversing with the Prophet, who was still alive, and had not even then fled from Mecca; for, after sojourning some time with the Prophet in Arabia,

Chuckerwutty

---

* This Footstep of Adam is, under the name of *Sreepud*, or the "Holy Foot," equally reverenced and resorted to by the *Hindus*, as appears by the relation of a journey made to visit it by a *Fakeer* of this last mentioned persuasion, called Praun Poory, now living at Benares, who has also travelled as far north as to *Moscow;* and has from memory (since he is disabled from writing, by being of the tribe of *Oordhbahu*, or whose arms and hands remain constantly in a fixed position above their heads) afforded me an opportunity of causing to be committed to writing, an interesting account of his various travels throughout India, as well as into other parts of *Asia;* and on the subject of these *Hindu Fakeers'* propensity to travelling. I may here add, that I saw a few months ago at Benares, one of them who had travelled as far as Pekin, which he described under the name of *Pechin;* and had passes from the Chinese government in his possession. He mentioned the name of a temple of Hindu adoration as being situated in *Pekin*.

Chuckerwutty (whom *Mahommed* had dignified with the title of *Sultaun Tauje ul Herid*, is mentioned in ZEIRREDDIEN's book to have died on his return, on the first day of the first year of the Hejira, answering to the 16th of July, of the year of our Lord 622, after, however, addressing recommendatory letters to the chiefs in Malabar in favour of sundry of his Mussulman brethren, who were thereby enabled to construct the first mosque or temple of their new faith in that country as early as the 21st year of the Hejira, or A. D. 642.

XII. But although ZEIRREDDIEN (the author I am now quoting) deemed it fit to allow a place in his work to the traditions that he found thus locally to obtain, he fairly avows his own disbelief in them; more especially as to what relates to the supposed conversion of *Shermanoo Permaloo*,* and his journey to visit the Prophet in Arabia; subjoining also his own opinion, that the Mussulman religion did not acquire any footing, either permanent or extensive, in *Malabar* till towards the latter end of the second century of the *Mahommedan* æra.

XIII. ZEIRREDDIEN next enters into some description of the existing manners of the Malabarians as he found them; after premising that the Malabar country was then divided into a number of more or less extensive independencies; in which there were chieftains, commanding from one to two and three hundred, and up to a thousand, and to five, ten, and thirty thousand; and even (which is perhaps an undue amplification) to a lack of men, and upwards; and describing that in some

of

---

* From this improbability, joined to the unlikely accounts delivered by the Hindus themselves, as to the departure of their chief governor, it may not perhaps be deemed too uncharitable, to suspect that *Shermanoo* disappeared like *Romulus* in a storm, as being, perhaps, found inconvenient to the new situation of independence that the Malabar Princes admit to have, on this occasion, either assumed, or been promoted to.

of thefe countries there were at the fame time two *Hakims*, or rulers; in others three, and in fome even more; having diftinct bodies of men attached to them refpectively; whence hatred and warfare were, he obferves, fometimes generated between them, which never, however, terminated in any entire feparation between the parties; and adding, that at that time the three greateft powers were the *Colaftrian* Rajah to the north, the *Samoory* or *Zamorin* in the centre; and farther fouth a Prince who ruled from the town of Kolum, or Coulim, to Cape Comorin, comprehending the ftates now held by the Rajah of Travancore.

XIV. The author next proceeds to an enumeration of what he confidered as the chief peculiarities in the manners of the Malabarians, from which I fhall literally tranfcribe, into the body of this narrative, the following particulars from the tranflation of ZEIRREDDIEN's original work; fubjoining in notes fuch particulars as my own enquiries, or other information, may tend to corroborate, define, or illuftrate, in refpect to fome of the circumftances he has related.

1ft. " If their ruler be flain in war, his army be-
" come quite defperate, and will fo violently attack
" and prefs upon their faid deceafed ruler's enemy, and
" upon the troops of the latter, and fo obftinately
" perfevere in forcing their way into his country, and
" to ruin it, that either they will completely in this
" way affect their revenge, or continue their efforts till
" none of them furvive; and therefore the killing of a
" ruler is greatly dreaded, and never commanded; and
" this is a very ancient cuftom of theirs, which in mo-
" dern times has, however, fallen with the majority
" into difuetude.

2d. " The rulers of Malabar are of two claffes or
" parties, one of which acts in fupport of the *Samoory*
Rajah,

"Rajah, whilst the other party acts in concert with
"the *Hakim* of *Cochin*; which is the general system,
"and only deviated from occasionally from particular
"causes; but as soon as these cease to operate, the
"party naturally returns again to the ancient usage.
"These leaders are never guilty of backwardness or
"failure in war, but will fix a day to fight on, and
"punctually adhere thereto; nor will they commit
"treachery in the conduct of it.

3d. "On the death of any principal or superior
"person among them, such as father, mother, and
"elder brother, in the cast of *Bráhmens*, (whilst among
"carpenters, and the lower casts, the superiors and
"principal persons are the mother and mother's
"brother, or one's own elder brother, as among the
"*Nayrs*,) when any one dies of the description of a
"superior, as above mentioned, his surviving relative
"is to remain apart for a twelvemonth; during which
"time he is not to cohabit with his wife, or to eat
"the flesh of animals, or to chew the beetle leaf, or
"cut the hair of his head, or his nails: Nor can any
"deviation be admitted from this practice, which is
"reckoned for the good of the defunct.

4th. "It is certain that among the body of *Nayrs*,
"and their relatives, the right of succession and in-
"heritance vests in the brother of the mother, or goes
"otherwise to the sister's son, or to some of the ma-
"ternal relations; for the son is not to obtain the
"property, country, or succession of the father; which
"custom hath for a long time prevailed; and I (the
"author) say, that among the *Moslems* of *Cannanore*
"they do not bequeath or give their heritage to their
"sons, which is also the rule with the inhabitants in
"that vicinity, notwithstanding that these said per-
"sons, who do thus exclude their sons, be well read
"in the *Koran*, and have imbibed its precepts, and
"are

"are men of study and piety.* However, among
"the *Bráhmens*, goldsmiths, carpenters, and iron-
"smiths, and *Teers*, or lower orders of husbandmen,
"and fishermen, &c. the son does succeed to the rights
"and property of the father; and marriage is prac-
"tised among these casts.

5th. "But the *Nayrs* practise not marriage, except
"as far as may be implied from their tying a thread
"round the neck of the woman at the first occasion;
"wherefore the acts and practical maxims of this sect
"are suited to their condition, and they look upon the
"existence or non-existence of the matrimonial con-
"tract as equally indifferent.

6th. "Among the *Bráhmens*, where there are more
"brothers than one, only their elder, or the oldest of
"all of them, will marry, provided he have had,
"or be likely to have, male issue; but these brothers
"who thus maintain celibacy, do nevertheless cohabit
"with *Nayr* women, without marriage, in the way
"of the *Nayrs*; and if, through such intercourse, a
"son should be born, they will not make such child
"their heir. But when it becomes known that the
"elder married brother (in a family of *Bráhmens*) will
"not have a son, then another of the brothers enters
"into the state of matrimony.

7th. "Among the *Nayrs* it is the custom for one
"*Nayr* woman to have attached to her two males,
"or four, or perhaps more;† and among these a
                                         "distribution

---

* I have, however, reason to believe, that this rule and custom is now wearing out among the *Mapillas*, or Malabar Mahommedans; continuing, however, to be still more particularly observed at Cannanore and Tellicherry: but, even in this last mentioned place, I was informed by KARIAT MOOSA, a principal merchant of this sect, that it is evaded by fathers dividing among their sons much of their property during their life-time.

† This description ought, I believe, to be understood of the *Nayrs* inhabiting the more southern parts of Malabar, from the Toorecherie, or Cotta river, to Cape Comorin; for to the northward of the said river the *Nayr* women are said to be prohibited
                                         from

"distribution of time is made so as to afford to each
"one night, in like manner as a similar distribution
"of time is made among the true believers of Malabar
"for cohabiting with their wives; and it but rarely
"happens that enmity and jealousy break out among
"them on this account.

8th. "The lower casts, such as carpenters, iron-
"smiths, and others, have fallen into the imitation of
"their superiors, the *Nayrs*, with this difference,
"however, that the joint concern in a female is,
"among these last, limited to the brethren and male
"relations by blood,* to the end that no alienation
"may take place in the course of the succession and the
"right of inheritance.

9th. "Among the *Nayrs* the whole body is kept
"uncovered, except a little about the middle. They
"make no difference in male or female attire; and
"among

from having more than one male connection at a time; for failure in which she is liable to chastisement; without, however, incurring loss of cast, unless the paramour be of a lower tribe than her own.

* "Alone in lewdness, riotous and free,
"No spousal rights withhold, and no degree;
"In unendear'd embraces free they blend,
"Yet but the husband's kindred may ascend
"The nuptial couch. Alas! too blest, they know
"Nor jealousy's suspense, nor burning woe;
"The bitter drops which oft from dear affection flow."
MICKLE's CAMOENS, Book vii.

This custom prevails among the five low casts of *Teer*; of *Agaree*, or carpenters; *Muzalie*, or brass-founders; *Tattam*, or goldsmiths; and *Kollen Perimcollen*, or blacksmiths; who live promiscuously with one or more women: and sometimes two, three, four, or more brothers cohabit with one woman. The child, or children, who are the offspring of this connection, inherit the property of the whole fraternity; and whenever the female of the house is engaged with either of the brethren, his knife is said to be hung up at the door of the apartment as a signal of its being occupied. It is, however, but justice to add, that this custom is said to be local, and practised only in a few of the southern districts; and even among these five casts there is no prohibition against any man's keeping for himself, either one or as many women as he can maintain.

" among their kings and lords, none of them think of
" shrouding their women from the sight of all man-
" kind; though among the *Bráhmens* this modesty
" and decorum are attended to.

10th. " Among the *Nayrs*, they dress out and
" adorn their women with jewels and fine apparel,
" and bring them out into large companies, to have
" them seen and admired by all the world.

11th. " Among the *Malabars*, priority in age
" stamps superiority and rule, were the difference only
" of a moment; and, notwithstanding that such party
" may be a fool, or blind, or aged, or otherwise, the
" rulership devolves to the sister's children; nor has
" it ever been heard that any one put to death his
" elder with a view of sooner attaining to dominion.*

12th. " In case the line of descent and succession
" become extinct among them, or be in danger of be-
" coming so, they do then bring an alien, (whether an
" adult or minor,) and him they constitute the inhe-
" ritor, as the substitute for a son, or for a brother, or for
" a sister's son; nor will any future difference be made
" between such adopted and a real heir; which custom
" is current and observed among all the infidels of
" Malabar, whether Rajahs or Shopkeepers, from the
" highest to the lowest; so that the line of descent
" becomes not extinct.†

13th.

---

* Thus in the *Zamorins*' families, and in that of the Rajahs of *Paulghaut*, there are from fifty to an hundred or more males of the same blood, i. e. descended from females of the Rajah's family, who are all entitled to, and do accordingly rise to. the chief rule, agreeably to their seniority in point of birth, without any other right or title of precedence.

† This is in general true: but there lately occurred an instance to the contrary, whereby the *Rauje* or Lordship of *Vittulnaad* has escheated to the Company. With respect to the provision occasionally made against such extinctions of families, it is very true that the Rajahs make it a practice, in case of any impending danger of this kind, to procure some males and females (though of the latter more than of the former) to keep up the regal line.

13th. "They have, moreover, subjected themselves
"to a multitude of inconveniencies, or difficult ob-
"servances, which they do, nevertheless, stedfastly ad-
"here to; as, for instance, they have arranged and
"limited the fitness of things as respectively appli-
"cable to the higher, middle, and lower ranks, in
"such manner, that if a person of the higher, and one
"of the lower, happen to meet, or rather to approach
"each other, the proper distance to be observed be-
"tween them is known and defined; and if this dis-
"tance be encroached upon, he of the higher cast must
"bathe; nor can he lawfully touch food before under-
"going this purification; or if he do, he falls from
"his dignity, to which he cannot be raised again; nor
"has he any other resource than to betake himself to
"flight, and, forsaking his abode, to proceed where
"his situation is unknown; and should he not thus
"flee, the ruler of the country is to apprehend him,
"and shall sell him to some mean person, should even
"the party incurring this disgrace be a child or a
"woman; or otherwise he may resort to the *Moslems*,
"and possess the *Islam*,* or else become a *Jogui*, or a
"*Fringy*, i. e. a *Christian*.

14th. "In like manner it is prohibited for those of
"a lower degree to dress food for a higher; and if any
"one partake of such a meal, he must fall from his rank.

15th. "Those who are entitled to wear the *Zunaar*,
"or *Bráhmenical* thread, are superior to, and more no-
"ble than, all the classes of the *Infidels* of Malabar;
"and

---

* This is one of the reasons assigned to me by a Rajah of the *Zamorin* family, for the number of *Mapilla Mussulmans* being now greater in the *Calicut* districts than the *Hindus* and *Nayrs*; namely, the nicety of their observances, and facility of losing cast; which drives the parties, from necessity, into the pale of *Islamism*. The same Rajah mentioned, on this occasion, the custom of the *Namboory Bráhmens*, who thus disposed of their own women, without incurring any disparagement of cast, to the *Mapillas*; which rule holds also good in respect to other females, as intimated in the second note page 13, and in the sequel of ZEIR-REDDIEN's text.

"and among these *Zunaar* wearers there are also the
higher, middle, and lower. Of the first are the
Bráhmens, who are above all others the most respectable; and these also have among themselves the
same distinctions of first, second, and third degrees.

16th. "The *Nayrs* of *Malabar* follow the martial
profession,* and exceed both in numbers and dignity,
having sundry degrees among themselves; and inferior to them in cast are the *Teers*, whose practice
it is to climb up the cocoa-nut trees, and to bring
down the fruit, and to extract the intoxicating juice
thereof, called *toddy*; and below these *Teers* are the
carpenters, smiths, goldsmiths, fishermen, &c. and
under these again, in respect of degree, are the *Poleres*, or *Poliars*, (i.e. ploughmen,) and those of other
base casts, engaged in the manual part of husbandry; and among whom also are other subordinate
degrees of distinction.†

* Poliar the labouring lower clans are named;
By the proud *Nayrs* the noble rank is claimed;
The toils of culture and of art they scorn:
The shining faulchion brandish'd in the right,
Their left arm wields the target in the fight.
CAMOËNS, Book vii.

These lines, and especially the two last, contain a good description of a *Nayr*, who walks along, holding up his naked sword
with the same kind of unconcern, as travellers in other countries
carry in their hands a cane or walking-staff. I have observed
others of them have it fastened to their back, the hilt being stuck
in their waistband, and the blade rising up, and glittering between the shoulders. It must not, however, be inferred, that all
the *Nayrs* betake themselves, at present, to the martial profession;
for, according to the information collected for me with much
care on the customs of that country by the late Lieutenant MAC
LEAN (who was *Malabar translator* to the commission of which I
was a member) there are supposed to be thirty distinct classes of
this general tribe; many of whom do now apply to the peaceable
arts of husbandry, penmanship and account, weaving, carpenter's work, pottery, oil making, and the like; though formerly
they are all said to have been liable to be called upon by their respective sovereigns to perform military service.

† For a farther account of these casts, see note page 5, and second note page 13.

17th. "If a stone light from a *Polere* on a woman of a superior rank on a particular night, which is marked out for this in the year, then that woman must be excluded from her rank; and although she shall not have seen the said man, nor been touched by him, yet still her lord shall make a conveyance of her by sale; or she shall become a *Moslem*, or a *Christian*, or a female *Jogui*; and this custom is general.*

18th. "In cases of fornication (or what is locally deemed the illicit intercourse between the sexes) if the parties differ much in degree, the higher loses his or her rank; nor has he or she any other resource than the one above-mentioned: yet, if a *Bráhmen* fornicate with a *Nayr* woman, he shall not thereby lose his cast; there being between those two old tribes that anciently established connection which hath been already noticed.

19th. "Such are the painful observances which they have entailed on themselves, through their own ignorance and want of knowledge, which God Almighty hath, however, in his mercy, rendered the means of encreasing the number of the faithful.†"

XV. Our *Mahommedan* author then proceeds to mention, that the towns built along the coast of *Malabar* owed their origin to, and were principally constructed

---

* I have allowed this paragraph of Zeirreddien's text to stand inserted in the order of his own enumeration, because it is connected with the one that follows; though the custom it refers to seems so unreasonable, that, as I never had occasion to hear it corroborated by the report of the natives, I cannot vouch for its being well founded.

† In the manner adverted to in the second note page 15. And here closes, for the present, the literal extract I have made from Zeirreddien's performance, which, for distinction sake, I have marked with inverted commas.

ſtructed by, the Mahommedan traders,* who, though not then amounting to a tithe of the general population, were much courted by the ſeveral Rajahs, and more eſpecially by the *Zamorin,* to frequent his port of Calicut, on account of the duty of ten per cent. that was levied on their trade.

XVI. The arrival of the fleets of the Portugueſe, the firſt under *Vaſco de Gama,* in the 904th year of the Higeree, (correſponding with the year of our Lord 1498,) and of that conducted by *Cabral,* a few years thereafter, with the negociations, jealouſies, and wars that enſued thereon, are next related by our author, in a manner eaſily enough reconcileable to the accounts of the ſame tranſactions already publiſhed throughout Europe. He aſcribes the Europeans reſorting to India, to their deſire to purchaſe pepper and ginger. Nor does he ſeek to conceal that, between them and the Mahommedan traders, a commercial jealouſy immediately ſprang up, which proved the cauſe of all the bitter wars that were afterwards carried on, by ſea and land, by the *Zamorins* and *Mahommedans* on the one part; and the Rajah of *Cochin* (to whoſe port the Portugueſe had ſailed, on their breach with the former Prince) and his *European* allies on the other; the former being afterwards reinforced from the Arabian Gulph by a large fleet fitted out under the command of *Ameer Hoſaine,* an officer in the ſervice of *Kaunis al Ghowry,* the then reigning Sultaun of Egypt; but theſe armaments failed of their object; and the *Ghowry* Prince was ſoon afterwards himſelf ſubdued by *Selim,* the Turkiſh Emperor: and of the treatment which the Mahommedan traders continued, in the mean time, to experience

---

* The principally current Malabar æra is ſtated in the account aſcribed to the Biſhop of Verapoli (as already quoted in the note page 2) to have been fixed from the building of the city of *Coulum,* (by us called Quiloan,) about twenty-four *cadums* (Malabar leagues) or eighty Britiſh miles, ſouth of Cochin. It was formerly very famous as the emporium of the coaſt, and founded in the 825th year of the Chriſtian æra.

experience from the *Portuguese,* the following description is literally taken from the translation of Nizameddien's Treatise.

1st. "The believers of Malabar were established
"in the most desirable and happy manner, by reason
"of the inconsiderable degree of oppression experienced
"from the rulers, who were acquainted with the an-
"cient customs, and were kind to, and protectors of,
"the Mussulmans; and the subjects lived satisfied and
"contented; but sinned so, that God turned from
"them, and did therefore command the Europeans of
"Portugal, who oppressed and distressed the Mahom-
"medan community by the commission of unlimited
"enormities, such as beating and deriding them;
"and sinking and stranding their ships; and spitting
"in their faces, and on their bodies; and prohibiting
"them from performing voyages, particularly that to
"*Mecca*; and plundering their property, and burning
"their countries and temples; and making prizes of
"their ships; and kicking and trampling on their (the
"believers) books, and throwing them into the flames.
"They also endeavoured to make converts to their
"own religion; and enjoined churches of their own
"faith to be consecrated; tempting people, for these
"objects, with offers of money: and they dressed out
"their own women in the finest ornaments and ap-
"parel, in order thereby to deceive and allure the wo-
"men of the believers. They did also put *Haji's*, and
"other Mussulmans, to a variety of cruel deaths; and
"they reviled and abused with unworthy epithets the
"Prophet of God; and confined the Mahommedans,
"and loaded them with heavy irons, carrying them
"about for sale, from shop to shop, as slaves; en-
"hancing their ill usage on these occasions, in order
"to extort the larger sum for their release. They con-
"fined them also in dark, noisome and hedious dun-
"geons; and used to beat them with slippers; tor-
"turing them also with fire; and selling some into,
"and retaining others, in their servitude as their
"slaves. On some they imposed the severest
"tasks,

" tafks, without admitting of the fmalleft relief or ex-
" emption. Others they tranfported into Guzerat,
" and into the Concan, and towards Arabia, being
" places which they themfelves ufed to frequent, in
" the view either of fettling or fojourning therein, or
" of capturing veffels. In this way they accumulated
" great wealth and property, making captives alfo of
" women of rank, whom they kept in their houfes till
" European iffue was procured from them. Thefe *Por-*
" *tuguefe* did in this manner alfo feize on many *Seyyuds*,
" learned and principal men, whom they retained in
" confinement till they put them to death; thus pre-
" judicing and diftreffing the Muffulmans in a thou-
" fand ways; fo as that I have not a tongue to tell or
" defcribe all the mifchiefs and mortifications attend-
" ant on fuch a fcene of evil.

2d. " After this they exerted their utmoft efforts
" (which they had, indeed, from firft to laft) to bring
" the Muffulmans within the pale of their religion;
" and they made at length peace with them for a con-
" fideration to be paid to them of ten in the hundred.

3d. " The Mahommedans refiding principally on
" the fea coafts, it was cuftomary for the newly arrived
" *Europeans* (who ufed to refort annually to India at
" the appointed feafons) deridingly to afk the perfons
" fettled of their nation at the fea-ports, whether, and
" why, they (thefe fettled *Portuguefe*) had not yet done
" away the appearance of thefe people the *Muffulmans?*
" reviling thereon their own chiefs for not abolifhing
" the Mahommedan religion; in the profecution of
" which view the heads of the Portuguefe defired the
" *Hakim* of *Cochin* to expel the *Muffulmans* from his
" city, promifing thereon to prove themfelves the
" means of his reaping double the profit which ac-
" crued to him from their traffick; but the *Hakim* of
" *Cochin* anfwered, ' Thefe are my fubjects from days
" of old; and it is they who have erected my city; fo
" that it is not poffible for me to expel them."

XVII. The war thus continued till the *Portuguese*, who had been originally permitted to conſtruct forts at Cochin and Cannanore, obliged the *Zamorin* to admit of their erecting one alſo at Calicut.

XVIII. They had alſo made themſelves maſters of Goa from the *Adel Sahi* dynaſty of the *Bejapoor* Kings in *Decan*; nor could any of the ſhips of the Mahommedans ſail in ſafety to either gulph, without being furniſhed with *Chriſtian paſſes*.

XIX. In the *Hejira* year 931, anſwering to A. D. 1524-5, the Mahommedans appear, by ZEIRREDDIEN's narrative, to have (countenanced, no doubt, and probably actively aſſiſted, by their friend the *Zamorin*) been engaged in a barbarous war, or attack, on the *Jews* of *Cranganore*, many of whom our author acknowledges their having put to death without mercy; burning and deſtroying, at the ſame time, their houſes and ſynagogues, from which devaſtation they returned, and enabled their great protector, the *Zamorin*, to expel, in the courſe of the following year, the *Portugueſe* from *Calicut*.

XX. But the latter ſhortly afterwards re-eſtabliſhed themſelves in the vicinity of that capital, and were even permitted to build a fort within a few miles of it, at a place called *Shaliaut*, of which they are related to have retained poſſeſſion for upwards of thirty years, and till, in or about the year 1571, they were, after a long ſiege, compelled to capitulate; whereupon the *Zamorin* is ſtated by NIZAMEDDIEN to have ſo completely demoliſhed their fortreſs, as not to leave one ſtone of it ſtanding on another.

XXI. The *Portugueſe* proved, however, more permanently ſucceſsful in an acquiſition they made in the province or (at that time) kingdom of *Guzerat*; where, according

according to my author, they, in the year 943, or A. D. 1536-7, obtained from *Behader Shah*, its monarch, (whom they are charged by ZEIRREDDIEN with having afterwards flain) the ceffion of the fortrefs of Diu, of which they ftill retain poffeffion.

XXII. The author, ZEIRREDDIEN, places within the following year the Portuguefe building a fort at Cranganore, and their fuccefsful refiftance at Diu, to an exepedition fitted out againft them from Egypt, by command of the Ottoman Emperor *Solyman*, whofe bafha, or commander, is reprefented to have retired in a difcreditable manner from the conteft.

XXIII. This author places fubfequent to the Hejira year 963, A. D. 1556, a difference that enfued between the Portuguefe and *Ali Rajah*,[*] the Mahommedan chief of Cannanore; and to whom belonged alfo the Laccadivian Iflands, which, on this occafion, ZEIRREDDIEN charges the Chriftians with having barbaroufly ravaged; and towards the clofe of his hiftorical detail, he inferts the following notice of the refult of the long and bloody competition between them and the Mahommedans for the trade of the eaft.

1ft. " It pleafing the Almighty to try the fidelity
" of his fervants, he gave fcope to the Portuguefe,
" and beftowed on them the maftery of a number of
" fea-ports; fuch as thofe in Malabar, and in Guze-
" rat, and in Concan, &c. and they became rulers in
" all the towns and cities, and fwarmed therein, and
" reared

---

[*] The head of this principality of Cannanore (of which a female, known by the name of the *Beeby*, is the prefent reprefentative) is alfo called *Ali Rajah*, which, in the Malabar tongue, may be interpreted " Lord of the Sea;" a diftinction affected (as I have heard) from this family's having long poffeffed the Laccadives, whence they have occafionally invaded the Maldives; the *Badfha*, or monarch, of which is faid to be to this day jealous of them on that account.

" reared fortreſſes in Hurmuz, (Ormus,) Saket, Diu
" Mehel, and in Sumatra, and at Malacca, and Mil-
" koop; and at Mylatoor, and Nagputtun, and Aju-
" ram, and in the ports of Shoulmundul, (Coroman-
" del,) with many alſo in thoſe of Ceylon. They na-
" vigated alſo as far as China; and their commerce
" extended throughout all theſe and other ports; and
" the Mahommedan merchants ſunk under their ſu-
" perior influence, and became obedient to them and
" their ſervants; having no longer any power to trade
" themſelves, unleſs in ſuch articles as the Portugueſe
" did not much like to deal in : nor requires it to be
" ſuggeſted, that their choice fell upon thoſe commo-
" dities that yielded the largeſt profit; all which they
" excluſively reſerved, without allowing any one elſe
" to trade therein."

XXIV. The traveller, CÆSAR FREDERICKE, having been on the Malabar coaſt about the time that ZEIRREDDIEN's hiſtory cloſes, it may tend to contraſt the preceding ſtate of facts according to our *Mahommedan* author's view of them, to ſubjoin his *Chriſtian* cotemporary's account of ſome of the ſame circumſtances.

XXV. Treating of Barcelore, a town on the northern part of the Malabar coaſt, FREDERICKE continues, (in the words of his old Engliſh tranſlator,)
" and from thence you ſhall go to a city called Cana-
" nore, which is a harquebuſh-ſhot diſtant from the
" chiefeſt city that the King of Cananore hath in his
" kingdom, being a King of the *Gentiles*; and he and
" his are very naughty and malicious people; always
" having delight to be in war with the *Portugals*; and
" when they are in peace, it is for their intereſt to let
" their merchandize paſs. From Cananore you go to
" Cranganore, which is another ſmall fort of the Por-
" tugals, in the land of the King of Cranganore,
" which is another King of the Gentiles, and a coun-
" try of ſmall importance, and of an hundred and
" twenty

" twenty miles, full of thieves, being under the King
" of Calicut, (the *Zamorin*,) a King alfo of the Gen-
" tiles, and a great enemy to the Portugals, with
" whom he is always in war; and he and his country
" are the neft and refting for ftranger thieves,
" and thofe be called *Moors of Carpofa*, becaufe they
" wear on their heads long red hats; and thieves part
" the fpoils that they take on the fea with the King of
" Calicut, for he giveth leave unto all that will go a
" roving, liberally to go; in fuch wife that all along
" that coaft there is fuch a number of thieves, that
" there is no failing in thofe feas, but with great fhips,
" and very well armed; or elfe they muft go in com-
" pany with the army of the Portugals."

XXVI. Upon the decline of the *Portuguefe* power, the *Dutch*, eftablifhing themfelves on the Malabar coaft, took from the former the fortreffes of Cannanore and Cochin: and about the fame period, or as early as 1664, the *Englifh Eaft India Company* appear, by the records at Tellicherry, to have begun to traffick in the *Zamorin's* dominions, in the fouthern diftricts of Malabar, as well as to have obtained, in 1708, in the northern parts of the fame coaft, a grant of the fort of Tellicherry, from the *Colaftry*, or *Cherical Rajah*, the limits of which they foon extended on the fouth fide, by the fuccefsful termination of a warfare, which they had in 1719 with the *Corngotto Nayr*, who alfo agreed that they fhould enjoy the exclufive trade of pepper duty free within his country; an acquifition which was followed, in 1722, by their obtaining a fimilar exclufive previlege (with a refervation in favour of the *Dutch* trade alone) throughout the more extenfive country of Cherical: and in 1725 they concluded a peace with the Rajah of the diftrict of Cartinad; by which they became entitled to the pre-emption of all the pepper and cardamums it produced; acquiring alfo fimilar exclufive privileges in Cottiote in 1759: and in this 'manner fo rapid appears to have been the extenfion of the power and influence of the Britifh

Nation

Nation on that part of the coaſt, that in 1727 the Company's ſervants at Tellicherry mediated a peace between the Kings of Canara and Colaſtria, under which circumſtances they added, in 1734-5, the iſland of Dermapatam, and the fort of Madacara, to their poſſeſſions, together with the entire laſt mentioned iſland in the year 1749, with power to adminiſter juſtice therein, on the ſame footing as at Tellicherry: and they appear, in ſhort, to have been from this period courted, reſpected, and feared, by all the Rajahs and Chiefs within the limits of the ancient Colaſtrian kingdom, with which their good intelligence ſuffered, however, a temporary interruption, in conſequence of the Company's Government having, in 1751, entered into a treaty with the Canareſe King of Bednore; whereby, for the conſideration of a factory at Onore, and a freedom of trade in his dominions, they agreed to aſſiſt him in the proſecution of that Prince's then meditated continuation of hoſtilities againſt the country of Colaſtria: but the former harmony was again eſtabliſhed in 1757, when a new treaty of mutual defence was concluded between the Company and the Rajah of Cherical; and ſuch appears to have been in general the progreſs of the Britiſh influence, that the *Engliſh Eaſt India Company* became every where entitled to ſuperior or excluſive advantages in purchaſing the valuable products of the country, viz. pepper, cardamums, and ſandal-wood; and at laſt obtained, in 1761, from the Rajah of Cherical, the further important privilege of collecting for their own behalf, the cuſtom-houſe duties and tolls within their own territories, for the moderate conſideration of a fixed quit-rent of 21,000 ſilver fanams, or 42,000 rupees per annum, to be paid to his government: in addition to all which, he and the other Rajahs had by this time ſucceſſively yielded up their right to all wrecks or ſtranding of the Company's veſſels or property; an article which, with the cuſtoms on merchandize, conſtituted two of the moſt inherent and acknowledged rights of the Malabar Princes at that period. XXVII.

XXVII. For otherwife thofe Rajahs' rights in general did not then extend to the exaction of any regular, fettled, or fixed revenue from their fubjects, the original conftitution of their government only entitling them to call on their vaffals, the *Bráhmen* and *Nayr* landholders, for military fervice: but, although this general exemption from any land-tax is ftated to have thus univerfally prevailed, in the early times of the Rajahs' governments, it is, however, allowed, that they were occafionally fubject to fome contribution for the extraordinary exigencies of defence againft the invafion of foreign enemies, fuch as the Canarefe and Portuguefe: and in Cherical, and alfo in the *Samoory's* dominions, the cuftom was at length introduced, or, perhaps, rather continued, from the earlieft period, (as intimated in Section VI.) of the Rajahs' levying from the lands (excepting, perhaps, thofe appertaining to the temples) a fettled revenue or income, in money or kind, equal to one fifth of the produce: and the Rajahs held alfo large domains of their own, which, with the cuftoms on trade, and mint duties, might have been fufficient for the maintenance of their ordinary ftate; more efpecially as, in addition to thefe rights, they, under the head of *Poorefhandrum*, exacted from the *Mapillas* (i. e. the defcendants of the Muffulmans *) a fhare of the eftates of all deceafed perfons;

* Of the term *Mahapilla*, or *Mapilla*, I have heard many derivations; one of which was given me by a *Cauzy* of their own tribe, who fcrupled not (whether jocularly, or otherwife, I cannot determine) to combine it of the two *Hindvee* words *Mah*, mother, and *Pilla*, a puppy; intimating, that it was a term of reproach fixed on them by the Hindoos, who certainly rate them below all their own creditable cafts, and put them on a footing with the *Chriftians* and *Jews*; to the former of whom (if not to both) they apply the fame name: and thus the Chriftians of St. Thomas are diftinguifhed by the name of the *Syrian Mapillas*: but I rather confide in the more reafonable derivation I obtained thro' Lieut. MAC LEAN's refearches, viz. that the term is indeed compounded of *Maha*, or *Mahai*, and *Pilla*, though not in the aforefaid *Cauzy's* offenfive fenfe, but as a denomination applied to the firft ftrangers who fettled in Malabar, by reafon of their being fuppofed to come from Mocha, which in Malabar is called

Mahai;

persons; whilst, under the donation of *Cheradayam*, they derived a considerable casual, though constant, revenue from the fines levied on crimes and offences; a well as from another article, called *Chungadum*, or protection money, received from the support and countenance granted by one Rajah to the subjects of another; and from the escheats of the estates of those of their Hindu subjects who died without heirs; and from *Talapanam*, (which was a kind of poll-tax;) and from the presents made by their subjects on the two annual festival days of ONAM and VISHOO; and other certain annual offerings; together with a few professional taxes paid by distillers, weavers, and fishermen, among the lower casts: besides all which, they claimed, as royalties, all gold ore*, and all elephants, and the teeth of that animal; and all game, together with cardamum and *Sagwan*, or teek trees, and bamboos, and honey, and wax, and the hides of tigers, and the fins of all sharks caught, (forming a considerable article of trade,) and the wreck (as above specified) of all vessels stranded on their coasts.

XXVIII. The Chiefs who (under the denomination of the Rajahs, with the exception of a few independent *Nayr* landholders) have thus, for so long a succession of centuries, governed Malabar, are mostly of the *Khetric*, or second tribe of Hindus; but the *Cherical* and *Samoory* (who were the two principal families in point of extent of dominions) are of the *Samunt* or *Erary*, (i. e. cowherd cast;) as is also the Rajah of Travancore, who is a branch of the original *Colastrian* or *Cherical* family: And the mode of succession that has time out of mind been established among these Princes (which I the rather add here, as ZEIRREDDIEN has not otherwise than by inference touched at all on this

part

Mahai; whilst *Pilla* is also another Malabar word for a child, or orphan; and from these two words the Mapillas are said to take their name of " Children or Natives, or (perhaps Outcasts) of Mahai, or Mocha."

* Gold dust is found in a hill called *Nellampoor Mella*, in the talook of *Ernaar* or *Ernaad*.

part of the general subject) is not, as in the rest of India, in favour of their own sons and children, but (as noticed by ZEIRREDDIEN in respect to the *Nayrs*) of their brethren in the female line, and of the sons of their sisters, who do not marry according to the usually received sense of that term in other parts of the world, but form connections of a longer or shorter duration, according to the choice of the parties, for the most part with Malabar *Bráhmens*, (called *Namboories*,*) and who differ essentially from others of that cast throughout the rest of India,) by whom are thus propagated the heirs to all the Malabar principalities, without, however, the reputed fathers having, or pretending to, any paternal claim to the children of these transitory engagements, who, divided under each Rajahship into distinct branches, called *Quilon*, or *Kolgum*, or *Kollum*, i. e. families or palaces, succeed (as has been already intimated) to the chief Rajahship, or supreme rule, by seniority; whilst the next senior, or heir-apparent, is stiled the first; and the others, or the heirs in expectancy, are (as for instance, in the *Samoory's* family) distinguished by the titles of the second, third, fourth, or fifth Rajahs; as far down as which they are called general Rajahs; and being deemed more especially to belong to the state, form a kind of permanent council to the *Zamorin*; whilst all those males of the family who are more than five removes from the senior, or

Zamorinship,

---

* *Namboory*, or *Namboodire*, is said by some (according to the explanation furnished to me by Lieutenant MAC LEAN) to be a corruption of *Nambie*, applicable to those whose privilege it is to attend to and perform the religious service in the temples; whilst others assert that the name is derived from *Nama*, and *Poogia*, or *Poogikanna*, to invoke, pray, or perform religious ceremonies. *Nambadie*, or *Nambidie*, a class of inferior *Bráhmens*, said to have become degraded from their ancestor, a *Namboorie*, having been employed by SHERMANOO PERMALOO, and the *Malabarians*, to cut off by treachery (which he effected) CHORA, a former *percimal*, or governor, whom KISSEN RAO had sent back with an army to supercede SHERMANOO, as intimated in Section VII. And besides these, there are above a dozen more subdivisions of the *Bráhmenical* tribe.

Zamorinship, continue to be distinguished as first, second, or third Rajah of such a Kolgum or palace, (meaning the house or branch of the family they were born in,) and rise thus, as it were, in their own corps, till, by reaching within four or five of the head, they become heirs general: and as from this mode of succession the chief Rajah is generally superannuated, either the heir-apparent, or one of the younger Rajahs, is often vested, under the title of Regent, with the active part of the administration.

XXIX. In this manner did the *Zamorins'* family, in particular, and the other Rajahs of *Malabar* in general, continue to carry on their government till the year 1766, when HYDER ALI KHAN made the descent on, and conquest of, their country;* of the manner and immediate consequences of which, as far as regards his own house, the following description was given to me by the present *Samoory* or *Zamorin*.

XXX. "In the Malabar year 941, A. D. 1765-6,
" HYDER ALI KHAN came with an army of fifty
" thousand men into *Mulyalum*, or *Mullewar*, (both
" terms meaning the Malabar country,) and waged war
" with my maternal uncle; and having defeated him,
" took possession of his dominion. My uncle sent a
" vakeel (or ambassador) to HYDER ALI KHAN, to
" request that his country might be restored to him,
" and agreed to pay any tribute which might be settled.
" *Hyder* gave a very favourable reception to the am-
" bassador, but informed him, that, as he could not
" place entire reliance on his word, he proposed
" himself to depute two persons, by name SREE
" NEWAUS RAO and MOOKUT RAO, to the Rajah, to
" communicate his views; adding, that the Rajah
" might trust to his honour, and go to meet him,
" when he would settle with him the terms that might
" be concerted between them. The vakeel came back
" with *Hyder's* men to the late Rajah, and informed him
" of

* This is to be understood with the exception of *Paulghaut*, which HYDER had possessed himself of four or five years before.

"of what had paſſed; whereupon the Rajah intimated
"his apprehenſions of *Hyder*, whom he ſpoke of as
"a man of a quarrelſome diſpoſition, and who had
"diſgraced many perſons of high rank, and who
"would probably be diſpoſed to inflict ſome mark of
"diſgrace upon him alſo; wherefore he (the Rajah)
"declared, that he would place his reliance not ſo
"much on *Hyder*, as upon the aſſurances from his
"two agents, who, being both *Brâhmens*, he would,
"on their ſwearing by their *Brâhmenical threads*, by
"the ſalgram, (a ſtone ſacred among the *Hindus*,)
"and by their ſwords, that he ſhould return in ſafety,
"conſent to accompany them, to have an interview
"with *Hyder*; to all which they agreed; and as *Hyder's*
"army was at Toorſhery, the Rajah, my uncle, went
"with *Sree Newaus Rao* and *Mookut Rao* to meet
"*Hyder*, who advanced to *Coorumnar*, where the meet-
"ing took place.

2d. "During the interview, they converſed about the
"country: But *Hyder* ſoon broke off the conference,
"by demanding of the Rajah a crore of gold mohurs;
"upon which the latter aſſured him, if he were to ſell
"the whole of the Calicut country, he could not get
"near that ſum for it; but that he would deliver the
"whole of his treaſure, and other property, and pay
"him as much as was in his power: yet *Hyder* was
"not ſatisfied with this offer, but cauſed the Rajah to
"be ſeized, and impriſoned; and ſent him under a
"guard of five hundred horſe, and two thouſand in-
"fantry, to the fort of Calicut; and the Rajah was
"confined in his own houſe without food, and was
"ſtrictly prohibited from performing the ceremonies
"of his religion; and as he thought that *Hyder*
"might inflict ſome further diſgrace upon him, either
"by cauſing him to be hanged, or blown from a gun,
"the Rajah ſet fire to the houſe with his own hand,
"and was conſumed in it."

XXXI. This firſt requiſition of Malabar by the late
Hyder Ali Khan was not of long duration; for the

Zamorin, and other Rajahs, took advantage of his entering into war with the *English East India Company* in 1768, to reinstate themselves: and they maintained possession till 1774, when *Hyder*, descending the Ghauts a second time with an army into the northern parts, and sending another, under *Sree Newaus Rao* through Paulghaut into the southern division, the Princess of the *Samcory's* family again fled into Travancore: and *Hyder's* direct and immediate government and administration appear from that period to have permanently pervaded, and become, in some degree, established, throughout all the southern division of Malabar.

XXXII. For some northern chieftains do not appear to have, on *Hyder's* first or second conquest, forsaken their countries, but agreed to become his tributaries; whilst the southern districts became a prey to almost constant dissensions, arising from the resistance and troubles which the Rajahs of the *Samcory's* family never discontinued to excite against the authority of *Hyder's* government, which was unable either effectually to quell these continued disturbances, or to punish, or even to expel, the authors of them; so that his officers were at length obliged to purchase that quiet which they could not command, by stipulating, in 1779, with one of the representatives of the *Samoory's* house, to allow him to levy a moderate ratable cess from the country for his own support; the effects of which conciliation could, however, hardly have produced any beneficial effects to the parties, or the inhabitants, before they were again embroiled by the consequences of the attack on and siege of Tellicherry, in 1779-80, and of the general war that followed; during which (that is, after the raising of the siege in question) the Rajahs of the *Samoory's* house took all the part in their power in favour of the British arms, and considerable successes attended their joint efforts in the capture, in 1782, of Calicut, and other places: but, by the peace of 1784, the Malabar countries being

being again given up, the fouthern as well as northern Rajahs were left at TIPPOO's mercy, which did not, however, prevent fome of the *Samocries* from ftill lurking in, and occafionally exciting alarm and difturbances, throughout the former part of thefe diftricts; fo that the officers of TIPPOO's government were obliged, in a like manner as their predeceffors under that of his father, to induce this family to a peaceable conduct, by beftowing a penfion in *Jaghire* upon RUVEE VURMA, one of the moft active of its members; which might, perhaps, have led to a clofer union between the exiled *Zamorin* and the Myfore government, had not the negociations to that end been interrupted in confequence of a refolution formed by TIPPOO (in the combined view of indulging his zeal as a *Mahommedan*, and of, at the fame time, rooting up, as he fondly might imagine, the caufes of that averfion which the *Malabar Hindus* had hitherto fhewn to his government) to attempt the forcible converfion of all his *Hindu* fubjects in *Malabar* to the *Muffulman* faith; for which purpofe, after ineffectually trying in perfon the effects of perfuafion, in a progrefs that he made into that country in April, 1788, he directed his officers of Calicut, to begin by feizing on the *Bráhmens*, and to render them examples to the other claffes, by enforcing circumcifion on them, and compelling them to eat beef; and accordingly many *Bráhmens* were feized in or about the month of July, 1788, and were thus forcibly deprived of their cafts; whilft others fought for fhelter with the Rajahs of the *Samoory*'s family, two or three of whom were then within the Calicut diftricts; and TIPPOO's having himfelf made fimilar conftrained converfions of a Rajah of the family of *Perepnaad*, (one of the fouthern *talooks*,) and of TICHERA TEROOPAR, a principal *Nayr* of *Nelemboor*, in the fame fouthern divifion of that country, together with fome other perfons, whom he had for various caufes carried up with him into Coimbitoor, thefe combined circumftances, and the return of the above named victims to his bigotry, fome fhort time thereafter

into

into *Malabar*, spread considerable alarm; and the injured parties, as well as the great body of *Nayrs* and *Hindus*, who justly feared for what might happen to themselves, rallied around, and looked principally up to, that Prince of the *Samoory*'s family, called the younger RUVEE VURMA, (who with his elder brother, of the same name, had some years before forced HYDER's officers to purchase their temporary and doubtful neutrality,) through whose assistance upwards of thirty thousand *Bráhmens* (including their wives and families) escaped from July to November, 1788, from the Calicut districts into Travancore; besides which, resenting these oppressions by TIPPOO on those of his sect and religion, RUVEE VURMA proceeded to open hostilities with the officers of TIPPOO's government, and proving victorious, and being assisted by the *Nelemboor* and *Perepnaad* converts, as well as by the *Nayrs* in general, and even by some of the *Mapillas*, a general insurrection took place throughout the southern districts, and the insurgents becoming masters of the open country, invested Calicut, so that TIPPOO found it necessary to dispatch *Monsieur Lally* with a strong force to its relief, on whose arrival the Rajah retreated, and was afterwards attacked in different places, without, however, being driven quite out of the field; insomuch that TIPPOO, fearing, perhaps, for the stability of his dominion in *Malabar*, followed *Monf. Lally* in person, in January or February, 1789; at which period his designs were generally reported to aim at the entire conversion, or extirpation, of the whole race of Rajahs, *Nayrs*, and other *Hindus*; many of whom were accordingly seized on, and circumcised; whilst others escaped; or, failing in the attempt, put themselves to death, to avoid loss of cast; one affecting instance of which is related of the Rajah of Cherical, who, finding that he was also to be circumcised, attempted to escape; and being pursued by TIPPOO's troops, and seeing no likelihood of being able to maintain any long resistance against them, he, after providing for the safety of his sister and her son, by sending them off to Travancore,

preferred

preferred for himself a voluntary death to the ignominy that he knew awaited his survivance; and he accordingly died either by his own hand, or by that of a friendly *Nayr*, whom he is said to have required to perform this last mournful office for him; whereupon TIPPOO, disappointed of his prey, seized on the dead Rajah's effects and country, which he continued to hold till finally deprived, by the *British* arms, of that, and the greater part of his Malabar territories, by the successful war that terminated by the peace, and his consequent cession of that country, in the year 1792; since which the *Zamorin*, and all the other Rajahs, have returned to their districts; into which they have been re-admitted, in full subordination to the Company's Government, which can alone beneficially conduct the administration of that coast in its present circumstances, and administer equal and impartial justice to the two great classes of *Hindus* and *Mahommedans*, of which the present society consists; and who, still smarting under the impression of the injuries they reciprocally inflicted and suffered during the turbulent and calamitous period of the *Mysore* dominion, can hardly be deemed to be in temper to qualify either to stand towards each other in the relation of sovereign and subject; more especially as the authority would have reverted, and the consequent retaliation have no doubt been exercised, (as was in some instances at first attempted,) by those who had been, during the last twenty years, the inferior and suffering party; for the *Mapillas*, or *Mahommedans*, finding themselves, during the preceding disastrous and unsettled administration of the religion of their new Prince, had availed themselves of that powerful circumstance in their favour, to molest, despoil, and (as far as in them lay) to ruin their former *Hindu* superiors; so that the bitterness of the enmity between the two sects had risen to the highest pitch of rancour, and will no doubt require a course of years to subside, or to give place to a re-establishment of the ancient amity.

C 2   XXXIII.

XXXIII. It has been already intimated, that the *Mapillas* in the southern districts exceed in numbers the remaining race of *Hindus*; and although many of them, who inhabit the towns on the coast, are industrious and quiet subjects, yet there is a large proportion, called the *Jungle Mapillas*, who, occupying the interior recesses near to the hills, have been so long inured to predatory habits, that some elapse of time must be required fully to reclaim them.

XXXIV. I have thus submitted to the Society the best account which, from the materials in my possession, I have been able to draw up of the History and Manners of the Inhabitants in the new acquisition of the *East India Company*, excepting as far as regards the *Nestorians*, and other *Christians*, and the *Jews*; the major part of both of whom living to the southward of what are properly the *British* limits, I have not hitherto had any sufficient opportunity of acquiring minute or accurate information respecting them.

II.

AN

ACCOUNT of TWO FAKEERS,

With their Portraits.

BY JONATHAN DUNCAN, Efq.

I BEG leave to lay before the Society the accompanying Pictures of two *Fakeers*, now living at *Benares*, which I had drawn there from the life. The firſt is named PURANA POORI, or (as uſually pronounced in Hindvee) PRAUN POORY, a *Sunyaſſy*, diſtinguiſhed by the epithet *Oordhbahu*, from his arms and his hands being in a fixed poſition above his head; and as he is a very intelligent man, and has been a great traveller, he conſented, in the month of May, 1792, to gratify my curioſity, by allowing to be committed to writing, by a ſervant of mine, from his verbal delivery in the Hinduſtan language, a relation of his obſervations in the various countries into which he has penetrated; but as his account is too long for inſertion in the *Aſiatick Reſearches*, (ſhould it even be deemed to merit a place in ſo reſpectable a repoſitory,) I have here extracted the principal parts of it, as an accompaniment to the portrait; having only farther to premiſe, that I have the utmoſt reliance on our traveller's not deſigning to impoſe in any part of his narrative; but allowance muſt be made for defects of memory, in a relation

relation extending through so many years, and comprehending such a number of objects.

II. PRAUN POORY is a native of *Canouge*, of the *Khetry* or *Raujepoot* tribe. At nine years of age he secretly withdrew from his father's house, and proceeded to the city of Bethour, on the banks of the Ganges, where he became a Fakeer, about the time (for he cannot otherwise fix the year) of MUNSOOR ALI KHAN's retreat from Dehli to Lucknow, and two or three years before the sack of Mat'hura by AHMED SHAH ABDALLI; which two events are in SCOTT's "*History of the Dekkan,*" related under the years 1751-2 and 1756; within which period he came to *Allahabad* to the great annual meeting of pilgrims, where hearing of the merits attached to what he describes as the eighteen different kinds of *Tupisya*, or modes of devotional discipline, he made choice of that of *Oordhbahu*, above noticed; the first operation of which he represents to be very painful, and to require preparation by a previous course of abstinence.

III. He then set out to visit Ramisher, opposite to Ceylon, taking his route by Kalpi, Oujeine, Burahanpoor, Aurungabad, and Elora; the surprising excavations at which place he notices: and crossing the Godavery at Tounker, he passed by Poona, Settara, and various other intermediate towns, to Bednore, of which a *Ranny*, or Princess, was then the sovereign; whence he went on to Seringapatam, then in possession of its Hindu Princes, whom he names NUND RAUJE and DEO RAUJE; leaving which, he descended through the Tamerchery Pass into Malabar, and arrived at Chochin; whence he crossed the Peninsula through a desart tract of country to Ramisher; after visiting which, he returned up the Coromandel coast to the temple of *Jaggernauth* in Orissa, specifying all the

the towns on this part of his route, which are too well known to require to be here enumerated.

From Jaggernauth our traveller returned by nearly the fame route to Ramifher, whence he paffed over into *Silan*, or Ceylon, and proceeded to its capital, which fome, he obferves, call *Khundi*, (Candi,) and others *Noora*; but that KHUNDI MAHA RAUJE is the Prince's defignation; and that further on he arrived at Catlgang, on a river called the Manic Gunga, where there is a temple of CARTICA, or CARTICEYA, the fon of MAHADEO, to which he paid his refpects, and then went on to vifit the *Sreepud*, or, "The Divine Foot," fituated upon a mountain of extraordinary height; and on one part of which there is alfo (according to this Fakeer's defcription) an extenfive miry cavity, called the *Bhoput Tank*, and which bears alfo the name of the Tank of RAVAN, or RABAN, (the *b* and *v* being pronounced indifferently in various parts of India,) one of the former Kings of this Ifland, well known in the Hindu legends for his wars with RAMA, and from whom this *Tapu*, or Ifland, may probably have received its ancient appellation of *Taprobane*, (i. e. the Ifle of RABAN.) But, however this may be, our traveller ftates, that, leaving this tank, he proceeded on to a ftation called *Seeta Koond*, (where RAMA placed his wife SEETA, on the occafion of his war with her ravifher RAVAN,) and then reached at length to the *Sreepud*, on a moft extenfive table or flat, where there is (he obferves) a *bungalow* built over the print of the divine foot; after worfhipping which, he returned by the fame route.

V. From Ceylon this *Sunyaffy* paffed over among the Malays, whom he defcribes as being *Muffulmans*; but there was one capital Hindu merchant, a native of Ceylon, fettled there, at whofe houfe he lodged for two months, and who then procured him a passage to Cochin, on the coast of Malabar, up which he proceeded by land; particularizing, with a wonderful tenacity of memory, the several towns and places through which he passed, with their intermediate distances: but as these are already well enough described in our own books of geography, his account of them need not be here inserted.

VI. In this direction he proceeded along the coast to Bombay, and passed on to Dwarac Tatta Hingulaj, or Henglaz, and through Multan, beyond the Attock, whence he changed his route to the eastward, and arrived at Hurdewar; where the *Ganges* enters the plains of Hindustan; and from that place of *Hindu* devotion he again departed in a westerly direction, through the upper parts of the Punjab to Cabul, and thence to Bamian, where he mentions with admiration the number of statues that still exist, though the place itself has been long deserted by its inhabitants.

VII. In the course of his rambles in this quarter of the country, he fell in with the army of AHMED SHAH ABDALLI, in the close vicinity of Ghizni; and that King, having an ulcer in his nose, consulted our Fakeer, to know if, being an Indian, he could prescribe a remedy for it: on which occasion the latter acknowledged that, having no knowledge of surgery or medicine, he had recourse to his wits, by insinuating to the Prince, that there most probably did subsist a connexion between the ulcer and his sovereignty, so that it might not be advisable to seek to get rid of the one, lest it should risk the loss of the other; a suggestion that met (he adds) with the approbation of the Prince and his Ministers.

VIII. PRAUN

VIII. Praun Poory afterwards travelled through *Khorafan*, by the way of Herat and Mufh-hed, to Aftrabad, on the borders of the Cafpian Sea, and to the Maha or Burce (i. e. larger) Jowalla Mookhi, or Juâla Mûchi, terms that mean a "Flaming Mouth," as being a fpot in the neighbourhood of Bakee, on the weft fide of the fea in queftion, whence fire iffues; a circumftance that has rendered it of great veneration with the Hindus; and Praun Poory adds, that locally it is called *Dagheftan*, a word which I underftand to mean in *Sanfcrit*, "The Region of Heat;" though the caufe is candidly afcribed by our traveller to the natural circumftance of the ground being impregnated with *naphtha* throughout all that neighbourhood.

IX. After fojourning eleven months at this Jowalla Mookhi, he embarked on the Cafpian, and obtained a paffage to Aftrachan; where he mentions to have been courteoufly received by the body of Hindus refiding in that place.

X. Praun Poory next proceeds to notice, that a river (meaning, no doubt, the Volga) flows under Aftrachan, and is, he fays, frozen over, fo as to admit of paffengers travelling on it during four months in the year; and thence, he mentions, in eighteen days journey, he proceeded to Mofcow, the ancient capital of Ruffia, (the Sovereign of which was, he obferves, a *Beeby*, or Lady,) and that he halted there during five days in the Armenian *Seray*; and he takes notice that there is an immenfe bell in this city, under which a hundred perfons may find room to ftand; adding, that he has heard, in a month's journeying beyond Mofcow, a traveller may reach Peterfburgh, and thence get to Great Britain.

XI. But Praun Poory proceeds no farther than Mofcow, from which place he returned by Aftrachan,

and

and passed through Persia, by the route of Shamaki, Sherwaun, Tubrez, Hamadan, and Ispahan; in which capital he sojourned during forty days, and then passed on to Shirauz; where he arrived during the government of KERIM SHAH, whom he describes as being then about forty years of age, as far as he could judge from an audience he had of him; and there were, he adds, two English gentlemen (one of whom he calls Mr. LISTER) at this King's court at the period of his visiting it.

XII. Embarking at Aboosheher, on the southern coast of Persia, he reached the Isle of *Kharek*, then governed by a chief called MEER MANNA, who had, he observes, taken it from the *Dutch*, and whom he represents as a chieftain living by carrying on a warfare against all his neighbours; and he mentions several Hindus as being settled here. He next arrived at the islands called *Bahrein*, on the coasts of which pearls are, he says, found; whence re-embarking for *Bussorah*, the vessel he was in was met and examined, and again released, by the *Bombay* and *Tartar* grabs, then carrying on hostilities (as he understood) against SOLYMAN, the Mahommedan chief of the Bahrein Isles. After this occurrence our traveller arrived at *Bussorah*, a well known town and sea-port, in which he found a number of Hindu houses of trade, as well as two idols or figures of VISHNU, known under his appellations of GOVINDA RAYA and CALYANA RAYA; or, according to the vulgar enunciation, and PRAUN POORY's pronunciation of their names, KULYAN Row and GOBIND Row.

XIII. After an ineffectual attempt to penetrate up the Tigris to Baghdad, he returned to Bussorah, whence descending the Persian Gulph, he arrived at Muscat, where he met also a number of *Hindus*; and from that place he reached Surat. From hence he again proceeded by sea to Mokha, where also he found a number
of

of Hindus; and he thence returned into India, landing on its weſt coaſt, in the port of Sanyanpoor, ſituated, I ſuppoſe, towards or in the Cutch or Sinde countries.

XIV. From this port he journeyed to Balkh (where he alſo mentions Hindus being ſettled) and to Bokhara, at which he notices having viewed the famous *Derjah* of KHAJA CHESTEE, and the loftieſt minar or ſpire he has ever ſeen. From this place, after twelve days journey, he arrived at Samarkand, which he deſcribes as a large city, having a broad river flowing under it: and thence our traveller arrived, after a ten days journey, at Budukhſhan, in the hills around which rubies are, he ſays, found; whence he travelled into Caſhmir; and from that paſſing over the hills towards Hinduſtan, he came to the Gungowtri, or "Decent of the "Ganges," where there is, he obſerves, a ſtatue of BAGHIRATHA; at which place the river may, he ſays, be leaped over: and he further notices, that thirty cofs to the ſouthward of Gungowtri there is a fountain, or ſpring, called the *Jumnowtri* or *Yumnowtri*, which he deſcribes as the ſource of the Jumna or Yamuna River.

XV. Our traveller, leaving this part of the country, came in a ſouth-eaſt direction into Oude, and went thence into Nepaul, the ſeveral towns in which he deſcribes, incluſive of its capital, Catmandee, where flow, he obſerves, the four rivers of Naugmutty, Biſhenmutty, Roodrmutty, and Munmutty; and at ſeven days journey beyond which, he notices a ſtation called *Goſſayn-thaun*, where MAHADEO took poiſon and ſlept, as related in the Hindu books; from which place (deſcribed by him as a ſnowy tract) he returned to Catmandee, and went thence in another direction into Thibet, croſſing in his way to it the Cofa river by a bridge compoſed of iron chains; and obſerving that at Leſtee, the third day's journey beyond the Cofa, is the boundary of Nepaul and Thibet, where

guards

guards are stationed on both sides; whence, in another day's travelling, PRAUN POORY arrived at Khaſſa, a town within *Bhote* or *Thibet*; (for by the former name the natives often underſtand what we mean by the latter;) hence he proceeded to *Chehang*, and from that to *Koortee*, where paſſes are given; and then croſſed over the hills (called in that country Lungoor) into the plain of Tingri, beyond which one day's journey is Gunguir; and at the end of the next *ſangee*, (from *ſangu*,) which means, he ſays, a *bridge* over a river there: after which our traveller proceeds to notice the other diſtances and ſtations of each *munzel*, or day's journey, (with other particulars, the inſertion of all which would render this addreſs too prolix,) till he reached Lahaſſa, and the mountain of *Patala*, the ſeat of the DELAI LAMA, whence he proceeded to Degurcha, which he mentions as that of the TAISHOO LAMA; and then, in a journey of upwards of eighty days, reached to the lake of Maun Surwur, (called in the Hindu books *Mânaſarôvara*;) and his deſcription of it I ſhall here inſert in a literal tranſlation of his own words.

XVI. "Its circumference (i. e. of the lake of
" Maun Surwur) is of ſix days journey, and around it
" are twenty or five-and-twenty *Goumaris*, or "re-
" ligious ſtations or temples, and the habitations of
" the people called *Dowki*, whoſe dreſs is like that of
" the Thibetians. The Maun Surwur is one lake;
" but in the middle of it there ariſes, as it were, a
" partition wall; and the northern part is called *Maun*
" *Surwur*, and the ſouthern *Lunkadh*, or *Lunkdeh*.
" From the Maun Surwur part iſſues one river, and
" from the Lunkadh part two rivers: The firſt is
" called *Brâhma*, where PURESRAM making *Tupiſya*,
" the *Brâhmaputra* iſſued out, and took its courſe to
" the eaſtward; and of the two ſtreams that iſſue
" from the Lunkadh, one is called the *Surju*, being
" the ſame which flows by Ayóddyà, or Oude; and
the

"the other is called *Sutroodra*, (or, in the *Puránas*,
"*Shutudru*, and vulgarly the *Sutluje*,) which flows
"into the *Punjaub* country; and two days journey
"west from the Maun Surwur is the large town of
"Teree Ládac, the former Rajahs of which were
"Hindus, but have now become Mahommedans.
"The inhabitants there are like unto the Thibetians.
"Proceeding from Ládac, seven days journey to the
"southward, there is a mountain called *Cailafa Cungri*,
"(*Cungur* meaning a *peak*,) which is exceedingly
"lofty; and on its summit there is a *Bhowjputr* or
"*Bhoorjputr* tree, from the root of which sprouts or
"gushes a small stream, which the people say is the
"*source* of the *Ganges*, and that it comes from *Vaicont'-*
"*ha*, or heaven, as is also related in the *Puránas*;
"although this source appears to the sight to flow
"from the spot where grows this *Bhowjputr* tree,
"which is at an ascent of some miles; and yet above
"this there is a still loftier summit, whither no one
"goes: but I have heard that on that uppermost
"pinnacle there is a fountain or cavity, to which a
"*Jagui* somehow penetrated; who, having immersed
"his little finger in it, it became petrified. At four
"days journey from Cailafa Cungri is a mountain
"called *Bráhmadanda*, or Bra'hma's *staff*, in which
"is the *source* of the *Aliknundra Ganga*; and five
"or six days journey to the south of that are si-
"tuated on the mountains the temples dedicated to
"Cedara, or Kedarnauth and Budranauth; and
"from these hills flow the streams called the *Kedar*
"*Ganga* and *Sheo Ganga*; the confluxes of which, as
"well as of the *Aliknundra*, with the main stream of
"the Ganges, take place near Kernpraug and Deo-
"praug, in the vicinity of Serinagur; whence they
"flow on in a united stream, which issues into the
"plains of Hindustan at the Hurdewar."

XVII. Praun Poory went back from this part
of the country into Nepaul and Thibet, from the capital

pital of which he was charged by the administration there with dispatches to the Governor General, Mr. HASTINGS, which he mentions to have delivered in the presence of Mr. BARWELL, and of the late Messrs. BOGLE and ELLIOTT; after which our traveller was sent to Benares with introductory letters to Rajah CHEYT SING and to Mr. GRAHAM, who was at that time the resident; and some years afterwards Mr. HASTINGS bestowed on him in *jaghire*, the village of *Assapoor*, which he continues to hold as a free tenure; though he is still so fond of travelling, that he annually makes short excursions into different parts of India, and occasionally as far as Nepaul.

XVIII. The name of the other Hindu Fakeer, or *Bráhmechary*, (whose picture reclining, in his ordinary position, on his bed of iron spikes, accompanies this,) is PERKASANUND; and he assumes the title or epithet of PURRUM SOATUNTRE, which implies *self-possession* or *independence*; and as his own relation of his mode of life is not very long, I deliver an English translation of it, as received from him in August, 1792; only observing that the *Jowalla Mookhi*, which he mentions to have visited, is not the one on the *Caspian*, but another; for there are at the least three famous places known to the Hindus under this general denomination; one near to Naugercote, another (whither PRAUN POORY went) in the vicinity of Bakee, and the third (as I have been informed by Lieut. WILFORD) at Corcoor, to the eastward of the *Tigris*; but whether it be the first or last of these *Jowalla Mookhis* that PERKASANUND visited, his narrative is not sufficiently clear to enable me to distinguish; neither are his general knowledge and intelligence at all equal to PRAUN POORY's, which may account for his observation as to the difficulty of reaching the Maun Surwur lake, whither not only PRAUN POORY, but other Fakeers, that I have seen at Benares, profess to have nevertheless penetrated; so that my present notice of PERKASANUND

to

to the Society, is principally on account of the ſtrange penance he has thought fit to devote himſelf to, in fixing himſelf on his *ſer-ſeja*, or bed of ſpikes, where he conſtantly day and night remains; and, to add to what he conſiders as the merit of this ſtate of mortification, in the hot weather he has often burning around him logs of wood; and in the cold ſeaſon, water falling on his head from a perforated pot, placed in a frame at ſome height above him; and yet he ſeems contented, and to enjoy good health and ſpirits. Neither do the ſpikes appear to be in any material degree diſtreſſing to him, although he uſes not the defence of even ordinary cloathing to cover his body as a protection againſt them: but as the drawing exhibits an exact likeneſs as well of his perſon as of this bed of ſeeming torture, I ſhall not here trouble the Society with any further deſcription of either, and conclude by mentioning, that he is now living at Benares, on a ſmall proviſion that he enjoys from government.

P. S. Had my official occupations, whilſt at Benares, admitted of my paying due attention to PRAUN POORY's narrative of his travels, the geographical information they contain, or rather point to, as to the ſource of the Ganges, Jumna, and other principal rivers, might have probably admitted of a fuller illuſtration, and greater degree of accuracy, from a farther examination of that *Sunyaſſy*, aided by the important aſſiſtance which I might in that caſe have obtained on this part of the ſubject from Lieutenant WILFORD, who has, through his own unwearied exertions, and chiefly at his own expence, collected a variety of valuable materials relative to the geography of the north of India; at the ſame time that, by a zealous application to the ſtudy of Hindu literature, joined to an intimate acquaintance with whatever the Greeks and Romans have left us, on their mythology, or concerning the general events of former ages, as far as their
knowledge

knowledge of the world extended, this gentleman is likely to throw much light on the earlier periods of the hiſtory of mankind.

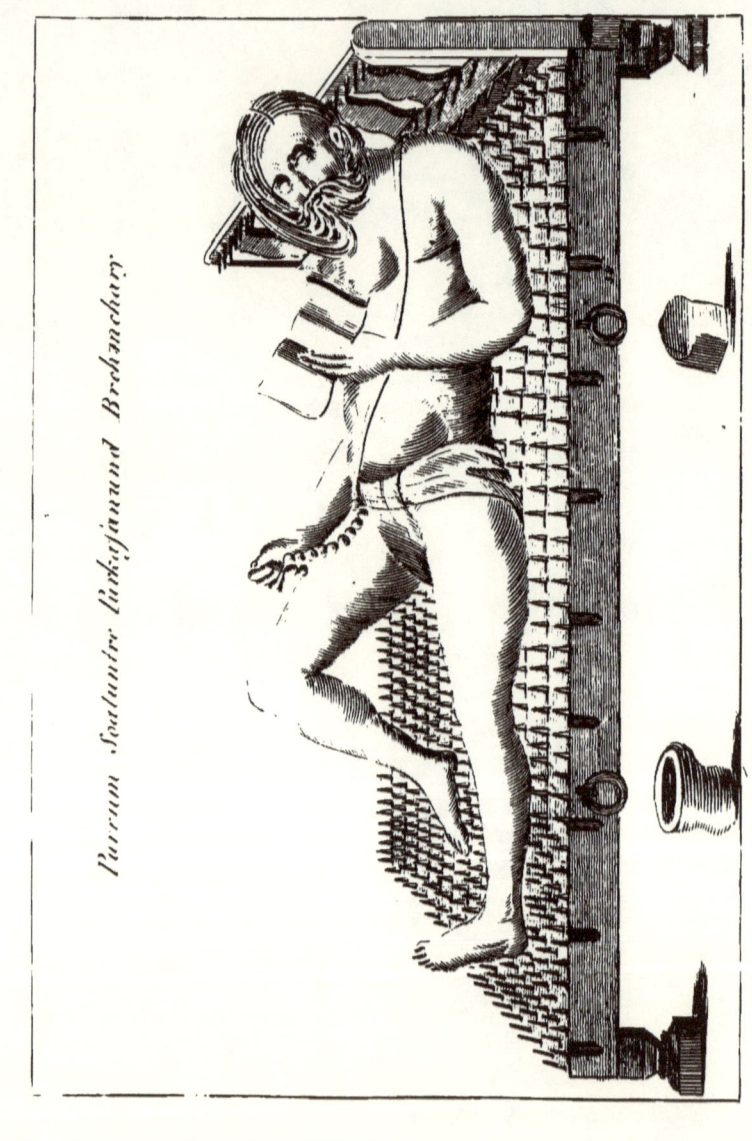

Translation of the Relation delivered by PURRUM SOATUNTRE PURKASANUND BREHMCHARY *of his Travels and Life; delivered on the* 14*th of August,* 1792.

I AM a *Bráhmen* of the *Yujerveda* sect, and of the line of *Práſher*. My ancestors are from the Punjaub. They had a long time ago come to visit at Jaggernauth, and had reached and were abiding at Gopegawn, where I was born. When I was only ten years of age, I used to give myself up to meditation and mortification, lying upon thorns and pebbles; a mode of life I had continued for ten years, when it was interrupted by my relations, who wanted me to think of marriage; whereupon, having attained to twenty years of age, I left my home, determined to devote myself to travelling. First, after coming out of my house, I went towards Ootrakhund, by way of *Nepaul* and *Bhote*. I went into the country of the Great and Little *Lama*, where the TEESHOO LAMA lives. In this tract is the *Maun Talaee*, (i. e. tank or lake,) as far as which is inhabited, but not beyond it; and the lake called *Maun Surwur* is seventeen *munzels*, or days' journey, farther on, in a jungly country, which prevents access to it. There are in this quarter the places known under the denominations of *Muni, Mahesho, Mahadeo*, and of *Teloke, Nauthjee,* and the *Debbees*, or cooking places, of *Nownauth*; and of the eighty-four *Sidhs*, or religious persons, thus distinguished; all situated on this side of the Maun Surwur. Into these Debbees, if one throw in either two loaves, or as many as are wanted; one in the name of the *Sidh*, and another in one's own name; that in the name of the *Sidh* remains at the bottom, and that in one's own name rises up baked. These places I visited. At the Maun Talaee the boundaries of four countries meet, viz. that of China, of the *Lama*'s country, of the Beseher country, and that of the Cooloo country.

Proceeding thus in religious progress from hill to hill, I passed through the Shaum country, and descending the hills, arrived in Cashmir, where I halted for devotional purposes, as well as to prosecute my studies. From Cashmir I went through Thibet to the Great Jowallah, which is situated in a country where fire rises out of the ground for the space of twelve cofs. In this Jowallah whoever wants to dress victuals, or boil water, they have only to dig a little fissure into the surface of the ground, and place the article thereon, which will serve without wood. On this side of Peishore, where the *Sendhe* salt is produced, there is a village called *Dudun Khan's Pend*, adjoining to the salt pits. The Rajah of that country was called Rajah BHENDA SINGH. I had here shut myself up in a *Gowpha*, or cell, where I vowed to remain doing penance for a period of twelve years. Vermin or worms gnawed my flesh, of which the marks still remain; and when one year had elapsed, then the Rajah opened the door of the cell, whereupon I said to him, " either take my " curse, or make me a *fer-feja*, or bed of spikes;" and then that Rajah made for me the *fer-feja* I now occupy. During the four months of the winter I made *jel-feja* upon this feat. *Jel-feja* is, that night and day water is let fall upon my head. From thence, by the Sindh country I went to Hingoolauje, (a mountain dedicated to *Debee*.) All the country to the west and south I travelled over upon this *fer-feja*, coming at length to Preyago, or Allahabad; and passing by Cashi, or Benares, I went to the temple of Jaggernauth; and visiting Balajee, proceeded on to Ramisher; and, after visiting that place, I journied on to Surat. In Surat I embarked in a vessel, and went by sea to Muscat in twelve days; and thence returning, came to Surat again. Mr. BODDAM was then at Surat; and he afterwards went to Bombay. I stayed two years at Surat. Mr. BODDAM granted me something to subsist on with my followers, and built a house for me; and still my *Cheilas*, or disciples, are there. It is is thirty-five years since I made *Tupisya* upon this *ser-seja*. I have been in several countries. How much shall I cause to be written? I have been at every place of religious resort, and have no longer any inclination to roam; but being desirous of settling in Benares, I have come hither. Three *Yugs* have passed, and we are now in the fourth; and in all these four ages there have been religious devotees, and their disciples; and they are first to make application to the Rajah, or to whoever is the ruler of the place; for even Rajahs maintain and serve us; and it is befitting that I obtain a small place, where I may apply to my religious duties, and that something may be allowed for my necessary expences, that I may bless you.

QUESTION.

In all the eighteen *Tupisyas*, or modes of penetential devotion, that are made mention of in the *Shaster*, the one you have chosen is not specified; wherefore it is inferable, that you must have committed some great offence, in expiation of which you have betaken yourself to the present very rude mode of discipline. Declare, therefore, what crime you have perpetrated.

ANSWER.

In the *Suthya Yug*, or first age, there was a *Rikh*, or holy-man, called AGNIBURNA, who performed this *ser-seja* discipline; as in the *Treta*, or second age, did RAVONO, for ten thousand years; and in the *Dwapar*, or third age, BHIKMA PITAMAHA, did the same; and in the *Cale Yug*, or present age, I have followed their example, during a period of thirty-five years; but not to expiate any crime or offence by me committed; in which respect if I be guilty, may VESHWEISHURA strike me a leper here in Benares.

QUESTION.

QUESTION.

When you went to Ramisher, at what distance was Lunka?

ANSWER.

We go to Ramisher to worship; and at the *Setbund*, or bridge there, there is a *ling* of sand, which I paid my respects to: but beyond that nobody from Hindustan has gone to Lunka. In the sea, your ships are always sailing about; but the current is such, that they cannot get thither; so, how can we go there? But from *Singuldeep*, or Ceylon, we can see the glitterings of Lunka. There I did not go; but my Cheilas have been there, who said that in *Singuldeep* is the seat of RAWON; and HUNOOMAN's twelve *Chokies*, or watch stations.

QUESTION.

Have you seen RAM's Bridge? If you have seen it, describe its length and breadth, and whether it be still found or broken.

ANSWER.

Ram's Bridge, which is called *Setbund*, is ascertained by the *Védas* to be ten *jojun* broad, and one hundred *jojun* long; but in three places it is broken. The people call it a bridge; or otherwise it appears to have wood growing on it, and to be inhabited.

ENUMERATION

III.

ENUMERATION *of* INDIAN CLASSES.

By H. T. COLEBROOKE, *Esq.*

THE permanent separation of Classes, with hereditary professions assigned to each, is among the most remarkable institutions of *India*; and, though now less rigidly maintained than heretofore, must still engage attention. On the subject of the mixed Classes, *Sanscrit* authorities, in some instances, disagree: Classes mentioned by one, are omitted by another; and texts differ on the professions assigned to some tribes. A comparison of several authorities, with a few observations on the subdivisions of Classes, may tend to elucidate this subject, in which there is some intricacy.

One of the authorities I shall use, is the *Játimálá*, or Garland of Classes; an extract from the *Rudra-yámala Tantra*, which, in some instances, corresponds better with usage and received opinions than the ordinances of MENU, and the great *D'herma-purána.*[*] On more important points its authority could not be compared with the *D'herma-sástra*; but, on the subject of Classes, it may be admitted; for the *Tantras* form

---

[*] The texts are cited in the *Viváddárnave sétu*, from the *Vrihad D'herma-purána*. This name I therefore retain; although I cannot learn that such a *purána* exists; or to what treatise the quotation refers under that name.

form a branch of literature highly esteemed, though at present much neglected. Their fabulous origin derives them from revelations of SIVA to PA'RVATI, confirmed by VISHNU, and therefore called *Agama*, from the initials of three words in a verse of the *Tódala Tantra*.

" Coming from the mouth of SIVA, heard by the " mountain-born goddess, admitted by the son of VA- " SUDE'VA, it is thence called *Agama*."

Thirty-six are mentioned for the number of mixed classes; but, according to some opinions, that number includes the fourth original tribe, or all the original tribes, according to other authorities: yet the text quoted from the great *D'herma-purána*, in the digest of which a version was translated by Mr. HALHED, name thirty-nine mixed classes; and the *Játimálá* gives distinct names for a greater number.

On the four original tribes it may suffice, in this place, to quote the *Játimálá*, where the distinction of *Bráhmanas*, according to the ten countries to which their ancestors belonged, is noticed: that distinction is still maintained.

" In the first creation, by BRA'HMA, *Bráhmánas* " proceeded, with the *Véda*, from the mouth of " BRA'HMA. From his arms *Cshatriyas* sprung; so " from his thigh, *Vaisyas*; from his foot *Súdras* were " produced: all with their females.

" The Lord of creation viewing them, said, " What " shall be your occupations?" They replied, " We " are not our own masters, oh, God! Command us " what to undertake.

" Viewing

"Viewing and comparing their labours, he made the firſt tribe ſuperior over the reſt. As the firſt had great inclination for the divine ſciences, (*Bráh-mevéda*,) therefore he was *Bráhmana*. The protector from ill, *(Cſhate)* was *Cſhatriya*; him whoſe profeſſion (*Véſa*) conſiſts in commerce, which promotes ſucceſs in war, for the protection of himſelf and of mankind; and in huſbandry, and attendance on cattle, called *Vaiſya*. The other ſhould voluntarily ſerve the three tribes, and therefore he became a *Súdra:* he ſhould humble himſelf at their feet."

And in another place:

"A chief of the twice-born tribe was brought by VISHNU's eagle from *Sáca dwipa:* thus have *Sáca dwipa Bráhmanas* become known in *Jambu dwipa*.

"In *Jambu dwipa Bráhmanas* are reckoned tenfold; *Sáreſwata, Cányacubja, Gauda, Maithila, Utcala, Drávidà, Marabáſhtrà, Tailanga, Gujjava*, and *Cáſmíra*, reſiding in the ſeveral countries *whence they are named.* (1.)

"Their ſons and grand-ſons are conſidered as *Cányacubja* prieſts, and ſo forth. Their poſterity, deſcending from MENU, alſo inhabit the ſouthern regions: others reſide in *Anga Banga* and *Calinga*; ſome in *Camrupa* and *Odra*. Others are inhabitants

(1.) Theſe ſeveral countries are *Sáreſwata*, probably the region watered by the river Serſutty, as it is marked in maps; unleſs it be a part of *Bengal*, named from the branch of the *Bhágirathí*, which is diſtinguiſhed by this appellation, *Cányacubja*, or *Canoj*: *Gaurá*, probably the weſtern *Gár*, and not the *Gaur* of *Bengal*: *Mit'hila*, or *Tirabhuſti*, corrupted into *Tirhut*; *Utcala*, ſaid to be ſituated near the celebrated temple of *Jagannát'ha; Drávidá*, pronounced *Dravira*; poſſibly the country deſcribed by that name, as a maritime region ſouth of *Carnata*, (*Aſ. Reſ.* vol. ii. p. 117.) *Marabáſhtrà*, or *Marhátta*; *Telinga*, or *Telingána*; *Gujjara*, or *Guzrat*; *Caſmíra*, or *Cáſhmír*.

" of *Sumbhadeſa:* and twice-born men, brought by for-
" mer Princes, have been eſtabliſhed in *Báda Mágadha,*
" *Varéndra, Chóla, Swernagráma, China Cula, Saca,*
" and *Berbera.*" (1.)

I ſhall proceed, without further preface, to enumerate the principal mixed claſſes, which have ſprung
from intermarriages of the original tribes.

1. *Murd'habhiſhicta,* from a *Bráhmana* by a girl of
the *Cſhatriya* claſs: his duty is the teaching of military exerciſes. The ſame origin is aſcribed in the
great *D'herma-purána* to the *Cumbhacára,* (2,) or pot-
ter, and *Tantraváya,* (3,) or weaver: but the *Tantraváya,* according to the *Játimálá,* ſprung from two
mixed claſſes, begotten by a man of the *Manibandha*
on a woman of the *Manicára* tribe.

2. *Ambaſht'ha,* or *Vaidya,* (4,) whoſe profeſſion is
the ſcience of medicine, was born of a *Vaiſya* woman,
by a man of the ſacerdotal claſs. The ſame origin is
given by the *D'herma-purána* to the *Canſacára,* (5,) or
brazier, and to the *Sanc'hacára,* (6,) or worker in ſhells.
Theſe again are ſtated, in the *Tantra,* as ſpringing
from the intermarriages of mixed claſſes; the *Canſacára* from the *Támracúta* and the *Sanc'hacára;* alſo
named *Sanchadáreca,* from the *Rájaputra* and *Gánd-
hica:* for *Rájaputras* not only denote *Cſhatriyas* as ſons
of

(1.) *Anga* includes *Bhágalpur. Benga,* or *Bengal* Proper, is a
part only of the Suba. *Varéndra,* or tract of inundation north
of the Ganges, is a part of the preſent Zila of *Rajeſháhi. Calinga*
is watered by the *Godáveri, (Aſi. Reſ.* vol. iii. p. 48.) *Camrupal,*
an ancient empire, is become a province of *Aſam. Odra* I underſtand to be *Oriſa* Proper. *Rada* (if that be the true reading)
is well known as the country weſt of the *Bhágirat'ha. Mágadha,*
or *Magadha,* is *Bahar* Proper; *Chóla* is part of Birbhum. Another
region of this name is mentioned in the Aſiatick Reſearches, vol.
iii. p. 48. *Swernagráma,* vulgarly *Sunargau,* is ſituated eaſt of
Dacca. *China* is a portion of the preſent Chineſe empire. On the
reſt I can offer no conjecture. *Saca* and *Berbera,* here mentioned,
muſt differ from the *Dwipa,* and the region ſituated between the
Cuſha and *Sancha Dwypas.* (2.) Vulgarly, *Cumár.* (3.) Vulgarly, *Tanti.* (4.) Vulgarly, *Baidya.* (5.) Vulgarly, *Cáſerá.*
(6.) Vulgarly, *Sac'héra.*

kings, but is also the name of a mixed class, and of a tribe of fabulous origin.

Rudra-Yámala Tantra: "The origin of *Rájapu-tras* is from the *Vaisya* on the daughter of an *Ambasht'ha*. Again, thousands of others sprung from the *foreheads of cows* kept to supply oblations."

3. *Nishada*, or *Párasava*, whose profession is catching fish, was born of a *Súdra* woman by a man of a sacerdotal class. The name is given to the issue of a legal marriage between a *Bráhmana* and a woman of the *Súdra* class. It should seem that the issue of other legal marriages in different classes were described by the names of mixed classes springing from intercourse between the several tribes. This, however, is liable to some question; and since such marriages are considered as illegal in the present age, it is not material to pursue the inquiry.

According to the *D'herma-purána*, from the same origin as the *Nishada* springs the *Varajíví*, or astrologer. In the *Tantra*, that origin is given to the *Bráhme-súdra*, whose profession is to make chairs or stools used on some religious occasions. Under the name of *Varajíví* (1) is described a class springing from the *Gópa* and *Tantraváya*, and employed in cultivating beetle. The profession of astrology, or, at least, that of making almanacks, is assigned, in the *Tantra*, to degraded *Bráhmanas*.

"*Bráhmanas*, falling from their tribe, became kinsmen of the twice-born class: to them is assigned the profession of ascertaining the lunar and solar days."

4. *Máhishya*

(1) Vulgarly, *Baraiya*.

4. *Máhishya* is the son of a *Cshatriya* by a woman of the *Vaisya* tribe. His profession is music, astronomy, and attendance on cattle.

5. *Ugra* was born of a *Súdra* woman by a man of the military class. His profession, according to MENU, is killing or confining such animals as live in holes: but, according to the *Tantra*, he is an encomiast or bard. The same origin is attributed to the *Nápita* (1) or barber; and to the *Maudaca*, or confectioner. In the *Tantra*, the *Nápita* is said to be born of a *Cuverina* woman by a man of the *Patticára* class.

6. *Carana* (2) from a *Vaisya*, by a woman of the *Súdra* class, is an attendant on princes, or secretary. The appellation of *Cáyast'ha* (3) is in general considered as synonimous with *Carana*; and accordingly the *Carana* tribe commonly assumes the name of *Cáyast'ha*: but the *Cáyast'has* of Bengal have pretensions to be considered as true *Súdras*, which the *Játimálá* seems to authorize; for the origin of the *Cáyast'ha* is there mentioned, before the subject of mixed tribes is introduced, immediately after describing the *Gópa* as a true *Súdra*.

One, named *Bhútidatta*, was noticed for his domestic assiduity, (4;) therefore the rank of *Cáyast'ha* was by *Bráhmanas* assigned to him. From him sprung three sons, *Chitrángada*, *Chitraséna*, and *Chitrágupta*: they were employed in attendance on princes.

The *D'herma-purána* assigns the same origin to the *Tambuli*, or beetle-seller, and to the *Tanlica*, or areca-seller, as to the *Carana*.

The

---

(1) Vulgarly, *Néya*, or *Nai*. (2) Vulgarly, *Caran*. (3) Vulgarly, *Cáit*. (4) Literally, *Staying at home*, (*Cáèy sansthitah*,) whence the etimology of *Cáyast'ha*.

The fix above enumerated are begotten in the direct order of the claffes. Six are begotten in the inverfe order.

7. *Suta*, begotten by a *Cſhatriya*, on a woman of the prieſtly claſs. His occupation is managing horſes, and driving cars. The ſame origin is given, in the *Purāna*, to the *Mālācāra* (1) or floriſt; but he ſprung from the *Carmacāra* and *Tailica* claſſes, if the authority of the *Tantra* prevails.

8. *Māgadha*, born of a *Cſhatriya* girl, by a man of the commercial claſs, has, according to the *Sāſtra*, the profeſſion of travelling with merchandize; but, according to the *Purāna* and *Tantra*, is an encomiaſt. From parents of thoſe claſſes ſprung the *Gōpa* (2) if the *Purāna* may be believed; but the *Tantra* deſcribes the *Gōpa* as a true *Sūdra*, and names *Gōpajivi* (3) a mixed claſs, uſing the ſame profeſſion, and ſpringing from *Tantravāya Manibandha* claſſes.

9 and 10. *Vaideha* and *Ayōgava*. The occupation of the firſt, born of a *Brāhmenī* by a man of the commercial claſs, is waiting on women: the ſecond, born of a *Vaiſya* woman by a man of the ſervile claſs, has the profeſſion of a carpenter.

11. *Cſhattri*, or *Cſhatta*, ſprung from a ſervile man by a woman of the military claſs, is employed in killing and confining ſuch animals as live in holes. The ſame origin is aſcribed by the *Purāna* to the *Carmacāra*, or ſmith, and *Dāſa*, or mariner. The one is mentioned in the *Tantra* without ſpecifying the claſſes from which he ſprung; and the other has a different origin, according to the *Sāſtra* and *Tantra*.

All

(1) *Mālī.* (2) *Gōp.* (3) *Gūariā-Gōp.*

All authorities concur in deriving the *Chándala* from a *Súdra* father and *Bráhmenì* mother. His profession is carrying out corpses, and executing criminals; and officiating in other abject employments for public service.

A third set of Indian classes originate from the intermarriages of the first and second set: a few only have been named by MENU; and, excepting the *Abhira*, or milkman, they are not noticed by the other authorities to which I refer. But the *Purána* names other classes of this set.

A fourth set is derived from intercourse between the several classes of the second set: of these also few have been named by MENU; and one only of the fifth set, springing from intermarriages of the second and third set; and another of the sixth set, derived from intercourse between classes of the second and fourth set. MENU adds to these classes four sons of outcasts.

The *Tantra* enumerates many other classes, which must be placed in lower sets*, and ascribes a different origin to some of the classes in the third and fourth sets.

These differences may be readily apprehended from the comparative table annexed. To pursue a verbose comparison would be tedious, and of little use; perhaps, of none; for I suspect that their origin is fanciful; and, except the mixed classes named by MENU, that the rest are terms for professions rather than classes; and they should be considered as denoting companies of artisans, rather than distinct races. The mode in which AMERA SINHA mentions the mixed classes and the professions of artisans, seems to support this conjecture.

However,

---

* See the annexed rule formed by our late venerable President.

However, the *Játimálá* expressly states the number of forty-two mixed classes, springing from the intercourse of a man of inferior class with a woman of superior class. Though, like other mixed classes, they are included under the general denomination of *Súdra*, they are considered as most abject, and most of them now experience the same contemptuous treatment as the abject mixed classes mentioned by MENU. According to the *Rudrayámala*, the domestic priests of twenty of these classes are degraded. "Avoid," says the *Tantra*, "the touch of the *Chandála*, and other
" abject classes; and of those who eat the flesh of kine,
" often utter forbidden words, and perform none of
" the prescribed ceremonies; they are called *Moléch-*
" *cha*, and going to the region of *Yavana*, have been
" named *Yavanas*.

" These seven, the *Rajaca*, *Chermacára*, *Nata*, *Ba-*
" *ruda*, *Caiverta*, and *Médabhilla*, are the last tribes.
" Whoever associates with them, undoubtedly falls from
" his class; whoever bathes or drinks in wells or pools
" which they have caused to be made, must be purified
" by the five productions of kine; whoever approaches
" their women, is doubtless degraded from his class."

" For women of the *Nata* and *Capála* classes, for
" prostitutes, and for women of the *Rajaca* and *Ná-*
" *pita* tribes, a man should willingly make oblations,
" but by no means dally with them."

I may here remark, that, according to the *Rudra-yamálá*, the *Nata* and *Natáca* are distinct; but the professions are not discriminated in that *Tantra*. If their distinct occupations, as dancers and actors, are accurately supplied, dramas are of very early date.

The *Pundraca* and *Pattasutracára*, or feeder of silk-worms, and silk-twister, deserve notice; for it has been said, that silk was the produce of *China* solely

until

until the reign of the Greek Emperor JUSTINIAN, and that the laws of *China* jealoufly guarded the exclufive production. The frequent mention of filk in the moft ancient *Sanfcrit* books would not fully difprove that opinion; but the mention of an Indian clafs, whofe occupation it is to attend filk-worms, may be admitted as proof, if the antiquity of the *Tantra* be not queftioned. I am informed, that the *Tantras* collectively are noticed in very ancient compofitions; but, as they are very numerous, they muft have been compofed at different periods; and the *Tantra* which I quote, might be thought comparatively modern. However, it may be prefumed that the *Rudra-yámala* is among the moft authentic, and, by a natural inference, among the moft ancient; fince it is named in the *Durgamebáta*, where the principal *Tantras* are enumerated*.

In the comparative Tables to which I have referred, the claffes are named, with their origin, and the particular profeffions affigned to them. How far every perfon is bound, by original inftitutions, to adhere rigidly to the profeffion of his clafs, may merit fome enquiry. Lawyers have largely difcuffed the texts of law concerning this fubject, and fome difference of opinion occurs in their writings. This, however, is not the place for entering into fuch difquifitions. I fhall therefore briefly ftate what appears to be the beft eftablifhed opinion, as deduced from the texts of MENU, and other legal authorities.

The regular means of fubfiftence for a *Bráhmana*, are affifting to facrifice, teaching the *Védas*, and receiving

---

* Thus enumerated, *Cali-Tantri, Mundmálá, Tárá, Nirbána-Tantra, Servar farun, Bira-Tantra, Singár-chana, Bhúta-Tantra, Uddifin* and *Cálicácalpa, Bhairavi-Tantra,* and *Bhairavicalpa, Todala, Mátribehédancha, Máya-Tantra, Birifwara, Bifeves-ara, Samayá-Tantra, Bráhma-Yámala-Tantra, Rudra-Yámala-Tantra, Sancáryámala-Tantra, Gayatri-Tantra. Cálicácula Servafwa, Culárnnava, Yégini-Tantra,* and the *Tantra Mehifhamaraddini.* Thefe are here univerfally known, Oh, BHAIRAVI, *greateft of-fouls!* And many are the *Tantras* uttered by SAMBHU.

ceiving gifts; for a *Cshatriya*, bearing arms; for a *Vaisya*, merchandize, attending on cattle, and agriculture; for a *Súdra*, servile attendance on the higher classes. The most commendable are, respectively for the four classes, teaching the *Véda*, defending the people, commerce, or keeping herds or flocks, and servile attendance on the learned and virtuous priests.

A *Bráhmana*, unable to subsist by his duties, may live by the duty of a soldier: if he cannot get a subsistence by either of these employments, he may apply to tillage, and attendance on cattle, or gain a competence by traffick, avoiding certain commodities. A *Cshatriya*, in distress, may subsist by all these means; but he must not have recourse to the highest functions. In seasons of distress, a further latitude is given. The practice of medicine, and other learned professions, painting and other arts, work for wages, menial service, alms and usury, are among the modes of subsistence allowed to the *Bráhmana* and *Cshatriya*. A *Vaisya*, unable to subsist by his own duties, may descend to the servile acts of a *Súdra*. And a *Súdra*, not finding employment by waiting on men of the higher classes, may subsist by handicrafts; principally following those mechanical occupations, as joinery and masonry; and practical arts, as painting and writing; by following of which he may serve men of superior classes: and, although a man of a lower class is in general restricted from the acts of a higher class, the *Súdra* is expressly permitted to become a trader or a husbandman.

Besides the particular occupations assigned to each of the mixed classes, they have the alternative of following that profession which regularly belongs to the class from which they derive their origin on the mother's side: those, at least, have such an option, who are born in the direct order of the classes, as the *Múrdhábhishicta*, *Ambasht'ha*, and others. The mixed classes

classes are also permitted to subsist by any of the duties of a *Súdra*; that is, by menial service, by handicrafts, by commerce, or by agriculture.

Hence it appears that almost every occupation, though regularly it be the profession of a particular class, is open to most other classes; and that the limitations, far from being rigorous, do, in fact, reserve only one peculiar profession, that of the *Bráhmana*, which consists in teaching the *Véda*, and officiating at religious ceremonies.

The classes are sufficiently numerous; but the subdivisions of classes have further multiplied distinctions to an endless variety. The subordinate distinctions may be best exemplified from the *Bráhmana* and *Cáyast'ha*, because some of the appellations, by which the different races are distinguished, will be familiar to many readers.

The *Bráhmanas* of Bengal are descended from five priests, invited from *Cányacubja*, by A'DISURA, King of *Gaura*, who is said to have reigned about three hundred years before Christ. These were *Bhatta Neráyna*, of the family of *Sahdila*, a son of *Casyapa*; *Dacsha*, also a descendant of *Casyapa*; *Védagarva*, of the family of *Vatsa Chandra*, of the family of *Saverna*, a son of *Casyapa*; and *Sri Hershu*, a descendant of *Bhavadwája*.

From these ancestors have branched no fewer than a hundred and fifty-six families, of which the precedence was fixed by BALLA'LA SE'NA, who reigned in the twelfth century of the Christian æra. One hundred of these families settled in *Varéndra*, and fifty-six in *Rara*. They are now dispersed throughout Bengal, but retain the family distinctions fixed by BALLA'LA SE'NA. They are denominated from the families to which their five progenitors belonged, and are still considered as *Cányacubja Bráhmanas*. At

At the period when these priests were invited by the king of *Gaura*, some *Sáreswata Bráhmanas*, and a few *Vaidicas*, resided in Bengal. Of the *Bráhmanas* of *Sáreswata* none are now found in Bengal; but five families of *Vaidicas* are extant, and are admitted to intermarry with the *Bráhmanas* of *Rárá*.

Among the *Bráhmanas* of *Váréndra*, eight families have pre-eminence, and eight hold the second rank.* Among those of *Rárá*, six hold the first rank.† The distinctive appellations of the several families are borne by those of the first rank; but in most of the other families they are disused; and *Serman*, or *Sermà*, the addition common to the whole tribe of *Bráhmanas*, is assumed. For this practice, the priests of Bengal are censured by the *Bráhmanas* of *Mit'hilá*, and other countries, where that title is only used on important occasions, and in religious ceremonies.

Vol. V.   E   In

* Va'ri'ndra Bra'hmanas.
Culi'na 8.

Moitra.	Bhima, or Cáli.	Rudra-Vágiṣi.	Sanyamini, or Sandyal.
Láhari.	Bhaduri.	Sadhu-Vágiṣi.	Bhadara.

The last was admitted by the election of the other seven.

Sudha Sro'tri' 8.
Cashta Sro'tri' 84.

The names of these families seldom occur in common intercourse.

† Ra'ri'ya Bra'hmanas.
Culi'na 6.

Muchuti, Vulgarly *Muc'kerja*. Ghóshàla.	Ganguli. Bandyagati, Vulgarly, *Banoji*.	Cánjelala. Chat'ati. Vulgarly, *Chatoji*.

Sro'tri' 50.

The names of these families seldom occur in common intercourse.

In *Mit'hilá* the additions are fewer, though distinct families are more numerous: no more than three sirnames are in use in that district, *T'hácura*, *Misra*, and *Ojhá*; each *appropriated* in any families.

The *Cáyast'has* of Bengal claim descent from five *Cáyast'has* who attended the priests invited from *Canyacubja*. Their descendants branched into eighty-three families, and their precedence was fixed by the same prince BALLA'LA SE'NA, who also adjusted the family rank of other classes.

In *Benga* and *Decshina Rárá* three families of *Cáyast'has* have pre-eminence; eight hold the second rank.* The *Cáyast'has* of inferior rank generally assume the addition of *Dása*, common to the tribe of *Súdras*, in the same manner as other classes have similar titles common to the whole tribe. The regular addition to the name of *Cshatriya* is *Verman*; to that of a *Vaisya*, *Gupta*; but the general title of *Déva* is commonly assumed; and, with a feminine termination, is also borne by women of other tribes.

The

* CA'YAST'HAS OF DECSHINA RA'RA' and BENGA.

CULI'NA 3.

Ghósha.	Vasu, Vulg. Bo'se.	Mitra.

SANMAULICA 8.

Dé.	Datta.	Cara.	Palita.
Séna.	Sinha.	Dása.	Guha.

MAULICA 72.

Guhan.	Gana.	Heda.	Huhin.	Naga.	Bhadre.
Sóma.	Pui.	Rudra.	Pála.	Aditya.	Chandra.
Sánya, or Sain.			Suin, &c.		
Syáma, &c.					
Téja, &c.					
Chácí, &c.					

The others are omitted for the sake of brevity; their names seldom occur in common intercourse.

The diſtinctions of families are important in regulating intermarriages. Genealogy is made a particular ſtudy; and the greateſt attention is given to regulate the marriages according to eſtabliſhed rulés, particularly in the firſt marriage of the eldeſt ſon. The principal points to be obſerved are, not to marry within the prohibited degrees; nor in a family known by its name to be of the ſame primitive ſtock; nor in a family of inferior rank; nor even in an inferior branch of an equal family; for within ſome families gradations are eſtabliſhed. Thus, among the *Culína* of the *Cáyaſt'has*, the rank has been counted from thirteen degrees; and in every generation, ſo long as the marriage has been properly aſſorted, one degree has been added to the rank. But ſhould a marriage be contracted in a family of a lower degree, an entire forfeiture of ſuch rank would be incurred.

The ſubject is intricate; but any perſon, deſirous of acquiring information upon it, may refer to the writings of *Gat'tácas*, or genealogiſts, whoſe compoſitions are in the provincial dialect, and are known by the name of *Culají*.

IV.

SOME ACCOUNT OF THE

SCULPTURES AT MAHABALIPOORUM;

Usually called the Seven Pagodas.

By J. GOLDINGHAM, Esq.

THESE curious remains of antiquity, situate near the sea, are about thirty-eight English miles southerly from *Madras*. A distant view presents merely a rock, which, on a near approach, is found deserving of particular examination. The attention passing over the smaller objects, is first arrested by a *Hindu* pagoda, covered with sculpture, and hewn from a single mass of rock; being about twenty-six feet in height, nearly as long, and about half as broad. Within is the *lingam*, and a long inscription on the wall, in characters unknown.

Near this structure, the surface of the rock, about ninety feet in extent, and thirty in height, is covered with figures in bas-relief. A gigantic figure of the god CRISHNA is the most conspicuous, with ARJOON, his favourite, in the *Hindu* attitude of prayer; but so void of flesh, as to present more the appearance of a skeleton than the representation of a living person. Below is a venerable figure, said to be the father of ARJOON; both figures proving the sculptor possessed no inconsiderable skill. Here are the representations of several animals, and of one which the *Bráhmens* name *singam*, or lion; but by no means a likeness of that animal, wanting the peculiar characteristick, the mane. Something intended to reprefent this is, indeed, vifible, which has more the effect of fpots. It appears evident, the sculptor was by no means fo well acquainted with the figure of the lion as with that of the elephant and monkey, both being well reprefented in this group. This fcene, I underftand, is taken from the *Mahabarat*, and exhibits the principal perfons whofe actions are celebrated in that work.

Oppofite, and furrounded by, a wall of ftone, are pagodas of brick, faid to be of great antiquity. Adjoining is an excavation in the rock, the maffy roof feemingly fupported by columns, not unlike thofe in the celebrated cavern in the Ifland of *Elephanta*, but have been left unfinifhed. This was probably intended as a place of worfhip. A few paces onward is another, and a more fpacious, excavation, now ufed, and I fuppofe originally intended, as a fhelter for travellers. A fcene of sculpture fronts the entrance, faid to reprefent CRISHNA attending the herds of ANANDA. One of the group reprefents a man diverting an infant, by playing on a flute, and holding the inftrument as we do. A gigantic figure of the god, with the *gopis*, and feveral good reprefentations of nature, are obferved. The columns fupporting the roof are of different orders, the bafe of one is the figure of a *Sphynx*. On the pavement is an infcription. (See Infcript.) Near is the almoft deferted village, which ftill retains the ancient name *Mahabalipoorum*. The few remaining *Bráhmens* vifit the traveller, and conduct him over the rock.

In the way up the rock a prodigious circular ftone is paffed under, fo placed by nature, on a fmooth and floping furface, that you are in dread of its crufhing you before you clear it. The diameter of this ftone is twenty-feven feet. The top of the rock is ftrewed with fragments of bricks, the remains, as you are informed, of a palace anciently ftanding on this fite. A rectangular polifhed polished slab, about ten feet in length, the figure of a *singam* couchant, at the south end, is shewn you as the couch of the DHERMA Rajah. A short way further, the bath used by the females of the palace is pointed out. A tale I suspect fabricated by the *Brâhmens* to amuse the traveller. That some of their own cast had chosen this spot, retired among rocks difficult of access to reside in, and that the bath, as it is called, which is only a rough stone hollowed, was their reservoir for water, would have an air of probability. The couch seems to have been cut from a stone accidentally placed in its present situation, and never to have made a part of the internal furniture of a building. The *singam*, if intended as a lion, is equally imperfect with the figures of the same animal before-mentioned.

Descending over immense beds of stone, you arrive at a spacious excavation; a temple dedicated to SI'VA, who is represented, in the middle compartment, of a large stature, and with four arms; the left foot rests on a bull couchant; a small figure of BRA'HMA on the right hand; another of VISHNU on the left; where also the figure of his goddess PARVATI' is observed. At one end of the temple is a gigantic figure of VISHNU, sleeping on an enormous *Cobra de Capella*, with several heads, and so disposed as to form a canopy over the head of the god. At the opposite end is the goddess SI'VA, with eight arms, mounted on a *singam*. Opposed to her is a gigantic figure, with a buffalo's head and human body. Between these is a human figure, suspended with the head downwards. The goddess is represented with several warlike weapons, and some armed dwarf attendants; while the monster is armed with a club. In the character of DURGA, or protector of the virtuous, the goddess is rescuing from the YEM Rajah (the figure with the buffalo's head) the suspended figure fallen improperly into his hands. The figure and action of the goddess are executed in a masterly and spirited style.

Over this temple, at a considerable elevation, is a smaller, wrought from a single mass of stone. Here is seen a slab similar to the DHERMA Rajah's couch. Adjoining is a temple in the rough, and a large mass of rock, the upper part roughly fashioned for a pagoda. If a conclusion may be drawn from these unfinished works, an uncommon and astonishing perseverance was exerted in finishing the structures here; and the more so, from the stone being a species of granite, and extremely hard.

The village contains but few houses, mostly inhabited by *Bráhmens*; the number of whom has, however, decreased of late, owing to a want of the means of subsisting. The remains of several stone edifices are seen here; and a large tank, lined, with steps of stone. A canopy for the pagod attracts the attention, as by no means wanting in magnificence or elegance. It is supported by four columns, with base and capital, about twenty-seven feet in height, the shaft tapering regularly upwards; is composed of a single stone, though not round, but sixteen sided; measuring at bottom about five and a half feet.

East of the village, and washed by the sea, which, perhaps, would have entirely demolished it before now, but for a defence of large stones in front, is a pagoda of stone, and containing the *lingam*, was dedicated to SI'VA. Besides the usual figures within, one of a gigantic stature is observed stretched out on the ground, and represented as secured in that position. This the *Bráhmens* tell you was designed for a Rajah who was thus secured by VISHNU; probably alluding to a prince of the VISHNU cast having conquered the country, and taken its prince. The surf here breaks far out over, as the *Bráhmens* inform you, the ruins of the city, which was incredibly large and magnificent. Many of the masses of stone near the shore appear to have been wrought. A *Bráhmen*, about fifty years of age, a native of the place, whom I have had an opportunity

opportunity of conversing with since my arrival at *Madras*, informed me, his grandfather had frequently mentioned having seen the gilt tops of five pagodas in the surf, no longer visible. In the account of this place by Mr. WILLIAM CHAMBERS, in the first volume of the *Asiatick Researches*, we find mention of a brick pagoda, dedicated to SI'VA, and washed by the sea; this is no longer visible; but as the *Bráhmens* have no recollection of such a structure, and as Mr. CHAMBERS wrote from memory, I am inclined to think the pagoda of stone mentioned above to be the one he means. However, it appears from good authorities, that the sea on this part of the coast is encroaching by very slow, but no less certain steps, and will perhaps in a lapse of ages entirely hide these magnificent ruins.

About a mile to the southward are other structures of stone, of the same order as those north, but having been left unfinished, at first sight appear different: the southermost of these is about forty feet in height, twenty-nine in breadth, and nearly the same in length, hewn from a single mass: the outside is covered with sculpture, (for an account of which see Inscriptions:) the next is also cut from one mass of stone, being in length about forty-nine feet, in breadth and height twenty-five, and is rent through the middle from the top to the bottom; a large fragment from one corner is observed on the ground: No account is preserved of the powerful cause which produced this destructive effect. Beside these, are three smaller structures of stone. Here is also the *singam*, or lion, very large, but, except in size, I can observe no difference from the figures of the same animal northerly. Near the *singam*, is an elephant of stone about nine feet in height, and large in proportion: Here, indeed, we observe the true figure and character of the animal.

The *Bráhmen* before mentioned informed me, that their *Puránas* contained no account of any of the structures here described, except the *stone pagodas near the sea*, and the *pagodas of brick at the village*, built by the DHERMA Rajah, and his brothers: He, however, gave me the following traditional account: That a northern prince (perhaps one of the conquerors) about one thousand years ago, was desirous of having a great work executed, but the *Hindu* sculptors and masons refused to execute it on the terms he offered: Attempting force I suppose, they, in number about four thousand, fled with their effects from his country hither, where they resided four or five years, and in this interval executed these magnificent works. The prince at length discovering them, prevailed on them to return, which they did, leaving the works unfinished as they appear at present.

To those who know the nature of these people, this account will not appear improbable. At present we sometimes hear of all the individuals of a particular branch of trade deserting their houses, because the hand of power has treated them somewhat roughly; and we observe like circumstances continually in miniature. Why the *Bráhmens* resident on the spot keep this account secret I cannot determine; but am led to suppose they have an idea, the more they can envelope the place in mystery, the more people will be tempted to visit and investigate, by which means they profit considerably.

The difference of style in the architecture of these structures, and those on the coast hereabouts, (with exceptions to the pagodas of brick at the village, and that of stone near the sea, both mentioned in the *Puránas*, and which are not different,) tends to prove that the artists were not of this country; and the resemblance of some of the figures and pillars to those in the *Elephanta* Cave, seems to indicate they were from the northward. The fragments of bricks,

at

SCULPTURES AT MAHABALIPOORUM. 75

at the top of the rock, may be the remains of habitations raised in this place of security by the fugitives in question. Some of the Inscriptions, however, (all of which were taken by myself with much care,) may throw further light on this subject.

INSCRIPTIONS *at* MAHABALIPOORUM.

On the lower Division of the Southern Structure and the Eastern Face.

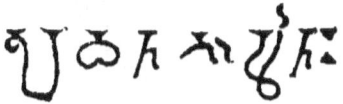

This Inscription is above a Figure apparently Female, but with only *one* Breast, (as at the Cave in *Elephanta* Island.) Four Arms are observed; in one of the Hands a Battle-axe, a Snake coiled up on the Right Side.

Above a Male Figure with four Arms.

Northern Face.

Above a Male Figure with Four Arms; a Battle-axe in one of the Hands.

Southern

Southern Front.

Above a Male Figure, with four Arms.

Above a Male Figure.

On the middle Division, Eastern Face.

Above a Male.

Above a Male, bearing a Weapon of War on the left Shoulder.

Northern

Northern Face.

Above a Male with four Arms, leaning on a Bull; the Hair plaited, and rolled about the Head; a *String* acrofs the left Shoulder, *as the* Bráhmens' *String* of *the prefent Day*.

Above two Figures, Male and Female. The former has four Arms, and the String as above; is leaning on the latter, who feems to ftoop from the Weight. The Head of the Male is covered with a high Cap, while the Hair of the Female is in the fame Form as that of the Female Figures at *Elephanta*.

Above two Figures, Male and Female. The former has four Arms, and the String.

[inscription]

Above a Male Figure, with four Arms, and the *Bráhmenical* String.

Southern Face.

[inscription]

Above a Male Figure, with four Arms.

[inscription]

Above a Male Figure, with four Arms, leaning on a Female, seeming to stoop under the Weight.

[inscription]

Above a Male, with four Arms. A Scepter appears in one Hand. This Inscription being very difficult to come at, is perhaps not quite correct.

SCULPTURES AT MAHABALIPOORUM. 79

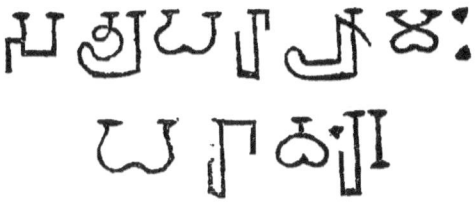

Above a Male Figure, with four Arms.

West Front.

Over a Male. The String over the left Shoulder, and a warlike Weapon on the Right.

Another Figure on this Face, but no Inscription above it.

On the Upper Division.

Each Front of this Division is ornamented with Figures, different in some Respects from those below: all, however, of the same Family.

On the Eastern Front is a Male Figure, (two Arms only.) He has two Strings or Belts; one crossing the other over the Shoulder.

Over

Over him is the following Inscription, the only one on this Division.

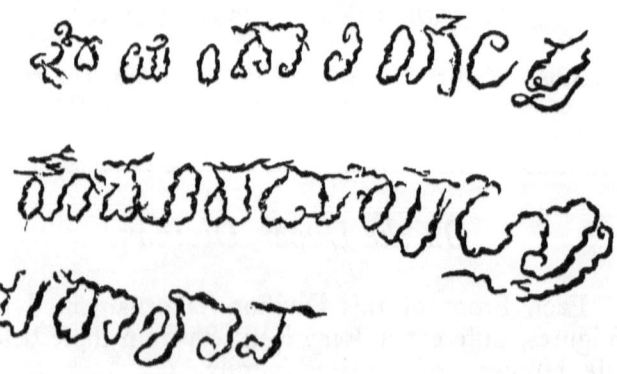

The Characters of this Inscription bear a strong Resemblance to those of the Inscription in the Stone Pagoda, near the Village mentioned in the first Part of the Account of the Place.

This Inscription is on the Pavement of the Choultry, near the Village, very roughly cut, and apparently by different Artists from those who cut the former.

Account

The Ambulatinea Moral Diagram

V.

Account of the Hindustanee Horometry.
By JOHN GILCHRIST, Esq.

THE inhabitants of *Hindustan* commonly reckon and divide time in the following manner; which exhibits a horography so imperfect, however, that its inaccuracy can only be equalled by the peoples' general ignorance of such a division, that, with all its imperfections and absurdities, must nevertheless answer the various purposes of many millions in this country. I shall therefore explain and illustrate so complex and difficult a subject, to the best of my ability and information from the natives, without presuming, in the discussion here, to encroach on the province of the chronologist or astronomer, who may yet investigate this matter with higher views, while my aim is, in the mean time, perhaps, not less usefully confined to ordinary cases and capacities entirely.

60 *Til* or *unoopul* (a sub-division of time, for which we have no relative term but *thirds*, as the series next to * *seconds*) are one *bipul*.

60 *Bipul* (which corresponds progressively only with our *seconds* or moments) one *pul*.

60 *Pul*

* On this principle one minute of ours being equal to 24 *puls*, and one moment to 24 *bipuls*, it is neither easy nor necessary to trace and mark the coincidence of such diminutives any farther. I may, however, add what the *Furhung Kardanee* contains, relative to these horal divisions, as follows.

4 *Renoo* constitute 1 *puluk*; 16 puluks, 1 *kast,ka* ; 30 kast,has, 1 *kula*; 30 kulas, 1 *guhun* ; 60 guhuns, 1 *dund* ; 2 dunds, 1 *g,huree*; 30 dunds, 1 *din*; 60 dunds, 1 *din o rat*. From this work it is evident that there exist various modes of dividing time in *India*, because a little farther on the author states the following also, viz.

60 *Zurru*, 1 *dum*; 60 dums, 1 *lumhu*, &c. which, as well as the many local modes in use, it would be superfluous to enumerate. I shall therefore attend only to the former, so far as they agree with our text. The *kast,ha* is equal to 4 *tils*, the *kula*, or two *bipuls* ; the *guhan* and *pul* are the same; so are the *dund* and *(kuchee) g,huree*; but the learner must advert to the *g,huree* in this note, being *pukkee*, or two of the former; as this distinction is frequently used when they allot only four *g,hurees* to the *puhur*; and *pukkee*, or *double*, is always understood.

60 *Pul* (correlative as above, in this sexagesimal scale with our *minutes* or *primes*) one *g,huree*, and 60 *g,huree* (called also *d,und*, which we may here translate *hour*) constitute our twenty-four hours,* or one whole day; divided into 4 *puhur din*, diurnal watches; 4 *puhur rat*, nocturnal watches.

During the equinoctial months, there are just 30 *g,hurees* in the day, and 30 also in the night; each *g,huree* properly occupying a space, *at all times*, exactly equal to 24 of our minutes; because 60 *g,hurees*, of 24 *English* minutes each, are of course 24 *English* hours of 60 *English* minutes each. For nations under or near the equator, this horological arrangement will prove convenient enough, and may yet be adduced as one argument for ascertaining with more precision the country whence the *Hindus* originally came, provided they are, as is generally supposed, the inventors of the system under consideration here. The farther we recede from the line, the more difficult and troublesome will the present plan appear. And as in this country the artificial day commences with the dawn, and closes just after sun-set, it becomes necessary to make the *puhurs* or *watches* contract and expand occasionally, in proportion to the length of the day, and the consequent shortness of the night, by admitting a greater or smaller number of *g,hurees* into these grand diurnal and nocturnal divisions alternately, and according to the sun's progress to or from the tropicks. The summer solstitial day will, therefore, consist of 34 *g,hurees*, and the night

---

* *Lumhu* and *dum*, perhaps, answer to our *minutes* and *seconds*, as the constituent parts of the *sa,ut*, or hour, 24 of which are said to constitute a natural day, and are reckoned from 1 o'clock after mid-day, regularly on through the night; also up to 24 o'clock the next noon, as formerly was the case, and which is still observed in some places on the continent; or, like ours, from 1 after noon to 12 at midnight; and again, from 1 after midnight to 12 o'clock the next noon. Whether those few who can talk of the *sa,ut* at all, have learnt this entirely from us or not, is a point rather dubious to me; but I suspect they have it from the Arabians, who acquired this with other sciences from the Greeks.

night of 26 only, or *vice verſa:* but, what is moſt ſingular in the *Indian* horometry, their *g,hurees* are unequally diſtributed among the day and night watches; the former varying from 6 to 9 in the *latter,* which are thus prevented from any definite coincidence with our time, except about the equinoctial periods only, when one *puhur* nearly correſponds to 3 *Engliſh* hours. I ſay *nearly,* becauſe even then the four middle watches have only 7 *g,hurees,* or 2 hours 48 minutes of ours; while the extremes have 8 *g,hurees* a-piece, or 24 *Engliſh* minutes more than the others, and conſequently agree with our 3 hours 12 minutes; while at other times the *puhur* is equal to no leſs than 3 hours 36 minutes; a fact which I believe has never yet been ſtated properly; though many writers have already given their ſentiments to the public on the ſubject before us; but they were probably miſled by ſaying 4-3s are 12 hours for the day, and the ſame for the night. Without conſidering the ſexageſimal diviſion, we muſt firſt make of the whole 24 hours, or 8 watches, 4 of which, during both equinoxes, having 7 *g,hurees* only, give 28: and the other 4 extreme watches, conſiſting at theſe periods alſo of 8 *g,hurees* each, form 32—60 in all; not 64 *g,hurees,** as ſome calculators have made it, who were not aware that the *g,huree,* or *dund,* never can be more nor leſs than 24 of our minutes, as I have proved above,

F 2 by

---

* One of thoſe vulgar errors originating in the crude and ſuperficial notions which none take the trouble to examine or correct, and being thus implicitly adopted, are not ſoon nor eaſily eradicated; nay, this very idea of *ſixty-four* may be ſupported from an old diſtich.

At,h puhur *choun ſut g,huree,* k,huree pokaroon pee,

Jee nikſe, Jo pee mile; nikus ja, e yih jee.

But I anſwer, the bard ſeems a ſorry aſtronomer, or he would not have followed the erroneous opinion of there being 8 *g,hurees* in each of the eight *puhur,* and 64 in the natural day: though this prevails among the illiterate Indians uncontroverted to the preſent hour; and, were I not to expoſe it here, might continue a ſtumbling-block for ever; and in this random way have we alſo imbibed the doctrine that 4 *puhur,* of three hours each, are twelve of courſe; and eight of theſe muſt give our 24. A brief, but truly incorrect, mode of ſettling this account.

by considering that 24 multiplied by 60, or 60 by 24, must be alike, which I shall make still more evident hereafter. In judicial and military proceedings, the present enquiry may, sometimes, assume considerable importance; and, as an acquaintance with it may also facilitate other matters, I have endeavoured to exhibit the Indian horometrical system contrasted with our own, upon a dial or horal diagram, calculated for one natural day of 24 hours, and adjusted to both the equinoctial and solstitial seasons, comprising four months of the twelve, that these may serve as some basis or data for a general coincidence of the whole, at any intermediate period, until men who are better qualified than the writer of this paper to execute such a task with precision, condescend to undertake it for us. He is even sanguine enough to hope that some able artist in Europe may yet be induced to construct the dials of clocks, &c. for the Indian market on the principles delineated here, and in *Persian* figures also. But we must now proceed to an explanation of the horal diagram adapted to the meridian of Patna, the central part of the Benares Zemindary, and the middle latitudes of *Hindustan*. The two exterior rings of this circle contain the complete 24 English hours, noted by the Roman letters, I, II, III, IV, &c. and the minutes are marked in figures, 24, 48, 12, 36, 60, agreeably to the sexagesimal scale, whereon the equi-distant intersections of this dial are founded; the meridional semicircles of which represent our semidian watch-plates, and for obvious reasons, with the modern horary repetition. See the note in page 82. I have distinguished the eight (4 diurnal and 4 nocturnal) watches, or *puhurs*, from I. to IV. by Roman letters also, with the *chime* (gujur) or number of bells struck at *each* in large figures, below the *puhur* letter, to which they belong, and in the same reiterated way; but these, instead of ranging from the meridian, like the English hours, commence with the equatorial and tropical lines alternately,

as

as their situations and spaces must regularly accord with the rising and setting of the sun at the vernal and autumnal equinoxes, as also at the summer and winter solstices. The days then differ in length alternately from 34 to 26 g,*burees*, as noted by the chime figures of every watch; all of which will be more evident from the mode of inserting them, and the manner that the plate has been shaded, to illustrate these circumstances fully. II. *puhur*, however, never varies; and being upon the meridional line, it of course constantly falls in with our XII. day and night. The fourth ring from the circumference shews the g,*burees*, when the day is longest, running with the sun to the top, and from this to VI. P. M. for the subdivisions of the day, and in the same manner by the bottom onwards for those of the night, throughout these concatenated circular figures 1. 2. 3. 4. 5. 6. 7. 8. 9, 1. 2, &c. q. v. in the plate. Still more interior appear the equinoctial g,*burees*, and on the same principles exactly. Within these come the winter solstitial g,*burees*, so clearly marked as to require no further elucidation here; except that in the three series of convergent figures now enumerated, the reader will recollect, when he comes to the highest number of g,*burees* in any *puhur*, to trace the *latter*, and its chime, or number of bells, out by the g,*buree* chord. For instance, when the days are shortest, begin 48 minutes after VI. A. M. and follow the coincident line inward to the centre, till you reach 9 and 34 for the closing g,*buree* and *gujur* of the night; thence go round in succession upwards with the day g,*burees* 1. 2. 3. 4. 5. 6. 7. the chord of which last terminates 36 minutes after IX. and has 7 upon it for 7 bells, and 1 for *ek puhur din*, the first watch of the day. In this way the whole may be compared with our time, allowing not only for the different meridians in this country, but for the several intermediate periods, and the difficulty of precisely ascertaining the real rising of the sun, &c. Nearest the centre I have inserted the prime divisions or *puls* of every *g,huree*, viz. 60, 50—15, 30, 45, 60, in two spaces only, because these are the invariable constituent minute parts of the *g,huree* at all seasons of the year, and consequently apply, (though omitted to prevent confusion,) as in the plate, to every one of the horal sections delineated there, into which the whole dial is equally divided. The intelligent reader may now consult the diagram itself, and I trust, with much satisfaction, as it, in fact, was the first thing that gave me any accurate knowledge of the *arrangement* and *coincidence* of the *Hindustanee* with the *English* hours, or of the rules on which their economy is founded. I certainly might have traced out and inserted the whole for a complete year, had not the apprehension of making the figure too intricate and crouded for general utility, determined me to confine it to the elucidation of four months only; especially as the real and artificial variations can be learned from an *Indian* astronomer, by those who may wish to be minutely accurate on this subject; whence every one will have it in his own power to note the exact horal coincidences at any given period, by extending the present scheme only a little farther; because the natives never add nor subtract a *g,huree* until the 60 *puls* of which it consists are accumulated, but, with their usual apathy, continue to distribute and reduce the constant increasing and decreasing temporal fractions among or from the several *puhurs* with little or no precision. Nay, they often have recourse to the last of the diurnal or nocturnal subdivisions for this purpose, when the grand horologist himself is about to inform them, that now is the time to wait for the whole of their lost minutes, before they proceed on a new score, at the risk, perhaps, of making the closing *g,huree* of the day or night as long as any two of the rest. On the other hand, when they have previously galloped too fast with time, the same ill fated hindmost *g,huree* may be reduced to a mere shadow, that the *G,huree,alee* may sound the exact number, without regarding its disproportion to the

the reft in the fame *puhur* at all. So much this and fimilar freedoms have been and can be taken with time in Hinduftan, that we may frequently hear the following ftory: While the faft of *Rumuzan* lafts, it is not lawful for the *Muffulmans* to eat or drink in the day; though at night they not only do both, but can uninterruptedly enjoy its other pleafures alfo; and upon fuch an occafion, a certain *Omra* fent to enquire of his *G,huree,alee*, if it was ftill night; to which the complaifant bellman replied in the true ftyle of oriental adulation, *Rat to ho chookee mugut peer moorfhid ke wafte do g,huree, myn luga rukee.* " Night is paft to " be fure; but I have yet two hours in referve for his " worfhip's conveniency." The apparatus with which the hours are meafured and announced, confifts of a fhallow bell-metal pan, named, from its office, *g,huree,al*, and fufpended fo as to be eafily ftruck with a wooden mallet by the *G,huree,alee*, who thus ftrikes the *g,hurees* as they pafs, and which he learns from an empty thin brafs cup (*kutoree*) perforated at bottom, and placed on the furface of water in a large veffel, where nothing can difturb it, while the water gradually fills the cup, and finks it in the fpace of one *g,huree*, to which this hour-cup or *kutoree* has previoufly been adjufted aftronomically by an aftrolabe, ufed for fuch purpofes in *India*. Thefe *kutorees* are now and then found with their requifite divifions and fubdivifions, very fcientifically marked in *Sanfcrit* characters, and may have their ufes for the more difficult and abftrufe operations of the mathematician or aftrologer: but for the ordinary occurrences of life, I believe the fimple rude horology defcribed above fuffices (perhaps divided into fourths of a *g,huree*) the Afiatics in general, who, by the bye, are often wonderfully uninformed refpecting every thing of this kind. The whole, indeed, appears, even to the better forts of people, fo perplexing and inconvenient, that they are very ready to adopt our divifions of time, when their refidence among or near us puts this in their power:

whence

whence we may, in a great measure, account for the obscurity and confusion in which this subject has hitherto remained among the *Indians* themselves; and the consequent glimmering light that preceding writers have yet afforded in this branch of oriental knowledge, which really seems to have been slurred over as a drudgery entirely beneath their notice and enquiry. The *first g,huree* of the *first puhur* is so far sacred to the Emperor of Hindustan, that his *G,huree,alee* alone strikes *one* for it. The second *g,huree* is known by two blows on the *G,huree,al*, and so on: one stroke is added for every *g,huree* to the highest, which (assuming the equinoctial periods for this statement) is eight, announced by eight distinct blows for the past *g,hurees;* after which, with a slight intermission, the *gujur* of eight bells is struck or rung, as noted in the diagram by the chime figure 8, and then one hollow sound publishes the first, or *ek puhur din* or *rat*, as this may happen, and for which consult the plate. In one *g,huree*, or 24 of our minutes, after this, the same reiteration takes place; but here stops, at the seventh or meridional *g,huree*, and is then followed with its *gujur*, or chime of 15; of which 8 are for the first watch, and 7 for the second, or *do puhur*, now proclaimed by two full distinct sounds. We next proceed with 7 more *g,hureees*, exactly noting them as before, and ringing the *gujur* of 22 strokes, after the seventh *g,huree*, or *teen puhur*, also known by three loud sounds. The fourth *puhur* has, like the first, 8 *g,hurees*, and differs in no other respect than having a *gujur* of 30 after the equatorial *g,huree* has been struck, the whole being closed by four loud blows on the *g,huree, al* for *char puhur din* or *rat;* the repetition being the same day and night during the equinoctial periods, which I have here given merely as an example more easy for the scholar's comprehension at first than the rest. The extreme *gujurs* may be properly termed the evening and morning *bell*; and, in fact, the word seems much restricted to these, as *puhur* alone is more commonly

commonly ufed for the middle *chimes* than *gujur* appears to be. Six or eight people are required to attend the eftablifhment of a *g,huree*; four through the day, and as many at night; fo that none but wealthy men, or grandees, can afford to fupport one as a neceflary appendage of their confequence and rank, which is convenient enough for the other inhabitants, who would have nothing of this fort to confult, as (thofe being excepted which are attached to their armies) I imagine there are no other public (*g,hurees*) clocks in all *India*.

VI.

On Indian Weights and Measures.

BY

H. T. COLEBROOKE, Esq.

COMMENTATORS reconcile the contradictions of ancient authors, on the subject of weights and measures, by a reference to different standards. To understand their explanations, I have been led to some enquiries, the result of which I shall state concisely, to alleviate the labour of others who may seek information on the same subject; omitting, however, such *measures* as are of very limited use.

Most of the authorities which I shall quote have not been consulted by myself, but are assumed from the citations in a work of GO'PA'LA BHATTA', on *Numbers* and *Quantities*, which is intitled *Sanc'hyaparimina*.

MENU, YA'JNYAWALEYA, and NA'REDA, trace all weights from the least visible quantity, which they concur in naming *trasarénu*, and describing as the very small mote which may be discerned in a sun-beam passing through "a lattice." Writers on medicine proceed a step further, and affirm, that a *trasarénu* contains thirty *paramánu*, or atoms: they describe the *trasarénu* in words of the same import with the definitions given by MENU, and they furnish another name for it, *vansì*. According to them, eighty-six *vansìs* make one *maríchi*, or sensible portion of light.

The

The legislators above named proceed from the *trasarénu* as follows:

8 *trasarénus*	=	1 *licsha*, or minute poppy seed.
3 *licshas*	=	1 *rája shershapa*, or black mustard seed.
3 *rája shershapas*	=	1 *gaura shershapa*, or white mustard seed.
6 *guara shershapas*	=	1 *yava*, or middle sized barley-corn.
3 *yavas*	=	1 *crĭshnala*, or seed of the *gunjà*.

This weight is the lowest denomination in general use, and commonly known by the name of *retti*, corrupted from *retticà*,* which, as well as *ractìcà*, denotes the red seed, as *crĭshnala* indicates the black seed of the *gunjà* creeper. Each *retti* used by jewellers is equal to $\frac{7}{8}$ths of a carat. The seeds themselves have been ascertained by Sir WILLIAM JONES, from the average of numerous trials, at $1\frac{1}{16}$ grain. But fictitious *rettis*, in common use, should be double of the *gunjà* seed; however, they weigh less than two grains and a quarter. For the sicca weight contains $179\frac{2}{3}$ grains nearly; the *másha*, $17\frac{3}{8}$ nearly; the *retti*, $2\frac{3}{16}$ nearly. Writers on medicine trace this weight from the smallest sensible quantity in another order.

30 *paramánus*, or atoms	=	1 *trasarénu*, or *vansi*.
86 *vansis*	=	1 *marichi*, or sensible quantity of light.
6 *marichis*	=	1 *rágicà*, or black mustard seed.
3 *rágicàs*	=	1 *shershapa*, or white mustard seed.
8 *shershapas*	=	1 *yava*, or barley-corn.
4 *yavas*	=	1 *gunjà*, or *ractìcà*.

* Asiatick Researches, vol. ii. page 154.

A *retticà* is alſo ſaid to be equal in weight to four grains of rice in the huſk: and Go'pa'la Bhatta' affirms that one ſeed of the *gunjà*, according to writers on aſtronomy, is equal to two large barley-corns. Notwithſtanding this apparent uncertainty in the compariſon of a ſeed of the *gunjà* to other productions of nature, the weight of a *ratticà* is well determined by practice, and is the common medium of compariſon for other weights. Theſe I ſhall now ſtate on the authority of Menu, Ya'jnyawaleya, and Na'reda.

Weights of Gold.

5 *chrĭſhnalas*, or *ratticàs* = 1 *máſha, máſhaca*, or *máſhica.*
16 *máſhas* = 1 *carſha, acſha, tólaca*, or *ſuverna.*
4 *carſhas*, or *ſuvernas* = 1 *pala*, (the ſame weight, which is alſo denominated *niſhca.*)
10 *palas* = 1 *dharana* of gold.

Ya'jnyawaleya adds, that five *ſuvernas* make one *pala* (of gold) according to ſome authorities.

Weights of Silver.

2 *ratticàs*, or ſeeds of the *gunjà* = 1 *máſhaca* of ſilver.
16 *máſhacas* = 1 *dharana* of ſilver, or *purána.*
10 *dharanas* of ſilver = 1 *ſatamána* or *pala* of ſilver.

But a *carſha*, or eighty *ratticàs* of copper, is called a *pana*, or *cárſhápana*.

Commentators differ on the application of the ſeveral terms. Some conſider *crĭſhnala* as a term appropriated to the quantity of one *ratticà* of gold; but Cullu'ca Bhatta' thinks the *ſuverna* only, peculiar to gold, for which metal it has alſo a name. A *pana*, or *cárſhápana*, is a meaſure of ſilver as well as of copper.

per. There is a further diversity in the application of the terms; for they are used to describe other weights. NA'REDA says a *másha* may also be considered as the twentieth of a *cárohápana*; and VRIHASPATI describes it as the twentieth part of the *pala*. Hence we have no less than four *máshas*: one *másha* of five *racticàs*; another of four *racticàs*, (according to NA'REDA;) a third of sixteen *racticàs*, according to VRIHASPATI;) and a fourth (the *máshaca* of silver) consisting of two *racticàs*; not to notice the *ma'shaca* used by the medical tribe, and consisting of ten, or, according to some authorities, of twelve, *racticàs*, which may be the same as the jeweller's *ma'sha* of six double *rettis*. To these I do not add the *má'sha* of eight *racticàs*, because it has been explained, as measured by eight silver *retti* weights, each twice as heavy as the seed; yet, as a practical denomination, it must be noticed. Eight such *rettis* make one *ma'sha*; but twelve *má'shas* compose one *tóla*. This *tóla* is no where suggested by the Hindu legislators. Allowing for a difference in the *retti*, it is double the weight of the legal *tóla*, or 210 grains instead of 105 grains.

A *nishca*, as synonimous with *pala*, consists of five *suvernas*, according to some authors. It is also a denomination for the quantity of one hundred and fifty *suvernas*. Other large denominations are noticed in dictionaries.

 108 *suvernas*, or *tólacas*, of gold, constitute an *urub-
  húshana*, *pala*, or *dínára*.
 100 *palas*, or *nishcas*, make one *tulá*; 20 *tulás*, or
  2000 *palas*, one *bhára*; and 10 *bhára*, one
  àchita.
 200 *palas*, or *nishcas*, constitute one *hára*.

According to DA'NAYO'GI'SWARA, the tenth of a *bhára* is called *ad'hára*, which is consequently synonimous with *hára*, as a term for a specifick quantity of gold.

GO'PA'LA

Go'pa'la Bhatta' alſo ſtates other weights, without mentioning by what claſſes they are uſed. I ſuſpect an error in the ſtatement, becauſe it reduces the *máſha* to a very low denomination, and I ſuppoſe it to be the jeweller's weight.

6 *rájicás (ractìcàs)*	=	1 *máſhaca, héma,* or *vánaca.*
4 *vánacas*	=	1 *ſala, dharana,* or *tanca.*
2 *tancas*	=	1 *cóna.*
2 *cónas*	=	1 *carſha.*

Probably it ſhould be *racticàs* inſtead of *rájicás*, which would nearly correſpond with the weights ſubjoined, giving twenty-four *retticás* for one *dharana* in both ſtatements. It alſo correſponds with the tables in the *Ayén Acberì*, (vol. iii. p. 94.) where a *tánc* of twenty-four *rettis*, fixed at ten barley-corns to the *retti*, contains two hundred and forty barley-corns; and a *máſha* of eight *rettis*, at ſeven and a half barley-corns each, contains ſixty *rettis*; conſequently four *máſhas* are equal to one *tanca*, as in the preceding table; and ſix jeweller's *rettis* are equal to eight double *rettis*, as uſed by goldſmiths.

The ſame author (Go'pa'la Bhatta') obſerves, that weights are thus ſtated in aſtronomical books:

2 large barley-corns	=	1 ſeed of the *gunjà*.
3 *gunjàs*	=	1 *balla.*
8 *ballas*	=	1 *dharana.*
2 *dharanas*	=	1 *alaca.*
1000 *alacas*	=	1 *dhatáca.*

The tale of ſhells, compared to weight of ſilver, may be taken on the authority of the *Lilavataì.*

20 *capardacas.*

20 *capardacas*, shells, or cowries = 1 *cácini*.
4 *cácini* = 1 *pana, cárshápana*, or *carshica*.
16 *para* (= 1 *purána* of shells) = 1 *bherma* of silver.
16 *bhermas* = 1 *nishca* of silver.

It may be inferred that one shell is valued at one *ractica* of copper; one *pana* of shells at one *pana* of copper; and sixty-four *panas*, at one *tólaca* of silver, which is equal in weight to one *pana* of copper. And it seems remarkable that the comparative value of silver, copper, and shells, is nearly the same at this time as it was in the days of Bha'scara*.

On the measures of grain Go'pa'la Bhatta' quotes the authority of several *puránas*.

Varáha purána:	1 *mushti*, or handful	= 1 *pala*.
	2 *palas*	= 1 *prasrĭti*.
	8 *mustis*	= 1 *cunchi*.
	8 *cunchis*	= 1 *pushcala*.
	4 *pushcalas*	= 1 *àd'haca*.
	4 *àd'hacas*	= 1 *dróna*.
Bhawishya purána:	2 *palas*	= 1 *prasrĭti*.
	2 *prasrĭtis*	= 1 *cudava*.
	4 *cudavas*	= 1 *prastha*.
	4 *prasthas*	= 1 *àd'haca*.
	4 *àd'hacas*	= 1 *dróna*.
	2 *drónas*	= 1 *cumb'ha*, or *súrpa*.
	16 *drónas*	= 1 *c'hárì*, or *shárì*.

---

* The comparative value of silver and copper was the same in the reign of Acber; for the *dám*, weighing five *tancs*, or twenty *máshas*, of copper, was valued at the fortieth part of the *Jelálì rupiya*, weighing twelve *máshas* and a half of pure silver; whence we have again the proportion of sixty-four to one.

Padme puràna: 4 *palas*   = 1 *cudava.*
       4 *cudavas*   = 1 *praſt'ha.*
       4 *praſt'has* = 1 *àd'haca.*
       4 *àd'hacas* = 1 *dróna.*
       16 *drónas*   = 1 *c'hári.*
       20 *drónas*   = 1 *cumb'ha.*
       10 *cumb'has* = 1 *báha*, or load.
Scanda puràna: 2 *palas*   = 1 *praſrĭti.*
       2 *praſrĭtis*   = 1 *cudava.*
       4 *cudavas*   = 1 *praſt'ha.*
       4 *praſt'has* = 1 *àd'haca.*
       4 *àd'hacas* = 1 *dróna.*
       2 *drónas*   = 1 *cumb'ha* according to some.
       20 *drónas*   = 1 *cumb'ha* according to others.

From these may be formed two Tables. The first coincides with texts of the *Varáha purána*, and is preferred by RAGHUNANDANA. The second, formed on the concurrent authority of the *Bhawiſhya*, *Padme* and *Scanda puránas*, is adopted in the *Calpateru*; rejecting, however, the *cumb'ha* of two *drónas*, and making the *pala* equal to the weight of three *tólacas* and a half.

Table I.

8 *muſhtis*, or handfuls, = 8 *palas* = 4 *praſrĭtis* = 1 *cunchi.*

8 *cunchis*   = 1 *puſhcala.*
4 *puſhcalas*   = 1 *àd'haca.*
4 *àd'hacas*   = 1 *dróna.*
20 *drónas*   = 1 *cumb'ha.*

Table II.

4 *palas* = 2 *prasritis*	= 1 *cudava* or *séttica*	14 *tólas*.
4 *cudavas*	= 1 *prast'ha*	56 ——
4 *prast'has*	= 1 *ád'haca*	224 ——
4 *ád'hacas*	= 1 *dróna*	896 ——
20 *drónas*	= 1¼ *c'hári* = 1 *cumb'ha*	17,920 ——
10 *cumb'has*	= 1 *báha*	179,200 ——

But some make two *drónas* equal to one *cumb'ha*.

Would it be unreasonable to derive the English coomb of four bushels from the *cumb'ha* of the *Hindus?* The *c'hári*, subsequently described, contains 5832 cubick inches, if the cubit be taken at eighteen inches. It would consequently be equal to two bushels, two pecks, one gallon, and two thirds; and the *cumb'ha*, equal to one *c'hári* and a quarter, will contain three bushels and three gallons nearly. According to LACSHMI'DHERA'S valuation of the *pala*, at three *tólacas* and a half, the *c'hári* weighs 14,336 *tólacas*, or 215 lb. avoirdupois nearly; and the *cumb'ha* 17,920 *tólacas*, or 268lb. which corresponds nearly to the weight of a coomb of good wheat; and a *báha* will be nearly equal to a wey, or a ton in freight.

The name of *séttica* for the fourth of a *prast'ha* is assumed from the *Varáha purána*; and HEMA'DRI accordingly declares it synonymous with *cudava*. The *Calpateru*, *Smrĭtisara*, *Retnácara*, and *Samayapradipa*, also make the *séttica* equal to the *cudava*, or a quarter of the *prast'ha*; but it contains twelve *prasrĭti* according to these commentaries, and the *prasrĭti* is described in the *Dánacánda*, by LACSHMI'DHERA, author of the *Calpateru*, as the quantity held in both hands by a man of the common fize. Twelve fuch handfuls fill a *cudava*, defcribed as a veffel four fingers wide, and as many deep, which is ufed in meafuring *small* wood, canes, iron, and other things. But VA'CHESPATIMISRA adopts this *cudava* of twelve *prafritis*, whence we have a third Table of legal Meafures in general ufe.

TABLE III.

12 double handfuls = 1 *cudava*.
4 *cudavas* = 1 *praft'ha*.
4 *praft'has* = 1 *àd'haca*.
4 *àd'hacas* = 1 *dróna*.
20 *drónas* = 1 *cumb'ha*.

Befides the difference already noticed on the fubject of the *cumb'ha*, commentators have fuggefted wider differences. According to CULLU'CA BHATTA', it contains twenty *drónas*; but this *dróna* contains two hundred *palas*.

In the *Dána vivéca* the *cumb'ha* is ftated at one thoufand *palas*; in the *Retnácara*, at twenty *praft'has*. But, according to JA'TU'CARNA, five hundred and twelve *palas* only conftitute a *cumb'ha*. This may be the fame quantity with the *dróna*, as a meafure or weight eftimated by the hand. It fhould confift of four *àd'hacas*, each equal to four *praft'has*; and each of thefe weighing, according to the *Atharva véda*, thirty-two *palas* of gold. This again feems to be the *praft'ha* of MAGAD'HA, defcribed by GO'PATHA BRA'HMANA.

4 *crĭfhnalas* = 1 *máfha*.
64 *máfhas* = 1 *pala*.
32 *palas* = 1 *praft'ha*, as ufed in MAGAD'HA.

Since the *pala* of gold weighs 420 troy grains, the *praſt'ha* contains one pound avoirdupois, fourteen ounces and three quarters nearly. The *dróna*, laſt mentioned, contains 30 lb. 11 oz. and a fraction; and a *cumb'ha* of twenty ſuch *drónas*, 614 lb. 6 oz. and a half nearly.

The meaſures of grain in common uſe, are probably derived from the ancient *cumb'ha* and *dróna*; but their names are not ſuggeſted by any of the preceding Tables. Twenty *cát'hás* make one *bíſí*; and ſixteen *bíſís* one *pautí*. The ſize of the *cát'há* varies in different diſtricts; in ſome containing no more than two and a half *ſér* of rice; in others five *ſér*, (80 ſicca weight;) or *even more*. In the ſouthern diſtricts of Bengal, a meaſure of grain is uſed which contains one *ſér* and a quarter. It is called *réc*. Four *récs* make one *páli*; twenty *pális*, one *ſoli*; and ſixteen *ſolis*, one *cáhen*.

The *Vrïhat Rájamartanda* ſpecifies meaſures which do not appear to have been noticed in other *Sanſcrit* writings.

  24 *tólacas* = 1 *ſér*.
   2 *ſér* = 1 *prabh*.

It is mentioned in the *Ayén Ackberí*, that the *ſér* formerly contained eighteen *dáms* in ſome parts of *Hinduſtan*, and twenty-two *dáms* in others; but that it conſiſted of twenty-eight *dáms* at the commencement of the reign of Acber, and was fixed by him at thirty *dáms*. The *dám* was fixed at five *táncs*, or twenty *máſhas*; or, as ſtated in one place, twenty *máſhas* and ſeven *rettis*. The ancient *ſér*, noticed in the *Ayén Ackberí*, therefore, coincided nearly with the *ſér* ſtated in the *Rájamartanda*. The double *ſér* is ſtill uſed in ſome places, but called by the ſame name (*panchaſérí*) as the weight of five *ſér* uſed in others.

For

For measures used in *Mit'hila*, and some other countries, we have the authority of CHANDE'SUARA, in the *Bála bhúshana*. They differ from the second table, interposing a *mánica* equal to a fourth of a *c'hárì*, and making the *báha* equal to twenty *c'hárìs*.

  4 *palas*   = 1 *cudava*.
  4 *cudavas* = 1 *prast'ha*.
  4 *prast'has* = 1 *àd'haca*.
  4 *àd'hacas* = 1 *dróna*.
  4 *drónas*   = 1 *mánica*.
  4 *mánicas* = 1 *c'hárì*.
  20 *c'hárìs*   = 1 *báha*.

GOPA'LA BHATTA' states another set of measures, without furnishing a comparison to any determinate quantity otherwise known.

  4 *áyus*   = 1 *sácsha*.
  4 *sácshas* = 1 *bilwa*.
  4 *bilwas*   = 1 *cudava*.
  4 *cudavas* = 1 *prast'ha*.
  4 *prast'has* = 1 *c'hárì*.
  4 *c'hárìs*   = 1 *gónì*.
  4 *gónìs*   = 1 *drónicá*.

I have already quoted a comparison of the *cudava* to a practical measure of length; and we learn from the *Lìlávatì*, that the *c'hárì*, or *c'hárìca*, of MAGAD'HA, should be a cube measured by one cubit. "A vessel "measured by a cubit, in every dimension, is a "*ghanahasta*, which, in MAGAD'HA, is called *c'hárìca*: "it should be made with twelve corners, *or angles* "*formed by surfaces;* *(that is, it should be made in the* "*form of a solid, with six faces.)*
            "The

"The *c'hárìca* of UTCALA is in general use on the south of the river *Gódáveri:* there the *dróna* is the sixteenth part of a *c'hárì*; (as in the Second Table;) the *àd'haca* the fourth of a *dróna*; the *praſt'ha*, the fourth of an *àd'haca*; and the *cudava*, a quarter of a *praſt'ha*. But the *cudava*, formed like a *ghanahaſta*, should be measured by three fingers and a half in every dimension. This vessel must be made of earth, or similar materials; for such alone is a *cudava*."

Both by this statement, and by the Second Table, a *c'hárì* consists of 1026 *cudavas*; and since the cubit must be taken at twenty-four fingers, or *angulas*, a solid cubit will contain 13,824 cubick *angulas* or fingers; and one *cudava* thirteen and a half cubick *angulas*. Its solid contents, therefore, are the half of a cube whose side is three fingers. A slight change in the reading would make the description quoted from the *Lílávatì* coincide with this computation; and the *c'hárìca* of UTCALA and MAGAD'HA would be the same.

However, LACSHMI'DHERA has described the *cudava* as a vessel four fingers wide, and as many deep, which makes a *cudava* of sixty-four cubick *angulas*, or twenty-seven cubick inches. This will exhibit an *àd'haca* of 432 inches, similar to a dry measure used at Madras, which is said to contain 423 cubick inches, and is the eighth part of a *marcal* of 3384 cubick inches, or nearly double the *dróna* of 1728 cubick inches. If the *cudava* of UTCALA be a cube whose side is three and a half fingers, containing forty-three cubick *angulas* nearly, or eighteen cubick inches and a fraction, the *c'hárìca* of UTCALA contains 44,118 cubick *angulas*, or 18,612 cubick inches, taking the cubit at eighteen inches.

On the measures of space, Go'pa'la Bhatta' quotes a text from *Vriddha* Menu, which traces these from the same minute quantity as weights.

8 *trasarénus* = 1 *rénu*.
8 *rénus* = 1 *bálágra*, or hair's point.
8 *bálágras* = 1 *licsha*, or poppy feed.
8 *licshas* = 1 *yúca*.
8 *yúcas* = 1 *yava*, or very small barley-corn.
8 *yavas* = 1 *angula*, or finger.

From this Menu proceeds to longer measures.

12 *angulas*, or fingers, = 1 *vitesti*, or span.
2 *vitestis*, or spans, = 1 *hesta*, or cubit.

In the Ma'rcande'ya *purána* measures are traced from atoms.

8 *paramánus*, or atoms, = 1 *para sucshma*, most minute substance.
8 *para sucshmas* = 1 *trasarénu*.
8 *trasarénus* = 1 *mehirajaés*, grain of sand or dust.
8 grains of sand = 1 *bálágra*, or hair's point.
8 *bálágras* = 1 *licsha*.
8 *licshas* = 1 *yúca*.
8 *yúcas* = 1 *yava*.
8 *yavas* = 1 *angula*, or finger.
6 fingers = 1 *pada*, or breadth of the foot.
2 *padas* = 1 *vitesti*, or span.
2 spans = 1 cubit (*hesta*)
2 cubits = the circumference of the human body.
4 cubits = 1 *dhanush*, *denda*, or staff.
2 *dendas* = 1 *naricá* (or *nádi*)

In another place the same *purána* notices two measures, one of which is often mentioned in rituals:

21 breadths of the middle of the thumb = 1 *retni*.
10 ditto   -   -   -   -   -   -   = 1 *pradeſya*, or ſpan, from the tip of the thumb to the tip of the fore-finger.

But, according to the *Calpateru*, it ſhould be ten breadths of the thumb and a half. And we learn from the ADITYA *purána*, that, according to VYA'SA, it ſhould be meaſured by the breadth of the thumb at the tip. The ſame *purána* makes two *retnis* (or 42 thumbs) equal to one *ciſhu*: but HA'RI'TA compares the *ciſhu* to the cubit, four of which it contains, according to his ſtatement: and four *ciſhus* make one *nalwa*. Here again the ADITYA *purána* differs, making the *nalwa* to contain thirty *dhanuſh*. It concurs with authorities above cited, in the meaſures of the cubits. *denda* and *nádì*; the firſt containing twenty-four fingers; the ſecond ninety-ſix fingers; and the *nádì* two *dendas*.

The ſame *purána* notices the larger meaſures of diſtance.

2000 *dhanuſh*   = 1 *cróſa*.
   2 *cróſas*   = *gavyuti*.
8000 *dhanuſh* = *gavyutis* = 1 *yójana*.

On one reading of the VISHNU *purána*, the *cróſa* contains only one thouſand *dhanuſh*. Accordingly GO'PA'LA BHATTA' quotes a text, which acquaints us that "Travellers to foreign countries compute the *yójana* at four thouſand *dhanuſh*:" but he adduces another text, which ſtates the meaſures of the *cróſa*, *gavyuti*, and *yójana*, as they are given in the ADITYA *purána*. The *Lílávatì* confirms this computation.

8 barley

8 barley-corns = 1 finger's breadth.
24 fingers = 1 *heſta*, or cubit.
4 cubits = 1 *denda* (= 1 *dhanuſh*.)
2000 *dendas* = 1 *cróſa* *
4 *cróſas* = 1 *yójana*.

The *Lílávatì* alſo informs us of the meaſures uſed for arable land, which are ſimilar to thoſe now in uſe.

10 hands = 1 *vanſa*, or bamboo cane.
20 *vanſas* (in length and breadth) = 1 *niranga* of arable land.

Diviſions of time are noticed in the firſt chapter of MENU, (v. 64.)

18 *niméſhas*, or the twinklings of an eye, = 1 *cáſht'hà*.
30 *cáſht'hàs* = 1 *calá*.
30 *calás* = 1 *cſhana*.
12 *cſhanas* = 1 *muhúrta*.
30 *muhúrtas* = 1 day and night, (according to mean ſolar time.)

From this he proceeds to the diviſions of the civil year.

15 days and nights (*ahórátra*) = 1 *pacſha*, or interval between the ſizygies.
firſt and laſt *pacſha* = 1 month.

2 months

---

* If the cubit be taken at eighteen inches, then 4000 yards = 1 ſtandard *cróſa* = 2 miles and a quarter nearly: and 2000 yards = 1 computed *cróſa* = 1 mile and one eighth: and MAJOR RENNEL ſtates the *crós* as fixed by ACBER at 5000 *gez* = 4757 yards = 2 Britiſh miles and 5 furlongs; and the average common *crós* at one mile ſtatute and nine tenths.

2 months = 1 feafon (*rĭtu*)
3 feafons = 1 *ayana* (half year)
2 *ayanas* = 1 year.

According to the *Súrya Siddhánta* (fee Af. Ref. vol. ii. p. 230.)

6 refpirations (*prá'ná'*) = 1 *vicalà*.
60 *vicalàs* = 1 *danda*.
60 *dandas* = 1 fydereal day.

The VISHNU *purá'na* ftates a mode of fubdividing the day, on which GO'PALA' BHATTA' remarks, that " it is founded on aftronomy," and fubjoins another mode of fubdivifion.

Ten long fyllables are uttered in one refpiration (*prá'ná'*.)

6 refpirations = 1 *vinàdicà*.
60 *vinàdicàs* = 1 *dhatà*.
60 *dhatàs* = 1 day and night, (or folar day.)

Proceeding to another Table, he fays, the time in which ten long fyllables may be uttered is equal to one refpiration.

6 refpirations = 1 *pala*.
60 *palas* = 1 *ghaticà*.
60 *ghaticàs* = 1 day and night.
30 days and nights = 1 month.
12 months = 1 year.

The VARA'HA *purá'na* concurs with the *Súrya Siddhá'nta* in another fubdivifion of time.

60 *cfhanas*

60 *cshanas*   = 1 *lava*
60 *lavas*   = 1 *nimésha*.
60 *nimeshas*   = 1 *cá'st'hà*.
60 *cá'st'hàs*   = 1 *atipala*.
60 *atipalas*   = 1 *vipala*.
60 *vipalas*   = 1 *pala*.
60 *palas*   = 1 *danda*.
60 *dandas*   = a night and day.
60 nights and days = 1 *ritu* or season.

But the BHAWISHYA *purá'na* subdivides the *nimésha* otherwise.

1 twinkling of the eye while a man is easy and at
   rest   = 30 *tatpanas*, or moments.
1 *tatpana* = 100 *trutis*.
1 *truti*   = 1000 *samcramas*.

RAGHUNANDANA, in the *Jyótishatatwa*, gives a rule for finding the planets which preside over hours of the day, called *hóra*. "Doubling the *ghatis* elapsed from "the beginning of the day (or sun-rise at the first me-"ridian) and dividing by five, the product shews the "elapsed hours, or *hóra's*. The sixth planet, counted "from that which gives name to the proposed day, "rules the second hour. The sixth counted from this "rules the third; and so on for the hours of the day: "but every fifth planet is taken for the hours of the "night." The order of the planets is ☾ ☿ ♀ ☉ ♂ ♃ ♄; consequently on a *Sunday* the regent of the several hours of the day and night are:

Day 1 2 3 4 5 6 7 8 9 10 11 12
     ☉ ♀ ☿ ☾ ♄ ♃ ♂ ☉ ♀ ☿   ☾   ♄
                                         Night

Night	1	2	3	4	5	6	7	8	9	10	11	12
	♂	♀	☾	♄	♃	☉	☿	♄	♂	♀	☾	♄	☉

As the days of the week are found by taking every fourth in the same series, we might proceed by this rule to the first *bórá* of the subsequent day, whose regent, the fourth from ☉, is ☾; and thence proceed by the above-mentioned rule to the regents of *hórás* for Monday.

I subjoin the original passage, which was communicated to me by Mr. DAVIS, and add a verbal translation.

বহ্নপুবতে ঘটিকাহিনিস্রাঃ কানাথা স্রোব্রাপতদঃ শবাষাঃ
দিনিস্রাণ সৃতৃবাণরত্যা নিস্রানাথা পেতমঃ শবল্যাঃ॥
বেথাশ্রু শবতো হবঃ সমোংস্যা পৈবত্রা স্রোকা
দেশাতব যোজযমিত বিযতীতিঃ শাদহীনাতিঃ॥ ১ ॥

"THE *ghatícas elapsed* from the beginning of the day being doubled, and divided by (five) arrows, *shew* the cords of time called *hórá*. In the day these cords are regulated by intervals of (six) seasons, counted from the particular regent of the day *proposed*; in the night by intervals of (five) arrows.

"The *commencement of the day*, at preceding or subsequent meridians, before or after sun-rise, *at the first meridian, is known* from the interval of countries, or *distance in longitude* measured by *yójanas*, and reduced into *ghatis*, after deducting a fourth *from the number of yójanas*."

The

The coincidence of name for the hour, or twenty-fourth part of the day, is certainly remarkable. But until we find the fame divifion of time noticed by a more ancient author than RAGHUNANDANA, it muft remain doubtful whether it may not have been borrowed from *Europe* in modern times.

VII.

OF THE

CITY OF PEGUE,

AND THE

TEMPLE OF SHOEMADOO PRAW.

By Captain MICHAEL SYMES.

THE limits of the ancient city *Pegue* may ſtill be accurately traced by the ruins of the ditch and wall that ſurrounded it. From theſe it appears to have been a quadrangle, each ſide meaſuring about a mile and a half. In ſeveral places the ditch is nearly filled by rubbiſh that has been caſt into it, or the falling in of its own banks: ſufficient, however, ſtill remains to ſhew that it once was no contemptible defence. The breadth I judged to be about 60 yards, and the depth ten or twelve feet; except in thoſe places where it is choaked up from the cauſes I have mentioned. There is ſtill enough of water to impede a ſiege; and I was informed, that when in repair, it ſeldom, in the hotteſt ſeaſon, ſunk below the depth of four feet.

The fragments of the wall likewiſe prove that this was a work of conſiderable magnitude and labour. It is not eaſy to aſcertain preciſely what was its exact height; but we conjectured it to have been at leaſt twenty-five feet; and in breadth at the baſe, not leſs than forty. It is compoſed of brick, badly cemented with clay mortar. Small equidiſtant baſtions, about 300 yards aſunder, are ſtill diſcoverable: but the whole is in a ſtate ſo ruinous, and ſo covered with weeds and briars, that it requires cloſe inſpection to determine the extent and nature of the defences.

In

In the center of each side there is a gateway, about thirty feet wide. These gateways were the principal entrances. The passage across the ditch is on a mound of earth, which serves as a bridge; and was formerly defended by a retrenchment, of which there are now no traces.

Nothing can exhibit a more striking picture of desolation than the inside of these walls. ALOMPRAW, when he carried the city by assault in the year 1757, razed every dwelling to the ground, and dispersed or led into captivity all the inhabitants. The pagodas, or praws, which are very numerous, were the only buildings that escaped the fury of the conquerors; and of these the great pagoda of SHOEMADOO has alone been attended to, and repaired. After the demolition of the city, ALOMPRAW carried the captive monarch with his family to *Ava*, where he remained many years a state prisoner. YANGOON, or RANGOON, founded about this time, was by a royal mandate constituted the seat of provincial government, and *Pegue* entirely abandoned.

The present king of the *Birmans*, whose government has been less disturbed than that of any predecessor of his family, entirely altered the system which had been adopted by his father, and observed during the successive reigns of his two brothers, NAMDOGE PRAW, and SEMBUAN PRAW, and of his nephew CHENGUZA. He has turned his attention to the population and improvement, rather than the extension, of his dominions; and seems more desirous to conciliate his new subjects by mildness, than to rule them through terror. He has abrogated several severe penal laws, imposed upon the *Taliens* or *Peguers:* justice is now distributed impartially; and the only distinction at present between a *Birman* and *Talien*, consists in the exclusion of the latter from all public offices of trust and power.

No

No act of the *Birman* government is more likely to reconcile the *Taliens* to the *Birman* yoke, than the reftoration of their ancient place of abode, and the prefervation and embellifhment of the Pagoda of SHOEMADOO. So fenfible was the King of this, as well as of the advantages that muft accrue to the ftate from an increafe of culture and population, that five years ago he iffued orders to rebuild Pegue, encouraged new fettlers by liberal grants, and invited the fcattered families of former inhabitants to return and repeople their deferted city.

The better to effect this purpofe, his *Birman* Majefty, on the death of TAOMANGEE, the late *Mayoon*, or Viceroy, which happened about five years ago, directed his fucceffor, MAIN LLA NO RETHEE, to quit Rangoon, and make Pegue his future refidence, and the feat of provincial government of the thirty-two provinces of *Henzawuddy*.

Thefe judicious meafures have fo far fucceeded, that a new town has been built within the fite of the ancient city; but Rangoon poffeffes fo many fuperior advantages, and holds out fuch inducements to thofe who wifh to dwell in a commercial town, that adventurers do not refort in any confiderable numbers to the new colony. The former inhabitants are now nearly extinct, and their families and defcendants fettled in the provinces of *Tanghoo*, *Martaban*, and *Talowmeou*; and many live under the protection of the *Siamefe*. There is little doubt, however, that the reftoration of their favourite temple of worfhip, and the fecurity held out to them, will, in the end, accomplifh the wife and humane intentions of the *Birman* Monarch.

Pegue, in its renovated ftate, feems to be built on the plan of the former city. It is a fquare, each fide meafuring about half a mile. It is fenced round by a stockade, from ten to twelve feet high. There is one main street, running east and west, which is intersected at right angles by two smaller streets, not yet finished. At each extremity of the principal street there is a gate in the stockade, which is shut early in the evening. After that hour, entrance during the night is confined to a wicket. Each of these gates is defended by a sorry piece of ordnance, and a few musqueteers, who never post centinels, and are usually asleep. There are also two other gates on the north and south sides of the stockade.

The streets of Pegue are spacious, as are the streets in all *Birman* towns that I have seen. The road is carefully made with brick, which the ruins of the old town plentifully supply. On each side of the way there is a drain, that serves to carry off the water. The houses even of the meanest peasants of Pegue, and throughout all the Birman empire, possess an advantage over Indian dwellings, by being raised from the ground either on wooden posts, or bamboos, according to the size of the building. The dwellings of the *Rahaans*, or priests, and higher ranks of people, are usually elevated eight or ten feet; those of the lower classes from two to four.

The houses of the inhabitants of Pegue are far from commodious, agreeably to European notions of accommodation; but I think they are at least as much so as the houses of Indian towns. There are no brick buildings either in Pegue or Rangoon, except such as belong to the King, or are dedicated to GAUDMA. The King has prohibited the use of brick or stone in private buildings, from the apprehension, I was informed, that, if people got leave to build brick houses, they might erect brick fortifications, dangerous to the security of the state. The houses, therefore, are all made of mats or sheathing-boards, supported on bamboos or posts. Being composed of such combustible materials,

materials, the inhabitants are under continual dread of fire, againft which they take every precaution. The roofs are lightly covered; and at each door ftands a long bamboo, with a hook at the end, to pull down the thatch: alfo another pole, with a grating of fplit bamboo at the extremity, about three feet fquare, to fupprefs flame by preffure. Almoft every houfe has earthen pots of water on the roof. And there is a particular clafs * of people, whofe bufinefs it is to prevent and extinguifh fires.

The *Mayoon's* habitation is a good building, in comparifon with all the other houfes of Pegue. It is raifed on pofts, ten feet high. There feems, from an outfide view, to be many apartments, befides the hall in which he gives audience. It is in the centre of a fpacious court, furrounded by a high fence of bamboo mats. There is in the hall, at the upper end, a fmall elevation in the floor, on which the Viceroy fits when he receives vifits in form.

The object in Pegue that moft attracts and moft merits notice, is, the Temple of SHOEMADOO †, or the

Golden

---

* Thefe people are called *Pagwaat*. They are flaves of the government; men who have been found guilty of theft, and through mercy have had their lives fpared. They are diftinguifhed by a black circle on each cheek, caufed by punctuation: alfo by having on their breafts, in BIRMAN characters, the word *Thief;* and the name of the article ftolen; as on one (that I afked an explanation of) *Putchoo Khoo*, or *Cloth Thief.*

Thefe men patrole the ftreets at night, to put out fires and lights after a certain hour. They act as conftables, and are the public executioners.

† *Shoe* is the *Birman* word for *golden;* and there can be little doubt that *Madoo* is a corruption of the *Hindu* MAHA DEVA or DEO. I could not learn from the *Birmans* the origin or etymology of the term; but it was explained to me as importing a *promontory that overlooked land and water.* *Praw* fignifies *Lord,* and is always annexed to the name of a facred building. It is likewife a fovereign and facerdotal title; and frequently ufed by an inferior when addreffing his fuperior. The analogy between the *Birmans* and the ancient *Egyptians*, in the application of this term, as well as in many other inftances, is highly deferving notice.

Phra was the proper name under which the *Egyptians* firft adored

Golden Supreme. This extraordinary edifice is built on a double terrace, one raised upon another. The lower and greater terrace is about ten feet above the natural level of the ground. It is quadrangular. The upper and lesser terrace is of a like shape, raised about twenty feet above the lower terrace, or thirty above the level of the country. I judged a side of the lower terrace to be 1391 feet, of the upper 684. The walls that sustained the sides of the terraces, both upper and lower, are in a state of ruin. They were formerly covered with plaister, wrought into various figures. The area of the lower is strewed with the fragments of small decayed buildings; but the upper is kept free from filth, and in tolerable good order. There is a strong presumption that the fortress is coeval with this building; as the earth of which the terraces are composed, appears to have been taken from the ditch; there being no other excavation in the city, or its neighbourhood, that could have afforded a tenth part of the quantity.

These terraces are ascended by flights of stone steps, broken and neglected. On each side are dwellings of the *Rahaans*, or priests, raised on timbers four or five feet from the ground. Their houses consist only of a single hall. The wooden pillars that support them are turned with neatness. The roof is of tile, and the sides of sheathing-boards. There are a number of bare benches in every house, on which the *Rahaans* sleep. We saw no furniture.

SHOEMADOO is a pyramid, composed of brick and plaister, with fine shell mortar, without excavation or aperture

---

adored the Sun, before it received the allegorical appellation of *Osiris*, or Author of Time. They likewise conferred it on their kings and priests. In the first book of MOSES, chap. xli. PHARAOH gives " JOSEPH to wife the daughter of *Potiphera*, or the Priest of ON." In the book of Jeremiah, a king of Egypt is styled, " PHARAOH OPHRA." And it is not a very improbable conjecture, that the title PHARAOH, given to successive kings of *Egypt*, is a corruption of the word *Phra*, or *Praw*; in its original sense signifying the *Sun*, and applied to the sovereign and the priesthood, as the representatives on earth of that splendid luminary.

aperture of any sort; actagonal at the base, and spiral at top. Each side of the base measures 162 feet. This immense breadth diminishes abruptly; and a similar building has not unaptly been compared in shape to a large speaking trumpet.*

Six feet from the ground there is a wide ledge, which surrounds the base of the building; on the plane of which are fifty-seven small spires, of equal size, and equidistant. One of them measured twenty-seven feet in height, and forty in circumference at the bottom. On a higher ledge there is another row, consisting of fifty-three spires, of similar shape and measurement. A great variety of mouldings encircles the building; and ornaments, somewhat resembling the fleur de lys, surround what may be called the base of the spire. Circular mouldings likewise gird this part to a considerable height; above which there are ornaments in stucco, not unlike the leaves of a *Corinthian* capital; and the whole is crowned by a *tee*, or umbrella of open iron-work, from which rises an iron rod with a gilded penant.

The *tee*, or umbrella, is to be seen on every sacred building in repair, that is of a spiral form. The raising and consecration of this last and indispensible appendage, is an act of high religious solemnity, and a season of festivity and relaxation.

The present King bestowed the *tee* that covers SHOEMADOO. It was made at the capital; and many of the principal nobility came down from *Ummerapoora* to be present at the ceremony of putting it on.

The circumference of the *tee* is fifty-six feet. It rests on an iron axis, fixed in the building, and is further

* Vide Mr. HUNTER's Account of *Pegue*.

further secured by large chains, strongly rivetted to the spire.

Round the lower rim of the umbrella are appended a number of bells, of different sizes, which, agitated by the wind, make a continual jingling.

The *tee* is gilt; and it is said to be the intention of the King to gild the whole of the spire. All the lesser pagodas are ornamented with proportionable umbrellas, of similar workmanship, which are likewise encircled by small bells.

The extreme height of the building, from the level of the country, is 361 feet; and above the interior terrace, 331 feet. On the south-east angle of the upper terrace there are two handsome saloons, or *keouns*, lately erected. The roof is composed of different stages, supported by pillars. I judged the length of each saloon to be about sixty feet, and the breadth thirty. The ceiling of one of them is already embellished with gold leaf, and the pillars lacquered; the other is not yet completed. They are made entirely of wood. The carving on the outside is very curious. We saw several unfinished figures, intended to be fixed on different parts of the building; some of them not ill shapen, and many exceedingly grotesque. Splendid images of GAUDMA (the *Birman* object of adoration) were preparing, which we understood were designed to occupy the inside of these *keouns*.

At each angle of the interior terrace is a pyramidical pagoda, sixty-seven feet in height, resembling, in miniature, the great pagoda. In front of the one in the

the south-west corner are four gigantic representations, in masonry, of PALLOO, or the *man-destroyer*, half beast, half human, seated on their hams, each with a large club on the right shoulder. The *Pundit* who accompanied me said, that they resembled the RAKUSS of the *Hindus*. They are guardians of the temple.

Nearly in the center of the east face of the area are two human figures in stucco, beneath a gilded umbrella. One standing, represents a man with a book before him, and a pen in his hand. He is called THAGIAMEE, the recorder of mortal merits, and mortal misdeeds. The other, a female figure kneeling, is MAHA SUMDERE, the protectress of the universe, as long as the universe is doomed to last: but when the time of general dissolution arrives, by her hand the world is to be overwhelmed, and destroyed everlastingly.

A small brick building, near the north-east angle, contains an upright marble slab, four feet high, and three feet wide, on which is a long and legible *Birman* inscription. I was told it was a recent account of the donations of pilgrims.

Along the north face of the terrace there is a wooden shed, for the convenience of devotees who come from a distance to offer up their prayers at SHOEMADOO.

On the north side of the great pagoda are three large bells, of good workmanship, suspended near the ground, between pillars. Several deers' horns are strewed around. Those who come to pay their devotions, first take up one of the horns, and strike the bell three times, giving an alternate stroke to the ground. This act, I was told, is to announce to the spirit of GAUDMA, the approach of a suppliant. There are several low benches near the bottom of the pagoda, on which the person who comes to pray places his offering, which generally consists of boiled rice, a plate of sweetmeats, or cocoa-nut fried in oil. When it is given, the devotee cares not what becomes of it. The crows and *pariah* dogs commonly eat it up in the presence of the donor, who never attempts to prevent or molest the animals. I saw several plates of victuals devoured in this manner, and understood it was the case with all that were brought.

There are many small pagodas on the areas of both terraces, which are neglected, and suffered to fall into decay. Numberless images of Gaudma lie indiscriminately scattered. A pious *Birman*, who purchases an idol, first procures the ceremony of consecration to be performed by the *Rahaans*, then takes his purchase to whatever sacred building is most convenient, and there places it either in the shelter of a *keoun*, or on the open ground before the temple: nor does he ever after seem to have any anxiety about its preservation, but leaves the divinity to shift for itself.

Some of those idols are made of alabaster, which is found in the neighbourhood of the capital of the *Birman* dominions, and admits of a very fine polish.

On both the terraces are a number of white cylindrical flags,* which are used by the *Rahaans* alone, and are considered as emblematic of purity and their sacred function. On the top of the staff there is commonly the figure of a *benza*, or goose, the symbol both of the Birman and Pegue nations.

From

---

* These flags are made of long stripes of white cloth, sewed together at the sides, and extended by hooks of thin bamboos.

From the upper ledge that surrounds the base of SHOEMADOO, the prospect of the country is extensive and picturesque; but it is a prospect of nature in her rudest state. There are few inhabitants, and scarcely any cultivation. The hills of *Martaban* rise to the eastward; and the *Sitang* river, winding along the plains, gives here and there an interrupted view of its waters. To the north-north-west, above forty miles, are the *Galladzet* hills, whence the Pegue river takes its rise; hills remarkable only for the noisome effects of their atmosphere. In every other direction the eye looks over a boundless plain, chequered by a wild intermixture of wood and water.

Previous to my departure from Pegue, I paid a visit to the *Siredaw*, or superior *Rahaan*, of the country. His abode was situated in a shady grove of tamarind trees, about five miles south-east of the city. Every object seemed to correspond with the years and dignity of the possessor. The trees were lofty. A bamboo railing protected his dwelling from the attack of wild beasts. A neat reservoir contained clear water. A little garden gave him roots; and his retreat was well stocked with fruit-trees. A number of younger *Rahaans* lived with him, and administered to his wants with pious respect. Though extremely emaciated, he seemed lively, and in full possession of his mental faculties. He said his age was eighty-seven. The *Rahaans*, although supported by charity, never accept of money. I therefore presented this venerable prelate of the order with a piece of cloth, which was repaid by a grateful benediction. He told me that, in the convulsions of the Pegue empire, most of their valuable records had been destroyed; but it was traditionally believed, that the temple of SHOEMADOO was founded two thousand three hundred years ago, by two brothers, merchants, who came to Pegue from *Talowmeou*, one day's journey east of *Martaban*. These pious traders raised a pagoda of one *Birman* cubit, twenty inches and a half in height. SIGEAMEE, or the spirit that presides over the elements, and directs the thunder and lightning, in the space of one night, increased the size of the pagoda to two cubits. The merchants then added another cubit, which SIGEAMEE likewise doubled in the same short time. The building thus attained the magnitude of twelve cubits, when the merchants desisted. That the pagoda was afterwards gradually increased by successive monarchs of Pegue; the registers of whose names, and the amount of their contributions, had been lost in the general ruin: nor could he inform me of any authentic archives that survived the wreck.

Of the deficiency of the foregoing account of the city of Pegue, and the temple of SHOEMADOO, I am fully sensible. Authentic documents were not to be procured; and the stories related, in answer to oral enquiries, were too extravagant to merit attention. That Pegue was once a great and populous city, the ruins of buildings within the walls, and the vestiges of its extensive suburbs, still extant, sufficiently declare. Of the antiquity of SHOEMADOO there is no reason to doubt: and as a pile of building, singular in its construction, and extraordinary for its magnitude, it may justly be numbered amongst the most curious specimens of oriental architecture.

VIII.

Description of the Tree called, by the Burmas, LAUNZAN.

BY

FRANCIS BUCHANAN, Esq. M. D.

BEFORE my setting out to accompany the late deputation to the court of *Ava*, I received some seeds, which had been sent to SIR JOHN SHORE from *Pegue*. It was conceived that they might be usefully employed to yield oil, with which they seemed to abound: I was therefore particular in making my enquiries after the plant producing them. I soon learned that they were produced only in the upper provinces of the kingdom; and, on my arrival there, I found myself still at a distance from the tree on which they grow. It is said only to be found on the mountains; and these I had no where an opportunity of examining. With some difficulty, however, I procured, whilst at *Amerapoora*, some young shoots, with abundance of the flowers, and several young plants in a growing state: and while at *Pagam*, on our return, I procured many branches with the young fruit. Unluckily, all the young plants died before I reached *Bengal*; otherwise, I believe, they might have been an acquisition of some value. The tree is said to be very lofty; and, from what I saw, must produce immense quantities of the fruit; as may readily be conceived from looking at the drawings; where it must be observed, that the fruit-bearing branch has had by far the greatest part of its produce shaken off by the carriage. In times of plenty, little use is made of the fruit, except for yielding oil, as had been expected; and besides, a small quantity of the seeds are gathered, and sent to all parts of the empire, where they are used for nearly the same purposes that almonds are amongst us; but the demand in this way cannot be considerable.

It is in times of scarcity that the fruit becomes valuable. It is said, when ripe, to be red; and, like a peach, consists of a succulent outer flesh, containing a hard shell, in which there is a single seed. The outer fleshy part is said to be agreeably acid, and safe to eat. When that is removed, the shells, by a slight beating, split in two, and are thus easily separated from the kernel. These kernels taste very much like a walnut; but are rather softer, and more oily. As they can, at those places where the trees grow, be afforded very cheap, in times of scarcity they are carefully gathered; and, when boiled with a little rice or *Indian* corn, furnish a great part of the food of the lower class of the natives.

I shall now add such a botanical description of the plant as will enable it to be reduced into the vegetable system; although not in every respect complete, owing to my not having seen the tree or the ripe fruit. I believe it will be found to constitute a new genus; but I do not venture to give it a name, till the *European* botanists have ascertained, whether or not it be reducible to any known genus of plants. In the botanical description I use the *Latin* language; as I am not yet sufficiently acquainted with the technical terms introduced into the *English* by the *Litchfield* Society, to use them with facility.

Character Essentialis. Cal. 1 phyll, petala 5, receptaculo inserta, stam. 10, receptaculo inserta. Nect. maximum, orbiculatum, 10 fulcum, germen involvens. Styli 5, conniventes. Drupa monosperma, nuce bivalvi. Habitat in montosis regni Barmanorum.

ARBOR elata ramis fuscis nùdis; ramulis foliosis. Ramuli floriferi glabri, rubicundi, viridé-punctati; fructiferi rimosi.

FOLIA

Folia approximata, alterna, petiolata, oblonga, bafi attenuata, integra, integerrima, retufa, glabra, venis reticulata.

Fulcra, petiolus anceps, acutangulus, breviffimus, glaber. Stipulæ, pubes, arma cirrhi nulla.

Inflorescentia. Paniculi axillares ad apices ramorum congefti, laxi, nudi, foliis longiores, ramoffiffimi; ramis teretibus, horizontalibus, fparfis. Flores parvi, albidi, plurimi, pedicellati, fparfi. Racemi fructiferi penduli, foliis multo longiores. Fructus rubri, acefcenti-dulces.

Cal. perianthum proprium monophyllum, concavum, corollâ brevius, quinquefidum: laciniis obtufis. Laciniæ calycis aliquando tres, fæpius quatuor.

Cor. petala quinque, rarius fex, receptaculo inferta, feffilia, fublinearia, obtufa, revoluta.

Nect. Maximum, in centro floris orbiculatum, depreffum, decem-ftriatum, germen involvens.

Stam. Filamenta decem, fubulata, erecta, petalis breviora, receptaculo inferta, antheræ parvæ, ovatæ.

Pist. Germen fuperum. Nectario tectum. Styli quinque fubulati, erecti, conniventes, longitudine ftaminum, ftigmata obtufa.

Per. Drupa compreffa, obovata, obtufa, obtufocarinata, unilocularis.

Sem. Nux unilocularis, compreffa, fub-bivalvis, dehifcens; femen folitarium, hinc acutum, inde craffum carinatum.

Affinis, ordine naturali, terminaliis proximus habitu, generi a Roxburgio *tfaroo mamaday* dicto, fed nectaria diverfiffima, characterem habet non nihil fimilem generi altero, a Roxburgio *chitraca* dicto, fed habitus diverfi; fingularis eft drupa monofperma cum ftylis quinque; fimile aliquod tamen occurrit in genere Roxburgiano *odina*.

A Saponaria diverfum genus, drupâ uniloculari.

IX.

Specimen of the Language

OF THE

PEOPLE INHABITING THE HILLS IN THE VICINITY OF BHAGULPOOR.

Communicated in a Letter to the Secretary,

BY

Major R. E. Roberts.

PERCEIVING that the very full and satisfactory account of the people inhabiting the hills in the vicinity of *Bhagulpoor*, by Lieutenant Shawe, in the Fourth Volume of the *Asiatick Researches*, is unaccompanied by any specimen of their language, should the following one be acceptable as a supplement to that account, or you deem it deserving the notice of the Society, I shall be obliged by your laying it before them, as I can rely on the correctness of it.

Mr. Shawe having observed that these people have no writing character, I just beg leave to add, that, when I was on duty at *Rajahmahl*, several years ago, a hill chief sent a verbal message to the commanding officer, expressing a wish to wait upon him. Being desired to appoint a day for that purpose, he transmitted a straw with four knots upon it, which was explained by the messenger who brought it, to intimate, that his master would come on the fourth day.

The Head	Cook.	The Eyelash	Cunmeer.
Eyebrow	Cunmudbâ.	Cheek	Cullâ.
Nose	Moēē.	Chin	Kyboo.
Throat	Cusser.	Tooth	Pul.
Armpit	Buddee puckda.	An Arm	Tât buddee.
Blood	Keefs.	Breast of a Woman	Doòdah.
A Finger	Angillee.		
The Breast	Bookah.	Heel	Teeknâ.
Belly	Coochah.	Flesh	Māāk.
Loins	Cudmah.	A Fever	Meed.
Back	Cookah.	Headake	Cooknogee.
A Vein	Narco.	Cholick	Coochoohoogee.
Toe	Cuddah Angillee.	A Tiger	Toot.
Hair	Tullee.	Dog	Alah.
An Eye	Cun.	Ant	Choobah.
Ear	Kydoob.	Kite	Chunneeâdee.
The Countenance	Tresoo.	Paroquet	Apud.
		Fly	Teeleur.
Beard	Pachoodee.	Bee	Ook.
Throat	Tood.	Heaver	Surruncussa.
Shoulder	Dupna.	A Star	Badekah.
A Nail (of Finger)	Ooruk.	Cloud	Badelee.
		Cow	Ooee.
A Lip	Boocootooda.	Jackal	Cheecáloo.
Navel	Cood.	Cat	Beerkah.
Buttock	Moodoocudmullâ.	Cock	Noogeer.
Liver	Cuckâlee.	Crow	Câcah.
The Foot	Chupta.	Dove	Poɔrah.
A Bone	Cocchul.	Pigeon	Cooteerah.
Forehead	Neepee.		

IN THE VICINITY OF BHAGULPOOR.   129

A Scorpion	Teelah.	Oil	Heefcun.
A Buffalo	Mung.	A Turband	Doomee, Cocudee.
A Hog	Keefs.	A Tree	Mun.
A Deer	Chutteedah.	Linen Cloth	Lookâ.
A Hen	Dooteegeer.	Cold	Kaidah.
A Bat	Cheedgoo.	Heat	Oomee.
A Snake	Neer.	A Houfe	Adâ.
A Fifh	Meen.	North	Colah.
Male, mafculine	Peechâlah.	South	Purrubmoha.
Sunfhine	Beer.	Weft	Beerhotroo.
Moonfhine	Beelah.	A Peacock	Choobah.
Lightning	Chudkah.	Sweet	Ameebade.
Light	Abublee.	Bitter	Câdkah.
Earth	Kycul.	Sour	Seeteed.
A Stone	Châchah.	Prayer, worfhip	Aydeeootee.
An Arrow	Châr.	*Hinduftan*	*Coler.*
A Bone	Eedut.	Wheat	Gyhoom.
Fire	Chuchah.	To fleep	Cooda.
Water	Oom.	To beget, procreate	Keena.
Grafs	Doobah.	To fleep	Cunderco.
Food	Jacoo.	To go	Aycoocoo.
Bread	Putteeâ.	To tear	Afeehee.
Cloth	Durjâ.	To fqueeze, prefs out }	Ayrcoo.
Black	Fudcooroa.		
White	Cheen burroo.	To grind	Tudyecâ.
Red	Kyfoo.	To know, underftand }	Booje een.
Yellow	Balcoo.		
Rice	Teekeel.	To rub	Mâleeâ.

Vol. V.   I

To break	Turrâ.	This	Bhee.
To found	Ahootee.	Him	Naheen.
To laugh	Alkee.	They	Nuckeed.
To weep	Boolkee.	Ignorant	Oo cullee mulla
To pull, draw	Bundra.	Justice	Muzcoor.
A River	Abeen.	Which	Chuchee.
Salt	Beek.	A Liar	Puffecarce.
A Cup	Coree.	A Rope, Cord	Meer.
Below, under	Tuttâ.	A Hill	Tookah.
A Tent Rope	Jumkâ.	Sick	Chootah.
High	Arkâ.	A Sheet	Chuppoodah.
A Door	Dowaree.	Left (Hand or Side)	Akdo.
A Flower	Kâdah.	Crooked	Deeza.
Game (Beasts of)	Cubbree.	Sand	Bâlah.
An Ideot	Bootah.	Accusation, Complaint	Mâfee.
The World	Oorahâ.		
A Mat	Tâlee.	A Garment, Vest	Joolee.
Before	Moodâhee.	Physick	Bhudder.
Why	Pundreek.	A Sash	Sujar.
Me, to me	Aykee.	A Mill	Mookah.

X.

An Account of the Discovery of Two Urns in the Vicinity of Benares.

By JONATHAN DUNCAN, Esq.

I HEREWITH beg leave to deliver to the Society a Stone and a Marble Vessel, found the one within the other, in the month of January, 1794, by the people employed by Baboo Juggut Sing in digging for stones from the subterraneous materials of some extensive and ancient buildings in the vicinity of a temple called *Sarnauth*, at the distance of about four miles to the northward of the present city of *Benares*.

In the innermost of these cases (which were discovered after digging to the depth of eighteen *hauts*, or cubits, under the surface) were found a few human bones, that were committed to the *Ganges*, and some decayed pearls, gold leaves, and other jewels of no value, which cannot be better disposed of than by continuing in the receptacle in which they must have so long remained, and been placed upon an occasion on which there are several opinions among the natives in that district. The first, that the bones found along with them, may be those of the consort of some former Rajah or Prince, who having devoted herself to the flames on the death of her husband, or on some other emergency, her relations may have made (as is said not to be unprecedented) this deposit of her remains as a permanent place of lodgment; whilst others have suggested, that the remains of the deceased may have probably only been thus temporarily disposed of, till a proper time or opportunity should arrive of committing them to the *Ganges*, as is usually observed in respect to these *pushpa*, or flowers; a term by which the *Hindus* affect to distinguish those residuary vestiges of their friends dying natural deaths, that are not consumed by the fire, to which their corpses are generally exposed, according to the tenets of their religion.

But I am myself inclined to give the preference to a conclusion differing from either of the two former, viz. that the bones found in these urns must belong to one of the worshippers of BUDDHA, a set of *Indian* heretics, who, having no reverence for the *Ganges*, used to deposit their remains in the earth, instead of committing them to that river; a surmise that seems strongly corroborated by the circumstance of a statue or idol of BUDDHA having been found in the same place under ground, and on the same occasion with the discovery of the urns in question, on which was an inscription, as per the accompanying copy of the original, ascertaining that a temple had between 7 or 800 years ago been constructed there for the worship of that deity.

नमोबुद्धाय वाराणासीसरस्यां गुरो: श्रीधामशशिपादाब्रम्
आराध्यनमितनृपति शिरोरुहै: शिवलाकीर्णम् १
भूपालचिन्द्रय व्यादि कीर्तिरत्नधराचय:
गौढाधिपोमदीपाल: काश्यांश्रीमानकारयत् २
मल्लजीकृत पांडित्यो वेद्वारावनिवर्त्तिनो
यो धर्मं राजिकं सांगे धर्मचक्र पुनर्नवम् ३
कृत वंतौ च नवीन मेसुमहास्थानशैलराजकुटीम्
हनांश्रीस्थिरपालो वर्मनपालोनुज: श्रीमान् ४
सम्वत् १०८३ पौष दिन ११

सधर्महेतु प्रकरो हेतुं तेषां तथाफले स्वदव्र
तेषांचयाविरोधावंतादी महाश्रमणा:

XI.

Account of some Ancient Inscriptions.

THE President lays before the Society a Fac Simile of some Ancient Inscriptions, received from Sir Charles Ware Mallet. They were taken by Mr. Wales, a very ingenious artist, who has employed himself in making designs of the excavations and sculptures at *Ellora*, and other parts on the western side of *India*. To the ingenuity of Lieutenant Wilford, the Society is indebted for an explanation of the Inscriptions. They are, as he observes, of little importance; but the publication of them may assist the labours of others in decyphering more interesting manuscripts or inscriptions. The following Extract of a Letter from Lieutenant Wilford, containing his Translation of the Inscriptions, accompanies them.

I HAVE the honour to return to you the fac simile of the several inscriptions, with an explanation of them. I despaired at first of ever being able to decypher them; for as there are no ancient inscriptions in this part of *India*, we never had, of course, any opportunity to try our skill, and improve our talents, in the art of decyphering. However, after many fruitless attempts on our part, we were so fortunate as to find at last an ancient sage, who gave us the key, and produced a book in *Sanscrit*, containing a great many ancient alphabets formerly in use in different parts of *India*. This was really a fortunate discovery, which hereafter may be of great service to us. But let us proceed.

Number II. and VI. are pure *Sanscrit;* and the character, though uncouth, is *Sanscrit* also.

The other numbers, viz. I. III. IV. and V. are written in an ancient vernacular dialect; and the characters, though very different from those now in use, are nevertheless derived from the original or primæval *Sanscrit*, for the elements are the same.

I have exhibited these numbers in one sheet. The Inscriptions are first written in their original dialect, but in *Sanscrit* characters. To this is annexed a translation in *Sanscrit*; and both the original dialect and the *Sanscrit* translation are exhibited in *English* characters.

The numbers I. III. IV. and V. relate to the wanderings of Yudishtira and the Pandovas through forests and uninhabited places. They were precluded, by agreement, from conversing with mankind; but their friends and relations, Vidura and Vya'sa, contrived to convey to them such intelligence and information as they deemed necessary for their safety. This they did by writing short and obscure sentences on rocks or stones in the wilderness, and in characters previously agreed upon betwixt them. Vya'sa is the supposed author of the *Puránas*.

No. I.

Consists of four distinct parts, which are to be read separately. In the first part, (1,) either Vidura or Vya'sa informs Yudishtira of the hostile intentions of Duryodhen.

" From what I have seen of him (Duryodhen,) " and after having fully considered (the whole tenor " of his conduct,) I am satisfied that he is a wicked " man. Keep thyself concealed, O chief of the il- " lustrious!"

In

In the 2d part of No. I.

"Having firſt broken the ſtone (that cloſes thy
"cave) come here ſecretly, old man, that thou mayeſt
"obtain the object of thy deſire. Thy ſufferings vex
"me ſore."

In the 3d part of No. I.

"O, moſt unfortunate, the *wicked* is come."

In the 4th part of No. I.

YUDISHTIRA and his followers being exhauſted with their ſufferings, made overtures of peace through VIDURA and VYA'SA. They had at firſt ſome hope of ſucceſs, when ſuddenly an end was put to the negociation, and affairs took another turn. This piece of intelligence they conveyed to YUDISHTIRA in the following manner:

4th. "Another word."

This expreſſion, is an adverbial form, is ſtill in uſe to expreſs the ſame thing.

No. III.

"O, worthy man, O, *Hara-bara*," (*Hara-bara*, the name of MAHADE'VA, twice expreſſed, is an exclamation uſed by people in great diſtreſs,) "aſcend into thy
"cave—Hence ſend letters—But into thy cave go ſe-
"cretly."

No. IV.

"Thou wilt ſoon perceive that they are leagued to-
"gether, and that their bellies (appetites) are the
"only rule of their conduct. Decline their friend-
"ſhip—See the door of yon cave—Break it open,
"(and conceal thyſelf therein.")

No. V.

"Go into the town immediately—But do not mix
"with them—Keep thyſelf ſeparate as the lotos (from
"the

" the waters in which it floats.)—Get into the house
" of a certain ploughman, and first remain concealed
" there; but afterwards keep thyself in readiness."

The two following numbers allude to the worship of BUDDHA.

No. II.

" Here is the statute of SA'CYA-UDA'RACA, (now a
" form of BUDDHA,) but who was before a *Brahmacári*,
" called SRI'-SOHILA."

No. VI.

" SA'CYA-PA'DA'MRATA made this statute."

My learned friends here insist that these Inscriptions were really written by the friends of YUDISHTIRA. I doubt this very much. These Inscriptions certainly convey little or no information to us: still our having been able to decypher them is a great point in my opinion, as it may hereafter lead to further discoveries, that may ultimately crown our labours with success. Indeed, your sending them to me has really been the occasion of my discovering the above-mentioned book, which I conceive to be a most fortunate circumstance.

F. WILFORD.

ANCIENT INSCRIPTIONS.

No. I.

बह्लाऊसा पकटरुटरवध गुप्तसुपुथितप	वरप्फुप्लुत वृद्ध पथरखंटुठठ पैपे	कृडूत रब रुपैपे	इत रधा वृत्त
Bhalá úhá pacat'ha vra'dhara bud'ha gupta fuputhitapa	*Varappru pluta vradd'ha pattharc'hatúi'ha t'ha paipé*	*Cra'árata c'ha-i paipé*	*Itaratthá vrattam*

The same in Sanſcrit.

बह्लातर्चनाप्रकटवृतः मूर्च्छनः सुप्रथितप	वरंप्राप्तुंगुप्तःवृद्ध पस्रंखंडयिंवाह् प्राप	कष्टरतन खलःप्राप्तः	अयथा वृतांतं
Babulá tarcaná pracatá vratah múrc'hah th'hannah fuprathitapa.	*Varam práptum guptah vraddha praſaramc'hun'dayitwá ha prápa.*	*Caſhtavata c'halah práptah.*	*Anyathá vrattántam.*

No. III.

रुविररुहररुट *Ruchara Hara-hara*

गुहांरुह्लांतेख्यानि *aruruba léhaé*

मेषघगूठःगछ *rurui guba ii.*

The same in Sanſcrit.

रुचरुहरुहर *Ruchira Hara-hara*

अरुरुहलेह्रा *gubám rubya léc'hyáni*

रुरुगुहरुई *préſhaya gú'dhad gach'ha.*

No. IV.

कलइजटहहेप हरुइ हेसेहर अहरेषगुहदरलट

Cala-i jat'hé rubahai paha-i thé fnébarah aruré fhaguhadara latá.

The same in Sanſcrit.

नानीहिनटरेहनःप्रहितंइछंतिसुषं हंआ हरएतदगुका दवारंलिछ

Jánihi jat'haré rú'dháb prahitam ich'hanti ſucham áhara étadguká dwáram lic'ha.

No. V.

ओब्रे इ ठ इ शो उ य ह धु ऽ ऽ ह ह ल स ह
स्सु ठे ह ज र ड्रा ऽ ढे इ र ह ह ल कु

Objé-i t'ha-i shégu sahru d'but'hara ruha hala ruha
basuté bajé ru-i-è gud'ha te i raru babaracru.

The same in *Sanscrit*.

अज्ज इ र तिं ष्टो शीं शा क्षां गिं सानें शा ह ऽ भ द
आन स चें अ य्या ति ष्ट व ठ स ः ति ष्ट प श्चा र उ चीगूं कु रु

Abja iva tishta sighram grámam jhatiti pravisabalad'hara
ávasathé adyápi gatwá guptah tishta pas'chát udhyogam curu.

Pure *Sanscrit*.

No. II.

श्रीसीहिलब्रस *Sri Sohila Brahma-*
चारिष्णांद्गाकारुद्रा *chúribhah Sácyaruda-*
रकप्रतिमेयं *raca pratiméyam.*

Pure *Sanscrit*.

No. VI.

शाकापाद्यमृतकृता प्रतिमा॥

Sácya Pádámrata cratá pratimá.

No. I. From *Veroel* or *Ellora*.

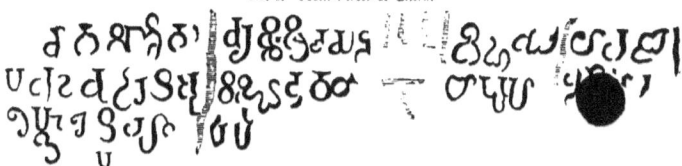

No. II. *Veroel* or *Ellora*.

No. III. *Ekvira* or *Jebire*.

No. IV. *Ekvira* or *Jebire*.

No. V. *Salsette*.

No. VI. *Veroel* or *Ellora*.

XII.

OBSERVATIONS on the ALPHABETICAL SYSTEM

OF THE

LANGUAGE of AWĂ and RĂC'HAIŇ.*

By CAPTAIN JOHN TOWERS.

THE annexed *Plate* † is a Specimen of the Alphabet of the Language of *Awă* and *Răc'haiṅ*, agreeably to the Arrangement adopted by the *Brăimmas* and *Mărămăs*, or Natives of thofe Kingdoms.

To avoid tedious and perplexing reference, it was thought advifeable to place under each fymbol its characteriftic reprefentative in *Roman* letters. In doing this, more than common attention has been paid to preferve the notation laid down in the elegant and perfpicuous "Syftem and Differtation on the Orthography of *Afiatick* Words in *Roman* Letters," commencing the Firft Volume of the Refearches of the Society; at leaft, as far as its typical arrangement correfponded with the fyftem under difcuffion; and where a variation rendered it neceffary, new combinations or fymbols have been introduced, and obfervations fubjoined for their elucidation.

The abecedary rules, as taught by the natives, are, in their aggregate capacity, called *Sáṅbuṅ*, or, *The Syftem of Inftruction.* They are claffed under three
                                                                  diftinct

---

* *Ava* and *Aracan.*   † Plate I.

distinct heads; and these again divided into thirty subordinate divisions, by the inflection of the primary letters, or alphabet properly so called, with the three classes of vowels *ărwi*, *ăsăiṅe*, and *ăsăiṭcri*, and four other marks. The instruction commences, however, with eighteen sounds, to prepare the pupil, as it is said, for the greater difficulties that are to follow. These sounds are included in what is taught subsequently, though ten of their symbols are not, which are therefore subjoined in the annexed Plate.

I.

Of the several series as they occur in the *Plate*, the first is *căgric'he*, or *the alphabet*; respecting which there is little to observe. In certain cases, to facilitate utterance, *c* is permuted with *g*, *ch* with *j*; the *second d* with the *second t*, *p* with *b*, and conversely. Of those sounds that have more than one symbol, the *first c'h*, *ch'h*, *l*; *second t*, *d*, *n*; and *third t'h*, are in general use; also the *second p'h*; except in those instances where it does not associate with the *four marks* that will appear under the following head.

II.

These are the *four marks* alluded to above. Their names, as they occur in the *Plate*, are *ăpāṅ*, *ărăiṭ*, *hṅăch'hwe*, *hmăch'hwe*, &c. according to the letter it is associated with, and *wăch'hwe*.

ăpāṅ.

The mark of this symbol is *y*; though it might more properly, and sometimes more conveniently, be marked by our third vowel, commencing a diphthong. The letters to which it is affixed, are *c*, *c'h*, (1,*) *g*, *t*, (2,) *p*, *p'h*, (1,) *b*, *m*, *l*, (1,) *s*. To this last it gives nearly

---

* The figures refer to the archetype in the *Plate*.

nearly the sound of our *sh*; which notation it is necessary to preserve, though probably not conformable to the strict rules of analogy. Possibly the constituent parts of this sound are the *palatial sibilant*, and *i*, coalescing with a following vowel.

Arărit.

This mark is typified by *r*, and is always prefixed to the letters with which it associates. These are *c, c'h,* (1,) *g, n, ch'h,* (1;) *t,* (2;) *p, p'h,* (1;) *b, m.* With *ch'h* it forms a very harsh combination. But it is to be observed, that it is the nature of this, as well as of all the marks, either separately, or in their several combinations, to coalesce into one sound with the associated letter as nearly as the organs of articulation will admit. Its name *ărăit* designates its natural form, meaning *erect* or *upright*.

Hmăch'hwe.

This extraordinary mark forms a new class of aspirates. Its name signifies *suspended*, from its situation with respect to the letter. The letters under which it is placed, are *n, ny, n,* (2;) *m, r, l,* (1;) *w, s;* before the *first seven* of which its type is *h*.* *s* it hardens into *z*, the appropriate symbol; or adds a syllable to the inherent vowel, as *sămi*, a daughter, which may be either written with the mark before us, or by *m*.† In the introductory part to *the system*,‡ it says, 'when the breath is obstructed by the pressure of the tongue (against the roots of the upper teeth, or probably against the palate) and forced between the teeth on either

---

* The aspirate *h* so evidently precedes the letter in pronunciation, that, however inclination may lead to make the symbol follow the letter, as is usual in the other aspirates, in this instance it cannot be done without an offensive violation of all analogy.

† See *Plate* I. *a.*

‡ That commences the *first* volume of the Researches of the Society. For the sake of brevity, it will be quoted throughout by this title.

either side of it, a liquid is formed peculiar to the *British* dialect of the *Celtick*.' We have found, however, this very sound in the mark before us when associated with *l*. If this be the sound represented by *ll*, as in the common surname *Lloyd*, the notation is but ill-suited to give an idea of its powers. In the combination of this mark with *ăpāṅ*, the only letters of association are *m* and *l*; and with *ārăit*, *ṅ* and *m*; the symbol being formed, as in the original, of the component parts.

Wăch'hwe,

or the *suspended w*, is subtended to every letter, excepting that with which it corresponds in the alphabet. Its symbol is *w*, but subject to certain changes and suppression, the particular instances of which will appear when the vowels come to be treated of. This mark with the letter *h*, and the one immediately preceding with the letter *w*, form two combinations for the same sound; which is that of *wh* in the word *what*. In its associations with the other marks, it is governed by the same rules, and governs the same letters as already related under their separate and combined forms; with an exception, however, to its homogeneous character in the alphabet. With *ăpāṅ*, and *ăpāṅ hmăch'hwe* and *hlăch'hwe*, we have the genuine sound of our *third* vowel forming a diphthong with the *fifth*; as *miuwă, hmiuwă, hliuwă*; the diphthong in these instances having precisely the same sound as in our word *lieu*: but, to preserve the notation here laid down, it must be typified by *y*, as *mywă, hmywă, hlywă*; though it might more properly be represented by its constituent parts, as in the first example.

3, 4, 5.

These are the *three series of vowels* and *nasal marks*. The first is called *ărwi*, or *written*, simply;* the second

---

* A letter is also said to be *ărwi* when uninflected.

cond *ăsăitne*, from the root *săit*, to ſtrike, (owing to the mark *ăsăit* or *tănc'hwăiň* that is ſtruck in writing from the top of the *final* letter) and *ňe*, ſmall; and the third *ăsăitcri*, from the ſame, and *cri*, large, great, in conſequence of the proportion of the *firſt* ſeries that is ingrafted into it being more than in the ſecond.

The alphabet, in its ſeveral aſſociations with *ăpăň*, *ărăit*, *hňăch'hwe*, and *wăch'hwe*, is, with only one exception, uniformly inflected throughout with the three ſeries of vowels and naſal marks in regular rotation as they occur in the Plate. The inſtance to the contrary is *wăch'hwe*, which is altogether excluded in the alphabetical inflection of *ăsăitcri*.

Except as a compound, the firſt vocal ſound, as deſcribed in the ſyſtem, has no place in the language before us. And there is yet a more ſtriking ſingularity; which is, that every ſyllable is liquid, as it were, in its termination, each letter having its peculiar vowel or naſal mark ſubjoined, and in no inſtance coaleſcing with a following letter. But, to elucidate it by inſtances from our own language: were a native of *Ava* or *Aracan* merely acquainted with the Roman letters, and that ſuch and ſuch ſymbols repreſented ſuch and ſuch ſounds, without knowing their rules of aſſociation, to read the words *book*, *boot*, *bull*, he would, agreeably to the powers he is taught to affix to the characters of his own language, pronounce them uniformly *bù*, or *bùcă*, *bùtă*, *bùlă*, reſpectively. And he could not poſſibly do otherwiſe; the organs of articulation being inadequate to give utterance to the final letters according to the abrupt mode by which we are inſtructed to terminate thoſe words. It need ſcarcely be obſerved, that hence each letter of the alphabet properly ſo called is uſed as a *ſyllabic initial*, and *never* as a *medial* or *final*, if we except the *naſals*. But here we only ſpeak as far as pronunciation is concerned. There is reaſon to ſuppoſe that this ſingularity is not peculiar to the language we are treating of, but that the *Chinese* is formed upon the same principle; and probably some of the *African* dialects, if the analogy observable in the mode in which some natives of that quarter of the globe pronounce exotick words, and that of the *Mŭrămăs*, be sufficient ground for the suggestion. Whether the language of *Tibet* be not also, a member of the Society may be possibly able to determine. A native of *Aracan*, of naturally strong parts, and acute apprehension, with whom more than common pains have been taken for many months past to correct this defect, can scarcely now, with the most determined caution, articulate a word or syllable in *Hindústani* that has a *consonant* for a *final*, which frequently occasions very unpleasant, and sometimes ridiculous equivocations; and such is the force of habit even to making the most simple and easy things difficult, that as obvious as the *first elementary sound* appears to our comprehension, in an attempt that was made to teach him the *Nágari* character, of which it is the *inherent* vowel, a number of days elapsed before he could be brought to pronounce it, or even to form any idea of it, and then but a very imperfect one.

The *Plate*, as has been already observed, shews the alphabetical arrangement adopted by the natives. It will be more convenient, however, in treating of the three series of vowels and nasal marks, to throw them into classes; not only for the sake of perspicuity, but to avoid the irksome task of endless repetition.

$$\breve{a}, \bar{a}, \overset{\circ}{a}, \breve{e}\breve{e}.$$

Our extended sound in *all*, and its contracted one in *fond*, are the basis of these four vowels. The first is pronounced with an accent peculiarly acute, by an inflection pretty far back of the tongue towards the palate,

late, terminated by a kind of catch. It seems, however, to drop this distinction when followed by a grave accent, as *tàrà*, just; a property that it would appear to possess in common with the other vowels distinguished by *acute* accents. It is inherent in every vowel, which may be the reason why it is placed last in the alphabet. The accent of the third is as remarkably *grave* as the other is *acute*; the second forming a medium between both, being our broad vowel in *all*; while the fourth is a guttural, analogous to the *Arabian kaf*; a suppression of the final utterance by which this is characterized as a consonant, being all that is necessary to form the sound before us.

i, ì, it.

The two first are accented in the same proportion as *ă* and *à*, only with somewhat less force. The last is pronounced with an effort unusually harsh, by a strong inflection of the centre part of the tongue towards the palate. It seems to form a sound between the third vowel of the system and the actual articulation of its final letter, with which a foreigner, from mere oral knowledge, would most probably be induced to write it. No doubt, however, exists of its being a vowel, as attention to the mode in which a native pronounces it will fully demonstrate. The constituent sound in *ăpān* being our third vowel, in the inflection of those letters which take that mark with the three vowels before us, the variation in their associated and unassociated capacity is not easily discernible at first, but the difference is discovered in a day or two's practice by the assistance of a native.

u, ù, up̆.

The *grave* and *acute* accents of the last series characterize the two first of the present; the third being

formed

formed by a sudden reciprocation of the tongue with an appulse nearly of the lips, so as to convey an idea of fulness; or, if the expression may be allowed, a remarkable roundness of sound united to an uncommonly obtuse and abrupt termination, a peculiarity that marks those vowels of the series *ăsăitŭe* and *ăsáitcri*, that have *mutes* for the double letter. To this observation, however, there is an exception, which will be taken notice of in its proper place. The sound of the letter, when associated with *wăch'hwe*, and inflected by the two first of these vowels, remains the same as in its unassociated form: but the sigma in this case appears to be considered by the natives themselves as redundant, for it has hitherto only been met with in their abecedary system.

e, è.

The *first* is the *e* of *the system*. It has two types; the *seventh* of the first series, and *the last but one* of the second, and which are often abbreviated in writing, as in the verbal termination *ze* and *rwe* in the Plate.*
By a strange irregularity, it is frequently written for *i*. The *second* is distinguished by the *grave* accent of the preceding series.

aò, ao; o, ò.

These vowels seem to be thus distinguished in the *system*: " By pursing up our lips in the least degree, we convert the simple element into another sound of the same nature with the *first* vowel, and easily confounded with it in a broad pronunciation: when this new sound is lengthened; it approaches very nearly to the *fourth* vowel, which we form by a bolder and stronger rotundity of the mouth." The two first may be often mistaken for the last; and, in some words,

* Plate I. *b.*

words, even for *ā* and *ằ*, when inflecting the other letters with *wăch'we*, suspended. Like *u*, *ù*, the symbol in association with *wăch'we*, when inflected with these four vowels, is redundant.

ăiĉ, ăip̃; aich, aiĉ.

Our diphthong in *ay*, or *joy*, which seems to be compounded of the broad vowel in *all*, or rather its correspondent short one, followed by the third, pronounced with the acute piercing accent described in treating of the first vowel, constitutes the sound of the two first of the present class of vowels; while the narrower sound in *eye* or *my*, with the obtuse abrupt termination mentioned under the third class of vowels, peculiarizes the two last. Taken in two's, as they appear above separated by the *semicolon*, their sounds are congenial. The two first form the exception taken notice of under the third class of vowels.

auĉ.

The diphthong of the *first* and *fifth* vowels, already so fully described in the system, with the guttural termination of *ăĉ*, is the sound of this vowel. It is sometimes abbreviated, by an elision of the *final* letter, when a point above is substituted in its room.*

The *nasals* are now only left for discussion; their peculiar vowels, as well as most of their nasal terminations, are to be found either in the system, or in the foregoing observations. The only thing therefore that remains, is arranging them into classes, and making a few trifling strictures.

ān, ǎ̀n.

No elucidation is here necessary. A species of abbreviation is sometimes observable in writing, when the

---

* See Plate I. *c*.

the double letter is placed above, inſtead of preceding, the following letter; as in the word *sāṅbuṅ*.*

iṅ.

The ſigma of this naſal in the original is not deduced analogouſly; its powers as a *ſyllabic initial* being that of the *dental* naſal, which ſound is altogether excluded from this language as a *final*.

um, uṅ.

The firſt of theſe is the regular ſymbol. Both ſounds have but one type in the original, that as a *labial* appearing to be reſtricted to thoſe inſtances where a labial follows; as *cumbup̄*, a *ſmall eminence*, or riſing ground. The naſal is frequently repreſented by a point above the letter.

ăiṅ, ăiṅ, aim; aiṅ, aiṅ.

The vowels of thoſe naſals are in the ſame proportion as *ăiṭ, aich*, pronounced without the acute accent and abrupt termination by which they are reſpectively diſtinguiſhed. The *obſcure* naſal,† formed by a ſlight inflection of the tongue towards the palate, with a trifling aid from the other organ, and which is ſo frequently to be met with in *Perſian* and *Hindi* vocables, is the ſound of the two firſt; the purpoſe of the third being ſeemingly to take their place when a *labial* follows, as in the word *căimp'hī*, the *earth*.‡ It may be proper

* See Plate I. *d*.
† This naſal appears to hold a middle place between the *dental* and *guttural* naſals conſidered as *finals*; with the laſt of which it has but one common type in *the Syſtem*.
‡ See Plate I. *e*; where it may be obſerved, the double letter has the one which ſhould follow it ſubtended to it, and takes the vowel with which it is inflected, the diſtinguiſhing mark *ăsăit* being ſuppreſſed; an abbreviation very common in the vowels and naſal marks formed by double letters, particularly where the double letter is the ſame with that which immediately follows it.

proper to observe here, that, like the *Hindi*, there is a slight nasality perceivable in the pronunciation of some words for which there is no symbol.

The diphthongs of *añ* and *aiñ* are permuted with *è* and *e* when inflecting *ny*, *y*, and the whole class of *äpāñ*; as *nyèñ*, *nyeñ*, &c. and *añ*, when inflecting those letters with *wăch'hwe* suspended, and the class *ăpīñwăch'hwe*; as *nywèñ*, &c. This last nasal, by an anomaly not to be accounted for, is very often written for *e*.

auñ, aùñ.

These compounds, formed of the first and fifth vowels and *guttural* nasal, close the three series of vowels and nasal marks, and with them the abecedary rules of this language.

There is, however, one observation more requisite, that could not have been introduced before without inconvenience, and which has therefore been reserved for this place. *ă* considered in its *syllabic initial* capacity, in its inflections of *ărwi* and *ăsāiñe* with *w"ch'hwe* suspended, is preceded by the fourth vowel, which, in this instance only, forms the symbol for *wăch'hwe*. The notation, therefore, for this deviation should be as follows: *oá, oa, oà, oaê, oañ, oàñ; o'i, o'ì; o'e o'è; o'ăit, o'ăip, o'ăiñ, oăìñ, o'ăim; o'aich, o'aiê, o'añ, o'aiñ.* There is a farther deviation observable in the *first six*, the primary vowel being changed in the present case into the simple element, with which the incipient letter coalesces into a diphthong. In the rest, the initial vowel is articulated separately, as the comma between indicates. As for *u, ù; aò, ao; o, ò;* they retain the same sound, as has been already observed, either with or without *wăch'hwe*.

The

The following extract, taken from a book entitled *Mănu Săingwăn*, or the *Iron Ring of Mănu*, is offered merely as a specimen of the notation here laid down. It scarcely, from its insignificancy, deserves a translation: however, one is subjoined.

*Măhăsămădă măn gri chăĉ' crăwălā sănchyā prain brain tăin dain piĉ', tă tăinchă hnaiĉ chhaun chye zaò tăchhe shaich'pà zaò thăimmăsăiĉ chăgà do go crà lo si lo mu'gà năin năĉ cri gā blyān a'hri zo myăĉ'hnā mu'rwe tămun chă hmă myăĉ'hnā chāin'dwăn pă nă chhe graŏ'rwe chăn gre jwā colăĉ co sup săn'rwe săin shăn jwā zaò co phrăn wăiĉ chă tăin'chhā chhăn bri zaò ămyo le'bà păriĉ'săiĉ do hnăn che we chrăin răin lyăĉ lăĉ up chyi hmă rădănā sumbà go hri'cho'rwe brăimmā chă zaò năiĉ sigrà do go hri'cho tain dăin u hmă blyăn i tăchhe shaich'pà thăimmăsăiĉ tărā chăgà go măhăsămădă măn gri ā crà pe lo zaò hnā.**

And Mănu said, "O, mighty Prince, Măhăsămădă! if thou hast an inclination to hear and understand the words of the eighteen holy books which I brought from the gate of *Chăĉ'răwălā*,† that enclose and form a barrier (to the earth) from thy palace; with thy face turned towards the east, cleaning thy teeth; washing thy eyes, mouth, cheeks, and ears, and wiping thy body and hands; and with a purified person, and having put on thy apparel and eat; and with the four friends ‡ assembled, and forming a circle, closing thy hands, and making obeisance to the three inestimable jewels, § and prostrating thyself before *Brăimmā*, (and

---

* For the original, see Plate II.

† Steep and stupendous mountains fabled to surround the earth, and beyond which no mortal can pass.

‡ MAN; the two classes of supernatural beings, NAIT and SIGRA, supposed to possess the peculiar guardianship of mankind; and *Brăimmā* through an attribute, it would seem, of ubiquity.

§ *Phurā, Tărā Sănc'hā*. The incarnate Deities, Divine Justice, and the Priests.

(and the two claſſes of beneficent Genii) *Näit* and *Sigrà*, and making known to them thy grievances (having performed all theſe acts, then) will I preſent unto thee, illuſtrious monarch, *Mähāsămădă*, and cauſe thee to hear the words of theſe eighteen books of Divine ordinances."

It is difficult to refrain obſerving, that the arrangement not only of the alphabet, but of the firſt ſeries of vowels (eight of which have diſtinct characters † which are not inflected) of the foregoing ſyſtem, has a ſtriking ſimilitude to the *Devanagâri*. In the alphabet, for inſtance, wherever it is defective, ſuch deficiency is ſupplied by double, and, in one caſe, quadruple, ſymbols for the ſame ſound; the firſt part being arranged into claſſes of four, each terminated by a naſal, forming together the number twenty-five; which exactly correſponds with the *Devanagâri*.

From information, there appears to be ſcarcely room to doubt, but that the *Siameſe* have one common language and religion with the *Brăimmās* and *Mărămăs*; and that in manners and cuſtoms the three nations form, as it were, one great family. How far theſe obſervations may extend to the inhabitants of *Aſam*, we ſhall be able to judge on the publication of the hiſtory of that country.

It may be ſufficient to obſerve in this place, that there is one ſad impediment to attaining a critical knowledge of the idiom of the language of *Ava* and *Aracan*, without which we may in vain expect from any pen accurate information reſpecting the religion, laws, manners, and cuſtoms, of theſe kingdoms; and that is, that there is no regular ſtandard of orthography, or the ſmalleſt trace of grammatical enquiry to

be

† See Plate I. Figure 6.

be found among the natives.† Much, however, may be done by patience and attention. The field is ample; and he who has leifure and perfeverance to attain a juft knowledge of its boundaries, will probably find his labours rewarded beyond his moft fanguine expectation.

† Every writing that has hitherto come under obfervation, has been full of the groffeft inaccuracies; even thofe ftamped by the higheft authority; fuch as official papers from the king of *Ava* to our government. How far the *Pălit*, or facred language, in which their religious ordinances are written, may be exempted from this remark, it is impoffible to fay. The *Priefts* are almoft the only people converfant in it, and few even among them are celebrated for the accuracy and extent of their knowledge. Between *Rámu* and *Iflámabád*, only *one* perfon has been heard of, and to him accefs has not hitherto been obtainable. Enquiry feems to favour an opinion, that an acquaintance with both languages is abfolutely neceffary to effect the important purpofes that at prefent introduce themfelves to our notice, and which are to prove the inhabitants of *Siam*, *Ava*, and *Aracan*, to be one and the fame people, in language, manners, laws, and religion; and features of the ftrongeft refemblance between them and thofe of *Afam*, *Népal*, and *Tibet*; and eventually to add another link to the chain of general knowledge, by furnifhing materials for filling up the interval that feems at prefent to feparate the *Hindus* from the *Chinefe*.

XIII.

SOME ACCOUNT OF THE

Elastic Gum Vine of Prince of Wales's Island,

AND OF

Experiments made on the milky Juice which it produces: With Hints respecting the useful Purposes to which it may be applied.

By JAMES HOWISON, Esq.

Communicated by JOHN FLEMING, Esq.

OUR first knowledge of the plant being a native of our *Island* arose from the following accident. In our excursions into the forests, it was found necessary to carry cutlasses for the purpose of clearing our way through the underwood. In one of those an elastic gum vine had been divided, the milk of which drying upon the blade, we were much surprized in finding it possess all the properties of the *American Caout-chouc*. The vine which produces this milk is generally about the thickness of the arm, and almost round, with a strong ash-coloured bark, much cracked, and divided longitudinally; has joints at a small distance from each other, which often send out roots, but seldom branches; runs upon the ground to a great length; at last rises upon the highest trees into the open air. It is found in the greatest plenty at the foot of the mountains, upon a red clay mixed with sand, in situations completely shaded, and where the mercury in the thermometer will seldom exceed summer heat.

In my numerous attempts to trace this vine to its top, I never succeeded; for, after following it in its different windings, sometimes to a distance of two hundred

hundred paces, I loft it, from its afcending among the branches of trees that were inacceffible either from their fize or height. On the weft coaft of *Sumatra* I underftand they have been more fuccefsful; *Doctor Roxburgh* having procured from thence a fpecimen of the vine in flowers, from which he has claffed it; but whofe defcription I have not yet feen.

With us the *Malays* have found tafting of the milk the beft mode of difcriminating between the elaftic gum vine and thofe which refemble it in giving out a milky juice, of which we have a great variety; the liquid from the former being much lefs pungent or corrofive than that obtained from the latter.

The ufual method of drawing off the milk is by wounding the bark deeply in different places, from which it runs but flowly, it being full employment for one perfon to collect a quart in the courfe of two days. A much more expeditious mode, but ruinous to the vine, is cutting it in lengths of two feet, and placing under both ends veffels to receive the milk. The beft is always procured from the oldeft vines. From them it is often obtained in a confiftence equal to thick cream, and which will yield two thirds of its own weight in gum.

The chemical properties of this vegetable milk, fo far as I have had an opportunity of examining, furprizingly refemble thofe of animal milk. From its decompofition in confequence of fpontaneous fermentation, or by the addition of acids, a feparation takes place between its *cafeous* and ferous parts, both of which are very fimilar to thofe produced by the fame proceffes from animal milk. An oily or butyrous matter is alfo one of its component parts, which appears

pears upon the surface of the gum so soon as the latter has attained its solid form. The presence of this considerably impeded the progress of my experiments, as will be seen hereafter.

I was at some trouble in endeavouring to form an extract of this milk so as to approach to the consistence of new butter, by which I hoped to retard its fermentative stage, without depriving it of its useful qualities; but as I had no apparatus for distilling, the surface of the milk, that was exposed to the air, instantly formed into a solid coat, by which the evaporation was in a great degree prevented. I, however, learned, by collecting the thickened milk from the inside of the coats, and depositing it in a jelly pot, that, if excluded from the air, it might be preserved in this state for a considerable length of time.

I have kept it in bottles, without any preparation, tolerably good, upwards of one year; for, notwithstanding the fermentation soon takes place, the decomposition in consequence is only partial, and what remains fluid, still retains its original properties, although considerably diminished.

Not having seen *M. Fourcroy's* memoir on *Caoutchouc*, I could not make trials of the methods proposed by him for preserving the milk unaltered.

In making boots, gloves, and bottles, of the elastic gum, I found the following method the best: I first made moulds of wax, as nearly of the size and shape of what they represented as possible; these I hung separately upon pins, about a foot from the ground, by pieces of cord wrought into the wax: I then placed under each a soup plate, into which I poured as much of the milk as I thought would be sufficient for one coat. Having dipped my fingers in this, I completely

pletely covered the moulds one after another, and what dropped into the plates was used as part of the next coat: the first I generally found sufficiently dry in the space of ten minutes, when exposed to the sun, to admit of a second being applied: however, after every second coat, the oily matter before mentioned was in such quantity upon the surface, that, until washed off with soap and water, I found it impossible to apply any more milk with effect; for, if laid on, it kept running and dividing like water upon wax.

Thirty coats I in common found sufficient to give a covering of the thickness of the bottles which come from *America*. This circumstance may, however, at any time be ascertained, by introducing the finger between the mould and gum, the one very readily separating from the other.

I found the fingers preferable to a brush, or any instrument whatever, for laying on the milk; for the moment a brush was wet with that fluid, the hair became united as one mass. A mode which at first view would appear to have the advantage of all others for ease and expedition in covering clay and wax moulds with the gum, viz. immersing them in the milk, did not at all answer upon trial; that fluid running almost entirely off, although none of the oily matter was present; a certain degree of force seeming necessary to incorporate by friction the milk with the new formed gum.

When, upon examination, I found that the boots and gloves were of the thickness wanted, I turned them over at the top, and drew them off, as if from the leg or hand, by which I saved the trouble of forming new moulds. Those of the bottles being smallest at the neck, I was under the necessity of dissolving in hot water.

The

The infide of the boots and gloves which had been in contact with the wax being by far the fmootheft, I made the outfide. The gloves were now finifhed, unlefs cutting their tops even, which was beft done with fciffars. The boots, however, in their prefent ftate, more refembled ftockings, having as yet no foles. To fupply them with thefe, I poured upon a piece of gunny a proper quantity of milk, to give it a thick coat of gum. From this, when dry, I cut pieces fufficiently large to cover the fole of the foot, which, having met with the milk, I applied; firft replacing the boot upon the mould to keep it properly extended. By this mode the foles were fo firmly joined, that no force could afterwards feparate them. In the fame manner I added heels and ftraps, when the boots had a very neat appearance. To fatisfy myfelf as to their impermeability to water, I ftood in a pond up to their tops for the fpace of fifteen minutes, when, upon pulling them off, I did not find my ftockings in the leaft damp. Indeed, from the nature of the gum, had it been for a period of as many months, the fame refult was to have been expected.

After being thus far fuccefsful, I was greatly difappointed in my expectations with regard to their retaining their original fhape; for, on wearing them but a few times, they loft much of their firft neatnefs, the contractions of the gum being only equal to about feven eighths of its extenfion.

A fecond difadvantage arofe from a circumftance difficult to guard againft, which was, that if, by any accident, the gum fhould be in the fmalleft degree weaker in one place than another, the effect of extenfion fell almoft entirely on that part, and the confequence was, that it foon gave way.

From what I had obferved of the advantage gained in fubftance and uniformity of ftrength, by making use of gunny as a basis for the soles, I was led to suppose, that if an elastic cloth, in some degree correspondent to the elasticity of the gum, were used for boots, stockings, gloves, and other articles, where that property was necessary, that the defects above mentioned might in a great measure be remedied. I accordingly made my first experiment with *Cossimbazar* stockings and gloves.

Having drawn them upon the wax moulds, I plunged them into vessels containing the milk, which the cloth greedily absorbed. When taken out, they were so completely distended with the gum in solution, that, upon becoming dry by exposure to the air, not only every thread, but every fibre of the cotton had its own distinct envelope, and in consequence was equally capable of resisting the action of foreign bodies as if of solid gum.

The first coat by this method was of such thickness, that for stockings or gloves nothing farther was necessary. What were intended for boots required a few more applications of milk with the fingers, and were finished as those made with the gum only.

This mode of giving cloth as a basis I found to be a very great improvement: for, besides the addition of strength received by the gum, the operation was much shortened.

Woven substances, that are to be covered with the gum, as also the moulds on which they are to be placed, ought to be considerably larger than the bodies they are afterwards intended to fit; for, being much contracted from the absorption of the milk, little alteration takes place in this diminution in size, even when dry, as about one third only of the fluid evaporates before the gum acquires its solid form.

Great

Great attention muſt be paid to prevent one part of the gum coming in contact with another while wet with the milk or its whey; for the inſtant that takes place, they become inſeparably united. But ſhould we ever ſucceed in having large plantations of our own vine, or in transferring the *American* tree (which is perhaps more productive) to our poſſeſſions, ſo that milk could be procured in ſufficient quantity for the covering various cloths, which ſhould be done on the ſpot, and afterwards exported to *Europe*, then the advantages attending this ſingular property of the milk would for ever balance its diſadvantages: cloths, and coverings of different deſcriptions, might then be made from this gum cloth, with an expedition ſo much greater than by the needle, that would at firſt appear very ſurprizing: the edges of the ſeparate pieces only requiring to be wet with the milk, or its whey, and brought into contact, when the article would be finiſhed, and fit for uſe. Should both milk and whey be wanting, a ſolution of the gum in either can always be obtained, by which the ſame end would be accompliſhed.

Of all the cloths upon which I made experiments, nankeen, from the ſtrength and quality of its fabric, appeared the beſt calculated for coating with the gum. The method I followed in performing this, was, to lay the cloth ſmooth upon a table, pour the milk upon it, and with a ruler to ſpread it equally. But ſhould this ever be attempted on a larger ſcale, I would recommend the following plan: To have a ciſtern for holding the milk a little broader than the cloth, to be covered with a croſs bar in the centre, which muſt reach under the ſurface of the milk, and two rollers at one end. Having filled the ciſtern, one end of the piece of cloth is to be paſſed under the bar, and through between the rollers; the former keeping the cloth immerſed in the milk, the latter in preſſing out what is ſuperfluous, ſo that none may be loſt. The cloth

cloth can be hung up at full length to dry; and the operation repeated until of whatever thickness wanted. For the reasons above-mentioned, care must be taken that one fold does not come in contact with another while wet.

Having observed that most of the patent catheters and bougies made with a solution of the elastic gum, whether in ether or in the essential oils, had either a disagreeable stickiness, or were too hard to admit of any advantage being derived from the elasticity of the gum, I was induced to make some experiments with the milk towards removing these objections.

From that fluid, by evaporation, I made several large sized bougies of pure gum, which, from their over-flexibility, were totally useless. I then took some slips of fine cloth covered with the gum, which I rolled up until of a proper size, and which I rendered solid by soaking them in the milk, and then drying them. These possessed more firmness than the former, but in no degree sufficient for the purpose intended. Pieces of strong catgut, coated with the gum, I found to answer better than either.

Besides an effectual cloathing for manufacturers employed with the mineral acids, which had been long a desideratum, this substance, under different modifications, might be applied to a number of other useful purposes in life; such as making hats, great coats, boots, &c. for sailors, soldiers, fishermen, and every other description of persons who, from their pursuits, are exposed to wet stockings; for invalids, who suffer from damps; bathing caps, tents, coverings for carriages of all kinds, for roofs of houses, trunks, buoys, &c.

This extraordinary vegetable production, in place of being injured by water, at its usual temperature is *is preserved by it. For a knowledge of this circumstance I am indebted to the *Chinese*. Having some years ago commissioned articles made of the elastic gum from *China*, I received them in a small jar filled up with water, in which state I have since kept them without observing any signs of decay.

Should it ever be deemed an object to attempt plantations of the elastic gum vine in *Bengal*, I would recommend the foot of the *Chittagong*, *Rajmahal* and *Bauglipore* hills, as situations where there is every probability of succeeding, being very similar in soil and climate to the places of its growth on *Prince of Wales's Island*. It would, however, be advisable to make the first trial at this settlement, to learn in what way the propagation of the plant might be most successfully conducted. A further experience may also be necessary, to ascertain the season when the milk can be procured of the best quality, and in the greatest quantity, with the least detriment to the vine.

* From an account of experiments made with the elastic Gum by M. Grossart, inserted in the *Annals de Chimie* for 1792, it appears, that water, when boiling, has a power of partially dissolving the gum so as to render one part capable of being finally joined to another by pressure only.

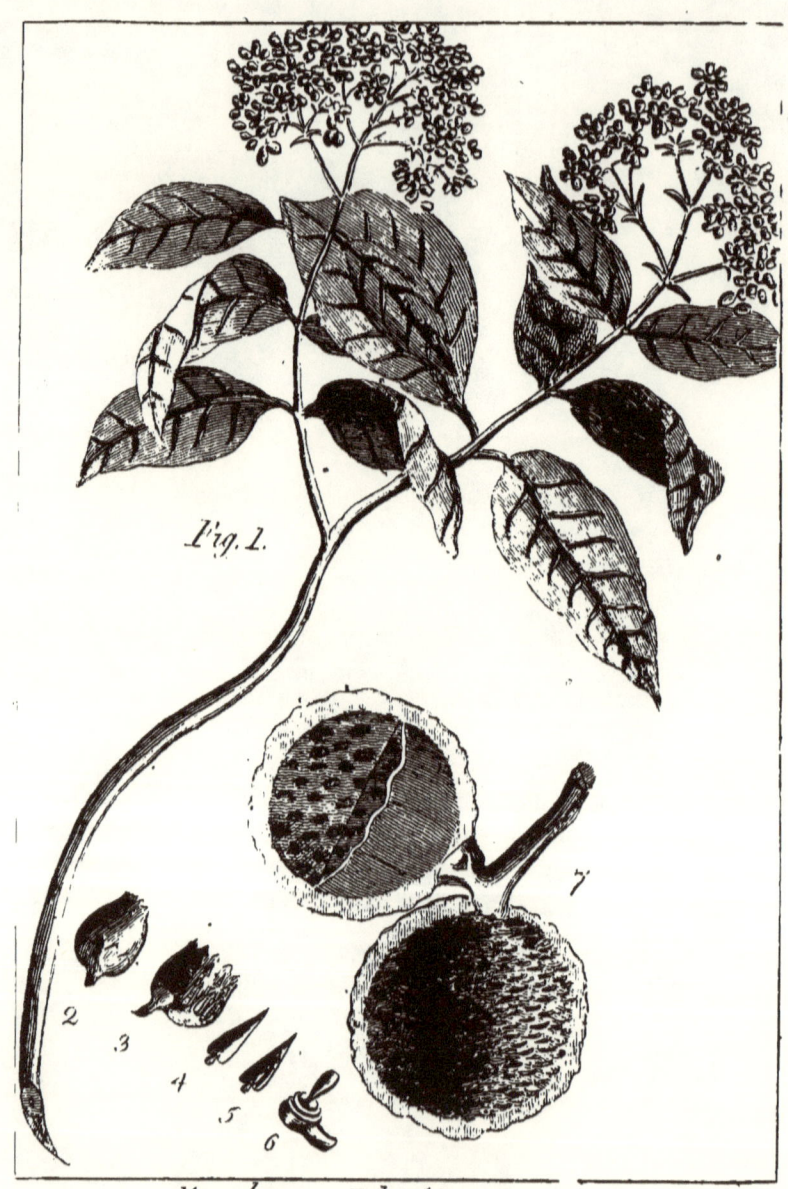

Urceola Elastica

XIV.

A BOTANICAL DESCRIPTION OF

URCEOLA ELASTICA, or CAOUT-CHOUC VINE of SUMATRA and PULLO-PINANG;

WITH AN

Account of the Properties of its inspissated Juice, compared with those of the

AMERICAN CAOUT-CHOUC.

By WILLIAM ROXBURGH, M. D.

FOR the discovery of this useful vine, we are, I believe, indebted to Mr. HOWISON, late *Surgeon* at *Pullo-pinang*; but it would appear he had no opportunity of determining its botanical character. To *Doctor* CHARLES CAMPBELL, of *Fort Marlborough*, we owe the gratification arising from a knowledge thereof.

About twelve months ago I received from that gentleman, by means of Mr. FLEMING, very complete specimens, in full foliage, flower, and fruit. From these I was enabled to reduce it to its class and order in the *Linnæan* System. It forms a new genus in the class *Pentandria*, and order *Monogynia*, and comes in immediately after *Tabernæmontana*, consequently belongs to the thirtieth natural order, or class called *Contortæ* by LINNÆUS in his natural method of classification or arrangement. One of the qualities of the plants of this order is, their yielding, on being cut, a juice which is generally milky, and for the most part deemed of a poisonous nature.

The generic name, *Urceola*, which I have given to this plant, is from the structure of the corol, and the specific name from the quality of its thickened juice.

So

So far as I can find, it does not appear that ever this vine has been taken notice of by any *European* till now. I have carefully looked over the *Hortus Malabaricus*, RUMPHIUS's *Herbarium Amboinense*, &c. &c. Figures of *Indian* Plants, without being able to find any one that can with any degree of certainty be referred to. A substance of the same nature, and probably the very same, was discovered in the Island of *Mauritius*, by M. POIVRE, and from thence sent to *France*; but, so far as I know, we are still ignorant of the plant that yields it.

The impropriety of giving to *Caout-chouc* the term gum, resin, or gum-resin, every one seems sensible of, as it possesses qualities totally different from all such substances as are usually arranged under those generic names: yet it still continues, by most authors I have met with, to be denominated elastic resin, or elastic gum. Some term it simply *Caout-chouc*, which I wish may be considered as the generic name of all such concrete vegetable juices (mentioned in this memoir) as possess elasticity, inflammability, and are soluble in the essential oils, without the assistance of heat.

In a mere definition, it would be improper to state what qualities the object does not possess; consequently it must be understood that this substance is not soluble in the menstruums which usually dissolve resins and gums.

East India Caout-chouc would be a very proper specific name for that of *Urceola elastica*, were there not other trees which yield juices so similar, as to come under the same generic character; but as this is really the case, I will apply the name of the tree which yields it for a specific one. E. G. *Caout-chouc* of *Urceola elastica*, *Caout-chouc* of *Ficus Indica*, *Caout-chouc* of *Artocarpus integrifolia*, &c. &c.

DESCRIPTION OF THE PLANT URCEOLA.
PENTANDRIA MONOGYNIA.

GEN. CHAR. calyx beneath five-toothed; corol one petaled, pitcher fhaped, with its contracted mouth five-toothed: nectary entire, furrounding the germs; follicles two, round, drupacious; feeds numerous, immerfed in pulp.

URCEOLA ELASTICA.

Shrubby, twining, leaves oppofite, oblong, panicles terminal, is a native of *Sumatra*, *Pullo-pinang*, &c. *Malay* countries.

Stem, woody, climbing over trees, &c. to a very great extent, young fhoots twining, and a little hairy, bark of the old woody parts thick, dark coloured, confiderably uneven, a little fcabrous, on which I found feveral fpecies of mofs, particularly large patches of *lichen*; the wood is white, light, and porous.

Leaves, oppofite, fhort-petioled, horizontal, ovate, oblong, pointed, entire, a little fcabrous, with a few fcattered white hairs on the under fide.

Stipules, none.

Panicles, terminal, brachiate, very ramus.

Flowers, numerous, minute, of a dull, greenifh colour, and hairy on the outfide.

Bracts, lanceolate, one at each divifion and fubdivifion of the panicle.

Calyx, perianth, one-leaved, five-toothed, permanent.

Corol, one petaled, pitcher fhaped, hairy, mouth much contracted, five-toothed, divifions erect, acute, nectary entire, cylindrick, embracing the lower two-thirds of the germs.

Stamens, filaments five, very fhort, from the bafe of the corol. Anthers arrow fhaped, converging, bearing their pollen in two grooves on the inside, near the apex; between these grooves and the insertions of the filaments they are covered with white soft hairs.

Pistil, germs two; above the nectary they are very hairy round the margins of their truncated tops. Style single, shorter than the stamens. Stigma ovate, with a circular band, dividing it into two portions of different colours.

Per. Follicles two, round, laterally compressed into the shape of a turnip, wrinkled, leathery, about three inches in their greatest diameters—one celled, two valved.

Seeds, very numerous, reniform, immersed in firm fleshy pulp.

EXPLANATION OF THE FIGURES.

1. A branchlet in flower, natural size.
2. A flower magnified.
3. The same laid open, which exposes to view the situation of the stamens inserted into the bottom of the corol, the nectarium surrounding the lower half of the two germs, their upper half with hairy margins, the style and ovate party-coloured; stigma appearing above the nectary.
4. Outside of one of the stamens ⎫
5. Inside of the same ⎬ much magnified.
6. The nectarium laid open, exposing to view the whole of the pistil.
7. The two seed vessels (called by Linnæus *follicles*), natural size; half of one of them is removed, to shew the seed immersed in pulp. A portion thereof is also cut away, which more clearly shews the situation and shape of the seed.

From wounds made in the bark of this plant there oozes a milky fluid, which on exposure to the open air,

air, separates into an elastic coagulum, and watery liquid, apparently of no use, after the separation takes place. This coagulum is not only like the American *caout-chouc* or Indian rubber, but possesses the same properties, as will be seen from the following experiments and observations made on some which had been extracted from the vine about five months ago. A ball of it now before me, is to my sense, totally void of smell, even when cut into, is very firm, nearly spherical, measures nine and a half inches in circumference, and weighs seven ounces and a quarter, its colour on the outside is that of American *caout-chouc*, where fresh cut into of a light brown colour till the action of the air darkens it; throughout there are numerous small cells, filled with a portion of light brown watery liquid above mentioned. This ball, in simply falling from a height of fifteen feet, rebounds about ten or twelve times, the first is from five to seven feet high, the succeeding ones of course lessening by gradation.

This substance is not now soluble in the above mentioned liquid contained in its cells, although so intimately blended therewith when first drawn from the plant, as to render it so thin, as to be readily applied to the various purposes to which it is so well adapted when in a fluid state.

From what has been said, it will be evident that this *caout-chouc*, possesses a considerable share of solidity and elasticity in an eminent degree. I compared the last quality, with that of American *caout-chouc* by taking small slips of each, and extending them till they broke; that of Urceola, was found capable of bearing a much greater degree of extension, (and contraction) than the American: however, this may be owing to the time the respective substances have been drawn from their plants.

The Urceola *caout-chouc*, rubs out the marks of a black lead pencil, as readily as the American, and is evidently the subſtance of which the Chineſe make their elaſtic rings.

It contains much combuſtible matter, burning entirely away, with a clear flame, emitting a conſiderable deal of dark-coloured ſmoke which readily condenſes into a large proportion of exceeding fine ſoot, or lamp-black; at the ſame time it gives but little ſmell, and that not diſagreeable; the combuſtion is often ſo rapid, as to cauſe drops of a black liquid, very like tar, to fall from the burning maſs; this is equally inflammable with the reſt, and continues when cold in its ſemi-fluid ſtate, but totally void of elaſticity; in *America* the *caout-chouc* is uſed for torches, ours appears to be equally fit for that purpoſe. Expoſed in a ſilver ſpoon to a heat, about equal to that which melts lead or tin, it is reduced into a thick, black, inflammable liquid, ſuch as drops from it during combuſtion, and is equally deprived of its elaſtic powers, conſequently rendered unfit for thoſe purpoſes, for which its original elaſticity rendered it ſo proper.

It is inſoluble in ſpirits of wine, nor has water any more effect on it, except when aſſiſted by heat, and then it is only ſoftened by it.

Sulphuric acid reduced it into a black, brittle, charcoal like ſubſtance, beginning at the ſurface of the *caout-chouc*, and if the pieces are not very thin, or ſmall, it requires ſome days to penetrate to their centre; during the proceſs, the acid is rendered very dark coloured, almoſt black. If the ſulphuric acid is previouſly diluted, with only an equal quantity of water, it does not then appear to have any effect on this ſubſtance, nor is the colour of the liquid changed thereby.

Nitric

Nitric acid reduced it in twelve hours to a foft, yellow, unelaftic mafs, while the acid is rendered yellow; at the end of two days, the *caout-chouc* had acquired fome degree of friability and hardnefs. The fame experiment made on American *caout-chouc* was attended with fimilar effects. Muriatic acid had no effect on it.

Sulphuric æther only foftened it, and rendered the different minute portions it was cut into eafily united, and without any feeming diminution of elafticity.

Nitric æther I did not find a better menftruum than the vitriolic, confequently, if the æther I employed was pure, of which I have fome doubt, this fubftance muft differ effentially from that of *America*, which BERNIARD reports to be foluble in nitric æther.

Where this fubftance can be had in a fluid ftate, there is no neceffity for diffolving or foftening it, to render it applicable to the various ufes for which it may be required; but where the dry *caout-chouc* is only procurable, fulphuric æther promifes to be an ufeful medium, by which it may be rendered fo foft as to be readily formed into a variety of fhapes.

Like American *caout-chouc*, it is foluble in the effential oil of turpentine, and I find it equally fo in Cajeput oil, an effential oil, faid to be obtained from the leaves of *Melaleuca Leucadendron*. Both folutions appear perfect, thick, and very glutinous. Spirits of wine, added to the folution in Cajeput oil, foon united with the oil, and left the *caout-chouc* floating on the mixture in a foft femi-fluid ftate, which, on being wafhed in the fame liquor, and expofed to the air, became as firm as before it was diffolved, and retained its elaftic powers perfectly, while in the intermediate ftates between femi-fluid and firm, it could be drawn out into long, tranfparent threads, refembling, in the polifh of their furface, the fibres of the tendons of animals; when they broke, the elafticity was fo great, that each end inftantaneoufly returned to its refpective mafs. Through all thefe ftages the leaft preffure with the finger and thumb united different portions, as perfectly as if they never had been feparated, and without any clamminefs, or fticking to the fingers, which renders moft of the folutions of *caout-chout*, fo very unfit for the purpofes for which they are required. A piece of catgut covered with the half infpiffated folution, and rolled between two fmooth furfaces, foon acquired a polifh, and confiftence very proper for bougies. Cajeput oil, I alfo found a good menftruum for American *caout-chouc*, and was as readily feparated by the addition of a little fpirit of wine, or rum, as the other, and appears equally fit for ufe, as I covered a piece of catgut with the wafhed folution, as perfectly as with that of *Urceola*. The only difference I could obferve, was a little more adhefivenefs from its not drying fo quickly; the oil of turpentine had greater attraction for the *caout-chouc*, than for the fpirits of wine, confequently remained obftinately united to the former, which prevented its being brought into that ftate of firmnefs fit for handling, which it acquired when Cajeput oil was the menftruum.

The Cajeput folution employed as a varnifh did not dry, but remained moift and clammy, whereas the turpentine folution dried pretty faft.

Expreffed oil of olives and linfeed proved imperfect menftruums while cold, as the *caout-chouc*, in feveral days, was only rendered foft, and the oils vifcid, but with a degree of heat equal to that which melts tin, continued for about twenty-five minutes, it was perfectly diffolved, but the folution remained thin and void of elafticity. I alfo found it foluble in wax, and

and in butter in the same degree of heat, but still these solutions were without elasticity, or any appearance of being useful.

I shall now conclude what I have to offer on the *caout-chouc*, or *Urceola elastica*, with observing that some philosophers of eminence have entertained doubts of the American *caout-chouc* being a simple vegetable substance, and suspect it to be an artificial production, an idea which I hope the above detailed experiments will help to eradicate, and consequently to restore the histories of that substance by M. *De la Condamine* and others, to that degree of credit to which they seem justly entitled, in support of which it may be further observed, that besides *Urceola elastica* there are many other trees, natives of the Torrid Zone, that yield a milky juice, possessing qualities nearly of the same nature, as *artocarpus integrifolia* (common jack tree) *ficus religiosus et Indica, Hippomane biglandulosa, Cecropia peltata*, &c.

The *caout-chouc* or *ficus religiosa*, the Hindus consider the most tenacious vegetable juice they are acquainted with; from it their best bird lime is prepared. I have examined its qualities as well as those of *ficus Indica* and *artocarpus integrifolia*, by experiments, similar to those above related, and found them triflingly elastic when compared with the American and Urceola *caout-choucs*, but infinitely more viscid than either; they are also inflammable, though in a less degree, and shew nearly the same phenomena when immersed in the mineral acids, solution of caustic alkali, alkohol, fat, and essential oils; but the solution in Cajeput oil could not be separated by spirits of wine and collected again like the solutions of the Urceola and American *caout-choucs*.

XV. SOME

XV.

SOME ACCOUNT OF THE
ASTRONOMICAL LABOURS
OF
JAYASINHA, RAJAH OF AMBHERE, OR
JAYANAGAR.

By WILLIAM HUNTER, Esquire.

WHILE the attention of the learned world has been turned towards the state of science in remote ages and countries, and the labours of the *Asiatick* Society have been more particularly directed to investigate the knowledge attained by the ancient inhabitants of Hindustan; it is a tribute due to a congenial spirit, to rescue from oblivion those among their descendants in modern times, who, rising superior to the prejudices of education, of national pride and religion, have striven to enrich their country with scientific truth derived from a foreign source.

The name of JAYASINHA is not unknown in *Europe*; it has been consigned to immortality by the pen of the illustrious Sir WILLIAM JONES: but yet, the extent of his exertions in the cause of science is little known; and the just claims of superior genius and zeal will, I hope, justify my taking up a part of the Society's time with a more particular enumeration of his labours.

JEY-SING or JAYASINHA succeeded to the inheritance of the ancient Rajahs of Ambhere, in the year *Vicramadittya* 1750, corresponding to 1693 of the *Christian* æra. His mind had been early stored with the knowledge contained in the Hindu writings, but he appears to have peculiarly attached himself to the
mathe-

mathematical sciences, and his reputation for skill in them stood so high, that he was chosen by the Emperor MAHOMMED SHAH to reform the calendar, which, from the inaccuracy of the existing tables, had ceased to correspond with the actual appearance of the heavens. JAYASINHA undertook the task, and constructed a new set of tables, which in honour of the reigning prince he named *Zeej Mahommedshahy*. By these almanacks are constructed at *Dehly*, and all astronomical computations made at the present time. The best and most authentic account of his labours for the completion of this work and the advancement of astronomical knowledge is contained in his own preface to the *Zeej Mahommedshahy*, which follows with a literal translation.

'*Praise* be to God, such that the minutely discerning genius of the profoundest geometers in uttering the smallest particle of it, may open the mouth in confession of inability; and such adoration, that the study and accuracy of astronomers who measure the heavens, on the first step towards expressing it, may acknowledge their astonishment and utter insufficiency. Let us devote ourselves at the altar of the King of Kings, hallowed be his name! in the book of the register of whose

بسم الله الرحمن الرحيم
ثناهي که خرد خورده بين هند سان عقده کشا در اداي دقيقه از ان زبان اعتراف بعجز و تصور کشايد و ستايشي که فکر اصابت قرين را صدان فلک پيماي يا ولين درجه آن شرح و بيان اقرار به تحير و نارسا بي نمايد نثار بارگاه شبهنا هي که طباق سموات بکند و رقيبست چند از دفتر ديوان قدرت

'power

ASTRONOMICAL LABOURS OF JAYASINHA. 179

'power the lofty orbs of
'heaven are only a few
'leaves; and the stars
'and that heavenly
'courser the sun, a small
'piece of money in the
'treasury of the empire
'of the Most High.

'If he had not adorned
'the pages of the table
'of the climates of the
'earth with the lines of
'rivers, and the cha-
'racters of grasses and
'trees, no calculator
'could have constructed
'the almanack of the
'various kinds of seeds
'and of fruits which it
'contains. And if he
'had not enlightened
'the dark path of the
'elements with the
'torches of the fixed
'stars, the planets, and
'the resplendent sun and
'moon, how could it
'have been possible to
'arrive at the end of
'our wishes, or to escape
'from the labyrinth, and

'the

'the precipices of igno-
'rance.

'From inability to
'comprehend the all-en-
'compassing beneficence
'of his power, HIPPAR-
'CHUS is an ignorant
'clown, who wrings the
'hands of vexation; and
'in the contemplation of
'his exalted majesty,
'PTOLEMY is a bat, who
'can never arrive at the
'sun of truth: The de-
'monstrations of Eu-
'CLID are an imperfect
'sketch of the forms of
'his contrivance; and
'thousands of JEMSHED
'CASHY, or NUSEER
'TOOSEE, in this at-
'tempt would labour in
'vain.

'But since the well-
'wisher of the works of
'creation, and the ad-
'miring spectator of the
'theatre of infinite wis-
'dom and providence,
'*Servai-Jeysing* from the
'first dawning of reason
'in his mind, and during
'its progress towards ma-
'turity, was entirely de-
'voted to the study of ma-
'thematical science, and
'the bent of his mind was
'constantly directed to
'the solution of its most

dif-

'difficult problems; by the aid of the supreme artificer he obtained a thorough knowledge of its principles and rules. —He found that the calculation of the places of the ſtars as obtained from the tables in common uſe, ſuch as the new tables of SEID GOORGANEE and KHACANEE, and the *Tuſheelat - Mula - Chand - Akber-ſhahee*, and the Hindu books, and the European tables, in very many caſes, give them widely different from thoſe determined by obſervation: eſpecially the appearance of the new moons, the computation of which does not agree with obſervation.

'Seeing that very important affairs both regarding religion and the adminiſtration of empire depend upon theſe; and that in the time of the riſing and ſetting of the planets, and the ſeaſons of eclipſes of the ſun and moon, many conſiderable diſagreements, of a ſimilar nature, were found; he repreſented

نصیبی کامل حاصل کرد چنان یافت که اسنتخراج تقادیم کواکب که از زیجهای متعارف مثل زیج جدید سعید کورکانی و خاقانی و تسهیلات ملاچاند اکبر شاهی و کتبهای هندی و زیج فرنکی میبشود اکثر و اغلب اوقات دور از مهر صود و عیان می یابند خصوصا روته اهله که جناب آن با مشاهده کم موافقت میکند

وحال آنكه کارهای سترک ارباب مال و محل و اصحاب دین و دول بدان منوط و مربوط است و همین طور در اوقات ظهور و خفای کواکب سیارات و ازمنه کسوفات و خسوفات اکثر تفاوت فاحش رومیدهد اینعنی را

'it to his majesty of dig-
'nity and power, the
'sun of the firmament
'of felicity and domini-
'on, the splendor of the
'forehead of imperial
'magnificence, the un-
'rivalled pearl of the sea
'of sovereignty, the in-
'comparably brightest
'star of the heaven of
'empire, whose standard
'is the Sun, whose reti-
'nue the Moon; whose
'lance is MARS, and his
'pen like MERCURY;
'with attendants like
'VENUS; whose thresh-
'old is the sky, whose
'signet is JUPITER;
'whose centinel SA-
'TURN; the Emperor
'descended from a long
'race of Kings; an
'ALEXANDER in digni-
'ty; the shadow of GOD;
'the victorious king,
'*Mahommed Shah*, may
'he ever be triumphant
'in battle!

'He was pleased to re-
'ply, since you, who are
'learned in the mysteries
'of science, have a per-
'fect knowledge of this
'matter; having assem-
'bled the astronomers
'and geometricians of the
'faith of ISLAM and the
'*Bramins* and *Pandits*,

'and

'and the astronomers of
'*Europe*, and having pre-
'pared all the apparatus
'of an observatory, do
'you so labour for the as-
'certaining of the point
'in question, that the dis-
'agreement between the
'calculated times of those
'phenomena, and the
'times in which they are
'observed to happen may
'be rectified.

'Although this was
'a mighty task, which
'during a long period of
'time none of the power-
'ful Rajahs had prose-
'cuted; nor, among the
'tribes of ISLAM, since
'the time of the martyr-
'prince, whose sins are
'forgiven, MIRZA ULU-
'GA BEG, to the present,
'which comprehends a
'period of more than
'three hundred years, had
'any one of the kings,
'possessed of power and
'dignity, turned his at-
'tention to this object;
'yet, to accomplish the
'exalted command which
'he had received, he *(Jey-
'sing.)* bound the girdle
'of resolution about the
'loins of his soul, and
'constructed here (at
'Dehly) several of the
'instruments of an obser-
'vatory,

'vatory, such as had been
' erected at *Samarcand*,
' agreeably to the *Musul-*
'*man* books: such as *Za-*
'*tul-huluck*, of brass, in
' diameter three *guz* of
' the measure now in use;
' (which is nearly equal to
' two cubits of the *Coram*)
' and *Zat-ul-shobetein*, and
' *Zat-ul-suchetein*, and
' *Suds-Fukheri*, and *sham-*
'*lah*. But finding that
' brass instruments did
' not come up to the ideas
' which he had formed of
' accuracy, because of the
' smallness of their size,
' the want of division in-
' to minutes, the shaking
' and wearing of their
' axes, the displacement
' of the centres of the cir-
' cles, and the shifting of
' the planes of the instru-
' ments; he concluded
' that the reason why the
' determinations of the
' cients, such as HIPPAR-
'CHUS and PTOLEMY
' proved inaccurate, must
' have been of this kind;
' therefore he construct-
' ed in *Dar-ul-khelâfet*
' *Shah-Jehanabad*, which
' is the seat of empire and
' prosperity, instruments
' of his own invention,
' such as *Jey-pergás* and
' *Ram-junter* and *Semrát-*

'*junter*, the semidiameter
' of which is of eighteen
' cubits, and one minute
' on it is a barley-corn
' and a half; of stone and
' lime, of perfect stabili-
' ty, with attention to the
' rules of geometry, and
' adjustment to the meri-
' dian, and to the latitude
' of the place, and with
' care in the measuring
' and fixing of them; so
' that the inaccuracies
' from the shaking of the
' circles, and the wear-
' ing of their axes, and
' displacement of their
' centres, and the inequa-
' lity of the minutes,
' might be corrected.
 ' Thus an accurate
' method of constructing
' an observatory was esta-
' blished; and the dif-
' ference which had ex-
' isted between the com-
' puted and observed
' places of the fixed stars
' and planets, by means
' of observing their mean
' motions and aberrations
' with such instruments,
' was removed. And, in
' order to confirm the
' truth of these observa-
' tions, he constructed
' instruments of the same
' kind in *Suvaï Jeypoor*,
' and *Matra*, and *Benares*,
' and *Oujein*.—When he
' compared these obser-
' vatories,

' vatories, after allowing
' for the difference of
' longitude between the
' places where they stood,
' the observations and
' calculations agreed.—
' Hence he determined
' to erect similar obser-
' vatories in other large
' cities, that so every per-
' son who is devoted to
' these studies, whenever
' he wishes to ascertain
' the place of a star, or
' the relative situation of
' one star to another,
' might by these instru-
' ments observe the phe-
' nomena. But, seeing
' that in many cases it is
' necessary to determine
' past or future pheno-
' mena, and also, that in
' the instant of their oc-
' currence, clouds or rain
' may prevent the obser-
' vation, or the power
' and opportunity of ac-
' cess to an observatory
' may be wanting, he
' deemed it necessary
' that a table be con-
' structed, by means of
' which the daily places
' of the stars being cal-
' culated every year, and
' disposed in a calendar,
' may be always in readi-
' ness.

' In the same manner
' as the geometers and astronomers

'astronomers of antiquity bestowed many years on the practice of observation, thus, for the establishment of a certain method, after having constructed these instruments, the places of the stars were daily observed. After seven years had been spent in this employment, information was received, that about this time observatories had been constructed in *Europe*, and that the learned of that country were employed in the prosecution of this important work; that the business of the observatory was still carrying on there, and that they were constantly labouring to determine with accuracy, the subtleties of this science. For this reason, having sent to that country several skilful persons along with PADRE MANUEL, and having procured the new tables which had been constructed there thirty years* before, and published under the name of *Leyyer*†, as well as

---

* JEYSING finished his tables in the year of the Hijira 1141, or A. D. 1728.

† DE LA HIRE, published the first edition of his tables in 1687, and the second in 1702.

'the

'the European tables an-
'terior to those; on ex-
'amining and comparing
'the calculations of these
'tables, with actual ob-
'servation, it appeared
'there was an error in the
'former, in assigning the
'moon's place, of half a
'degree: although the
'error in the other pla-
'nets was not so great, yet
'the times of solar and lu-
'nar eclipses he found to
'come out later or earlier
'than the truth, by the
'fourth part of a *ghurry*
'or fifteen *puls**. Hence
'he concluded that, since
'in *Europe*, astronomical
'instruments have not
'been constructed of
'such a size, and so large
'diameters, the motions
'which have been ob-
'served with them may
'have deviated a little
'from the truth; since, in
'this place, by the aid of
'the unerring artificer,
'astronomical instru-
'ments have been con-
'structed with all the ex-
'actness that the heart
'can desire; and the mo-
'tions of the stars have,
'for a long period, been
'constantly observed

* 'Equal to six minutes of our time, an error of three minutes in
' the moon's place would occasion this difference in time, and as it
' is improbable, that LA HIRE's tables should be inaccurate to the
' extent mentioned above, of half a degree, I conceive there must
' be an error in the original.

'' with

'with them; agreeably
'to observation the mean
'motions and equations
'were established. He
'found the calculation to
'agree perfectly with the
'observation; and al-
'though even to this day
'the business of the ob-
'servatory is carried on,
'a table under the name
'of his Majesty, the sha-
'dow of God, compre-
'hending the most accu-
'rate rules, and most per-
'fect methods of com-
'putation was construct-
'ed; that so, when the
'places of the stars, and
'the appearance of the
'new moons, and the
'eclipses of the sun and
'moon, and the con-
'junctions of the heaven-
'ly bodies, are comput-
'ed by it, they may ar-
'rive as near as possible
'to the truth, which, in
'fact, is every day seen
'and confirmed in the
'observatory.

'It therefore behoveth
'those who excel in this
'art, in return for so great
'a benefit, to offer up
'their prayers for long
'continuance of the pow-
'er and prosperity of so
'good a King, the safe-
'guard of the earth, and
'thus obtain for them-
'selves a blessing in
'both worlds.

The five observatories constructed by *Jayasinha* still exist, in a state more or less perfect. Having had the opportunity of examining four of the number, I shall subjoin a short description of them.

The observatory at *Dehly* is situated without the walls of the city, at the distance of one mile and a quarter; it lies S. 22 deg. W. from the *Jummah Musjid*, at the distance of a mile and three quarters, its latitude 28 deg. 37 min. 37 sec. N.* longitude 77 deg. 2 min. 27 sec. E. from Greenwich; it consists of several detached buildings:

1. A large Equatorial Dial, of the form represented at the letter A in Sir *Robert Barker's* description of the Benares observatory, (Ph. Transf. vol. LXVII.) its form is pretty entire, but the edges of the gnomon, and those of the circle on which the degrees were marked, are broken in several places. The length of the gnomon, measured with a chord, I found to be 118 feet seven inches, reckoning its elevation equal to the latitude of the observatory, 28 deg. 37 min.; this gives the length of the base 104 feet one inch, and the perpendicular height 56 feet nine inches; but, the ground being lower at the north end, the actual elevation at the top of the gnomon above it is more than this quantity. This is the instrument called by *Jayasinha*, *semrat Yunter* (the prince of dials). It is built of stone, but the edges of the gnomon and of the arches, where the graduation was, were of white marble, a few small portions of which only remain.

2. At a little distance from this instrument towards the N. W. is another equatorial dial, more entire, but smaller, and of a different construction. In the middle stands a gnomon, which, as usual in these buildings, contains a stair up to the top. On each side of

* The latitude assigned to it in the *Zeej Mahommedshaby* is 28 deg. 37 min.

this

this gnomon are two concentric femicircles, having for their diameters the two edges of the gnomon; they have a certain inclination to the horizon: at the fouth point, I found it to be twenty-nine degrees (nearly equal to the latitude,) but at fome diftance from that point it was thirty-three degrees. Hence it is evident, that they reprefent meridians, removed by a certain angle upon the meridian of the place. On each fide of this part is another gnomon, equal in fize to the former; and to the eaftward and weftward of them, are the arches on which the hours are marked. The ufe of the centre part above defcribed, I have never been able to learn. The length of the gnomon, which is equal to the diameter of the outer circle, is thirty-five feet four inches. The length of a degree on the outer circle is 3.74 inches. The diftance between the outer and inner circle is two feet nine inches. Each degree is divided into ten parts, and each of thefe is fubdivided into fix parts or minutes.

3. The north wall of this building connects the three gnomons at their higheft end, and on this wall is defcribed a graduated femicircle, for taking the al titudes of bodies, that lie due eaft or due weft from the eye of the obferver.

4. To the weftward of this building, and clofe to it, is a wall, in the plane of the meridian, on which is defcribed a double quadrant, having for centres the two upper corners of the wall, for obferving the altitudes of bodies paffing the meridian, either to the north or fouth of the Zenith. One degree on thefe quadrants meafured 2.833 inches, and thefe are divided into minutes.

5. To the fouthward of the great dial are two buildings, named

Uftuanah.

Uſtuanah. They exactly resemble one another, and are designed for the same purpose, which is to observe the altitude and azimuth of the heavenly bodies, they are two in number, on purpose that two persons may observe at the same time, and so compare and correct their observations.

These buildings are circular, and in the centre of each is a pillar of the same height with the building itself, which is open at top. From this pillar, at the height of about three feet from the bottom, proceed radii of stone horizontally to the circular wall of the building. These radii are thirty in number; the spaces between them are equal to the radii themselves, which measure in breadth as they recede from the pillar, so that each radius and each intermediate space forms a sector of six degrees.

The wall of the building at the spaces between the radii forms recesses internally, being thinner at those places than where it joins the radii. In each of these recesses are two windows, one over the other; and in the sides of the recess are square holes, at about the distance of two feet, above one another, by means of which a person may climb to the top. On the edges of these recesses are marked the degrees of the sun's altitude, or rather the tangents of those degrees shewn by the shadow of the centre pillar; and numbered from the top, from one degree to forty-five. For the altitude, when the sun rises higher, the degrees are marked on the horizontal radii; but they are numbered from the pillar outwards, beginning with one, so that the number here pointed out by the shadow, is the complement of the altitude. These degrees are subdivided into minutes. The spaces on the wall, opposite to the radii, are divided into six equal parts, or degrees, by lines drawn from top to bottom, but these degrees are not subdivided. By observing on which

which of these the shadow of the pillar falls, we may determine the sun's azimuth. The parts on the pillar opposite to the radii, and the intermediate spaces, in all sixty, are marked by lines reaching to the top, and painted of different colours.

In the same manner that we determine the altitude and azimuth of the sun, we may also observe those of the moon, when her light is strong enough to cast a shadow. Those of the moon at other times, or of a star, may also be found by placing the eye either on one of the radii, or at the edge of one of the recesses in the wall (according as the altitude is greater or less than forty-five degrees,) and moving along till the top of the pillar is in a line with the object. The degree at which the eye is placed will give the altitude, or its complement, and the azimuth is known from the number of the radius to which the eye is applied.

The dimensions of the building are as follow:

	Ft.	In.
Length of the radius from the circumference of the centre pillar to the wall; being equal to the height of the wall above the radii - - - - - - - -	24	6¾
Length of one degree on the circular wall		5¼
Which gives for the whole circumference	172	6
Circumference of the pillar { measured by a handkerchief carried round it }	17	0¾
{ Deduced from its coloured divisions measured with compasses - - - }	17	2¼

I do not see how observations can be made when the shadow falls on the spaces between the stone radii or sectors; and from reflecting on this, I am inclined to think, that the two instruments, instead of being duplicates, may be supplementary one to the other; the

the sectors in one corresponding to the vacant spaces in the other, so that in one or other an observation of any body visible above the horizon, might at any time be made. This point remains to be ascertained.

6. Between these two buildings and the great equatorial dial, is an instrument called *shamlah*. It is a concave hemispherical surface, formed of mason work, to represent the inferior hemisphere of the heavens. It is divided by six ribs of solid work, and as many hollow spaces; the edges of which represent meridians at the distance of fifteen degrees from one another. The diameter of the hemisphere is twenty-seven feet five inches.

The next in point of size and preservation among those which I have had the opportunity of examining, is the observatory at Oujein. It is situated at the southern extremity of the city in the quarter called *Jeysingpoorah*, where are still the remains of a palace of *Jayasinha*, who was soubahdar of Meliva, in the time of *Mahommed Shah*. The parts of it are as follow:

1. A double mural quadrant, fixed in the plane of the meridian. It is a stone wall, twenty-seven feet high, and twenty-six feet in length. The east side is smooth and covered with plaister, on which the quadrants are described; on the west side is a stair, by which you ascend to the top. At the top, near the two corners, and at the distance of twenty-five feet one inch from one another, were fixed two spikes of iron, perpendicular to the plane of the wall; but these have been pulled out. With these points as centres, and a radius equal to their distance; two arcs of 90 degrees are described intersecting each other. These are divided in the manner represented in the margin. One division in the upper circle is equal to six degrees; in the second

second one degree, (the extent contained in the specimens) in the third six minutes, and in the fourth one minute. One of these arcs serves to observe the altitude of any body to the north, and the other of any body to the south of the Zenith; but the arc which has its centre to the south, is continued to the southward beyond the perpendicular, and its centre about half a degree, by which, the altitude of the sun, can at all times be taken on this arc. With this instrument *Jayasinha* determined the latitude of Oujein to be 23° 10′ N.

Supposing the latitude, here meant, to be (as is most probable) that of the observatory, I was anxious to compare it with the result of my own observations (Asiatick Researches, vol. IV. p. 150. 152.) and, for that purpose, I made an accurate measurement from our camp, at SHAH DAWUL's *durgah*, to the mural quadrant of the observatory. I found the southing of the quadrant from our camp to be one mile 3.9 furlongs, which makes 1′ 17″ difference of latitude.

The latitude of the camp, by medium of two observations, of the sun is	23°	11′	54″
Deduced from the medium of six observations of fixed stars, taken at RANA KHAN's garden, at different latitude 7″ S.	23	11	45
From observation of the sun at the same place	23	11	37
From two observations of ♈, taken at the house in town, at different latitude 32″ S.	23	11	28
			164
Latitude of *Shah Dawul's* durgar, by medium of all observations	23	11	41
Difference of latitude, camp and observatory		1	17
Gives the latitude of the observatory	23	10	24

A closer

A closer coincidence could not be expected, especially as no account is made of seconds in any of the latitudes given in the *Zeej Mahommedshahy*. But, if farther refinement were desired, we might account for the difference, by the Hindu observers not having made any allowance for refraction. Thus, if we suppose the sun's altitude to have been observed, when on the equator, the result will be as follows:

Latitude of the observatory	23°	10'	24"
Its complement, being the true altitude of the sun on the equator	66	49	36
Refraction			24
Sun's apparent altitude	66	50	0
Latitude of the observatory from observation of the sun upon the equator without allowing for refraction	23	10	0

But (besides that I do not pretend, that the mean of my own observations can be relied on, to a less quantity than fifteen seconds,) when we consider, that a minute on the quadrant of the observatory is hardly .09 of an inch, without any contrivance for subdivision, we shall find it needless to descend into such minuteness: and as *Jayasinha* had European observers, it is not likely the refraction would be neglected, especially as the *Zeej Mahommedshahy* contains a table for that purpose. This table is an exact copy of M. DE LA HIRE's, which may be seen in the Encyclopedie, art. Refraction.

This instrument is called, *Yam-utter-bhitti-yunter*. With one of the same kind at Dehly, (No. 4, Dehly observatory,) in the year 1729, *Jayasinha* says, he determined the obliquity of the ecliptic to be 23° 28'. In the following year (1730) it was observed by GODIN 23° 28' 20".

2. On

2. On the top of the mural quadrant is a small pillar, the upper circle of which being two feet in diameter, is graduated for observing the amplitude of the heavenly bodies, at their rising and setting; it is called *Agra Yunter*. The circles on it are very much effaced.

3. About the middle of the wall the parapet to the eastward is increased in thickness, and on this part is constructed a horizontal dial called *Puebha Yunter*. Its length is two feet four inches and a half, but the divisions on it are almost totally effaced.

4. *Dig anfa Yunter*, a circular building, 116 feet in circumference. It is now roofed with tiles, and converted into the abode of a Hindu deity, so that I could not get access to examine its construction; but the following account of it is delivered in the *Sem'rat Siddhanta*, an astronomical work composed under the inspection of *Jayasinha*.

On a horizontal plane describe the three concentric circles A B C, and draw the north, south, east, and west lines, as in the figure. Then, on A build a

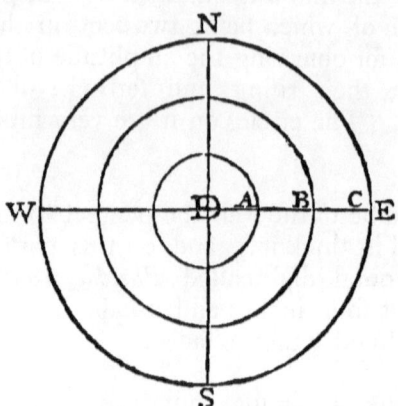

solid pillar, of any height at pleasure; on B build a wall, equal in height to the pillar at A; and on C a wall of double that height. From the north, south, east, and west points, on the top of the wall C stretch the threads N.S. W.E. intersecting each other in the point D, directly above the centre of the pillar A. To the centre of that pillar fasten a thread, which is to be laid over the top of the wall C, and to be stretched by a weight suspended to the other end of it.

The use of this instrument is for observing the azimuth *(dig-anfa)* of the heavenly bodies; and the observations with it are made in the following manner: The observer standing at the circumference of the circle B, while an assistant manages the thread moveable round the circle C, places his eye so that the object to be observed, and the intersection of the threads N.S. W.E. may be in one vertical plane, while he directs the assistant to carry the moveable thread into the same plane. Then the degrees on the circle C cut off by the moveable thread, give the azimuth required. In order to make this observation with accuracy, it seems necessary that the point D, and the centre of the pillar A, should be connected by a thread

thread perpendicular to the horizon; but no mention is made of this in the original description.

5. *Náree-wila-yunter*, or equinoctial dial, is a cylinder, placed with its axis horizontally, in the north and south line, and cut obliquely at the two ends, so that these ends are parallel to the equator *(Náree-wila)*. On each of these ends a circle is described, the diameter of which in this instrument is 3 feet 7 inches and a half. These are divided into *g,hurries*, of six degrees, into degrees and subdivisions, which are now effaced. In the centre of each circle, was an iron pin (now wanting) perpendicular to the plane of the circle, and consequently parallel to the earth's axis. When the sun is in the southern signs, the hours are shewn by the shadow of the pin in the south, and when he is in the northern signs by that to the north. On the meridian line on both sides are marked the co-tangent, to a radius equal to the length of the centre pin. The shadow of the pin on this line at noon, points out the sun's declination.

6. *Semrát-yunter*, also called *Náree-wila*, another form of equinoctial dial. (Fig. A of Sir ROBERT BARKER's plate.) It consists of a gnomon of stone, containing within it a stair. Its length is 43 feet 3.3 inches; height from the ground, at the south end, 3 feet 9.7 inches; at the north end 22 feet, being here broken. On each side is built an arc of a circle, parallel to the equator, of 90 degrees. Its radius is 9 feet 1 inch; breadth from north to south 3 feet 1 inch. These arcs are divided into *g,hurries* and subdivisions; and the shadow of the gnomon among them points out the hours. From the north and south extremities of the intersection of these arcs with the gnomon, are drawn lines upon the gnomon, perpendicular to the line of their intersection. These are

are confequently radii of the arcs; and from the points on the upper edge of the gnomon where thefe lines cut it, are conftructed two lines of tangents, one to the northward, and another to the fouthward, to a radius equal to that of the arc. To find the fun's declination, place a pin among thefe divifions, perpendicular to the edge of the gnomon; and move it backwards and forwards, till its fhadow falls on the north or fouth edge of the arc below: the divifion on which the pin is then placed, will fhew the fun's declination. In like manner, to find the declination *(kránti)* of a ftar, and its diftance in time, from the meridian *(net-ghurry)* place your eye among the divifions of the arc, and move it till the edge of the gnomon cut the ftar, while an affiftant holds a pin among the divifions on the edge of the gnomon, fo that the pin may feem to cover the ftar. Then the divifion on the arc at which the eye was placed, will fhew the diftance of the ftar from the meridian; while the place of the pin, in the line of tangents, will fhew its declination.

At *Matra* the remains of the obfervatory are in the fort, which was built by *Jayafinha* on the bank of the *Jumna*. The inftruments are on the roof of one of the apartments. They are all imperfect, and in general of fmall dimenfions.

1. An Equinoctial Dial, being a circle nine feet two inches in diameter, placed parallel to the plane of the equator, and facing northwards. It is divided into g,*hurries* of fix degrees each: each of thefe is fubdivided into degrees, which are numbered as *puls* 10, 20, 30, 40, 50, 60: laftly, each fubdivifion is farther divided into five parts, being 12 minutes, or two *puls*. In the centre is the remains of the iron ftyle, or pin, which ferved to caft the fhadow.

2. On

2. On the top of this instrument is a short pillar, on the upper surface of which is an amplitude instrument (like that described No. 2, *Oujein* observatory, called *Agra-yunter*); but it is only divided into octants. Its diameter is two feet five inches.

3. On the level of the terrace is another amplitude instrument, divided into sixty-equal parts. Its diameter is only thirteen inches.

4. On the same terrace is a circle, in the plane of the horizon, with a gnomon similar to that of a horizontal dial, but the divisions are equal, and of six degrees each. It must therefore have been intended for some other purpose than the common horizontal dial, unless we may conceive it to have been made by some person who was ignorant of the true principles of that instrument. This could not have been the case with *Jayasinha* and his astronomers; but the instrument has some appearance of being of a later date than most of the others: they are all of stone or brick, plaistered with lime, in which the lines and figures are cut; and the plaister of this instrument, though on the level of the terrace, and consequently more exposed to accidents than the others, is the freshest and most entire of all.

5. On the east wall, but facing westward, is a segment, exceeding a semicircle, with the arch downwards. It is divided into two parts, and each of these into fifteen divisions. Its diameter is four feet. On the west wall, facing eastwards, is a similar segment, with the arch upwards, divided in the same way as the former. Its diameter is seven feet nine inches.

The observatory at *Benares* having been described by Sir ROBERT BARKER, and Mr. WILLIAMS, I have

have only a few remarks to offer, in addition to the account delivered by those gentlemen.

I. A. (of Sir *Robert Barker's* plate) is the *Semrat-yunter*, described *Dehly* observatory, No. I. and *Oujein* observatory, No. VI. The arcs on each side are carried as far as ninety-six degrees, which are subdivided into tenth parts. Each space of six degrees is numbered from the bottom of the arc towards the top, sixteen in each arc. Each of these is equal to twenty-four minutes of our time, which answers to the *Hindu* astronomical *g,hurry*. Besides the stair contained in the gnomon, one ascends along a limb of each arc. The dimensions have been given by Mr. *Williams*, with an accuracy that leaves me nothing to add on that head. With respect to the reason of the name I am somewhat in doubt. It may have been given from its eminent utility; but the Rajah had conferred on one of his principal *Pandits* the title of *Semrat* or Prince; and perhaps this instrument, as well as the *Semrat-siddhanta*, may have been denominated in compliment to him; as another instrument (which I have not been able to find out) was called *Jey-pergas* in allusion to the Rajah's name.

B is the equinoctial dial or *Naree-wila* of No. V. *Oujein* observatory. The name given by the *Pandits* to Mr. *Williams (gentu-rage)* probably ought to be *yunter* or *yunter-raj*, q. d. the royal dial.

C is a circle of iron, faced with brass, placed between two stone pillars, about the height of the eyes, and revolving round one of its diameters, which is fixed parallel to the axis of the world. The breadth of the rim of the circle is two inches, the thickness of iron one inch, of brass three tenths of an inch. The diameter mentioned before is not the same breadth, and

and thickness with the rim. The limb is divided into 360 degrees, each degree into four equal parts; and there are larger divisions, containing six degrees each. The size of a degree is .3 of an inch. Round the centre revolves an index of brass; the end of which is formed as in the margin; and the line A B, which produced, passes through the centre of the circle, marks the degrees. From this description, it appears that the circle when placed in a vertical position, is in the plane of the meridian of Benares; when it declines from that position, it represents some other meridian. Were there any contrivance for measuring 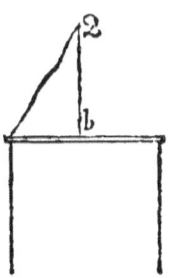 the quantity of this deviation, it would answer the purpose of an equatorial instrument, for determining the place of a star, or any other phænomenon in the heavens. For by moving the circle and its index, till the latter points exactly to the object, the degrees of deviation from the vertical position would mark the distance of the object from the meridian; and the degrees on the circle, intersected between the index and the diameter, which is perpendicular to that on which it revolves, would shew its declination. This last may indeed be observed with the instrument in its present state; but I am inclined to think, that there has been some contrivance for the former part also; having been informed by a learned Pandit, that in two rings of this kind in the *Jeyanagar* observatory such contrivance actually exists. On one of the pillars that support the axis, a circle is described parallel to the equator, divided into degrees and minutes; to the axis of the moveable circle is fixed an index, which is carried round by the motion of the circle; and thus points out, among the divisions on the immoveable circle, the distance from the meridian of the body to be observed.

Observations with this instrument cannot have admitted of much accuracy, as the index is not furnifhed with fights; and the pin by which it is fixed to the centre of the circle is fo prominent, that the eye cannot look along the index itfelf.

The literal meaning of the *Sanfcrit* term *Kranti-writ*, is *circle of declination*, which may, with fome propriety, have been applied to this inftrument, as mentioned by Mr. *Williams*. But this name is, in the *Hindu* aftronomical books, peculiarly appropriated to the ecliptic; and as the *Sem'rat Sid-dhanta* contains the defcription of an inftrument called *Kranti-writ-yunter*, wherein a circle is made, by a particular contrivance, to retain a pofition parallel to the ecliptic, I am inclined to believe that the appellation has been erroneoufly given by the ring above defcribed.

D is the *Dig-anfa-yunter*, No. 4. Oujein obfervatory. The " iron pins," with fmall holes in them, on the top of the outer wall, at the four cardinal " points," are undoubtedly as the Pandits informed Mr. *Williams* for ftretching the wires, or threads, the ufe of which is fully explained above.

The quadrant defcribed by Sir *Robert Barker*, but not reprefented in his plate, is the *Yam-utter-bhitti-yunter*, defcribed *Oujein* obfervatory, No. 1.

On the fouth-eaft corner of the terrace is a fmall platform raifed above its level, fo that you mount upon it by a flight of fteps. Upon this we find a circle of ftone, which Mr. *Williams* found to be fix feet two inches in diameter, in a pofition inclined to the horizon. Mr. *Williams* fays it fronts the weft, and that he could not learn the ufe of it.

I dare not, without further examination, oppofe to this what I find in my notes, taken in 1786, that it ftands in the plane of the equinoctial. If that is the cafe it has been clearly intended for a dial of the fame same kind as fig. B. and probably, as Mr. *Williams* says, never completed, as I found no appearance of graduation on the circle.

Having described those among the observatories constructed by *Jayasinha*, which have fallen under my observation, I proceed to give some account of the tables intitled *Zeej Mahommedshahy*. But here I should regret that, not having access to the *Tabulæ Ludovicia* of *La Hire*, I am unable to determine, whether those of *Jayasinha* are merely taken from the former, by adapting them to the *Arabian* lunar year; or, whether, as he asserts, they are corrected by his own observations; did not the zeal for promoting enquiries of this nature, manifested in the queries proposed to the Asiatick Society by Professor PLAYFAIR (to whom I intend to transmit a copy of the *Zeej Mahommedshahy*) convince me, that he will ascertain, better than I could have done, the point in question.

I. TABLES of the SUN consist of

1. Mean longitudes of the sun, and of his apogee, for current years of the *Hejira* from 1141 to 1171 inclusive.

2. Mean motions of the sun, and of his apogee, for the following periods of *Arabian* years, viz. 30, 60, 90, 120, 150, 180, 210, 240, 270, 300, 600, 900, 1200.

3. Mean motions of the Sun, and of his apogee, for *Arabian* months.

4. The same for days from 1 to 31.

5. The same for hours, 24 to a natural day; but these are continued to 61; so that the numbers answering to them, taken for the next lower denomination, answer for minutes.

6. The same for years complete of the *Hejira*, from 1 to 31.

7. The equation of time.

8. The sun's equation, or equation of the orbit. Argument, his *mean anomaly*, corrected by the equation of time. If this is in the northern signs, the equation is to be subtracted from his place corrected by the equation of time; if in the southern, to be added.

9. The sun's *distance*, his *horary motion*, and *apparent* diameter. Argument, his equated anomaly.

II. TABLES of the MOON,

1—6. Contain the mean longitudes and motions of the Moon, of her *apogee* and *node*, for the same period, as the corresponding tables of the sun.

7. The moon's first *equation*, or *elliptic equation*. Argument, her mean anomaly corrected by the equation of time, to be applied to her place; corrected by the equation of time, in the same manner as the equation of the sun to his.

8. The moon's *second equation*, is to be applied in three places; viz. to her *longitude* and *apogee*, corrected by the first equation and to the node. It has two arguments.

1. From the moon's longitude once equated, subtract the sun's equated place. The signs and degrees of this are at the top and bottom of the table.

2. From the moon's place once equated, subtract the place of the sun's apogee. The signs and degrees of this are on the right and left of the table.

The equation is found at the intersection of the two arguments. If the second argument is in the first half of the zodiac, and the first argument in the first or fourth quarter, the equation is to be added; in the second or third, to be subtracted. But if the second argument is in the second half of the *zodiac*, and the

first

first argument in the first or fourth quarter, it is subtractive; and in the second or third quarter, it is additive.

9. The moon's *third equation*, has also two arguments;

1. From the moon's place, corrected by the second equation, subtract the sun's true longitude; the signs and degrees of this are at the top and bottom of the table.

2. The moon's mean anomaly, corrected by the second equation; the signs and degrees are on the right and left of the table.

The equation is found at the intersection of the arguments; and is to be applied to the moon's longitude twice equated, by addition or subtraction, as expressed in the table, to give her true place in the *felckmayee* or in her *orbit*.

10. Equation of the node.

Argument, the moon's longitude thrice equated, diminished by that of the sun. The equation is to be added to, or subtracted from, the place of the node, as expressed in the table.

In the same table is a second column, entitled *correction of the node*. The numbers from this is to be referred and applied farther on.

11. The moon's fourth equation, or reduction from her *orbit*, to the *ecliptic*. From the moon's longitude thrice equated, subtract the equated longitude of the node, the remainder is the *argument of latitude*; and this is also the argument of the fourth equation; which is to be subtracted, if the argument is in the first or third quarter, from the moon's place in her *orbit*; and if the argument is in the second or fourth quarter, added to the same to give her longitude in the *munuffil*, i. e. reduced to the ecliptic.

12. Table of the moon's latitude, contains two columns, *latitude* and *adjustment of the latitude*. Both of these are to be taken out by the signs and degrees of the argument of latitude.

Multiply into one another, the correction of the node and the adjuſtment of the latitude, and add the product to the latitude of the moon, as taken out of the table, to give the latitude correct; which is northern if the argument of latitude be in the firſt half of the zodiac, and *vice verſa*.

III. TABLES of SATURN.

1—6. Contain the mean longitudes and motions of *Saturn*, of his apogee and node, for the ſame periods as the correſponding tables of the Sun and Moon.

7. Firſt equation. Argument *Saturn's* mean anomaly; if in the firſt ſix ſigns, ſubtraction, and *vice verſa*.

8. Equation of the node. Argument, the argument of latitude, found by ſubtracting the longitude of the node, from that of *Saturn* once equated; additive in the firſt and fourth quarters, ſubtractive in the ſecond and third.

9. *Saturn's* ſecond equation, or reduction of his orbit to the ecliptic. Argument, the corrected argument of latitude or difference between *Saturn's* longitude once equated and the equated longitude of the node. This equation to be added to, or ſubtracted from, the planet's longitude once equated, (or his place in his orbit,) in the ſame caſes as indicated in the correſponding table of the moon.

10. Table of *Saturn's* inclination. Argument, the argument of latitude.

11. Table of *Saturn's* diſtance. Argument, his mean anomaly corrected by the ſecond equation.

IV. TABLES of JUPITER, correſpond with thoſe of *Saturn*, excepting that there is no equation of the node, ſo that they are only ten in number.

V.

V. VI. VII. Tables of MARS, VENUS, and MERCURY, agree in number, denomination, and use, with those of *Jupiter*.

For several parts of the foregoing information, I am indebted to the grandson of a *Pandit*, who was a principal co-adjutor of *Jayasinha* in his astronomical labours. The Rajah bestowed on him the title of *Jyotish-ray*, or *Astronomer-royal*, with a *jageer* which produced 5000 rupees of annual rent. Both of these descended to his posterity; but from the incursions and exactions of the *Mahrattas* the rent of the *jageer* land was annihilated. The young man finding his patrimonial inheritance reduced to nothing, and that science was no longer held in estimation, undertook a journey to the *Decan*, in hopes that his talents might there meet with better encouragement; at the same time, with a view of visiting a place of religious worship on the banks of the *Nerbuddah*. There he fell in with RUNG RAW APPAH, dewan of the powerful family of POWAR, who was on his march to join ALY-BAHADUR in *Bundelcund*. With this chief the *Pandit* returned, and arrived at *Oujein* while I was there. This young man possessed a thorough acquaintance with the Hindu astronomical science contained in the various *Sid,dhantas,* and that not confined to the mechanical practice of rules, but founded on a geometrical knowledge of their demonstration; yet he had inherited the spirit of *Jayasinha* in such a degree, as to see and acknowledge the superiority of European science. In his possession I saw the translation into *Sanscrit* of several European works, executed under the orders of *Jayasinha*, particularly EUCLID's *Elements* with the treatises of plain and *spherical trigonometry*, and on the construction and use of logarithms, which are annexed to CUNN's or COMMANDINE's edition. In this translation, the inventor is called *Don* JUAN NAPIER, an additional presumption that *Jayasinha*'s European astronomers were of the Portuguese nation. This indeed, requires little confirmation,

firmation, as the son of one of them, *Don* PEDRO DE SYLVA, is still alive at *Jayanagar*; and *Pedro* himself, who was a physician as well as astronomer, has not been dead more than five or six years. Besides these, the *Pandit*, had a table of logarithms and of logarithmic sines and tangents to seven places of figures; and a treatise on conic sections. I have always thought, that after having convinced the Eastern nations of our superiority in policy and in arms, nothing can contribute more to the extension of our national glory than the diffusion among them of a taste for European science. And as the means of promoting so desirable an end, those among the natives who had penetration to see, and ingenuously to own, its superior accuracy and evidence, ought to be cherished. Among those of the Islamic faith, TYFFUZZUL HUSSEIN KHAN, who, by translating the works of the immortal NEWTON, has conducted those imbued with Arabick literature to the fountain of all physical and astronomical knowledge, is above my praise. I hoped that the *Pandit Jyotish Ray*, following the steps of his ancestors and of his illustrious master, might one day render a similar service to the disciples of *Brahma*. But this expectation was disappointed by his sudden death at *Jayanagar* soon after our departure from *Oujein*: and with him the genius of *Jayasinha* became extinct. URANIA fled before the brazen fronted *Mars*, and the observatory was converted into an arsenal and foundery of cannon.

The Hindu astronomy, from the learned and ingenious disquisitions of Mr. BAILY and professor PLAYFAIR, appears to carry internal marks of antiquity which do not stand in need of confirmation by collateral evidence. Else, it is evident, from the foregoing account, that such could not be derived from the observatories which have been described by travellers; those being of modern date, and as probably

of

of European as of Hindu construction. The assistance derived by *Jayasinha* from European books also inclines me to think, that the treatise entitled *Cshetradersa*, which was inspected by *Captain* WILFORD's *Pandit*, (Asiat. Ref. vol. IV. p. 178.) was not confined to geometrical knowledge, of purely *Brahminical origin*.

XVI.

DESCRIPTION *of a Species of* MELOE, *an insect of the* FIRST *or* COLEOPTEROUS *Order in the* LINNEAN *System: found in all Parts of* BENGAL, BEHAR, *and* OUDE; *and possessing all the Properties of the* SPANISH *blistering Fly, or* MELOE *Vesicatorius.*

By Captain HARDWICKE,
Communicated by Mr. W. HUNTER.

ANTENNÆ MONILIFORM, short, consisting of eleven articulations, increasing in size from the second to the apex; the first nearly as long as the last; each a little thicker upwards than at the base, and truncated, or as if cut off, the last excepted, which is egg-form.

Palpi—four, inequaled, clubbed, the posterior pair of three, and the anterior, of two articulations.

Maxillæ or jaws—four, the exterior horney, slightly curved inwards, three toothed—the two inferior teeth very small; the exterior pair, compressed and brush-like.

Head, gibbous; eyes prominent, large, reticulated; labium or upper lip, hard, emarginated.

Thorax—convex above, broader towards the abdomen, and encompassed by a narrow marginal line.

Elytra, crustaceous, the length of the abdomen, except in flies pregnant with eggs, when they are shorter by one ring; convex above, concave beneath; yellow, with three transverse, black, irregular, undulated bands; the one at the apex broadest, and that at the base dividing the yellow longitudinally, into two spots: porcated, or ridged; the ridges longitudinal and parallel,

parallel to the future; in number, three equal, one unequal, the ridges not very prominent.

Alæ or wings—membraneous, a little exceeding the elytra in length, and the ends folded under.

The tarsi of the two first pair of feet consists of five articulations; and of the posterior pair, four only.

Every part of the insect, excepting the wings and elytra, is black, oily to the touch, and covered more or less with dense hairs; a few scattered hairs are also evident on the elytra. All the crustaceous parts of the insect are pitted minutely. It is about the bigness of the *Meloë Proscarabæus* of LINN. and a full grown one, when dry and fit for use, is to the *M. Vesicatorius* in weight as 4¼ to 1.

They come into season with the periodical rains, and are found from the month of *July* to the end of *October*, feeding on the flowers of *cucurbitaceous* plants, but more frequently on the species of *Cucumis* called by the natives *Turiey*; with a cylindrical, smooth, ten angled fruit. Also on the *Raam Turiey*; or *Hibiscus Esculentus Hibiscus, Rosa Senfis*—and in jungles where these plants are not to be found, they are to be met with on two or more species of *Sida*, which flourish in that season.

In the failure of flowers, they will feed on the leaves of all these plants, except the *Turiey*—which I have not observed them eat. They are great devourers, and will feed as freely in confinement as at large.

In September they are full of eggs, which seems to be the best state in which they can be taken for medical use, at that time abounding more abundantly in

an

an acrid yellow oil, in which, probably, refides their moft active property.

This fluid feems the animal's means of rendering itfelf obnoxious to others; for, on the moment of applying the hand to feize it, it ejects a large globula from the knee joint of every leg, and this, if fuffered to dry on the fingers, foon produces an uncommon tingling in the part, and fometimes a blifter. This is the only inconvenience attending the catching of them, for they make no refiftance: on the contrary, they draw in the head towards the breaft as foon as touched, and endeavour to throw themfelves off the plant they are found on.

The female produces about 150 eggs, a little fmaller than a caraway feed, white and oblong oval. Their larvæ I have not feen, therefore as yet know not where they depofit their eggs.

Their flight from plant to plant is flow, heavy, and with a loud humming noife, the body hanging almoft perpendicularly to the wings.

They vary in the colour of the elytra, from an orange red to a bright yellow; but, I do not find this variety conftitutes any difference in fex.

The natives of this part of the country know the infect by the name of *tel-eene*, expreflive of its oily nature: they are acquainted with its bliftering properties, but I do not find they make any medicinal ufe of it.

The drawing which accompanies this defcription, exhibits the fly of its natural fize.

Futte-Ghur, September, 1796.

REPORT ON THE MELOE, OR LYTTA.

By W. Hunter, Esq.

The circumstance respecting your new species of Meloe or *Lytta*, which I lately had occasion to observe, was shortly as follows:

Tincture of them was directed as an external application to a man's arm, which was paralytic in consequence of rheumatism. On the first application several vesications were raised, as completely distended with serum, as if a blister had been applied. I am not particularly informed, what proportion the flies bore to the menstruum; but, I think it was something greater than that directed by the London college for the tincture of the officinal kind.

March 9th, 1796.

REPORT ON THE EFFECT PRODUCED BY A SPECIES OF MELOE, FOUND IN BENGAL, BEHAR, AND OUDE.

By W. R. Monroe, Esq.

I received your packet containing the specimens of the new blistering fly, a few days ago, whilst I was busily employed in preparations for my departure from this station. I lost no time, however, in making a trial of their efficacy on three different patients who required blistering. They succeeded in each trial; though the effect was in none produced completely in less than ten hours; and the vesications even then were filled with a serum rather gelatinous than fluid.

As far as these few trials authorise a conclusion, we may safely consider them a valuable substitute for the cantharides; though I should think they will not, in general, be found so active as the *Spanish* fly, in its most perfect state of preservation. Captain Hardwicke

WICKE has certainly, however, made a moſt uſeful addition to our *Aſiatick Materia Medica*; and, he may rely on it, that if I ſhould inadvertently mention the diſcovery, I ſhall not fail to give him alſo the merit he is ſo fairly entitled to for it. The country people, I find, give the fly different names, ſo that there are, I ſuppoſe, many ſpecies of it, the moſt efficacious of which he will, in his account of it, particularize.

REFERENCES.

A. A full grown inſect of its natural ſize.

B. The ſame reverſed, to ſhow the under part of the body and limbs.

C. The eggs.

D. An elytron of another fly, to ſhew the difference of colour and ſpots at the baſe.

E. A wing diſplayed.

F. The head magnified.

G. The labium or lip.

H. The horny or exterior jaws.

I. The hairy interior ditto.

K. The poſterior pair or palpi.

L. The anterior or leſſer ditto.

XVII.

A COMPARATIVE VOCABULARY

OF SOME OF THE LANGUAGES SPOKEN IN THE

BURMA EMPIRE.

By FRANCIS BUCHANAN, M. D.

TO judge from external appearance, that is to say, from shape, size, and feature, there is one very extensive nation that inhabits the east of *Asia*. It includes the eastern and western *Tartars* of the *Chinese* authors, the *Calmucs*, the *Chinese*, the *Japponese*, the *Malays*, and other tribes inhabiting what is called the Peninsula of *India* beyond the *Ganges*; and the islands to the south and east of this, as far at least as *New Guinea*. This, however, is speaking in a very general sense, many foreign races being intermixed with the nation, and, perhaps, many tribes belonging to it being scattered beyond the limits I have mentioned.

This nation may be distinguished by a short, squat, robust, fleshy stature, and by features highly different from those of an *European*. The face is somewhat in shape of a lozenge, the forehead and chin being sharpened, whilst at the cheek bones it is very broad: unless this be what is meant by the conical head of the *Chinese*, I confess myself at a loss to understand what that is. The eyebrows, or supercillary ridges, in this nation project very little, and the eyes are very narrow, and placed rather obliquely in the head, the external angles being the highest. The nose is very small, but has not, like that of the negro, the appearance of having been flattened; and the apertures of the nostrils, which in the *European* are linear and parallel, in them are nearly circular and divergent; for the *septum marium* being much thickest towards the face, places them entirely out of the parallel line. The mouths of this nation are in general well shaped; their hair is harsh, lank, and black. Those of them that live even in the warmest climates, do not obtain the deep hue of the negro or *Hindu*; nor do such of them as live in the coldest countries, acquire the clear bloom of the *European*.

In adventitious circumstances, such as laws, customs, government, political maxims, religion, and literature, there is also a strong resemblance among the different states composing this great nation; no doubt arising from the frequent intercourse that has been among them.

But it is very surprising, that a wonderful difference of language should prevail. Language of all adventitious circumstances, is the surest guide in tracing the migrations and connections of nations; and how in a nation, which bears such strong marks of being one, radically the same, languages totally different should prevail, I cannot, at present, pretend to conjecture: but, in order to assist, in accounting for the circumstance, having, during my stay in the *Burma* empire, been at some pains to collect a comparative vocabulary of such of the languages spoken in it as opportunity offered, I have thought it might be curious to publish it. I am sensible of its many imperfections: but it is a beginning, which I hope hereafter to make more complete; and, where I fail, others, without doubt, will be more successful.

In all attempts to trace the migrations and connections of tribes by means of language, it ought to be carefully remembered, that a few coincidences, obtained by searching through the whole extent of two dictionaries,

dictionaries, it is by no means the least affinity; for our organs being only capable of pronouncing a certain, and that a very limited number of sounds, it is to be expected, according to the common course of chance, that two nations, in a few instances, will apply the same sound to express the same idea. It ought also to be observed, that in tracing the radical affinities of languages, terms of art, men's names, religious and law phrases, are, of all words, the most improper: as they are liable constantly to be communicated by adventitious circumstances from one race of men to another. What connection of blood have we, *Europeans*, with the *Jews*, from whom a very great proportion of our names and religious terms are derived? Or what connection have the natives of *Bengal* with the *Arabs* or *English*, from whom they have derived most of their law and political terms? With the former they have not even had political connection; as the phrases in question were derived to them through the medium of the *Persians* and *Tartars*. Two languages, therefore, ought only to be considered as radically the same, when, of a certain number of common words chosen by accident, the greater number have a clear and distinct resemblance. A circumstance, to which, if antiquarians had been attentive, they would have been saved from the greater part of that etymological folly, which has so often exposed their pleasing science to the just ridicule of mankind.

In the orthography I have had much difficulty. Two people will seldom write in the same way, any word or language with which they are unacquainted. I have attempted merely to convey to the *English* reader, without any minute attention to accent, or small variations of vowels, a sound similar to that pronounced; nor have I paid any attention to the orthography of the natives. This, in the *Burma* language, I might have done; but as I am not acquainted with the writing of the other tribes, I thought

thought it the safest method, to express the sound merely. The following scheme of vowels, in order to read my vocabulary correctly, must be kept in mind:

A—pronounce as in the *English* words bad, bat, had, hat.

Aw—or broad *Scotch* o, as in bawd.

Ay—as the *English* a, in babe, bake, bare; day, pay, hay.

Ee—in order to avoid confusion, I use for the *English* e; as they have exactly the same sound.

Æ—I use for the *French* and *Scotch* é open.

U—I always found as in the word duck; using oo for its other sound, as in book.

Ou—I found as in found, bound.

Au—is nearly similar, but broader, a sound scarcely to be met with in the *English* language.

Ei—I use as the vowel in bind, find, &c.

Ai—nearly the same but broader

Oe—I use to to express the *French* u.

} These two sounds, as far as I remember, are not used by the *English*.

It is to be observed, that the pronunciation, among all these tribes, to a stranger appears exceedingly inarticulate. In particular they hardly ever pronounce the letter R; and T, D, TH, S, and Z, are almost used indiscriminately. The same may be said of P and B. Thus the word for water which the *Burma's* universally pronounce *yee*, is written *rae*; and the *Palli* name for their capital city *Amarapoora*, is commonly pronounced *Amaapooya*. This indistinct pronunciation probably arises from the excessive quantity of betel, which they chew. No man of rank ever speaks without his mouth being as full as possible of a mixture of betel and nut, tobacco, quicklime, and spices. In this state he is nearly deprived of the use of his tongue in articulation, which,

which, although not the only organ of speech, is yet of such use in articulation, as to be commonly considered as such. Hence it is, that an indistinct articulation has become fashionable, even when the tongue is at liberty.

I shall begin with the *Burma* language as being at present the most prevalent. There are four dialects of it, that of the *Burma* proper, that of *Arakan*, that of the *Yo*, and that of *Tenaserim*.

The people called by us *Burmas, Barmas, Vermas, Brimmas*, &c. stile themselves *Myammaw*. By the people of *Pegu*, they are named *Pummay*; by the *Karaya*, *Yoo*; by the people of *Cussay*, *Awaw*; by the *Cussay shan, Kammau*; by the *Chinese* of *Younan*, *Lawneen*: and by the *Aykobat*, *Anwa*. They esteem themselves to be descended from the people of *Arakan*, whom they often call *Myammaw gyee*, that is to say, great *Burmas*.

The proper natives of *Arakan*, call themselves *Yakain*, which name is also commonly given to them by the *Burmas*. By the people of *Pegu* they are named *Takain*. By the *Bengal Hindus*, at least by such of them as have been settled in *Arakan*, the country is called *Rossawn*, from whence, I suppose, Mr. RENNELL has been induced to make a country named *Roshawn* occupy part of his map, not conceiving that it would be *Arakan*, or the kingdom of the *Mugs*, as we often call it. Whence this name of *Mug*, given by *Europeans* to the natives of *Arakan*, has been derived, I know not; but, as far as I could learn, it is totally unknown to the natives and their neighbours, except such of them as by their intercourse with us have learned its use. The *Mahommedans* settled at *Arakan*, call the country *Rovingaw*, the *Persians* call it *Rekan*.

The third dialect of the *Burma* language is spoken by small tribe called *Yo*. There are four governments of this nation, situated on the east side of the *Arakan* mountains, governed by chiefs of their own, but tributary to the Burmas.

The fourth dialect is that of what we call the coast of *Tenasserim*, from its city now in ruins, whose proper name was *Tanayntharee*. These people, commonly called by the *Burmas*, *Dawayza* and *Byeitza*; from the two governments, of which their country consists, have most frequently been subjected to *Siam* or *Pegu*; but at present they are subjects of the *Burma* king.

Although the dialects of these people, to one another, appear very distinct, yet the difference consists chiefly in such minute variations of accent as not to be observable by a stranger. In the same manner as an *Englishman* at first is seldom able to distinguish even the *Aberdeen* accent from that of the other shires of Scotland, which to a Scotchman appears so different; so, in most cases, I could perceive no difference in the words of these four languages, although among the *Burmas*, any of the provincials, speaking generally, produced laughter, and often appeared to be with difficulty understood. I shall, therefore, only give a list of the *Burma* words; those of the other dialects are the same, where difference is not mentioned.

1. English.	Myammaw.	Yakain.	Tanayntharee.	Yo.
1 Sun	Nay	—	—	—
2 Moon	La	—	—	—
3 Star	Kyee	Kyay	—	Kay
4 Earth	Myacgyee	—	—	—
5 Water	Yæ	Ree	—	Rae
6 Fire				

LANGUAGES OF THE BURMA EMPIRE.

English.	Myammaw.	Yakain.	Tanayntharee.	Yo.
6 Fire	Mee	—	—	
7 Stone	Kiouk	—	—	Kioukay
8 Wind	Læ	Lee	—	—
9 Rain	Mo	—	—	—
10 Man	Loo	—	—	—
11 Woman	Meemma	—	—	—
12 Child	Loogalay	*Looshee	—	—
13 Head	Kaung	—	—	—
14 Mouth	Parat	—	—	—
15 Arm	Læmmaung	—	—	—
16 Hand	Læk	—	—	Laik
17 Leg	Kæthalour	—	—	Saloongfa
18 Foot	Kiæbamo	—	—	—
19 Beast	Taraitram	—	—	—
20 Bird	Hugæk	—	—	Knap
21 Fish	Ngaw	—	—	—
22 Good	Kaung	—	—	—
23 Bad	Makaung	—	—	—
24 Great	Kyee	—	—	—
25 Little	Ngay	—	—	—
26 Long	Shay	—	—	Shæ
27 Short	Ato	—	—	To
28 One	Teet	—	—	—
29 Two	Hueet	—	—	—
30 Three	Thoum	—	—	—
31 Four	Lay	—	—	—

* Literally, a little man.

English	Myammaw	Yakain	Tanayntharee	Yo
32 Five	Ngaw	—	—	—
33 Six	Kiouk	—	—	—
34 Seven	Kuhneet	—	—	—
35 Eight	Sheet	—	—	—
36 Nine	Ko	—	—	—
37 Ten	Tazay	—	—	—
38 Eat	Zaw	—	—.	—
39 Drink	Thouk	—	—	—
40 Sleep	Eit	—	—	—
41 Walk	Xleen	Hlay	—	Hlay
42 Sit	Tein	—	—	—
43 Stand	Ta	Mateinay	—	Mateenahay
44 Kill	That	Sot	—	Afatu
45 Yes	Houkkay	—	—	—
46 No	Mahouppoo	—	—	—
47 Here	Deeinaw	—	—	Thaman
48 There	Homaw	—	—	—
49 Above	Apomaw	—	—	Apobau
50 Below	Houkmaw	—	—	Auk

The next most prevalent language in *India* beyond the *Ganges*, is what we call the *Siammese*, a word probably corrupted from the *Shan* of the *Burmas*. The *Siammese* race occupies the whole frontier of *Yunan*, extending on the east to *Tonquin* and *Cochinchina*, and on the south, down to the sea. It contains many states or kingdoms, mostly subject or tributary to the *Burmas*. I have only procured vocables of three of its dialects, which I here give compleat, as they differ confiderably.

The

The first dialect is that of the kingdom of *Siam*, the most polished people of eastern *India*. They called themselves to me simply *Tai*; but Mr. LOUBERE says, that in order to distinguish themselves from a people to be afterwards mentioned, they add the word *Nay*, which signifies little. By the *Burmas*, from the vulgar name of their former capital city, they are called *Yoodaya*; by the people of *Pegu* they are named *Seem*; and by the *Chinese* of *Yunan*, *Syianlo* or *Kyenlo*.

The second dialect of the *Siammese* language which I shall mention, is that of a people, who, to me, also called themselves simply *Tai*. I believe, however, they are the *Tai-yay*, or great *Tai*, of Mr. LOUBERE. They have been long subject to the *Burmas*, who call them *Myelapshan*; by the people of *Pegu* they are named *Sawn*; *Thay* by the *Karayn*; *Looktai* by the *Katheeshan*; *Kabo* by the people of *Kathee* or *Cussay*; *Pawee* by the *Chinese*; and to me they were named *Lau* by the *Siammese* proper. Their country towards the north lies between the west side of *Yunan* and the *Erawade* or great *Burma* river, descending down its eastern bank a considerably way; it then extends along the south side of *Yunan* till it comes to the *Loukiang* or river of *Martaban*, which forms its eastern boundary; on the south it extends to no great distance from *Martaban*; and on the west it is separated from *Burma* proper by a chain of mountains, that pass about fifteen miles to the east of *Ava*.

The third dialect of the *Siammese* language is that of a people called, by the *Burmas*, *Kathee Shawn*; to themselves they assume the name of *Tai-loong* or great *Tai*. They are called *Moitay Kabo*, by the *Kathee* or people of *Cussay*. They inhabit the upper part of the *Kiayn duayn* river, and from that west to the *Erawade*. They have, in general, been subject to the king of *Munnypura*; but, at present, are tributary to the *Burma* monarch.

II. English.	Tainay.	Taiyay.	Tai-loong.
1 Sun	Rocn	Kawan	Kangoon
2 Moon	Sun	Loen	Noon
3 Stars	Dau	Lau	Nau
4 Earth	Deen	—	Neen
5 Water	Nam	Nawh or Naum	Nam
6 Fire	Fai	Fai	Pui
7 Stone	Hin	—	Heen
8 Wind	Lam	Loum	Loom
9 Rain	Fon	Foon	Poon
10 Man	Kon	Kon	Koon
11 Woman	Pooen	Paeyen	Pawneen
12 Child	Daeknooe	Lawen	Lookwoon
13 Head	Seeza	Ho	Hoo
14 Mouth	Pawk	Tsop	Pawk
15 Arm	Kayn	Komooee	Moo
16 Hand	Moo	Mooee	Pawmoo
17 Leg	Naung	Koteen	Hooko
18 Foot	Langteen	Swateen	Lungdin
19 Beast	Sawt	—	Nook
20 Bird	Noup	Naut	Nook
21 Fish	Plaw	Paw	Paw
22 Good	Dee	Lee	Wanoo
23 Bad	Maidee	Malee	Mowan
24 Great	To	Loung	Loong
25 Little	Layt	Laik	Unleek
26 Long	Yan	Yan	Anyou
27 Short	San	Lot	Unlot

28 One

English.	Tai-nay.	Tai-yay.	Tai-long.
28 One	Noong	Noo	Aning
29 Two	So	Sang	Sowng
30 Three	Sam	Sam	Sam
31 Four	See	Shee	Shee
32 Five	Haw	Haw	Haw
33 Six	Hok	Houk	Hook
34 Seven	Kyæt	Sayt	Seet
35 Eight	Payt	Payt	Pæt
36 Nine	Kawo	Kaw	Kau
37 Ten	Seet	Sheet	Ship
38 Eat	*Kyeen Kau	Kyeen Kau	Kyeen Kau
39 Drink	Kyeen Nam	Kyeen Nawm	Kyeen Nam
40 Sleep	Non	Non	Non
41 Walk	Teeo	Hoe	Pei
42 Sit	Nanon	Nawn	Nung
43 Stand	Yoon	Lootfook	Peignung
44 Kill	Kaw	Po	Potai
45 Yes	O	Sai	Munna
46 No	Maifhai	Mofai	Motfau
47 Here	Teenee	Teenai	Teenay
48 There	Teenon	Teepoon	Ponaw
49 Above	Bonon	Teenaipoon	Nooa
50 Below	Kang lang	Teetai	—

The next language, of which I fhall give a fpecimen, is that of the people who call themfelves *Moitay*.

---

* Kau is rice, and Nam is water. Here, therefore, we have a nation with no word to exprefs the difference between eating and drinking. The pleafures of the table muft be in little requeft with them.

Their country is situated between *Sylhet* in *Bengal* and that of the *Tailoong* above mentioned: to the north of it is *Assam*; on the south *Arakan*, and the rude tribes bordering on that kingdom. Their capital city they name *Munnypura*. By the people of *Bengal* they are called *Muggaloos*, an appellation with which those we saw at *Amarapura* were totally unacquainted. This name, however, *Europeans* have applied to the country, turning it at the same time into *Meckley*. *Kathee* is the name given to this people by the *Burmas*, which we also have taken for the name of the country, and corrupted into *Cussay*. Mr. RENNEL having from *Bengal* obtained information of *Meckley*, and from *Ava* having heard of *Cussay*, never conceived that they were the same, and, accordingly, in his map of *Hindustan*, has laid down two kingdoms *Cussay* and *Meckley*; for which, indeed, he had sufficient room, as by Captain BAKER's account he had been induced to place *Ava* much too far to the east.

III.

	English.	*Moitay.*		*English.*	*Moitay.*
1	Sun	Noomeet	13	Head	Kop Kok
2	Moon	Taw	14	Mouth	Seembaw
3	Stars	Towang Meezat	15	Arm	Pambom
			16	Hand	Khoit
4	Earth	Leipauk	17	Leg	—
5	Water	Eesheen	18	Foot with the ankle	Kho
6	Fire	Mee			
7	Stone	Noong Loong	19	Beast	—
8	Wind	Noosheet	20	Bird	Oosaik
9	Rain	No	21	Fish	Ngaw
10	Man	Mee	22	Good	Pawee or Pai
11	Woman	Noopee	23	Bad	Pattay
12	Child	Peeka	24	Great	Sauwee
			25	Little	

English.	Moitay.	English.	Moitay.
25 Little	Apeekauk	38 Eat	Sat
26 Long	Afamba	39 Drink	Tawee
27 Short	Ataymba	40 Sleep	Keepee
28 One	Amaw	41 Walk	Kwnee
29 Two	Anee	42 Sir	Pummee
30 Three	Ahoom	43 Stand	Lapee
31 Four	Maree	44 Kill	Hallo
32 Five	Mangaw	45 Yes	Manee
33 Six	Torok	46 No	Nattay
34 Seven	Tarayt	47 Here	Mafhee
35 Eight	Neepaw	48 There	Ada
36 Nine	Mapil	49 Above	Mataka
37 Ten	Tarraw	50 Below	Maka

In the intermediate space between *Bengal*, *Arakan*, the proper *Burma*, and the kingdom of *Munnaypura*, is a large mountainous and woody tract. It is occupied by many rude tribes. Among these, the most distinguished, is that by the *Burmas* called *Kiayn*, from whom is derived the name of the great western branch of the *Erawade*, for *Kiaynduayn* signifies the fountain of the *Kiayn*. This people calls itself *Koloun*, and it seems to be a numerous race, universally spoken of, by its neighbours, as remarkable for simple honesty, industry, and an inoffensive disposition.

IV.

English.	Koloun.	English.	Koloun.
1 Sun	Konee	4 Earth	Day
2 Moon	Klow	5 Water	Tooee
3 Star	Affay	6 Fire	May

7 Stone

English	Koloun.	English	Koloun.
7 Stone	Aloong	29 Two	Palmee
8 Wind	Klee	30 Three	Patoon
9 Rain	Yoo	31 Four	Poonhee
10 Man	Kloun	32 Five	Poonho
11 Woman	Patoo	33 Six	Poofonk
12 Child	Saemee	34 Seven	Pooæfæ
13 Head	Mulloo	35 Eight	Pooæfay
14 Mouth	Mawkoo	36 Nine	Poongo
15 Arm	Maboam	37 Ten	Poohaw
16 Hand	Mukoo	38 Eat	Kayawæ
17 Leg	Manwam	39 Drink	Koyawee
18 Foot	Kopaung	40 Sleep	Eitfha
19 Beaft	Pakyoo	41 Walk	Hlayæfhoe
20 Bird	Pakyoo	42 Sit	Own
21 Fifh	Ngoo	43 Stand	Undoon
22 Good	Poælahoe	44 Kill	Say,oe
23 Bad	Sælahoe	45 Yes	Afhæba
24 Great	Ahlayn	46 No	Seehay
25 Little	Amee	47 Here	Næa
26 Long	Afaw	48 There	Tfooa
27 Short	Sooæhay	49 Above	Akloengung
28 One	Moo	50 Below	Akoa

Another rude nation, which fhelters itfelf in the receffes of hills and woods, from the violence of its infolent neighbours, is named by the *Burmas Karayn*; and *Kadoon* by the people of *Pegu*. They are moft numerous in the *Pegu* kingdom, and like the *Kiayn* are

are diftinguifhed for their innocence and induftry. By the *Burmas* they are faid to be of two kinds; *Burma* and *Tulain Karayn*. Some of them, with whom I converfed, feemed to underftand this diftinction, calling the former *Paffooko* and the latter *Maploo*. This, however, probably arofe from thefe individuals being better acquainted with the *Burma* ideas, than the generality of their countrymen; for the greater part of thofe, with whom I converfed, faid that all *Karyn* were the fame, and called them *Play*. I am, however, not certain if I underftood them rightly; nor do I know, that I have obtained the proper name of this tribe. I have given a vocabulary of each of thefe, who feemed to underftand the diftinction of *Burma* and *Tailain Karayn*, and two of different villages who did not underftand the difference; for in this nation I found the villages differing very much in dialect; even where not diftant, probably owing to their having little communication one with another. It muft be obferved, that in ufing an interpreter, one is very liable to miftakes, and thofe I had were often very ignorant.

V. *Englifh*.	*Paffooko*.	*Maploo*.	*Play*, No. 1.	*Play*, No. 2.
1 Sun	Moomay	Moo	Mooi	Moomay
2 Moon	Law	Law	Law	Poolaw
3 Stars	T'Saw	Shceaw	Shaw	Shaw
4 Earth	Katchaykoo	Kolangkoo	Kako	Laukoo
5 Water	Tee	Tee	Tee	Tee
6 Fire	Mee	Meeung	Meea	Mee
7 Stone	Loe	Loong, Noong-Lung	—	Loung
8 Wind	Kallee	Lee	Lee	Lee
9 Rain	Tachoo	Tchatchang	Moko	Moko
10 Man	Paganyo	Pafhaw	Pafha	Paploom or Pafha
11 Woman	Pomoo	Pomoo	Pummee	Pammoe

VOL. V. P 12 Child

English.	Paſſooko.	Maploo.	Play, No. 1.	Play, No. 2.
12 Child	Pozaho	Poſſaw	Napootha	Apoza
13 Head	Kozohui	Kohui	Kohui	Pokoohui
14 Mouth	Patako	Pano	Ganoo	Pano
15 Arm	Tchoobaw-lee	Tchoobaw-lee	Atſyoodoo	Tchoobaw-lee
16 Hand	Patchoo	Poitchoo	Kutſhoo	Tchooaſee
17 Leg	Kadoe	Pokaw	Kandoo	Kandoo
18 Foot	Konyawko	Kanyakoo	Kanyako	Kanyaſaw
19 Beaſt	T'hoo	Too	—	—
20 Bird	T'hoo	Too	Kalo	To
21 Fiſh	Nyaw.	Zyaw	Ya	Ya
22 Good	Ngeetchawmaw	Ngee	Gyee	Gyee
23 Bad	Taw ngee baw	Nguay	Gyeeay	Gyeeay
24 Great	Pawdoo	Hhoo	Uddo	Doo
25 Little	Tchecka	Tchei	Atſei	Atſee
26 Long	To atcho maw	T'ho	Loeya	Ato
27 Short	P'hecko	P'hoe	Apoe	Apoe
28 One	Taydoe	Nadoe	Laydoe	Laydoe
29 Two	Kee-doe	Nee-doe	Nee-doe	Nee-doe
30 Three	So-doe	Song-doe	Soung-doe	Soung-doe
31 Four	Looee-doe	Lee-du	Lee-doe	Lee-doe
32 Five	Yay-doe	Yay-doe	Yay-doe	Yay-doe
33 Six	Hoo-doe	Hoo doe	Koo-doe	Koo-doe
34 Seven	Nooee-doe	Noay-doe	Noæ-doe	Noæ-du
35 Eight	Ho-doe	Ho-doe	Ko-doe	Ko-doe
36 Nine	Kooee-doe	Kooee doe	Kooee-doe	Kooee-doe
37 Ten	Tatchee	Leitchee	Taſſee	Laytſee
38 Eat	Po, o	Aw	Ang	Ang

39 Drink

English.	Paſſooko.	Maploo.	Play, No. 1.	Play, No. 2.
39 Drink	Oo	O	O	O
40 Sleep	Prammee	Mee	Mee	Mee
41 Walk	Latcholia	Leetalay	Rakuæ	Lakuæ
42 Sit	Tcheenaw	Tſeingaw	Tyſana	Tſayna
43 Stand	Tchoćto	Tchonto	Tſayna la-gay	Gnaythoe
44 Kill	Klo	P'hee	Pætegui	Paythee
45 Yes	Maylee	Moayyoo	Moiyoo	Moithay
46 No	Tamaybaw	Moæ	Moi	Moi
47 Here	Loeee	Layee	Leyoo	Layee
48 There	Lubanee	Loo	Læyo	Læyo
49 Above	Mokoo	Mokoo	Læpanko	Læpanko
50 Below	Hokoo	Lankoo	Læpaula	Læpaula

To this kingdom, the natives of which call themſelves *Moan* we have given the name of *Pegu*, a corruption of the vulgar appellation of its capital city *Bagoo*; the polite name of the city among its natives having been *Dam Hanga*, as among the *Burmas Hanzawade*. This people are named *Talain* by the *Burmas* and *Chineſe* of *Yunan*; *Lawoo* by the *Karayn*; and *Tarain* by the *Tai-loong:* their kingdom extends along the mouths of the two great rivers *Erawade* and *Thauluayn*, or of *Ava* and *Martaban*, from the frontiers of *Arakan* to thoſe of *Siam*.

VI.

English.	Moan.	English.	Moan.
1 Sun	Knooay Tangooay	5 Water	Nawt
2 Moon	Katoo	6 Fire	Komot
3 Stars	Shawnaw	7 Stone	—
4 Earth	Toe	8 Wind	Kyeaw
		9 Rain	

English.	Moan.	English.	Moan.
9 Rain	Proay	31 Four	Pou
10 Man	Puce	32 Five	Soon
11 Woman	Preau	33 Six	Teraw
12 Child	Koon	34 Seven	Kapo
13 Head	Kadap	35 Eight	Tatfam
14 Mouth	Paun	36 Nine	Kaflee
15 Arm	Toay	37 Ten	Tfo
16 Hand	Kanna Toay	38 Eat	Tfapoung. Poung, I
17 Leg	Kadot-prawt		believe, is rice.
18 Foot	Kanat zein	39 Drink	Saung nawt. Nawt
19 Beast	—		is water
20 Bird	Seen ngat	40 Sleep	Steik
21 Fish	Kaw	41 Walk	Au
22 Good	Kah	42 Sit	Katcho
23 Bad	Hookah	43 Stand	Katau
24 Great	Mor	44 Kill	Taw
25 Little	Bok	45 Yes	Taukua
26 Long	Kloein	46 No	Auto
27 Short	Klee	47 Here	Noomano
28 One	Mooi	48 There	Taoko
29 Two	Bau	49 Above	Tatoo commooee .
30 Three	Pooi	50 Below	Tauamo

These six are all the languages of this great *eastern* nation, of which, during my stay in the *Burma* empire, I was able to procure vocables sufficient for my purpose. Although they appear very different at first sight, fight, and the language of one race is totally unintelligible to the others; yet I can perceive in them all some coincidences, and a knowledge of the languages, with their obsolete words, their phrases, their inflections of words; and elisions, *euphoniæ causâ*, would, perhaps, shew many more. Those that have the greatest affinity are in Tab. I. IV. and V. Mr. GILCHRIST, whose knowledge of the common dialects in use on the banks of the *Ganges* is, I believe, exceeded by that of no *European*, was so obliging as to look over these vocabularies, but he could not trace the smallest relation between the languages.

I shall now add three dialects, spoken in the *Burma* empire, but evidently derived from the language of the *Hindu* nation.

The first is that spoken by the *Mohammedans*, who have been long settled in *Arakan*, and who call themselves *Rooinga*, or natives of *Arakan*.

The second dialect is that spoken by the *Hindus* of *Arakan*. I procured it from a *Bráhmen* and his attendants, who had been brought to *Amarapura* by the king's eldest son, on his return from the conquest of *Arakan*. They called themselves *Rossawn*, and, for what reason I do not know, wanted to persuade me that theirs was the common language of *Arakan*. Both these tribes, by the real natives of *Arakan*, are called *Kulaw Yakain*, or stranger *Arakan*.

The last dialect of the *Hindustanee* which I shall mention is, that of a people called by the *Burmas Aykobat*; many of whom are slaves at *Amarapura*. By one of them I was informed, that they called themselves *Banga*; that formerly they had kings of their own, but that, in his father's time, their kingdom had been overturned by the king of *Munnypura*, who carried away a great part of the inhabitants to his residence. When that was taken laſt by the *Burmas*, which was about fifteen years ago, this man was one of the many captives who were brought to *Ava*. He ſaid alſo, that *Banga* was ſeven days journey ſouth weſt from *Munnypura*; it muſt, therefore, be on the frontiers of *Bengal*, and may, perhaps, be the country called in our maps *Caſhar*.

Mr. *Gilchriſt* has been ſo good as to examine partʲ‑cularly theſe two dialects, and to mark thus (*) thoſe words, which come neareſt the *Hinduſtanee* ſpoken on the *Ganges*; and thus (†) thoſe not ſo evidently in connection with the ſame, but which ſhęw reſem‑blance by analogy.

Engliſh.	*Rooinga.*	*Roſſawn.*	*Banga.*
1 Sun	Bel	*Sooja	Bayllee
2 Moon	Sawn	Sundſa	Satkan
3 Stars	Tara	*Nokyoto	*Tara
4 Earth	Kool	Murtika	*Matee
5 Water	Pannæ	*Dſol	*Pannæ
6 Fire	Auin	*Aagance	Zee
7 Stone	Sheel	*Sheel	*Heel
8 Wind	Bau	*Pawun	*Bo
9 Rain	Jorail	†Biſtee	*Booun
10 Man	Manuſh	†Moonuſa	*Manoo
11 Woman	Meealaw	Stree	Zaylan
12 Child	Gourapa	*Balouk	Sogwo
13 Head	Mata	Muſtok	Teekgo
14 Mouth	Gall	Bodon	Totohan

15 Arm

English.	Rooinga.	Roffawn.	Banga.
15 Arm	Bahara	*Baho	Paepoung
16 Hand	Hat	Ofto	Hatkan
17 Leg	Ban	†Podo	Torooa
18 Foot	Pau	Pata	Zankan
19 Beaft	—	Zoomtroo	Safee fangee
20 Bird	Paik	†Pookyee	†Pakya
21 Fifh	Maws	Mootiæ	†Mas
22 Good	Goom	Gam	Hoba
23 Bad	Goom nay	Gumnay	Hoba nay
24 Great	Boddau	Dangor	Domorgo
25 Little	Thuddee	*Tfooto	Hooroogo
26 Long	Botdean	Deengol	Deengul
27 Short	Banick	*Batee	*Batee
28 One	Awg	*Aik	*Ak
29 Two	Doo	*Doo	De
30 Three	Teen	*Teen	*Teen
31 Four	Tchair	*Tfar	*Saree
32 Five	Panfoee	*Paus	*Pas
33 Six	Saw	*Tfo	*Tfæ
34 Seven	Sat	*Sat	*Hat
35 Eight	Awtoa	†Afto	*Awt
36 Nine	Nonaw	*No	*No
37 Ten	Dufloa	*Dos	*Dos
38 Eat	Kau	*Kawai	†Kæk
39 Drink	Karin	Kawo	†Peek

P 4   40 Sleep

English.	Rooinga.	Roſſawn.	Banga.
40 Sleep	Layrow	†Needſara	Hooleck
41 Walk	Pawkay	Bayra	†O·tcea-ootca
42 Sir	Boihow	†Bocſho	†Bo
43 Stand	Tcheilayto	*Karao	†Oot
44 Kill	Marim	*Maro	*Mar
45 Yes	Hoi	Oir	Oo
46 No	Etibar	*Noay	*Naway
47 Here	Hayray	Etay	Erang
48 There	Horay	Horay	Orung
49 Above	Ouchalo	*Ooper	Gos
50 Below	Ayray	Hayray	†Tol

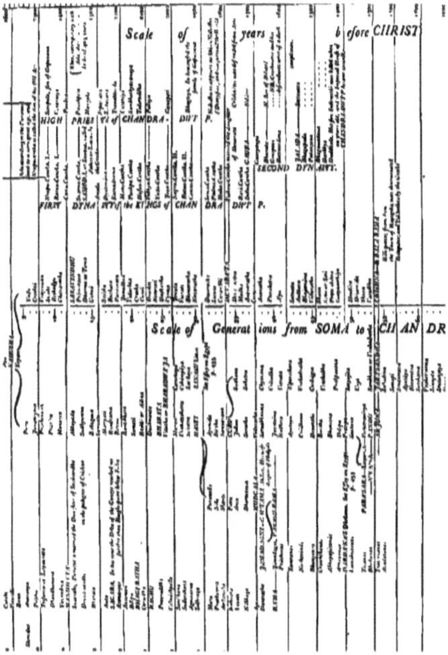
Scale of years before CHRIST
Scale of Generations from SOMA to CHANDR
FIRST DYNASTY of the KINGS of CHANDRA-DUTT
HIGH PRIESTS of CHANDRA-DUTT
SECOND DYNASTY

XVIII.

ON THE

CHRONOLOGY OF THE HINDUS.

BY CAPTAIN FRANCIS WILFORD.

THE accompanying genealogical table is faithfully extracted from the VISHNU *purána*, the BHA'GAVAT, and other *puránas*, without the least alteration whatever. I have collected numerous MSS. and with the affiftance of fome learned *Pundits* of *Benares*, who are fully fatisfied of the authenticity of this table, I exhibit it as the only genuine chronological *record* of Indian hiftory that has hitherto come to my knowledge. It gives the utmoft extent of the chronology of the *Hindus*; and as a certain number of years only can be allowed to a generation, it overthrows at once their monftrous fyftem, which I have rejected as abfolutely repugnant to the courfe of nature, and human reafon.

Indeed their fyftems of geography, chronology, and hiftory, are all equally monftrous and abfurd. The circumference of the earth is faid to be 500,000,000 *yojanas*, or 2,456,000,000 Britifh miles: the mountains are afferted to be 100 *yojanas*, or 491 Britifh miles high. Hence the mountains to the fouth of *Benares* are faid, in the *puránas*, to have kept the holy city in total darknefs, till *Matra-deva* growing angry at their infolence, they humbled themfelves to the ground, and their higheft peak now is not more than 500 feet high. In *Europe* fimilar notions once prevailed; for we are told that the *Cimmerians* were kept in continual darknefs by the interpofition of immenfely high mountains. In the CA'LICA *purána*, it is faid that the mountains have funk confiderably, fo that the higheft is not above one *yojana*, or five miles high.

When

When the *Puranics* speak of the kings of ancient times, they are equally extravagant. According to them, king YUDHISHT'HIR reigned seven and twenty thousand years; king NANDA, of whom I shall speak more fully hereafter, is said to have possessed in his treasury above 1,584,000,000 pounds sterling, in gold coin alone: the value of the silver and copper coin, and jewels, exceeded all calculation; and his army consisted of 100,000,000 men. These accounts geographical, chronological, and historical, as absurd and inconsistent with reason, must be rejected. This monstrous system seems to derive its origin from the ancient period of 12,000 natural years, which was admitted by the *Persians*, the *Etruscans*, and, I believe, also by the *Celtic* tribes; for we read of a learned nation in *Spain*, which boasted of having written histories of above six thousand years.

The *Hindus* still make use of a period of 12,000 divine years, after which a periodical renovation of the world takes place. It is difficult to fix the time when the *Hindus*, forsaking the paths of historical truth, launched into the mazes of extravagance and fable. MEGASTHENES, who had repeatedly visited the court of CHANDRA GUPTA, and of course had an opportunity of conversing with the best informed persons in *India*, is silent as to this monstrous system of the *Hindus*: on the contrary, it appears, from what he says, that in his time they did not carry back their antiquities much beyond six thousand, or even five thousand years, as we read in some MSS. He adds also, according to CLEMENS of *Alexandria*, that the *Hindus* and the *Jews* were the only people, who had a true idea of the creation of the world, and the beginning of things. There was then an obvious affinity between the chronological systems of the *Jews* and the *Hindus*. We are well acquainted with the pretensions of the *Egyptians* and *Chaldeans* to antiquity. This they never attempted to conceal. It

is

is natural to suppose, that the *Hindus* were equally vain: they are so now; and there is hardly a *Hindu* who is not persuaded of, and who will not reason upon, the supposed antiquity of his nation. MEGASTHENES who was acquainted with the antiquities of the *Egyptians*, *Chaldeans*, and *Jews*, whilst in *India*, made enquires into the history of the *Hindus*, and their antiquity: and it is natural to suppose that they would boast of it as well as the *Egyptians* or *Chaldeans*; and as much then as they do now. Surely they did not invent fables to conceal them from the multitude, for whom on the contrary these fables were framed.

At all events, long before the ninth century the chronological system of the *Hindus* was as complete, or rather, perfectly the same as it is now; for ALBUMAZAR, who was contemporary with the famous ALMAMUN, and lived at his court at *Balac* or *Belkh*, had made the *Hindu* antiquities his particular study. He was also a famous astronomer and astrologer, and had made enquiries respecting the conjunctions of the planets, the time of the creation of the world, and its duration, for astrological purposes; and he says, that the *Hindus* reckoned from the Flood to the *Hejira* 720,634,442,715 days, or 3725 years[*]. Here is a mistake, which probably originates with the transcriber or translator, but it may be easily rectified. The first number, though somewhat corrupted, is obviously meant for the number of days from the creation to the *Hejira*; and the 3725 years are reckoned from the beginning of the *Cali-yug* to the *Hejira*. It was then the opinion of ALBUMAZAR, about the middle of the ninth century, that the æra of the *Cali-yug* coincided with that of the Flood. He had, perhaps, data which no longer exist, as well as ABUL-FA-

---

[*] See *Bailly's* Astron. Anc. p. 30. and Mr. *Davis's* Essay in the second volume of the Asiatick Researches, p. 274.

ZIL in the time of AKBAR. Indeed, I am sometimes tempted to believe, from some particular passages in the *Puránas*, which are related in the true historical style, that the *Hindus* have destroyed, or at least designedly consigned to oblivion, all genuine records, as militating against their favourite system. In this manner the *Romans* destroyed the books of NUMA, and consigned to oblivion the historical books of the E-TRURIANS, and I suspect also those of the TURDE-TANI in *Spain*.

The *Puráns* are certainly a modern compilation from valuable materials, which I am afraid no longer exist: an astronomical observation of the heliacal rising of *Canopus*, mentioned in two of the *Puránas*, puts this beyond doubt. It is declared there, that certain religious rites are to be performed on the 27th of *Bhádra*, when *Canopus*, disengaged from the rays of the sun, becomes visible. It rises now on the 18th of the same month. The 18th and 27th of *Bhádra* answer this year to the 29th of August and 7th of September. I had not leisure enough to consult the two *Puránas* above mentioned on this subject. But as violent disputes have obtained among the learned Pandits, some insisting that these religious rites ought to be performed on the 27th of *Bhádra*, as directed in the *Puránas*, whilst others insist, it should be at the time of the *udáya*, or appearance of *Canopus*; a great deal of paper has been wasted on this subject, and from what has been written upon it, I have extracted the above observations. As I am not much used to astronomical calculations, I leave to others better qualified than I am to ascertain from these data the time in which the *Puránas* were written.

We learn from MANETHO, that the *Egyptian* chronology enumerated fourteen *dynasties*, the particulars of which he omitted as unworthy of notice. In the same manner the *Hindu* chronology presents us with a
series

series of fourteen Dynasties, equally repugnant to nature and reason; six of these are elapsed, we are in the seventh, which began with the Flood, and seven more we are taught to expect. These fourteen Dynasties are hardly ever noticed by the *Hindus* in their legendary tales, or historical poems. The rulers of these Dynasties are called MENUS: and from them their respective Dynasty, *antara*, or period, is called a *Manwantara*. Every Dynasty ends with a total destruction of the human race, except the *Menu* or ruler of the next period, who makes his escape in a boat, with the seven *Rishis*. The same events take place; the same persons, though sometimes under different names, re-appear.

Thus the history of one Dynasty serves for all the rest. In reality history, according to the *Hindus* themselves begins with the Flood, or the seventh *Menu*. Each period consists of 12,000 years, which the *Hindus* call *divine*. The *Persians* are not unacquainted with these renovations of the world, and periods of 12,000 years; for the bird *Simurgh* is introduced, telling CAHERMAN that she had lived to see the earth seven times filled with creatures, and seven times a perfect void, (it should be six times a perfect void, for we are in the seventh period,) and that she had already seen twelve great periods of 7000 years. This is obviously wrong; it should be seven great periods of 12,000 years.

The antediluvian history, being considered by the *Hindus* in different points of view, is related in various ways, having little connection with each other. We are told first that BRA'HMA created *ten* BRA'MADICAS or children of BRA'HMA, who were to be the progenitors of the *moveable* and *immoveable* parts of the creation, by which they understand *animals* and *vegetables*. Their names are MANICHI, ATRI, ANGIRAS, PULASTYA, PULAHA, CRITU, DACSHA, VASISHTHA, BURIGU, and NARADA. These sprang immediately from BRA'HMA,

MA, and produced the Gods, the *Daityas,* good and bad genii, animals, and plants of all sorts. The *Puránics* are not agreed as to the number of *Brahmádicas.* In the *Bhágavat* it is declared that they were *ten*; but in other *puránas* they reckon nine; whilst in the *Scanda-purána* it is declared that there were only seven *Brahmádicas,* whose names are MARICHI, ATRI, ANGIRA'SA, PULASTYA, PULA'HA, CRITA, and VOSISHTA; nor are there wanting authorities to reduce them to three, namely, the three sons of SWAYAMBHUVA, who was BRAHMA himself in a human shape.

It is declared, that the seven MENUS, who have made their appearance, sprang from the *Brahmádicas:* their names are, SWAYAMBHUVA, SWA'ROCHISHA, UTTAMA, TA'MASA, RAIVATA, CHACSHUSHA, and SATYAVRATA or NOAH.

The seven RISHIS sprang immediately from BRA'HMA, and their names are, CASYAPA, ATRI, VOSISHTA, VISVAME'TRA, GAUTAMA, JAMADAGNI, and BHA'RADWA'JA. These holy penitents, by their salutary counsels, and the example of their austerities, discover the path of rectitude and virtue to mankind. It is remarked of *Atri,* that he was both a *Brahmádica* and a *Ríshi*; and, perhaps, the seven *Menus,* the seven *Brahmádicas,* with the seven *Ríshis,* are the same, and make only seven individual persons. The seven *Brahmádicas* were *prajápatis* or lords of the *prajas* or creatures. From them mankind were born, and they are probably the same with the seven *Menus,* who, when far advanced in years, withdrew from the world, and became *Ríshis* or holy penitents, as, according to the *Puránas,* was the general practice of mankind in former ages. These seven grand ancestors of the human race were first *Brahmádicas* or children of *Bráhma,* and created for the purpose of replenishing the earth with inhabitants; having fulfilled their mission they became sovereigns of the universe, or *Menus*; and in their old age they withdrew to solitary places

to

to prepare for death, and become *Ríshis*. *Swayambhu-va*, or the son of the self-exifting, was the firft *Menu*, and the father of mankind: his confort's name was *Satarupa*. In the fecond *Veda*, the Supreme Being is introduced thus fpeaking: " From me *Bráhma* was born: he is above all; he is *pitama*, or the father of all men; he is *Aja* and *Swayambhu*, or felf-exifting." From him proceeded *Swayambhuva*, who is the firft *Menu:* they call him *Adima* (or the firft, or *Protogonus:*) he is the firft of men, and *Parama-purufha*, or the firft male. His help-meet *Pricriti* is called alfo *Satarupa:* fhe is *Adima* (2) or the firft: fhe is *Viſva-jenni*, or the mother of the world: fhe is *Iva* or like *I*, the female energy of nature, or fhe is a form of, or defcended from *I*: fhe is *Para* or the greateft: both are like, *Maha-deva* and his *Sacti* (the female energy of nature) whofe names are alfo *Iſa* and *Iſi*.

Swayambhuva is *Bráhma* in a human fhape, or the firft *Bráhma*: for *Bráhma* is man individually, and alfo collectively, mankind; hence *Bráhma* is faid to be born and to die every day, as there are men fpringing to life, and dying every day. Collectively he dies every hundred years, this being the utmoft limits of life in the *Cali-yug*, according to the *Puránas*: at the end of the world, *Bráhma* or mankind is faid to die alfo, at the end of a hundred divine years. *Swa-yambhuva*, in the prefent *calpa*, is *Viſhnu* in the character of *Bráhma-rupi Javardana*, or the *Viſhnu* with the countenance of *Bráhma*. To underftand this it is neceffary to premife, that it has been revealed to the *Hindus*, that, from the beginning to the end of things, when the whole creation will be annihilated and abforbed into the Supreme Being, there will be five great *calpas*, or periods. We are now in the middle of the fourth *calpa*, fifty years of

---

(2) *Adima* is the feminine gender from *Adima* or *Adimas*.

Bráhma

Bráhma being elapsed; and of the remainder the first *calpa* is begun. These five great *calpas* include 500 years of *Bráhma*, at the end of which nothing will remain but the self-existing. Every *calpa*, except the first, is preceded by a renovation of the world, and a general flood: whilst the flood that precedes every *Manwantara* is in great measure, a partial one, some few high peaks and some privileged places, as *Benares*, being excepted; the peaks remaining above the waters, and *Benares* and other privileged places being surrounded by the waters as with a circular wall.

These five *calpas* have five deities, who rule by turns, and from whom the *calpas* are denominated. These five deities are, *Dévi*, *Surya* or the Sun, *Ganésa*, *Vishnu*, and *Is'wara*. *Bráhma* has no peculiar *calpa*: he is intimate to every one of them. Every deity, in his own period, is *Calsva-rupi* or *Chronus*. We are now under the reign of the fourth *Chronus*. The Western mythologists mention several ruling deities of that name. *Calsva-rupi* signifies he who has the countenance of *Cála*, *Chronus*, or *Time*. This is now the *calpa* of *Vishnu*, who, to create, thought on *Bráhma*, and became *Bráhma-rupi-Janardana*. He preserves and fosters the whole creation in his own character; and will ultimately destroy it through *Is'wara* or *Rudra*. The *calpa* of *Vishnu* is called also the *Puchna* or *Lotos period*. It is declared in the *puránas* that all animals and plants are the *Ling* or *Phallus* of the *Calsva-rupi* deity; and that at the end of his own *calpa* he is deprived of his *Ling* by his successor, who attracts the whole creation to himself, to swallow it up or devour it, according to the Western mythologists; and at the end of his *calpa* he disgorges the whole creation. Such is the origin of *Chronus* devouring his own offspring; of *Jupiter* disgorging it through a potion administered to him by *Metis*; and of *Chronus* castrating his own father. According to this, *Swayambhuva*

is

is conjointly and individually, *Bráhma*, *Vishnu*, and *Isá* or *Maha-deva*. To *Swayambhuva* were born three daughters, *Acuti*, *Deva-sruti*, and *Vyruti* or *Prasuti*. *Bráhma* created three great *Rajapátis*, to be their husbands; *Cardama*, *Dacsha*, (the same who was also a *Bráhmadica*,) and *Ruchi*. *Cardama* is acknowledged to be a form of *Siva*, or *Siva* himself: and *Dacsha* to be *Bráhma*; hence he is often called *Dacsha Bráhma*; and we may reasonably conclude that the benevolent *Ruchi* was equally a form of *Vishnu*. It is said in the *védas*, as I am assured by learned *pundits*, that these three gods sprang in a mortal shape from the body of *Adima*; that *Dacsha Bráhma* issued mystically from his navel, *Vishnu* from his left, and *Siva* from his right side. It is declared in the *puránas*, that *Iswara* cut off one of the heads of *Bráhma*, who being immortal was only maimed. The same mystical rancour was manifest when they assumed a mortal shape; as appears from the following relation: The pious *Dacsha* desiring to perform sacrifice, invited gods and men to assist at it, but did not ask *Siva* on account of his bad conduct and licentious life. The wife of *Siva*, who was the daughter of *Dacsha*, could not brook this neglect, and determined to go: her husband expostulated with her, but to no purpose. When she arrived, her father took no notice of her, which enraged her so much, that after having spoiled the sacrifice, she jumped into the sacred fire, and expired in the flames. *Siva* hearing of her misfortune, went to *Dacsha*; and, reproaching him for his unnatural conduct towards his own daughter, cut off his head. *Dacsha* had no male offspring, but many daughters, whose alliance was eagerly sought for by the most distinguished characters. It is asserted in the *puránas* that from *Cardama*, *Dacsha*, and *Ruchi*, the earth was filled with inhabitants: yet in the same *puránas* we are told, that *Bráhma*, being disappointed, found it necessary to give two sons to *Adima*, from whom, at last, the earth was filled with inhabitants. These two sons were PRIYAVRATA and UTTA'NAPA'DA, who appear to be the same with CARDAMA and RUCHI. Here the antediluvian history assumes a different shape; and the *puránics*, abandoning their idle tales of the seven *Menus* and renovations of the world, between the time of SWAYAMBHUVA and the flood of SATYAVRATA, presents us with something more consistent with reason and historical truth; but which at once overthrows their extravagant fabrick. PRIYAVRATA was the first born of ADIMA; and the particulars recorded of his progeny have no small affinity with the generations exhibited by SANCHONIATHO, as will appear from the following comparative Table:

I. ADIMA, and ADIMA or I'VA.

I. PROTOGONUS, synonimous with ADIM: AION or AEON from I'VA or I'VAM, in the second case.

II. PRIYAVRATA. He married BARHISMATI, the daughter of VISVACARMA, the chief engineer of the Gods.

II. GENUS, GENEA.

III. AGNIDHRA and his seven brothers, whose names signify fire and flame. By one wife he had three sons: they became *Menus*; and were named, UTTAMA, TAMASA, and RAIVATA. By another wife, AGNIDHRA had nine sons, who gave their names to the mountainous tracts of *Nabhi*.

III. PHOS, PHUR, PHLOX; that is, light, fire, and flame.

IV. Cimpurusha, Hari-varsha, Ila'varta, Ra'ma'naca, Curu, Bhadrasva, Ce'tuma'la, and Hiranmaya.	IV. They begat sons of vast bulk, whose names were given to the mountains on which they seized, viz. *Cassius, Libanus, Anti-Libanus, Brathys.*
V. Rïshabaha, son of Nabahi.	V. Memrumus, Hypsuranius, and Usous.
VI. Bharata, who gave his name to the country of *Bharata-varsha*.	VI. Agreæs, Haliæus.
VII. Sumarti, Dhumra-ce'tu, whose name signifies a fiery meteor.	VII. Chrysaor.
VIII. Devajita 9. Pratihara 10. Pratihata { said by some to be brothers. The names of the two last imply beating, hammering, &c. }	VIII. Technites, Geïnus, Autochton.
IX. Aja and Bhuma'na. Then follows a list of sixteen names, supposed by some to be so many generations in a direct line; by others, this is denied: but as nothing is recorded of them, they are omitted.	IX. Agrowerus, or Agrotes. Aja in *Sanscrit*, is synonimous nearly with *Autochton*, and Bhu'mana answers to *Agrowerus* and *Agrotes*.

The posterity of Adima or Adim (for the letter A in this name has exactly the sound of the *French* *e* in the word *j'aime*) through Utta'napa'da, is as follows:

I. Adim

I. ADIM and I'VA. I'VA founds exactly like EVE, pronounced as a diffyllable E-VE.

II. UTTA'NAPA'DA. He had two wives, SURUCHI and SURUTI: by the firft he had UTTAMA, and by the fecond DHRUVA. *Uttánapáda* was exceedingly fond of *Suruchi*, which gave rife to the following circumftances. Whilft he was careffing *Uttama* his fon *Dhruva* went to him and was repulfed. *Dhruva* burft into tears, and complained to his mother, who advifed him to withdraw into the defarts. He followed her advice, and retired into a foreft on the banks of the *Jumna*, where he gave himfelf up to the contemplation of the Supreme Being, and the performance of religious aufterities. After many years the Supreme Being appeared to him, and commanded him to put an end to his aufterities and return to his father, who had relented. He went accordingly to his father, who received him with joy, and refigned the kingdom to him. *Dhruva*, like *Enoch* in Scripture is commended for his extraordinary piety, and the falutary precepts he gave to mankind. He did not tafte death, but was tranflated to heaven, where he fhines in the polar ftar. Here *Enoch* and *Enos* are confounded together. *Uttama*, whofe education had been neglected, gave himfelf up to pleafure and diffipation. Whilft hunting he happened to quarrel with the *Cuveras*, and was killed in the fray. *Dhruva*, at the head of a numerous army, took the field to revenge the death of his brother: many had fallen on both fides, when *Swayambhuva* or *Adim* interpofed, and a lafting peace was concluded between the contending parties.

III. DHRŬVA. He had by his first wife two sons, VATSARA and CALMAVATSARA; by ILA he had a son called UTCALA, and a daughter.

IV. VATSARA, by his wife SWACATAI had six sons, the eldest of whom was called PUSHPA'RNA.

V. PUSHPA'RNA had by his wife DOSHA three sons, and by NAD'WALA, CHACSHUSHA, who became a *Menu*.

VI. CHACHUSHA had twelve sons, the eldest of whom was called ULMACA.

VII. ULMACA had six sons, the eldest of whom was ANGA.

VIII. ANGA had an only son called VENA.

IX. VENA, being an impious and tyrannical prince, was cursed by the BRA'HMENS; in consequence of which curse he died without leaving issue. To remedy this evil they opened his left arm, and with a stick churned the humours till they at last produced a son, who proved as wicked as his father, and was of course set aside: then opening the right arm, they churned till they produced a beautiful boy, who proved to be a form of VISHNU under the name of PRĪTHU.

X. PRĪTHU. Gods and men came to make obeisance to him, and celebrate his appearance on earth. He married a form of the goddess LACSHMI. In his time, the earth having refused to give her wonted supplies to mankind,

Prĭthu began to beat and wound her. The earth, aſſuming the ſhape of a cow, went to the high grounds of *Meru*, and there laid her complaint before the ſupreme court, who rejected it; as ſhe acknowledged, that ſhe had refuſed the common neceſſaries of life, not only to mankind in general, but to Prĭthu himſelf, whoſe wife ſhe was in a human ſhape. Prĭthu and his deſcendants were allowed to beat and wound her in caſe of noncompliance with the decree of the ſupreme court. The earth ſubmitted reluctantly, and ſince that time mankind are continually beating and wounding her, with ploughs, harrows, hoes, and other inſtruments of huſbandry. We are told alſo, in more plain language, that Prĭthu cut down whole foreſts, levelled the earth, planted orchards, and ſowed fields with all ſorts of uſeful ſeeds. From her huſband Prĭthu, the earth was denominated Prĭthwĭ.

Prĭthu was a religious prince, fond of agriculture, and became a huſbandman; which is to be underſtood by his quarrel with the earth. This induces me to think, that he is the ſame with Satyavrata, or Noah, whoſe mortal father is not mentioned in the *puránas*, at leaſt my *Pundits* have not been able to find it. His heavenly father was the Sun; and Satyavrata is declared alſo to be an incarnation of Vishnu. Here I muſt obſerve, that at night, and in the weſt, the Sun is Vishnu: he is Bra'hma in the eaſt, and in the morning; from noon to evening he is Siva.

XI. Prĭthu had five children. Vijitasva, who became ſovereign over his four brothers, and had the middle part of the kingdom to his own ſhare; Huryacsha ruled over *Prachi*, or the eaſt, and built the town of *Rájgriha*, now *Ráj-mehal*; Dhumracé'sha, who ruled in the ſouth, as Vrica did in the weſt, and Dravina'sa in the north.

XII. Vĭsi-

XII. Vi'sitaswa had by one of his wives three fons, called Pavaca, Pavamana, and Suchi, all names of fire. He became *Antardhana* at pleafure, that is to fay, he appeared and difappeared whenever he chofe; and he withdrew his foul from his body at pleafure. He was born again of his own wife, and of himfelf, under the name of Havirdhana. Havirdhana married Havirdhani, by whom he had fix children, known by the general appellation of *Prachina-barhi*.

XIII. Varishada, the eldeft of them, married Satadruti the daughter of Oceanus, and had by her two fons called the *Prachetas*.

XIV. The famous Dacsha before mentioned, was born again one of them. His brothers, bidding adieu to the world, withdrew to forefts in diftant countries towards the weft, where they beheld the tranflation of Dhruva into heaven. And here ends the line of Utta'napa'da, which I now exhibit at one view, with fome variations.

I. Swayambhuva or Adim.

II. Utta'napa'da, who was probably the fame with Ruchi.

III. Dhruva, eminent for his piety.

IV. Vatsara.

V. Pushparna, called alfo Ripunjaya.

VI. Chacshusha, Menu.

VII. Ulmaca or Uru.

VIII. Anga.

IX. Venu.

X. Prithu, fuppofed to be Noah.

XI. Vigitasva.

XII. Havir-

XII. HAVIRDHANA.   SWAYAMBHUVA dies.
XIII. VARISHADA.
XIV. The ten PRA'CHETA's. DHRUVA is translated
                       into heaven.

By supposing *Prĭthu* to be *Noah*, and *Dhruva* to be *Enos*, this account agrees remarkably well with the computation of the *Samaritan Pentateuch*. *Enos* lived 433 years after the birth of *Noah*, and, of course, the great-grand-children of the latter could be witnesses of the translation of *Dhruva* into heaven. *Swayambhuva* or *Adam* lived 223 years after the birth of *Noah*, according to the computation of the *Samaritan Pentateuch*; and it is said of *Prĭthu*, that the earth having assumed the shape of a cow, he made use of this grand ancestor *Swayambhuva* as a calf to *milk her*. Perhaps the old sire took delight in superintending the fields and orchards, and attending the dairies of his beloved *Prĭthu*.

The only material difficulty in supposing *Prĭthu* to be the same with *Noah*, respects his offspring to the fourth generation before the flood. But, when we consider that *Noah* was 500 years old when *Japheth* and his two sons were born, it is hardly credible that he should have had no children till that advanced age. The *purănics* insist, that *Satyavrata* had many before the Flood, but that they perished with the rest of mankind, and that SHARMA or SHAMA, CHARMA, and JYA'PATI, were born after the Flood: but they appear to have no other proof of this, than that they are not mentioned among those who escaped with *Noah* in the ark. I shall now give a table of the *seven Menus* compared with the two lines descended from ADIM and I'VA.

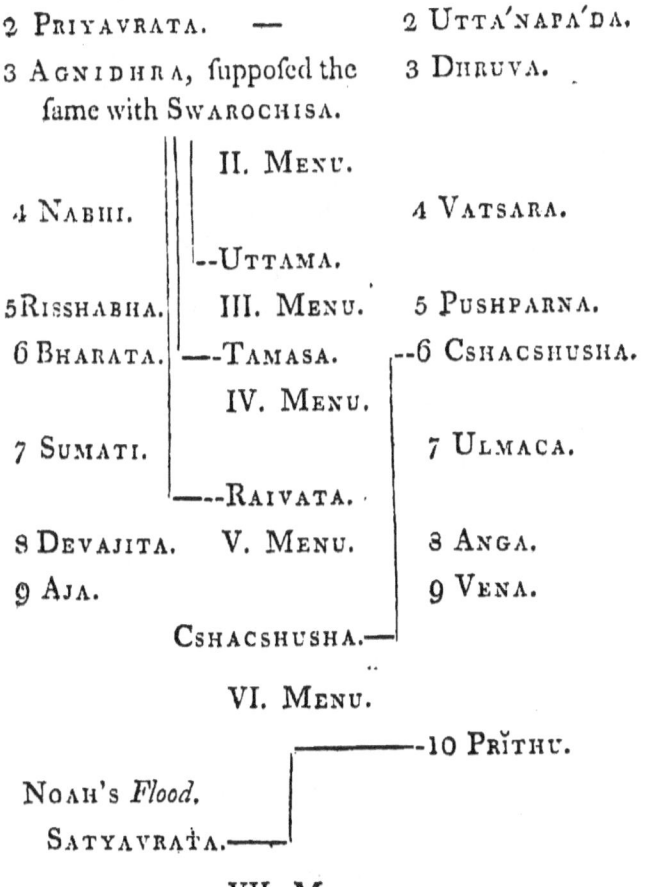

This table completely overthrows the fyftem of the *Menwantaras,* previous to the Flood; for it is declared in the *puránas,* that at the end of every *Menwantara,*

wantara, the whole human race is destroyed, except one *Menu*, who makes his escape in a boat with the seven *Ríshis*. But, according to the present table, *Swayambhuva* went through every *Menwantara* and died in the sixth; *Dhruva* also saw five *Menwantaras* and died on the sixth. *Uttama*, *Tamasa*, and *Raivata*, being brothers, lived during the course of several *Menwantaras*, and when *Uttama* made his escape in a boat, besides the seven *Ríshis*, he must have taken with him his two brothers, with *Dhruva* and *Swayambhuva*. Of these *Menus* little more is recorded in the *puránas*, than that they had a numerous offspring; that certain *Devatas* made their appearance; and that they discomfited the giants. The mortal father of *Swarochisa* is not known. His divine father was *Agni*; hence, he is supposed by some to be the same with *Agnidhra*.

During the reign of the fourth *Menu*, occurred the famous war between the *elephants* and the *crocodiles*, which, in the *puránas*, is asserted to have happened in the *sacred isles* in the west. What was the origin of it we are not told; but whenever the *elephants* went to a lake, either to drink or to bathe, the *crocodiles* laying in wait, dragged them into the water and devoured them. The *Gujendra* or *Nag'náth*, the lord of the *elephants*, was once attacked by the chief of the *grahas* or *crocodiles* on the bank of a *lake*, in one of the *sacred isles* called *Suvarnéya*; a dreadful conflict took place, and the *Nag'náth* was almost overpowered, when he called on *Heri* or *Vishnu*, who rescued him, and put an end to the war. What could give rise to such an extravagant tale I cannot determine, but some obvious traces of it still remain in the *sacred isles in the west*, for almost every lake in *Wales* has a strange story attached to it, of battles fought there between an *ox* and a *beaver*, both of an uncommon size. At night the lowing of the *ox* and the rattling of the chain, with which the *Ychain-bannawg* or great *ox* endeavours to pull out of the water the *avanc* or *beaver*, are often heard.

heard. It is well known that *elephants* were called *oxen* in the west, and the ancient *Romans* had no other name for them. It may be objected, that if there had been *elephants*, in the *sacred isles*, the inhabitants would have had names for them; but the *Cymri* are certainly a very modern tribe, relatively to the times we are speaking of; and probably there were no *elephants* or *crocodiles* when they settled there; but, hearing of a strange story of battles between a large land animal and an amphibious one, they concluded that these two animals could be no other than the *ox* and *beaver*, the largest of the kind they were acquainted with, *nag′,náhhá st′han*, or the place of the *nag′náth*, or lord of the elephantine race, is well known to the antiquaries of *Juvernia*.

During the sixth *dynasty* came to pass the famous *churning of the ocean*, which is positively declared in the *purána* to have happened in the *sea of milk*, or more properly, as it is often called also the *White Sea*, which surrounds the *sacred isles* in the west, and is thus denominated according to the *Treloca-derpan*, because it washes the shores of the *white island*, the principal of the *sacred isles*. The *white island* in *Sanscrit*, *sweta-dwip* or *chira-dwip*, is as famous in the east as it is in the west. It may seem strange, that islands so remote should be known to the *puránics*; but the truth is, that the *védas* were not originally made known to mankind in *India*. The *Bráhmens* themselves acknowledge that they are not natives of *India*, but that they descended into the plains of *Hindustan* through the pass of *Heridwar*.

The old continent is well described in the *puránas*, but more particularly the countries in which the *védas* where made public; and in which the doctrine they contain flourished for a long time. Accordingly the *sacred isles* in the west, the countries bordering on the *Nile*, and, last of all, *India*, are better and more minutely

nutely defcribed than any other country. *Atri* called *Edris*, and *Idris*, in the countries to the weft of *India*, carried the *védas* from the abode of the gods on the fummit of *Meru*, firft, to the *facred ifle*; thence to the banks of the *Nile*; and, laftly, to the borders of *India*. The place of his abode, whilft in the *facred ifles*, became afterwards a famous place of worfhip under the name of *Atri-ft'han* the *place* or *feat* of *Atri* or *Idris*. It is often mentioned in the *puránas*, and defcribed to be on a high mountain, not far from the fea fhore.

I fhall pafs over the four ages, as they do not appear to anfwer any purpofe, either aftronomical or hiftorical. They are called by the fame names that were ufed by the *Greek* mythologifts; except the fourth, which is called by the *Hindus*, the *earthen* age. I fhall only remark, that *Menu* in his Inftitutes fays, that in the firft or *golden* age*, men, free from difeafe, lived four hundred years; but in the fecond, and the fucceeding ages, their lives were leffened gradually by one quarter; that in the *cali-yug*, or prefent age, men live only one hundred years. This may ferve to fix the period and duration of the firft ages; for it is obvious, that the whole paffage refers to natural years.

I fhall now conclude this account of *antediluvian* hiftory by obferving, that the firft defcendants of *Swayambhuva* are reprefented in the *puránas*, as living in the mountains to the north of *India* toward the fources of the *Ganges*, and downwards as far as *Serinágara* and *Hari-áwár*. But the rulers of mankind lived on the fummit of *Meru* towards the north; where they appear to have eftablifhed the feat of juftice, as the *puránas* make frequent mention of the oppreffed repairing thither for redrefs. *India*, at that time, feems to have been perfectly infulated; and we know, that

---

* Inftitutes of *Menu*, p. 11.

from

from the mouth of the *Indus* to *Dehli*, and thence to the mouth of the *Ganges*, the country is perfectly level, without even a single hillock; but this subject is foreign to my present purpose, and may be resumed hereafter. The generations after the Flood, exhibited in the accompanying table, begin with the famous *Atri*, and end with *Chandra-Gupta*, who was contemporary with *Alexander the Great*. *Buddha*, the grandson of *Atri* married *Ila*, daughter of *Satyavrata* or *Noah*, who was born to him in his old age.

Atri for the purpose of making the *védas* known to mankind, had three sons; or, as it is declared in the *puránas*, the *Trimurti*, or *Hindu Triad*, was incarnated in his house. The eldest called *Soma*, or the moon in a human shape, was a portion or form of *Bráhma*. To him the *sacred isles* in the west were allotted. He is still alive though invisible, and is acknowledged as the chief of the sacerdotal tribe to this day.

The second, a portion of *Vishnu*, was called *Datta* or *Date* and *Dattátréya*. The countries bordering on the *Nile* fell to his share. He is the *Toth* of the *Egyptians*.

The third was a cholerick saint called *Durvásás*. He was a portion of *Mahádéva*, but had no fixed place assigned to him; and he is generally rambling over the world, doing more mischief than good; however, we find him very often performing *Tapasya* in the mountains of *Armenia*. A dreadful conflagration happened once in that country, which spreading all over *Cusha-dwipa* destroyed all the *animals* and *vegetables*. *Arama*, the *son* of a *son* of *Satyavrata* (and consequently the *Aram* of Scripture) who was hunting through these mountains,

mountains, was involved with his party in the general conflagration; a punishment inflicted, it is supposed, for his having inadvertently wounded the foot of *Durvásis* with an arrow. The death of *Arama* happened three hundred years after the Flood, according to the *puránas* *, as noticed in a former essay on *Egypt*.

Chandra-Gupta, or he who was saved by the interposition of *Lunus* or the *Moon*, is called also *Chandra* in a poem quoted by Sir William Jones. The *Greeks* call him *Sandracuptos, Sandracottos,* and *Androcottos*. *Sandrocottos* is generally used by the historians of *Alexander*; and *Sandracuptos* is found in the works of *Athenæas*. *Sir William Jones*, from a poem written by *Somadeva*, and a tragedy called the coronation of *Chandra* or *Chandra-Gupta*†, discovered that he really was the *Indian* king mentioned by the historians of *Alexander*, under the name of *Sandracottos*. These two poems I have not been able to procure; but, I have found another dramatic piece, intitled *Mudra-Rácshasa*, or the *seal* of *Rácshasa*, which is divided into two parts: the first may be called the coronation of *Chandra-Gupta*, and the second the reconciliation of *Chandra-Gupta* with *Mantri-Rácshasa*, the prime minister of his father.

The history of *Chandra-Gupta* is related, though in few words, in the *Vishnu-purána*, the *Bhagawat*, and two other books, one of which is called *Brahatcathu*, and the other is a lexicon called *Camandaca*: the two last are supposed to be about six or seven hundred years old.

---

* Essay on *Egypt*, in the *Asiat. Res.* vol. III. p. 38.
† *Asiatick Researches*, vol. IV. p. 6. 11.

In the *Vishnu-purána* we read, " unto *Nanda* shall
" be born nine sons ; *Cotilya*, his minister shall de-
" stroy them, and place *Chandra-Gupta* on the throne."

In the *Bhagawat* we read, " from the womb of *Su-*
" *dri, Nanda* shall be born. His eldest son will be
" called *Sumalya*, and he shall have eight sons more ;
" these, a *Bráhmen* (called *Cotilya, Vatsayana,* and *Cha-*
" *nacya* in the commentary) shall destroy, after them
" a *Maurya* shall reign in the *Cali-yug.* This *Bráh-*
" *men* will place *Chandra-Gupta* on the throne." In
the *Brahatcatha* it is said, that this revolution was effected in seven days, and the nine children of *Nanda*
put to death. In the *Camandaca, Chanacyas* is called
Vishnu-Gupta. The following is an abstract of the
history of *Chandra-Gupta* from the *Mudra-Rácshasa :*

Nanda, king of *Prachi*, was the son of *Maha Nandi*,
by a female slave of the *Sudra* tribe : hence *Nanda*
was called a *Sudra*. He was a good king, just and
equitable, and paid due respect to the *Bráhmens :* he
was avaricious, but he respected his subjects. He was
originally king of *Magada*, now called *South-Bahar*,
which had been in the possession of his ancestors since
the days of *Crishna* ; by the strength of his arm he subdued all the kings of the country, and like another
Parasu-Ráma destroyed the remnants of the *Cshettris*.
He had two wives, *Ratnavati* and *Mura*. By the first
he had nine sons, called the *Sumalyadicas*, from the
eldest, whose name was *Sumalya* (though in the *dramas*, he is called *Sarvarthasidd'hi*) ; by *Mura* he had
Chandra-Gupta, and many others, who were known
by the general appellation of *Mauryas,* because they
were born of *Mura.*

Nanda,

Nanda, when far advanced in years, was taken ill suddenly, and to all appearance died. He soon revived, to the great joy of his subjects: but his senses appeared to be greatly deranged, for he no longer spoke or acted as before. While some ascribed the monarch's imbecillity to the effects of a certain poison, which is known to impair the faculties at least, when it proves too weak to destroy the life of those to whom it is administered, *Mantri-Rácshasa*, his prime minister was firmly persuaded, according to a notion very prevalent among the *Hindus*, that upon his master's death, some magician had entered into the lifeless corpse which was now re-animated and actuated by his presence. He, therefore, secretly ordered, that strict search might be made for the magician's own body: for, as according to the tenets of their superstition, this would necessarily be rendered invisible, and continue so, as long as its spirit informed another body; so he naturally concluded the magician had enjoined one of his faithful followers to watch it, until the dissolution of the spell should end the trance. In consequence of these orders, two men being discovered keeping watch over a corpse on the banks of the *Ganges*, he ordered them to be seized and thrown into the river, and caused the body to be burnt immediately. It proved to belong to *Chandra-das*, a king of a small domain in the western part of *India* beyond the *Vindhyan* hills, the capital whereof is called *Vicat-palli*. This prince having been obliged to save himself by flight, from the *Yavanas* or *Greeks*, who had dispossessed him of his kingdom, had assumed, with the garb of a penitent, the name of *Suvid'ha*. *Mantri-Rácshasa* having thus punished the magician for his presumption, left the country.

When *Nanda* recovered from his illness he became a tyrant, or, rather, having entrusted *Sacatara*, his prime minister, with the reins of government, the latter ruled with absolute sway. As the old king was one day hunting with his minister, towards the hills to the south of the town, he complained of his being

ing thirsty, and quitting his attendants, repaired with *Sacatara* to a beautiful *reservoir*, under a large spreading tree, near a cave in the hills, called *Patalcandira*, or the passage leading to the infernal regions; there *Sacatara* flung the old man into the *reservoir*, and threw a large stone upon him. In the evening he returned to the imperial city, bringing back the king's horse, and reported, that his master had quitted his attendants and rode into the forest; what was become of him he knew not, but he had found his horse grazing under a tree. Some days after *Sacatara*, with *Vacranara*, one of the secretaries of state, placed *Ugradhanwa*, one of the younger sons of *Nanda*, on the throne.

The young king being dissatisfied with *Sacatara's* account of his father's disappearance, set about farther enquiries during the minister's absence, but these proving as little satisfactory, he assembled the principal persons of his court, and threatened them all with death, if, in three days, they failed to bring him certain intelligence what was become of his father. This menace succeeded, for, on the fourth day, they reported, that *Sacatara* had murdered the old king, and that his remains where concealed under a stone in the *reservoir* near *Patalcandra*; *Ugradhanwa* immediately sent people with camels, who returned in the evening, with the body and the stone that had covered it. *Sacatara* confessed the murder, and was thereupon condemned to be shut up with his family in a narrow room, the door of which was walled up, and a small opening only left for the conveyance of their scanty allowance. They all died in a short time, except the youngest son *Vicatara*, whom the young king ordered to be released, and took into his service. But *Vicatara* meditated revenge; and the king having directed him to call some *Bráhman* to assist at the *sraddha* he was going to perform,

perform, in honour of his ancestor, *Vicatara*, brought an ill-natured priest, of a most savage appearance, in the expectation that the king might be tempted, from disgust at so offensive an object, to offer some affront to the *Bráhmen*, who, in revenge, would denounce a curse against him. The plan succeeded to his wish: the king ordered the priest to be turned out, and the latter laid a dreadful imprecation upon him, swearing at the same time, that he would never tie up his *shicá* or lock of hair, till he had effected his ruin. The enraged priest then ran out of the palace exclaiming, whoever wishes to be king let him follow me. *Chandra-Gupta* immediately arose, with eight of his friends, and went after him. They crossed the *Ganges*, with all possible dispatch, and visited the king of *Népal*, called *Parvateswara*, or the lord of the mountains, who received them kindly. They entreated him to assist them with troops and money, *Chandra-Gupta* promising, at the same time, to give him the half of the empire of *Práchi*, in case they should be successful. *Parvateswara* answered, that he could not bring into the field a sufficient force to effect the conquest of so powerful an empire; but, as he was on good terms with the *Yavans* or *Greeks*, the *Sacas* or *Indo-Scythians*, the people of *Camboja* or *Gayni*, the *Ciratas* or inhabitants of the mountains to the eastward of *Népal*, he could depend on their assistance. *Ugradhanwa* enraged at the behaviour of *Chandra-Gupta*, ordered all his brothers to be put to death.

The matter, however, is related differently in other books, which state, that *Nanda*, seeing himself far advanced in years, directed that, after his decease, his kingdom should be equally divided between the *Sumalyadicas*, and that a decent allowance should be given to the *Mauryas* or children of *Mura*, but the *Sumalyadicas* being jealous of the *Mauryas*, put them all to death, except *Chandra-Gupta*, who, being saved through the protection of *Lunus*, out of gratitude assumed the name of *Chandra-Gupta*, or saved by the moon: but to resume the narrative,

Parvá-

Parvátes̀wara took the field with a formidable army, accompanied by his brother *Virochana* and his own son *Malaya-Cetu*. The confederates soon came in sight of the capital of the king of *Prachi*, who put himself at the head of his forces, and went out to meet them. A battle was fought, wherein *Ugradhanwa* was defeated, after a dreadful carnage, in which he himself lost his life. The city was immediately surrounded, and *Sawartha-Siddhi*, the governor, seeing it impossible to hold out against so powerful an enemy, fled to the *Vindhyan* mountains, and became an anchoret. *Racshasa* went over to *Parvátes̀wara* *. *Chandra-Gupta*, being firmly established on the throne, destroyed the *Sumalya-dicas*, and dismissed the allies, after having liberally rewarded them for their assistance: but he kept the *Yavans* or *Greeks*, and refused to give the half of the kingdom of *Prachi* to *Parvátes̀wara*, who, being unable to enforce his claim, returned to his own country meditating vengeance. By the advice of *Racshasa* he sent a person to destroy *Chandra-Gupta*; but *Vishnu-Gupta*, suspecting the design, not only rendered it abortive, but turned it back upon the author, by gaining over the assassin to his interest, whom he engaged to murder *Parvátes̀wara*, which the villain accordingly effected. *Racshasa* urged *Mataya-Cetu* to revenge his father's death, but though pleased with the suggestion, he declined the enterprize, representing to his councellor, that *Chandra-Gupta* had a large body of *Yavans* or *Greeks* in his pay, had fortified his capital, and placed a numerous garison in it, with guards of *elephants* at all the gates; and finally, by the defection of their allies, who were either overawed by his power, or conciliated by his favour, had so firmly established his authority, that no attempt could be made against him with any prospect of success.

---

* *Racshasa* on hearing of the death of *Sacatara* returned, and became prime minister of *Ugra-dhanwa*.

In the mean time *Vishnu-Gupta*, being conscious that *Chandra-Gupta* could never be safe so long as he had to contend with a man of *Racshasa*'s abilities, formed a plan to reconcile them, and this he effected in the following manner: there was in the capital a respectable merchant or banker, called *Chandana-Das*, an intimate friend of *Racshasa*. *Vishnu-Gupta* advised *Chandra-Gupta* to confine him with his whole family: some time after he visited the unfortunate prisoner, and told him that the only way to save himself and family from imminent destruction, was to effect a reconciliation between the king and *Racshasa*, and that, if he would follow his advice, he would point out to him the means of doing it. *Chandana-Das* assented, though, from the known inveteracy of *Racshasa* against *Chandra-Gupta*, he had little hope of success. Accordingly, he and *Vishnu-Gupta*, betook themselves privately to a place in the northern hills, where *Racshasa* had a country seat, to which he used to retire from the bustle of business. There they erected a large pile of wood, and gave out that they intended to burn themselves. *Racshasa* was astonished when he heard of his friends' resolution, and used every endeavour to dissuade them from it; but *Chandana-Das* told him, he was determined to perish in the flames with *Vishnu-Gupta*, unless he would consent to be reconciled to *Chandra-Gupta*. In the mean time the prince arrived with a retinue of five hundred men; when, ordering them to remain behind, he advanced alone towards *Racshasa*, to whom he bowed respectfully and made an offer of delivering up his sword. *Racshasa* remained a long time inexorable, but at last, overcome by the joint entreaties of *Vishnu-Gupta* and *Chandana-Das*, he suffered himself to be appeased, and was reconciled to the king, who made him his prime minister. *Vishnu-Gupta*, having succeeded in bringing about this reconciliation, withdrew to resume his former occupations; and *Chandra-Gupta* reigned afterwards many years, with justice and equity, and adored by his subjects.

By

By *Prachi* (in Sanscrit) or the east, is understood all the country from *Allahabad* to the easternmost limits of *India*: it is called also *purva*, an appellation of the same import, and *puroh* in the spoken dialects. This last has been distorted into *purop* and *prurop* by European travellers of the last century. From *prachi* is obviously derived the name of *Prasii*, which the Greeks gave to the inhabitants of this country. It is divided into two parts: the first comprehends all the country from *Allahabad* to *Raj-mehal* and the western branch of the *Ganges*; the second includes *Bengal*, the greatest part of which is known in Sanscrit under the name of *Gancara-desa*, or country of *Gancara*, from which the Greeks made *Gangaridas* or *Gangaridai*, in the first case. *Gancara* is still the name of a small district near the summit of the *Delta*.

Perhaps from these two countries called *Purva* is derived the appellation of *Parvaim* in Scripture, which appears with a dual form. According to Arrian's *Periplus*, *Bengal* was famous for its highly refined gold, called *Keltin* in the *Periplus*, and *Camden* or *Calden* to this day. It is called *Kurden* in the *Ayeen Ackbery**.

The capital city of *Prachi* proper, or the western part of it, is declared to be *Raj-griha*, or the royal mansion. According to the *puránas* it was built by a son of king *Prithu*, called *Haryacsha*. It was taken afterwards by *Bala-Rama*, the brother of *Crishna*, who rebuilt it, and assigned it as a residence for one of his sons, who are called in general *Baliputras*, or the children of *Bala*. From this circumstance it was called *Balipura*, or the town of the son of *Bala*; but in the spoken dialects it was called *Bali-putra*, because a *putra*, or son of *Bali*, resided in it. From *Bali-putra* the Greeks made *Palipatra* and *Pali-bothra*, and

---

* Vol. III. p. 234.

the inhabitants of the country, of which it was the capital, they denominated *Palibothri*, though this appellation more properly belongs to another tribe of *Hindus*, of whom I gave some account in a former essay on Egypt.

DIODORUS SICULUS, speaking of *Palibothra*, says, that it had been built by the Indian *Hercules*, who, according to *Megasthenes*, as quoted by *Arrian*, was worshipped by the *Suraseni*. Their chief cities were *Methora* and *Clisobora*; the first is now called *Mutra*(*), the other *Mugu-nagur* by the Musulmans, and *Calisa-pura* by the Hindus. The whole country about *Mutra* is called *Surasena* to this day by learned *Bráhmens*.

The Indian *Hercules*, according to *Cicero*, was called BELUS. He is the same with BALA, the brother of CRISHNA, and both are conjointly worshipped at *Mutra*; indeed, they are considered as one *Avatara*, or incarnation of *Vishnu*. *Bala* is represented as a stout man with a club in his hand. He is called also *Bala-Rama*. To decline the word *Bala* you must begin with *Balas*, which I conceive to be an obsolete form, preserved only for the purpose of declension, and etymological derivation. The first *a* in *Bala* is pronounced like the first *a* in *America*, in the eastern parts of *India*: but in the western parts, and in *Benares*, it is pronounced exactly like the French *e* in the pronouns *je*, *me*, *le*, &c. thus the difference between *Balas* and *Belus* is not very great. As *Bala* sprung from *Vishnu*, or *Heri*, he is certainly *Heri-cula*, *Heri-culas*, and *Hercules*. Diodorus Siculus says, that the posterity of *Hercules* reigned for many centuries in *Pali-bothra*, but that they did nothing worthy of being recorded; and, indeed, their names are not even mentioned in the *puránas*.

(*) In Sanscrit it is called *Mat'hura*.

In the *Ganga-mahatmya*, in which all places of worship, and others of note, on the banks of the *Ganges*, are mentioned, the prefent town of *Raj-mehal* is pofitively declared to be the ancient city of *Raj-griha* of the *puránas*, the capital of *Prachi*, which afterwards was called *Bali-putra*.

Raj-griha, and *Raj-mehal* in *Perfian*, fignify the fame thing. It is alfo called by the natives *Raj-mandalam*, and by *Ptolemy Palibothra-mandalon* for *Bali-putra-mandalam*: the firft fignifies the royal manfion, and the fecond the manfion of the *Bala-putras*. In a more extenfive fenfe *mandalam* fignifies the circle, or country belonging to the *Bali-putras*. In this fenfe we fay *Coro-mandel*, for *Cholo* or rather *Jala-mandal*.

Here I muft obferve, the prefent *Raj-mehal* is not precifely on the fpot where the ancient *Raj-griha*, or *Bali-putra*, ftood, owing to the ftrange devaftation of the *Ganges* in that part of the country for feveral centuries paft. Thefe devaftations are attefted by univerfal tradition, as well as by hiftorical records, and the concurring teftimony of RALPH, FITCH, TAVERNIER, and other *European* travellers of the laft century. When I was at *Raj-mehal* in January laft, I was defirous of making particular enquiries on the fpot, but I could only meet with a few *Bráhmens*, and thofe very ignorant; all they could tell me was, that in former ages *Raj-mehal*, or *Raj-mandal*, was an immenfe city, that it extended as far as the eaftern limits of *Boglipoore* towards *Terriagully*, but that the *Ganges*, which formerly ran a great way towards the N. E. and Eaft, had fwallowed it up; and that the prefent *Raj-mehal*, formerly a fuburb of the ancient city, was all that remained of that famous place. For farther particulars they referred me to learned *pundits* who unfortunately lived in the interior parts of the country.

In the *Mudrá-rácſhaſa*, it is declared, that the city in which *Chandra-Gupta* reſided, was to the north of the hills, and, from ſome particular circumſtances that will be noticed hereafter, it appears that they could not be above five or ſix miles diſtant from it. *Megaſthenes* informs us alſo, that this famous city was ſituated near the confluence of the *Erannoboas* with the Ganges. The Erannoboas has been ſuppoſed to be the Sone, which has the epithet of *Hirán-ya-baha*, or *gold-waſting*, given to it in ſome poems. The Sone, however, is mentioned as a diſtinct river from the Erannoboas, both by *Pliny* and *Arrian*, on the authority of *Megaſthenes*: and the word *Hirán-ya-baha*, from which the Greeks made Erannoboas, is not a *proper* name, but an *appellative* (as the Greek *Chryſorhous*), applicable, and is applied, to any river that rolls down particles of gold with its ſands. Moſt rivers in *India* as well as in *Europe*, and more particularly the Ganges, with all the rivers that come down from the northern hills, are famous in ancient hiſtory for their golden ſands. The *Coſhanus* of *Arrian*, or *Coſſoagus* of *Pliny*, is not the river *Cooſy*, but the *Coſſanor Cattan*, called alſo *Coſſay*, *Coſſar*, and *Caſſay*, which runs through the province of *Midnapoor*, and joins the remains of the weſtern branch of the Ganges below *Nanga-Cuſſan*.

The Erannoboas, now the Cooſy, has greatly altered its courſe for ſeveral centuries paſt. It now joins the Ganges, about five and twenty miles above the place where it united with that river in the days of *Megaſthenes*; but the old bed, with a ſmall ſtream, is ſtill viſible, and is called to this day *Puranah-bahah* the old *Cooſy*, or *the old channel*. It is well delineated in Major Rennell's Atlas, and it joins an arm of the Ganges, formerly the bed of that river, near a place called *Nabob-gunge*. From *Nabob-gunge* the Ganges formerly took an extenſive ſweep to the eaſtward, towards *Hyatpoor*, and the old banks of the river are ſtill viſible in that direction. From theſe facts, ſupported

ported by a close inspection of the country, I am of opinion, *Baliputra* was situated near the confluence of the old Cooſy with the Ganges, and on the ſpot where the villages of *Mynyaree* and *Biſſuntpoor-gola* now ſtand; the Ganges proceeding at that time in an eaſterly direction from *Nabob-gunge*, and to the north of theſe villages. The fortified part of *Palibothra*, according to *Megaſthenes*, extended about ten miles in length, while the breath was only two. But the ſuburbs, which extended along the banks of the Ganges, were, I doubt not ten or fifteen miles in length. Thus *Dehli*, whilſt in a flouriſhing ſtate, extended above thirty miles along the banks of the *Jumna*, but, except about the centre of the town, conſiſted properly of only a ſingle ſtreet, parallel to the river.

The ancient geographers, as *Strabo*, *Ptolemy*, and *Pliny*, have deſcribed the ſituation of *Palibothra* in ſuch a manner that it is hardly poſſible to miſtake it.

Strabo*, who cites *Artemidorus*, ſays, that the Ganges on its entering the plains of India, runs in a ſouth direction as far as a town called *Ganges*, *(Ganga-puri,)* now *Allahabad*, and from thence, with an eaſterly courſe as far as *Palibothra*, thence to the ſea (according to the *Chreſtomathia* from *Strabo)* in a ſoutherly direction. No other place but that which we have aſſigned for the ſite of *Bali-putra*, anſwers to this deſcription of *Artemidorus*.

Pliny, from *Megaſthenes*, who, according to *Strabo*, had repeatedly viſited the court of *Chandra-Gupta*, ſays, that *Palibothra* was 425 Roman miles

---

* B. XV. p. 719.

from the confluence of the Jumna with the Ganges. Here it is necessary to premise, that *Megasthenes* says the highways in India were measured, and that at the end of a *certain Indian measure* (which is not named, but is said to be equal to *ten stadia,*) there was a *cippus* or sort of *column* erected. No Indian measure answers to this but the *Brahmeni*, or astronomical cols, of *four* to a *yojana*. This is the Hindu *statute* cols, and equal to 1,227 British miles. It is used to this day by astronomers, and by the inhabitants of the *Panjab*, hence it is very often called the *Panjabi-cofs*: thus the distance from *Lahor* to *Multan* is reckoned, to this day to be 145 *Panjabi*, or 90 *common cofs*.

In order to ascertain the number of *Brahmeni* cols reckoned formerly between *Allahabad* and *Palibothra*, multiply the 425 Roman miles by eight (for Pliny reckoned so many stadia to a mile) and divide the whole by ten (the number of stadia to a cols according to Megasthenes) and we shall have 340 *Brahmeni* cols, or 417.18 British miles; and this will bring us to within two miles of the confluence of the old Coosy with the Ganges.

Strabo informs us also that they generally reckoned 6000 stadia from *Palibothra* to the mouth of the Ganges; and from what he says, it is plain, that these 6000 stadia are to be understood of such as were used at sea, whereof about 1100 make a degree. Thus 6000 of these stadia give 382 British miles. According to Pliny they reckoned more accurately 6380 stadia or 406 British miles, which is really the distance by water between the confluence of the old Coosy with the Ganges, and Injellee at the mouth of the Ganges. Ptolemy has been equally accurate in assigning the situation of Palibothra relatively to the towns on the banks of the Ganges, which he mentions above and below it. Let us begin from the confluence of the Tuso, now the Tonse, with the Ganges.

Tuso,

Tufo, now the *Tonfe*, (See Major *Rennel's* courfe of the Ganges.)

Cindia, now *Conteeah*.

Sagala (in Sanfcrit *Suchela*, but in the vulgar dialects *Sokheila*) now Vindya Vatni near Mirzapoor.

Sanbalaca, in Sanfcrit *Sammalaca*. It is now called *Sumbulpoor*, and is fituated in an ifland oppofite to Patna. It is called Sabelpoor in Major *Rennel's* Map of the courfe of the Ganges, but the true name is Sumbulpoor. It derived its celebrity, as well as its name, from games (for fo the word Sammallaca imports) performed there every year in honour of certain heroes of antiquity. During the celebration of thefe games, Sammallaca was frequented by a prodigious concourfe of merchants, and all forts of people, inafmuch that it was confidered as the greateft fair in the country. This place is mentioned in the *Harichhetra Maha-tmya*, which contains a defcription of the principal places of worfhip in North Bahar,

Borœca, now *Borounca*, oppofite to Bar and Rajowly, near Mowah on the Byar, about three miles from the Ganges, which formerly ran clofe by it. It was the place of refidence of the kings of the Bhur tribe, once very powerful in this country.

Sigala, Mongier. In *Ptolemy's* time it was fituated at the junction of the river Fulgo with the Ganges, which he derives from the mountains of Uxentus, as that word probably is, from *Echác-dés*, or country of *Echác*, or, as it written in the maps *Etchauk*: there are five or fix places of this name in the mountains of Ramgur. The river Fulgo is the Cacuthis of *Arrian*, fo called from its running through the country of Cicata. According to the fame author, the Andomatis or Dummoody had its fource in the fame mountains.

The

The Ganges formerly ran almoſt in a direct line from Borounka to Monghier, the Fulgo uniting with it near this place; but ſince the river taking a ſoutherly courſe, has made great encroachments upon the northern boundary of Monghier, which ſtretched out a conſiderable diſtance in that direction to a hill of a conical ſhape, which the ſtream has totally waſhed away. This fact is aſcertained on the evidence of ſeveral Hindu ſacred books, particularly of the *Gangamahatmya*; for, at the time this was written, one half of the hill ſtill remained. *Sigala* appears to be corrupted from the Sanſcrit *Sirhala, a plough*. At the birth of CHRISHNA a ſheet of fire like the garments of the gods, appeared above the place called Vindhyavaſni, near Mirzapoor. This appearance is called *Suchéla*, or, in the vulgar dialects, *Sukhela* or *Sukhaila*, from which the Greeks made *Sagala*. This fiery meteor forced its way through the earth, and re-appeared near Monghier, tearing and furrowing up the ground like a plough, or *ſirhala*. The place where it re-appeared is near Monghier, and there is a cave formed by lightning ſacred to *Devi*.

Palibothra. Near the confluence of the old Coofy with the Ganges.

Aſtha-Gura, now *Jetta-gurry*, or *Jetta-coory*, in the inland parts of the country and at the entrance of a famous paſs through the Raj-mehal hills.

Corygazus, near Palibothra, and below it, is derived from the Sanſcrit *Gauri-Goſchi*, or the *wilderneſs of Gauri*, a form of *Devi*. The famous town of Gaur derives its name from it. It is called by *Nonnus* in his *Dionyſiacs* Gagus for Goſcha, or the Goſcha by excellence. He ſays it was ſurrounded with a net-work, and that it was a journey of two days in circumference. This ſort of incloſure is ſtill practiſed in the eaſtern

eastern parts of *India*, to prevent cattle from straying, or being molested by tigers and other ferocious animals. The kings of *Persia* surround their Haram, when encamped, with a net-work; and formerly, the *Persians* when besieging a town, used to form a line of contravallation with nets. The northern part only, towards *Cotwally*, was inhabited at that early period.

Tondota. Tanda-haut (haut is a market). This name, in different MSS. of *Ptolemy*, is variously written, for we read also, *Condota* and *Sondota*: and unfortunately, these three readings are true *Hindu* names of places, for we have *Sanda-haut*, and *Cunda-haut*. However, *Tanda-haut*, or in *Sanscrit*, *Tandá-haut* appears to be *Tandá*, formerly a market place, called also *Tanrah*, *Tarrah*, *Tardah*, and *Tanda*. It is situated near the southern extremity of the high grounds of *Gaur*, on the banks of the old bed of the *Ganges*.

Tamalites. Samal-haut. No longer a *Hát*, but simply *Samal-poore*. *Tamal-hat* is not a *Hindu* name, and, I suppose here, a mistake of the transcriber. It is between *Downapoor* and *Sooty*. (See *Rennell's* map.) The *Ganges* ran formerly close to these three places; and Mr. *Bernier*, in his way from *Benares* to *Cossimbazar*, landed at *Downapoor*.

Elydna is probably *Laudannah*.

Cartinaga, the capital of the *Cocconagæ*, or rather *Cottonaga*, is called now *Cuttunga*, it is near *Soory*; the *Portuguese*, last century, called it *Cartunga* and *Catrunga*.

Cartisina now *Carjuna*, or *Cajwana*, is near *Beudwau*. I shall just observe here, that the three last mentioned towns are erroneously placed, in *Mercator's* map, on the banks of the *Ganges*. *Ptolemy* says no such thing.

The next place on the banks of the *Ganges* is

Oreo-

Oreophanta. Hararpunt or *Haryárpunt* in the vulgar dialects; in Sanscrit it is *Hararparna* from *Hara* and *Arpana*, which implies a piece of ground consecrated to *Hara* or *Mahá-deva*. The word *Arpana* is always pronounced in the spoken dialects, *Arpunt*; thus they say, *Crishnarpunt*. It is now *Rangamatty*. Here was formerly a place of worship, dedicated to *Mahá-deva* or *Hara*, with an extensive tract of ground appropriated to the worship of the God; but the Ganges having destroyed the place of worship, and the holy ground having been resumed during the invasions of the Musulmans, it is entirely neglected. It still exists, however, as a place of worship, only the image of the Phallus is removed to a greater distance from the river.

Aga-nagara, literally the *Nagara*, or town of *Aga*. It is still a famous place of worship in the *dwipa* (island or peninsula) of Aga, called, from that circumstance, *Aga-dwip*: the true name is *Agar-dwip*. A few miles above Aga-nagara, was the city called *Catadupe* by *Arrian* from *Cativa-dwip*, a place famous in the *puránas*. It is now called Catwa.

Ganges-regia, now *Satgauw*, near *Hoogly*. It is a famous place of worship, and was formerly the residence of the kings of the country, and said to have been a city of an immense size, so as to have swallowed up one hundred villages, as the name imports: however, though they write its name *Satgauw*, I believe it should be *Sátgauw*, or the *seven villages*, because there were so many consecrated to the Seven *Rishis*, and each of them had one appropriated to his own use.

Palura, now *Palorah*, or *Pollerah*, four or five miles to the west of *Oolbarya* below *Budge-budge*. A branch of the Ganges ran formerly to the west of it, and after passing by Naga-basan, or Nagam-bapan, fell into the sea towards Ingellee. From Nagam-basan the western branch of the Ganges was

was denominated *Cambuſon Oſtium* by the Greeks. This place is now ridiculoufly called *Nanga-baſſan*, or the naked abode; whereas its true name is *Naga-baſan*, or the abode of ſnakes, with which the country abounds.

Sir WILLIAM JONES fays, " the only difficulty in " deciding the fituation of Palibothra to be the fame " as Patali-putra, to which the names and moſt cir- " cumſtances nearly correſpond, aroſe from hence, " that the latter place extended from the confluence " of the Sone and the Ganges to the fite of Patna, " whereas Palibothra ſtood at the junction of the " Ganges and the Erannoboas; but this difficulty has " been removed, by finding in a claſſical Sanſcrit book, " near two thouſand years old, that Hiranyabahee, or " golden armed, which the Greeks changed into Eran- " noboas, or the river with a lovely murmur, was, in " in fact, another name for the Sona itſelf, though " *Megaſthenes*, from ignorance or inattention, has " named them ſeparately." *Vide Aſiatic Reſearches*, *vol. IV. p.* 11.

But this explanation will not be found ſufficient to ſolve the difficulty, if Hiranyabaha be, as I conceive it is not, the proper name of a river; but an appellative, from an accident common to many rivers.

Patali-putra was certainly the capital, and the refi- dence of the kings of Magadha or ſouth Behar. In the *Mudra Rácſhaſa*, of which I have related the argument, the capital city of *Chandra-Gupta* is called Cuſumapoor throughout the piece, except in one paſſage, where it ſeems to be confounded with Patali- putra, as if they were different names for the ſame place. In the paſſage alluded to, *Rácſhaſa* afks one of his meſſengers, " If he had been at Cuſumapoor?" the man replies, " Yes, I have been at Patali-putra." But

Sumapon

Sumapon, or Phulwaree, to call it by its modern name, was, as the word imports, a pleasure or flower garden, belonging to the kings of Patna, and situate, indeed, about ten miles W.S.W. from that city, but, certainly, never surrounded with fortifications, which *Ananta*, the author of the *Mudra Rácshasa* says, the abode of *Chandra-Gupta* was. It may be offered in excuse, for such blunders as these, that the authors of this, and the other poems and plays I have mentioned, written on the subject of *Chandra-Gupta*, which are certainly modern productions, were foreigners; inhabitants, if not natives, of the Deccan; at least *Ananta* was, for he declares that he lived on the banks of the Godaveri.

But though the foregoing considerations must place the authority of these writers far below the ancients, whom I have cited for the purpose of determining the situation of Palibothra; yet, if we consider the scene of action, in connexion with the incidents of the story, in the *Mudra Rácshasa*, it will afford us clear evidence, that the city of *Chandra-Gupta* could not have stood on the site of Patna; and, a pretty strong presumption also, that its real situation was where I have placed it, that is to say, at no great distance from where Rajé-mehal now stands. For, first, the city was in the neighbourhood of some hills which lay to the southward of it. Their situation is expressly mentioned; and for their contiguity, it may be inferred, though the precise distance be not set down from hence, that king Nanda's going out to hunt, his retiring to the reservoir, among the hills near Patalcandara, to quench his thirst, his murder there, and the subsequent return of the assassin to the city with his master's horse, are all occurrences related, as having happened on the same day. The messengers also who were sent by the young king after the discovery of the murder to fetch the body, executed their commission and returned to the city

the

the fame day. Thefe events are natural and probable, if the city of *Chandra-Gupta* was on the fite of Raje-mehal, or in the neighbourhood of that place, but are utterly incredible, if applied to the fituation of Patna, from which the hills recede at leaft thirty miles in any direction.

Again, *Patalcandara* in Sanfcrit, fignifies *the crater* of a volcano; and in fact, the hills that form the glen, in which is fituated the place now called *Moo-tijarna*, or the *pearl dropping fpring*, agreeing perfectly in the circumftances of diftance and direction from Raje-mehal with the refervoir of Patalcandara, as defcribed in the poem, have very much the appearance of a crater of an old volcano. I cannot fay I have ever been on the very fpot, but I have obferved in the neighbourhood, fubftances that bore undoubted marks of their being volcanic productions: no fuch appearances are to be feen at Patna, nor any trace of there having ever been a volcano there, or near it. *Mr. Davis* has given a curious defcription of Mootijarna, illuftrated with elegant drawings. He informs us there is a tradition, that the refervoir was built by *Sultan Suja*: perhaps he only repaired it.

The confufion *Ananta*, and the other authors above alluded to, have made in the names of Patali-putra and Bali-putra, appears to me not difficult to be accounted for. While the fovereignty of the kings of Maghadha, or fouth Bahar, was exercifed within the limits of their hereditary dominions, the feat of their government was Patali-putra, or Patna: but *Janafandha*, one of the anceftors of *Chandra-Gupta*, having fubdued the whole of Prachi, as we read in the *puránas*, fixed his refidence at Bali-putra, and there he fuffered a moft cruel death from *Crifhna* and *Bala Rama*, who caufed him to be fplit afunder. *Bala* reftored thefon, *Sahadéva*, to his hereditary dominions; and from that time the kings of Maghadha, for twenty-four generations, reigned peaceably at Patna,

Patna, until *Nanda* ascended the throne, who, proving an active and enterprising prince, subdued the whole of Prachi; and having thus recovered the conquests, that had been wrested from his ancestor, probably re-established the seat of empire at Bali-putra; the historians of Alexander positively assert, that he did. Thus while the kings of Palibothra, as *Diodorus* tells us, sunk into oblivion, through their sloth and inactivity, (a reproach which seems warranted by the utter silence observed of the posterity of *Bala Rama* in the *Puránas*, not even their names being mentioned;) the princes of Patali-putra, by a contrary conduct, acquired a reputation that spread over all India: it was, therefore, natural for foreign authors, (for such at least, *Ananta* was.) especially in compositions of the dramatic kind, where the effect is oftentimes best produced by a neglect of historical precision, of two titles, to which their hero had an equal right to distinguish him by the most illustrious. The author of *Sacontala* has committed as great a mistake, in making Hastinapoor the residence of *Dushmánta*, which was not then in existence, having been built by *Hasti*, the fifth in descent from *Dushmánta*; before his time there was, indeed, a place of worship on the same spot, but no town. The same author has fallen into another error, in assigning a situation of this city not far from the river Malini, (he should rather have said the *rivulet* that takes its name from a village now called *Malyari*, to the westward of Lahore: it is joined by a new channel to the Ravy;) but this is a mistake; Hastinapoor lies on the banks of the old channel of the Ganges. The descendants of *Peru* resided at Sangala, whose extensive ruins are to be seen about fifty miles to the westward of Lahore, in a part of the country uninhabited. I will take occasion to observe here, that *Arrian* has confounded *Sangala* with *Salgada*, or *Salgana*, or the mistake has been made by his copyists. *Frontinus* and *Polyænus* have preserved the true name of this place, now called *Calanore*; and close to it is a deserted village, to this day called

called *Salghéda*; its situation answers exactly to the description given of it by *Alexander's* historians. The kings of Sangala are known in the Persian history by the name of Schangal, one of them assisted *Afrasiab* against the famous *Caicosru*; but to return from this digression to Patali putra.

The true name of this famous place is, *Patali-pura*; which means the town of *Patali*, a form of *Devi* worshipped there. It was the residence of an adopted son of the goddess *Patali*, hence called *Patali-putra*, or the son of *Patali*. Patali-putra and Bali-putra are absolutely inadmissable, as Sanscrit names of towns and places; they are used in that sense, only in the spoken dialects; and this, of itself, is a proof, that the poems in question are modern productions. Patali-pura, or the town of Patali, was called simply Patali, or corruptly Pattiali, on the invasion of the Musulmans: it is mentioned under that name in Mr. *Dow's* translation of *Ferishta's* history. It is, I believe, the *Patali* of *Pliny*. From a passage in this author compared with others from *Ptolemy*, *Marcianus*, *Heracleota*, and *Arrian* in his *Periplus*, we learn that the merchants, who carried on the trade from the Gangetic Gulph, or Bay of Bengal, to Perimula, or Malacca, and to Bengal, took their departure from some place of rendezvous in the neighbourhood of Point Godavery, near the mouth of the Ganga Godavery. The ships used in this navigation, of a larger construction than common, were called by the Greek and Arabian sailors, *colandrophonta*, or in the Hindustani dialect, *coilan-di-pota*, *coilan boats or ships*: for *pota* in Sanscrit, signifies a boat or a ship; and *di* or *da*, in the western parts of India, is either an adjective form, or the mark of the genitive case. *Pliny* has preserved to us the track of the merchants who traded to Bengal from Point Godavery.

They went to Cape Colinga, now Palmira; thence to Dandagula, now Tentu-gully, almost opposite to Fultati*; thence to Tropina, or Triveni and Trebeni, called Tripina by the Portuguese, in the last century; and, lastly, to Patale, called Patali, Patiali as late as the twelfth century, and now Patna. *Pliny*, who mistook this Patale for another town of the same name, situate at the summit of the Delta of the Indus, where a form of *Devi*, under the appellation of *Patali* is equally worshipped to this day, candidly acknowledges, that he could by no means reconcile the various accounts he had seen about Patale, and the other places mentioned before.

The account transmitted to us of *Chandra-Gupta*, by the historians of *Alexander*, agrees remarkably well with the abstract I have given in this paper of the *Mudra Rácshasa*. By *Athenæus*, he is called *Sandracoptos*, by the others *Sandracottos*, and sometimes *Androcottos*. He was also called *Chandra* simply; and, accordingly, *Diodorus Siculus* calls him *Xandrames* from *Chandra*, or *Chandram* in the accusative case; for in the western parts of India, the spoken dialects from the Sanscrit do always affect that case. According to *Plutarch*, in his life of *Alexander*, *Chandra-Gupta* had been in that prince's camp, and had been heard to say afterwards, that *Alexander* would have found no difficulty in the conquest of Práchi, or the country of the Prasians had he attempted it, as the king was despised, and hated too, on account of his cruelty.

In the *Mudra Rácshasa* it is said, that king *Nanda*, after a severe fit of illness, fell into a state of imbecillity, which betrayed itself in his discourse

---

* This is the only place in this essay not to be found in *Rennell's* Atlas.

and

and actions; and that his wicked minister, *Sacatara*, ruled with despotic sway in his name. *Diodorus Siculus* and *Curtius* relate, that *Chandram* was of a low tribe, his father being a barber. That he, and his father *Nanda* too, were of a low tribe, is declared in the *Vishnu-purána* and in the *Bhágavat Chandram*, as well as his brothers, was called *Maurya* from his mother *Mura*; and as that word* in Sanscrit signifies a barber, it furnished occasion to his enemies to asperse him as the spurious offspring of one. The Greek historians say, the king of the Prasū was assassinated by his wife's paramour, the mother of *Chandra*; and that the murderer got possession of the sovereign authority, under the specious title of regent and guardian to his mother's children, but with a view to destroy them. The *puránas* and other Hindu books, agree in the same facts, except as to the amours of *Sacatara* with *Mura*, the mother of *Chandra-Gupta*, on which head they are silent. *Diodorus* and *Curtius* are mistaken in saying, that *Chandram* reigned over the Prasū, at the time of *Alexander's* invasion: he was contemporary with *Seleucus Nicator*.

I suspect *Chandra-Gupta* kept his faith with the Greeks or Yavans no better than he had done with his ally, the king of Nepal; and this may be the motive for *Seleucus* crossing the Indus at the head of a numerous army; but finding *Sandro-coptos* prepared, he thought it expedient to conclude a treaty with him, by which he yielded up the conquests he had made; and, to cement the alliance, gave him one of his daughters in marriage †. *Chandra-Gupta* appears to have agreed on his part to furnish

---

* See the *Jutivivcca*, where it is said, the offspring of a barber, begot by stealth, of a female of the Sudra tribe, is called *Maurya*: the offspring of a barber and a slave woman is called *Maurya*.

† *Strabo*, B. 15, p. 724.

Seleucus annually with fifty elephants; for we read of *Antiochus* the Great going to India, to renew the alliance with king *Sophagasenus*, and of his receiving fifty elephants from him. *Sophagasenus*, I conceive, to be a corruption of *Shivaca-Sèna*, the grandson of *Chandra-Gupta*. In the *puránas* this grandson is called *Aśécavard-dhana* or *full of mercy*, a word of nearly the same import as *Aśéca-séna* or *Shivaca-séna*; the latter signifying *he whose armies are merciful do not ravage and plunder the country*.

The son of *Chandra-Gupta* is called *Allitrochates* and *Amitrocates* by the Greek historian. *Seleucus* sent an ambassador to him; and after his death the same good intelligence was maintained by *Antiochus* the son or the grandson of *Seleucus*. This son of *Chandra-Gupta* is called *Varisára* in the *puránas*; according to *Parasara*, his name was *Dasaratha*; but neither the one nor the other bear any affinity to *Amitrocates*: this name appears, however, to be derived from the Sanscrit *Mitra-Gupta*, which signifies *saved by Mitra* or *the Sun*, and therefore probably was only a surname.

It may be objected to the foregoing account, the improbability of a Hindu marrying the daughter of a Yavana, or, indeed, of any foreigner. On this difficulty I consulted the Pundits of Benares, and they all gave me the same answer; namely, that in the time of *Chandra-Gupta* the Yavanas were much respected, and were even considered as a sort of Hindus though they afterwards brought upon themselves the hatred of that nation by their cruelty, avarice, rapacity, and treachery in every transaction while they ruled over the western parts of India; but that at any rate the objection did not apply to the case, as *Chandra-Gupta* himself was a *Sudra*, that is to say, of the lowest class. In the

Vishnu-

Viſhnu-purána, and in the *Bhagawat*, it is recorded, that eight Grecian kings reigned over part of India. They are better known to us by the title of the Grecian kings of Bactriana. *Arrian* in his *Periplus*, enumerating the exports from Europe to India, ſets down as one article beautiful virgins, who were generally ſent to the market of Baroche. The Hindus acknowledged that, formerly, they were not ſo ſtrict as they are at this day; and this appears from their books to have been the caſe. *Strabo* does not poſitively ſay that *Chandra-Gupta* married a daughter of *Seleucus*, but that *Seleucus* cemented the alliance he had made with him by connubial affinity, from which expreſſion it might equally be inferred that *Seleucus* married a daughter of *Chandra-Gupta*; but this is not ſo likely as the other; and it is probable the daughter of *Seleucus* was an illegitimate child, born in Perſia after *Alexander's* conqueſt of that country.

Before I conclude, it is incumbent on me to account for the extraordinary difference between the line of the *Surya Varſas* or children of the ſun, from *Ichſwacu* to *Daſaratha-Rama*, as exhibited in the ſecond volume of the *Aſiatick Reſearches*, from the *Viſhnu-purana* and the *Bhagawat*, and that ſet down in the Table I have given with this Eſſay. The line of the *Surya Varſas*, from the *Bhagawat* being abſolutely irreconcileable with the anceſtry of *Arjuna* and *Chriſhna*, I had at firſt rejected it, but, after a long ſearch, I found it in the *Ramayen*, ſuch as I have repreſented it in the table, where it perfectly agrees with the other genealogies. *Daſaratha-Rama* was contemporary with *Paraſu Rama*, who was, however the eldeſt; and as the *Ramayen* is the hiſtory of *Daſaratha-Rama*, we may reaſonably ſuppoſe, his anceſtry was carefully ſet down and not wantonly abridged. I ſhall now conclude this Eſſay with the following remarks:

I. It has been asserted in the second volume of the *Asiatick Researches*, that *Paraſara* lived about 1180 years before *Chriſt*, in conſequence of an obſervation of the places of the colures. But Mr. *Davis*, having conſidered this ſubject with the minuteſt attention, authorizes me to ſay, that this obſervation muſt have been made 1391 years before the Chriſtian æra. This is alſo confirmed by a paſſage from the *Paraſara Sanhita* in which it is declared, that the *Udaya* or *heliacal* riſing of *canopus*, (when at the diſtance of thirteen degrees from the ſun, according to the Hindu aſtronomers,) happened in the time of *Paraſara*, on the 10th of *Cartica*; the difference now amounts to twenty-three days. Having communicated this paſſage to Mr. *Davis*, he informed me, that it coincided with the obſervation of the places of the colures in the time of *Paraſara*.

Another ſynchroniſm ſtill more intereſting, is that of the flood of *Deucalion*, which, according to the beſt chronologers, happened 1390 years before *Chriſt*. *Deucalion* is derived from *Déo-Calyún* or *Déo Caljún*: the true Sanſcrit name is *Déva-Cála-Yavana*. The word *Cála-Yavana* is always pronounced in converſation, and in the vulgar dialects *Cá-lyún* or *Cálijún*: literally, it ſignifies the devouring *Yavana*. He is repreſented in the *puránas*, as a moſt powerful prince, who lived in the weſtern parts of India, and generally reſided in the country of *Camboja*, now *Gazni*, the ancient name of which, is *Sahni* or *Saſna*. It is true, they never beſtow upon him the title of *Déva*; on the contrary, they call him an incarnate *demon*: becauſe he preſumed to oppoſe *Criſhna*; and was very near defeating his ambitious projects; indeed *Criſhna* was nearly overcome and ſubdued, after ſeventeen bloody battles; and, according to the expreſs words of the *puránas*, he was forced to have recourſe to treachery: by which means *Cályún* was totally defeated in the eighteenth engagement. That his followers and deſcendants ſhould beſtow on him the title of *Déva*, or *Deo*,

is

is very probable; and the numerous tribes of Hindus, who, to this day, call *Crĭſhna,* an impious wretch, a merciless tyrant, an implacable and moſt rancorous enemy. In ſhort, theſe Hindus, who conſider *Crĭſhna* as an incarnate demon, now expiating his crimes in the fiery dungeons of the loweſt hell, conſider *Cályûn* in a very different light, and, certainly, would have no objection to his being called *Deo-Cályûn.* Be it as it may, *Deucalion* was conſidered as a *De'va* or *Deity* in the weſt, and had altars erected to his honour.

The Greek mythologiſts are not agreed about him, nor the country, in which the flood, that goes by his name, happened: ſome make him a Syrian; others ſay, that his flood happened in the countries, either round mount Etna, or mount Athos; the common opinion is, that it happened in the country adjacent to Parnaſus; whilſt others ſeem to intimate, that he was a native of India, when they aſſert that he was the ſon of *Prometheus,* who lived near Cabul, and whoſe cave was viſited by *Alexander,* and his Macedonians. It is called in the *puránas Garuda-ſt'han,* or the place of the *Eagle,* and is ſituated near the place called *Shibi,* in Major *Rennell's* map of the weſtern parts of India; indeed, *Pramathaſi* is better known in Sudia by the appellation of *Sheba* *. *Deo-Cályûn,* who lived at Gazni, was obliged on the arrival of *Crĭſhna,* to fly to the adjacent mountains, according to the *puránas;* and the name of theſe mountains was formerly *Parnaſa,* from which the Greeks made *Parnaſus;* they are ſituated between Gazni and Peſhower. *Crĭſhna,* after the defeat of *Cályûn,* deſolated his country with fire and ſword. This is called in Sanſcrit *Pralaya;* and may be effected by water, fire, famine, peſtilence, and war: but in the vulgar dialects, the word *Pralaya,* ſignifies only a

---

* *Bamian* (in Sanſcrit *Vamiyan*) and Shibr lay to the N.W. of Cabul.

flood or inundation. The legends relating to *Deo-Cálydn*, *Prometheus* and his *cave*, will appear in the next differtation I fhall have the honour to lay before the Society.

II. *Megafthenes* was a native of Perfia, and enjoyed the confidence of *Sibyrtius* *, governor of Arachofia, (now the country of Candahar and Gazni,) on the part of *Seleucus*. *Sibyrtius* fent him frequently on the embaffies to *Sandrocuptos*. When *Seleucus* invaded India, *Megafthenes* enjoyed alfo the confidence of that monarch, who fent him, in the character of ambaffador, to the court of the king of Prachi. We may fafely conclude, that *Megafthenes* was a man of no ordinary abilities, and as he fpent the greateft part of his life in India, either at Candahar or in the more interior parts of it; and, as from his public character, he muft have been daily converfing with the moft diftinguifhed perfons in India, I conceive, that if the Hindus, of that day, had laid claim to fo high an antiquity, as thofe of the prefent, he certainly would have been acquainted with their pretenfions, as well as with thofe of the Egyptians and Chaldæans; but, on the contrary, he was aftonifhed to find a fingular conformity between the Hebrews and them in the notions about the beginning of things, that is to fay, of ancient hiftory. At the fame time, I believe, that the Hindus, at that early period, and, perhaps, long before, had contrived various aftronomical periods and cycles, though they had not then thought of framing a civil hiftory, adapted to them. Aftrology may have led them to fuppofe fo important and momentous an event as the creation muft have been connected with particular conjunctions of the heavenly bodies; nor have the learned in Europe been entirely free from fuch notions. Having once laid down this pofition,

* *Arrian*, B. 5. p. 203.

they did not know where to stop; but the whole was conducted in a most clumsy manner, and their new chronology abounds with the most grofs abfurdities; of this, they themfelves are confcious, for, though willing to give me general ideas of their chronology, they abfolutely forfook me, when they perceived my drift in a ftricter inveftigation of the fubject.

The lofs of *Megafthenes*' works is much to be lamented. From the few fcattered fragments, preferved by the ancients, we learn that the hiftory of the Hindus did not go back above 5042 years. The MSS. differ; in fome we read 6042 years; in others 5042 and three months, to the invafion of India by *Alexander*. *Megafthenes* certainly made very particular enquiries, fince he noticed even the months. Which is the true reading, I cannot pretend to determine; however, I incline to believe, it is 5042, becaufe it agrees beft with the number of years affigned by *Albumazar*, as cited by Mr. *Bailly*, from the creation to the flood. This famous aftronomer, whom I mentioned before, had derived his ideas about the time of the creation and of the flood, from the learned Hindus he had confulted; and he affigns 2226 years, between what the Hindus call the laft renovation of the world, and the flood. This account from *Megafthenes* and *Albumazar*, agrees remarkably well with the computation of the *Septuagint*. I have adopted that of the *Samaritan Pentateuch*, as more conformable to fuch particulars as I have found in the *puránas*; I muft confefs, however, that fome particular circumftances, if admitted, feem to agree beft with the computation of the *Septuagint*: befides, it is very probable, that the Hindus, as well as ourfelves, had various computations of the times we are fpeaking of.

Megafthenes informs us alfo, that the Hindus had a lift of kings, from *Dionyfius* to *Sandrocuptos*, to the number of 153. Perhaps, this is not to be underftood stood of successions in a direct line: if so, it agrees well enough with the present list of the descendants of *Nausha*, or *Deo-Naush*. This is what they call the genealogies simply, or the great genealogy, and which they consider as the basis of their history. They reckon these successions in this manner: from *Nausha* to *Crishna*, and collaterally from *Naush* to *Parichshita*; and afterwards from *Jarasandha*, who was contemporary with *Crishna*. Accordingly the number of kings amounts to more than 153: but, as I wanted to give the full extent of the Hindu chronology, I have introduced eight or nine kings, which, in the opinion of several learned men, should be omitted, particularly six, among the ancestry of *Crishna*.

Megasthenes, according to *Pliny* and *Arrian*, seems to say, that 5042 years are to be reckoned between *Dionysius*, or *Deo-Nausha*, and *Alexander*, and that 153 kings reigned during that period: but, I believe, it is a mistake of *Pliny* and *Arrian*; for 153 reigns, or even generations, could never give so many years.

Megasthenes reckons also fifteen generations between *Dionysius* and *Hercules*, by whom we are to understand, *Crishna* and his brother *Bala-Rama*. To render this intelligible, we must consider *Naush* in two different points of view: *Naush* was at first a mere mortal, but on mount Meru he became a *Déva* or *God*, hence called *Déva-Naush* or *Deo-Naush*, in the vulgar dialects. This happened about fifteen generations before *Crishna*. It appears that like the spiritual rulers of Tartary and Tibet (which countries include the holy mountains of Meru), *Deo-Naush* did not, properly speaking, die, but his soul shifted its habitation, and got into a new body whenever the old one was worn out, either through age or sickness. The names of three of the successors of *Nausha* have been preserved by *Arrian*; they are *Spartembas*, *Budyas*, and *Cradevas*. The

first

firſt ſeems derived from the Sanſcrit *Prachinvan*, generally pronounced *Prachinban*, from which the Greeks made *Spartemban* in the accuſative caſe; the two others are undubitably Sanſcrit, though much diſtorted, but I ſuſpect them to be titles, rather than proper names.

III. This would be a proper place to mention the poſterity of *Noah* or *Satyavrata*, under the names of *Sharma* or *Shama* (for both are uſed,) *Charma* and *Jyapti*. They are mentioned in five or ſix *puránas*, but no farther particulars concerning them are related, beſides what is found in a former eſſay on Egypt. In the liſt of the thouſand names of *Viſhnu*, a ſort of Litany, which Bráhmens are obliged to repeat on certain days, *Viſhnu* is called *Sharma*, becauſe, according to the learned, *Sharma* or *Shama*, was an incarnation of that deity. In a liſt of the thouſand names of *Siva*, as extracted from the *Padma-purána*, the 371ſt name is *Shama-Jaya*, which is in the fourth caſe, anſwering to our dative, the word *praiſe* being underſtood: *Praiſe* to *Sharmaja*, or *to him who was incarnated in the houſe of Sharma*.

The 998th name is *Sharma-putradáya*, in the fourth caſe alſo, *praiſe to him who gave offspring to Sharma*. My learned friends here inform me, that it is declared in ſome of the *puránas*, that *Sharma*, having no children, applied to *Siva*, and made *Tapaſya*, to his honour. *Iſwara* was ſo pleaſed, that he granted his requeſt and condeſcended to be incarnated in the womb of *Sharma*'s wife, and was born a ſon of *Sharma*, under the name of *Baleswara*, or *Iſwara* the infant. *Baleswara*, or ſimply *Iſwara*, we mentioned in a former eſſay on *Semiramis*; and he is obviouſly the *Aſſur* of Scripture.

In another list of the thousand names of SIVA (for there are five or six of them extracted from so many *puránas*) we read, as one of his names, BALESA ISA or ISWA'RA the *infant*. In the same list SIVA is said to be VARAHI-PALACA, or he who *fostered* and cherished VARAHI, the consort of VISHNU, who was incarnated in the character of SHARMA. From the above passages the learned here believe that SIVA, in a human shape, was legally appointed to raise seed to SHARMA during an illness thought incurable. In this sense JAPHET certainly dwelt in the tents of SHEM. My chief *pandit* has repeatedly, and most positively, assured me, that the posterity of SHARMA to the tenth or twelfth generation, is mentioned in some of the *puránas*. His search after it has hitherto proved fruitless, but it is true, that we have been able to procure only a few sections of some of the more scarce and valuable *puránas*. The field is immense, and the powers of a single individual too limited.

V. The ancient statues of the gods having been destroyed by the Mussulmans, except a few which were concealed during the various persecutions of these unmerciful zealots, others have been erected occasionally, but they are generally represented in a modern dress. The statue of *Bala-Rama* at Mutra has very little resemblance to the Theban *Hercules*, and, of course, does not answer exactly to the description of *Megasthenes*. There is, however, a very ancient statue of *Bala-Rama* at a place called *Baladeva*, or *Baldeo* in the vulgar dialects, which answers minutely to his description. It was visited some years ago by the late Lieutenant STEWART, and I shall describe it in his own words: "*Bala-Rama* or *Bala-deva* is represented *there* with a ploughshare in his left hand, with which he hooked his enemies, and in his right hand a thick cudgel, with which he cleft their sculls; his shoulders are covered with the skin of a tyger. The village of Baldeo is thirteen miles E. by S. from Muttra."

Here I shall obferve, that the ploughfhare is always reprefented very fmall fometimes omitted; and that it looks exactly like a harpoon, with a ftrong hook, or a *gaff*, as it is ufually called by fifhermen. My *pandits* inform me alfo, that *Bala-Rama* is fometimes reprefented with his fhoulders covered with the fkin of a lion.

XIX.

REMARKS ON THE NAMES OF THE *CABIRIAN DEITIES,*

AND ON SOME WORDS USED IN THE MYSTERIES OF ELEUSIS.

BY CAPTAIN FRANCIS WILFORD.

IN the *Adhuta-cosa* we find the following legends, which have an obvious relation to the Deities worshipped in the mysteries of *Samothrace*.

In *Patala* (or the infernal regions) resides the sovereign queen of the *Nagas* (large snakes or dragons:) she is beautiful, and her name is Asyoruca. There, in a cave, she performed *Tapasya* with such rigorous austerity, that fire sprang from her body, and formed numerous *agni-tiraths* (places of sacred fire) in *Patala*. These fires, forcing their way through the earth, waters, and mountains, formed various openings or mouths, called from thence the *flaming mouths*, or *juála-muc'hi*. By Samudr (Oceanus) a daughter was born unto her called Ramá-de'ví. She is most beautiful; she is Lacshmi; and her name is A'syo'tcersha' or A'syo'tcrishta. Like a jewel she remains concealed in the ocean.

The Dharma-Raja, or King of Justice, has two countenances; one is mild and full of benevolence; those alone who abound with virtue, see it. He holds a court of justice, where are many assistants, among whom are many just and pious kings: Chitragupta acts as chief secretary. These holy men determine what is *dharma* and *adharma*, just and unjust. His (*Dharma rajas*) servant is called CARMALA: he brings the righteous on celestial cars, which go of themselves, whenever holy men are to be brought in, according to the directions of the DHARMA-RAJA, who is the sovereign of the Pitris. This is called his *divine countenance*, and the righteous alone do see it. His other *countenance* or *form* is called YAMA; this the wicked alone can see. It has large teeth, and a monstrous body. Yama is the lord of Patala; there he orders some to be beaten, some to be cut to pieces, some to be devoured by monsters, &c. His servant is called CASHMALA, who, with ropes round their necks, drags the wicked over rugged paths, and throws them headlong into hell. He is unmerciful, and *hard* is his heart: every body trembles at the sight of him. According to MNASEAS, as cited by the scholiast of *Appollonius Rhodius*, the names of the Cabirian Gods were AXIEROS, or CERES, or the EARTH; AXIOCERSA or PROSERPINE; AXIOCERSOS or PLUTO; to whom they add a fourth called CASMILLUS, the same with the infernal MERCURY.

AXIEROS is obviously derived from *Asyoruca*, or rather from *Asyoru*, or *Asyorus*; for such is the primitive form; which signifies literally, *she whose face is most beautiful*.

AXIOCERSA is derived from *Asyotcersa*, a word of the same import with the former, and which was the sacred name of PROSERPINE. This is obviously derived from the Sanscrit *Prasarparni*, or *she who is surrounded by large snakes and dragons*. *Nonnus* represents her as surrounded by two enormous snakes who constantly watched over her. She was ravished by *Jupiter* in the shape of an enormous dragon. She was generally supposed to be his daughter; but the Arcadians, according to *Pausanias*, insisted that she was the daughter of *Ceres* and *Neptune*; with whom the ancient mythologists often confound *Oceanus*.

As

As she is declared, in the sacred books of the Hindus, to be the same with *Lacshmi*, her consort of course is *Vishnu*, who rules, according to the *puránas*, in the west, and also during the greatest part of the night. In this sense *Vishnu* is the *Dis* of the western mythologists, the *black Jupiter* of *Statius* ; for *Vishnu* is represented of a *black*, or *dark azure* complexion: *Pluto* or *Yama* is but a form of *Vishnu*. The titles of *Dis* or *Ades* appear to me to be derived from *A'di* or *A'din*, one of the names of *Vishnu*. When Cicero says *, *Terrena autem vis omnes atque natura,* Diti *patri dedicata est* ; that is to say, That nature, and the powers or energy of the earth, are under the direction of *Dis*. This has no relation to the judge of departed souls, but solely belongs to *Vishnu*.

Axiocersos, or in Sanscrit *A's'yotcersa*, or *A's'yotcersas*, was *Pluto* or *Dis*, and was meant for *Vishnu*. *Vishnu* is always represented as extremely beautiful; but I never found *A's'yotcersa* among any of his titles : he is sometimes called *Atcersa*, a word of the same import.

Cashmala' or Cashmala's is obviously the *Casmilus* of the western mythologists. The appellation of *Cabiri*, as a title of these deities is unknown to the Hindus; and, I believe, by the Cabirian gods, we are to understand the gods worshipped by a nation, a tribe or a society of men called *Cabires*. The *Cuveras* or *Cuberas*, as it is generally pronounced are a tribe of inferior deities, possessed of immense riches, and who are acquainted with all places under, or above ground, abounding with precious metals and gems. Their history in the *puránas*, begins with the first *Menu*, and no mention is made in it of floods, at least my learned friends tell me so. They are represented with *yellow eyes*,

* *Cic. De Natura Deorum.*

like the *Pingacſhas* (of whom we ſpoke in a former eſſay on Egypt,) and perhaps may be the ſame people; certain it is the *Pingacſhas* worſhipped the Cabirian gods. *Diodorus Siculus* ſays, that the invention of fire, and the working of mines was attributed to them: and we find a *Cabirus* repreſented with a hammer in his hand.

At the concluſion of the myſteries of ELEUSIS, the congregation was diſmiſſed in theſe words: Κογξ, Ὄμ, Παξ; *Conx, Om, Pax*. Theſe myſterious words have been conſidered hitherto as inexplicable; but they are pure Sanſcrit, and uſed to this day by Bráhmens at the concluſion of religious rites. They are thus written in the language of the Gods, as the Hindus call the language of their ſacred books, *Canſcha, Om, Pacſha.*

CANSCHA ſignifies the object of our moſt ardent wiſhes.

OM is the famous monoſyllable uſed both at the beginning and concluſion of a prayer, or any religious rite, like *Amen*.

PACSHA exactly anſwers to the obſolete Latin word *Vix*: it ſignifies change, courſe, ſtead, place, turn of work, duty, fortune. It is uſed particularly after pouring water in honour of the Gods and *Pitris*. It appears alſo from HESYCHIUS,

I. That theſe words were pronounced aloud at the concluſion of every momentous tranſaction, religious or civil.

II. That when Judges, after hearing a cauſe gave their ſuffrages, by dropping of pebbles of different colours into a box, the noiſe, made by each pebble was

was called by one of these three words (if not by all three) but more probably, by the word *Pacsha*; as the *turn*, or *pacsha* of the voting judge, was over.

When lawyers pleaded in a court of justice, they were allowed to speak two or three hours, according to the importance of the cause; and for this purpose, there was a *Clepsydras*, or *water clock* ready, which, making a certain noise at the end of the expired *pacsha*, *vix*, or *turn*, this noise was called *Pacsha*, &c.

The word *Pacsha* is pronounced *Vacsh* and *vact* in the vulgar dialects, and from it the obsolete Latin word *vix* is obviously derived. The *Greek* language has certainly borrowed largely from the Sanscrit; but it always affects the spoken dialects of India; the language of the Latins in particular does, which is acknowledged to have been an ancient dialect of the Greek.

XX.

ACCOUNT OF THE
PAGODA AT PERWUTTUM.

EXTRACT OF A JOURNAL BY CAPTAIN COLIN
MACKENZIE,

COMMUNICATED BY MAJOR KIRKPATRICK.

THE Pagoda of Perwuttum, hitherto unknown to Europeans, is fituated near the fouth bank of the Kiftna, in a wild tract of country, almoft uninhabited, except by the Chinfuars, about

Horizontal distance { 65 miles W. of Inawada in Guntoor.
63 miles E. N. E. of Canoul.
And fuppofed to be 103 miles S. and ¼ E. of Hydrabad.

March 14th, 1794.—Having fent notice to the manager of the revenues (the principal officers of the circar) that I was defirous of feeing the Pagoda, provided there was no objection, I was informed at noon, that I might go in. The manager did not appear very defirous of paying any of the common civilities, but the Bráhmens crowded round to conduct me into the place. On entering the fouth gate, we defcended by fteps, and through a fmall door, to the inner court, where the temples are: in the centre was the Pagoda of *Mallecarjee,* the principal deity worshipped here. It is fquare, and the roof is terminated by a pyramid of fteps; the whole walls and roof on the outfide, are covered with brafs plates, which have been gilt, but the gilding is now worn off. Thefe plates are joined together by fmall bars and fockets, fo that the whole may be taken off without damage the fpire or pyramid is not above thirty feet from the ground; the plates are plain,

plain excepting a few embossed figures of women, some small ornaments, and on the friezes of the doors, the pannels of which are also plated. A statue with three legs is placed over each of the three entries; to support this uncommon figure, a post is carried up, which, at first sight, gives it the appearance of being empaled. On the west side of the pagoda inscriptions are engraved very neatly on three sheets of brass plates. Opposite to the south side, on a neat basement and pedestal ornamented with brazen figures of cows, is a slender pillar about twenty-four or thirty feet high, entirely composed of brass plates; it is bent; and from the joints, which plainly appear in the plating, it seems to be laid on a bamboo enclosed within. The four sides of the pedestal are covered with inscriptions, two in Gentoo or Tellinga, one in Grindam, and one in Naggerim: the first seven lines of the latter in large well defined characters, I copied; five smaller lines followed, which I could not copy so exactly, the character being small, and the pedestal highly elevated. Some characters are also engraved on the fillet and ornamental parts of the moulding. From hence I was conducted to the smaller and more ancient temple of MALLECARJEE, where he is adored in the figure of a rude stone, which I could just distinguish through the dark vista of the front building on pillars. Behind this building an immense fig tree covers with its shade the devotees and attendants, who repose on seats placed round its trunk and carpeted. Among these was one *Byraggy* who had devoted himself to a perpetual residence here; his sole subsistence was the milk of a cow, which I saw him driving before him: an orange coloured rag was tied round his loins and his naked body was besmeared with ashes.

Some of the Bráhmens came in the evening, with a copy of the inscriptions on two of the brass plates: they professed not to know exactly, the meaning

meaning of them, being, they said, *Sanscrittum Jigum*. The same ignorance of the language of their religious books, seems to prevail through all these countries. The Bráhmens in attendance here, are relieved at stated times, from Autcowr and other places, as this place is unwholesome and the water bad. One of them said, he had books at Autcowr, explanatory of the history of the Pagoda, and of the figures carved on the walls. Though they had never heard that any European had been here before, they did not express any surprise at this visit. Some of them applied for medical aid, but no fever prevailed among them at that time.

During the troubles of *Sevi-row*, the Chinsuars occupied the Pagoda, who stripped it of some ornaments and damaged it. Since *Sevi-row* had submitted the revenues derived from the resort of pilgrims, are collected for the *canoul circar* by a manager or aumildar, who resides within the enclosure, as do the sebundies and peons, stationed here to protect the pilgrims, who come from all parts at certain stated festivals.

The red colour, that predominates in the rock of this country, (which is a granite,) is very remarkable. The superstratum, which, in many places, forms the naked superfices of the soil, is of a black colour, and from the smooth shining surface it frequently exhibits, appears to have been formerly in a state of fusion, but goes to no great depth; the next stratum is composed of grains of a reddish colour, mixed with others of a white shining quartz, in greater proportion and of a larger size, so as to give the stone, when quarried, a greyish colour, which is more observable after it has been cut or chiseled. Iron is found in several parts of this mountainous tract, and so are diamonds, but the labour is so great, and the chance of meeting with the veins so very uncertain, that

that the digging for them has been long discontinued; the following places were mentioned as producing them, viz.

1. *Saringamutta*, near *Jatta Reow*, on the other side the *Kistna*, where the ferry and road to *Amirabad* crosses. N. B. A Pagoda here.

2. *Routa Pungala*, two parous distant, near *Pateloh Gunga*.

3. *Gossah Reow*, twelve parous down the river. N. B. a ferry or ford there. After the heavy rains, when the rivers fall, they are found sometimes in the beds. This place is near the ruins of *Chundra-goomply-putnam*, formerly a great town on its north bank, and now belonging to *Amraritty*.

The weather being warm, I was desirous of getting over as much of this bad road as I could before noon: my tents and baggage had been sent off at four, A. M. and I only remained at the Pagoda, with the intention of making some remarks on the sculptures of its wall as soon as day light appeared. But the Bráhmens with the *Rajpoot amuldar* (who had hitherto shewn a shiness that I had not experienced in any other parts of the journey,) came to request, that, as I was the first European, who had ever came so far, to visit *Mallecarjee* and had been prevented from seeing the object of their worship, by yesterday not being a lucky day, I would remain with them that day, assuring me, that the doors would be opened at ten o'clock. I agreed to wait till that hour, being particularly desirous of seeing, by what means, the light was reflected into the temple, which the unskilfulness of my interpreter could not explain intelligibly to my comprehension. Notice being at last given, at about half past eight, that the sun was high enough, the doors on the east side the gilt Pagoda were thrown open, and a mirror, or reflecting speculum,

speculum, was brought from the *Rajpoot amuldar's* house. It was round, about two feet in diameter, and fixed to a brass handle, ornamented with figures of cows; the polished side was convex, but so foul that it could not reflect the sun beams; another was therefore brought, rather smaller and concave, surrounded by a narrow rim and without a handle. Directly opposite to the gate of the Pagoda is a stone building, raised on pillars, enclosing a well, and ending in a point; and, being at the distance of twelve or fourteen feet, darkens the gateway by its shadow, until the sun rises above it: this, no doubt, has been contrived on purpose to raise the expectation of the people, and by rendering the sight of the idol more rare, to favour the imposition of the Bráhmens. The moment being come, I was permitted to stand on the steps in front of the threshold without, (having put off my shoes, to please the directors of the ceremony, though it would not have been insisted on,) while a crowd surrounded me, impatient to obtain a glimpse of the aweful figure within. A boy, being placed near the door-way, waved and played the concave mirror, in such a manner, as to throw gleams of light into the Pagoda, in the deepest recess whereof was discovered, by means of these coruscations, a small, oblong, roundish white stone, with dark rings, fixed in a silver case. I was permitted to go no farther, but my curiosity was now sufficiently satisfied. It appears, that this god *Mallicarjee* is no other than the *Lingam*, to which such reverence is paid by certain casts of the Gentoos; and the reason why he is here represented by stones unwrought, may be understood from the Bráhmens' account of the origin of this place of worship. My interpreter had been admitted the day before into the *sanctum sanctorum*, and allowed to touch the stone, which he says is smooth, and shining, and that the dark rings or streaks are painted on it; probably it is an agate, or some other stone of a silicious kind, found near some parts of the Kishna, and of an uncommon size. The speculums were of a whitish metal, probably a mixture of tin and brass.

These

These arts, designed to impose on the credulity of the ignorant superstitious crowd, seem to have been cultivated successfully here, and the difficulties attending the journey, with the wild gloomy appearance of the country, no doubt, add to the aweful impression made on their minds.

The Bráhmens having given me the following account of the origin of the Pagoda, I insert it here, as it may lead to farther enquiry, and by a comparison with other accounts, however disguised by fable or art, some light may be thrown on the history, and manners of a people so very interesting.

" At Chundra-gumpty-patnum, twelve parous down
" the river on the north side, formerly ruled a Raja
" of great power, who, being absent several years
" from his house, in consequence of his important
" pursuits abroad, on his return fell in love with his
" own daughter, who had grown up during his long
" absence. In vain the mother represented the im-
" piety of his passion: proceeding to force, his daugh-
" ter fled to these deserts of Perwuttum, first utter-
" ing curses and imprecations against her father; in
" consequence of which, his power and wealth de-
" clined; his city, now a deserted ruin, remains a monu-
" ment of divine wrath; and himself, struck by the
" vengeance of Heaven, lies deep beneath the waters
" of Puttela-gunga, which are tinged green by the
" string of emeralds that adorned his neck." Here is a fine subject for a fable; it may, however, furnish a clue to history, as the ruins of this once opulent city are still said to exist. This account of the origin of the devotion here, bears a great resemblance to that of the pilgrimage to Mouserrat in Catalonia, mentioned in *Baretti's* travels.

" The princess was called *Mallica-davi*, and lived
" in this wilderness. Among her cattle, was a remarka-
" bly fine black cow, which she complained to her
" herdsmen,

"herdsmen, never gave her milk. He watched be-
"hind the trees, and saw the cow daily milked by an
"unknown person. *Malica-Divi* informed of this,
"placed herself in a convenient situation, and be-
"holding the same unknown person milking the cow,
"ran to strike him with an iron rod or mace, which
"she held in her hand; but the figure suddenly disap-
"peared, and to her astonishment, nothing remained
"but a rude shapeless stone. At night the god ap-
"peared to her in a dream, and informed her, he
"was the person that milked the cow; she, therefore
"on this spot, built the first temple that was consecrated
"to the worship of this deity represented by a rude
"stone." This is the second temple that was shewn
yesterday, where he is exhibited in the rude state
of the first discovery, and is called *Mudi-Mulla-Car-
jee* or *Mallecarjee*; the other temples were afterwards
built in later times, by Rajas and other opulent
persons. The lingam, shewn by reflected light in the
gilded temple, has also its history and stories, still
more absurd and wonderful, attached to it. It was
brought from the (now deserted) city of Chun-
dra-goompty-patnam. The princess, now worshipped
as a goddess, is also called *Brama-Rumbo*, or *Stri-
chillum-Rumbo*, from whence this Pagoda is called
Strichillum. She delights peculiarly in Perwuttum,
but is called by eighteen other names.

It may be proper here, to take notice of the carvings on the outer walls, as they are remarkable for
their number, and contain less of those monstrous figures than other buildings of this kind. It would
appear that the stories represented on several divisions,
or compartments, are designed to impress on the
mind some moral lesson, or to heighten the reverence
inculcated for the object of adoration here. The
customs and manners of the Gentoos: their arms,
dress, amusements, and the parade and state attendant on their sovereigns, in former times, might be
elucidated by a minute inspection of the figures represented

sented on the walls; drawings of which, and translations of, or extracts from, any books or inscriptions, that might be found, having relation to them, would be useful to that end.

The several Pagodas, Choultries, and Courts, are enclosed by a wall 660 feet long and 510 feet broad. In the centre of this inclosure are the more ancient buildings already described. Below the level of the principal gate, a road or avenue, twenty-four feet broad, goes parallel without to this wall, from whence is a descent by steps to gardens on the north side; from the east gate a double colonade runs, 120 yards, forming a street; an oblong tank is on the west side, from which water was conducted to reservoirs in the gardens, but these are now entirely neglected; the town or pettah covered the south side, and the S. E. angle; the form of the inclosure is an oblong square, with one square projection to the west. The great gateways are, as usual, supported by stone pillars, leaving apartments for the guard on each side the entrance: they are covered with spires of brick work; and this, with the pillar between, being retired some feet within the line of walls, shews that they are of more modern construction, though the spires are rather ruinous: and it may be proper to remark, that these brick spires, formed of several stories with small pilasters, of no regular order, and the niches ornamented with figures in plaister, seem to be the latest invention used in the Pagodas; those with pyramidal roofs, step-fashion, and the summit crowned, sometimes by a globe, are more ancient and of several sizes, so low as four feet in height; built of stone, and seem to be the first improvement on the early rude temples of rough stones set up on end to cover the image of the god. These first attempts are frequently seen among the hills. The wall of the inclosure is built of hewn blocks of the greyish stone, from six to seven feet long by three high, exactly squared and laid together, and about eight or nine rows of these, from the level of the interior

pavement

pavement, leaves its height, from twenty-four varied to twenty-seven feet; the whole of the wall on the outside (being 2,100 feet by twenty-four, allowing 240 for the opening of the gates and square projection on the west side) is covered with carvings and figures sculptured out of the block. Every single block has a rim, or border, raised round it, within which, the carving is raised on a level with the rim, designed evidently, to protect the figures from injury, while raised upon the wall.

The first and lowest row of these stones is covered with figures of elephants, harnessed in different ways, as if led in procession, many of them twisting up trees with their trunks.—2nd. The second row is chiefly occupied with equestrian subjects; horses led ready saddled and their manes ornamented, others tied up to pillars, some loose; a great many horsemen are represented, engaged in fight, at full gallop, and armed with pikes, swords, and shields; others are seen hunting the tyger, and running them through with long spears. The riders are represented very small in proportion to the horses, probably to distinguish the size of the latter, as a smaller cast seems intended to be represented among the led horses, where a few are seen lower in size, something resembling the Acheen breed of horses. All these figures are very accurately designed. It is remarkable, that several figures are represented gallopping off as in flight, and at the same time drawing the bow at full stretch; these Parthian figures seem to have entirely dropped the bridle, both hands being occupied by the bow; some of them are seen advancing at full speed, and drawing the bow at the same time. This mode appears to have been practised by the Indians, as it is highly probable, that the arts of common life only, are here represented in the lower row.— 3d. On the third row, a variety of figures are represented, many of them hunting pieces; tygers (and in one place a lion) attacked by several persons;

crowds

crowds of people appear on foot, many armed with bows and arrows, like the Chinfuars; many figures of Byrraggies or Jogies are feen diftinguifhed by large turbans, carrying their sticks, pots, and bundles, as if coming from a journey; some leaning on a stick as if tired, or decrepid from age; others approaching with a mien of refpect and adoration.—The fourth, fifth, sixth, and seventh rows, are filled (as it would appear from the fcanty information I was able to obtain) with representations of several events regarding the deities of the place, or expreffive allegories of the moral and religious dogmas of the Bráhmens; and probably some may record particular events of real history.—The eighth has fewer carvings than the reft, some ftones are occupied by a single flower of large fize, perhaps intended for the facred flower *(lotos)*: and some, though but a few, by the figure of a god.—The ninth, or upper row, is cut into openings, in the manner of battlements, and the ftones, between each of thefe apertures, are alternately fculptured with the figures of the Lingam, and a cow fhaded by an umbrella, to fignify its pre-eminence.

To examine the particular groups reprefented, would have taken up much more time than I could fpare, but I particularly noticed the following: 1ft, a figure with five heads, weighing two figures in a balance: one of them appears to have a little out-balanced the other. From what I could underftand from the Bráhmens, this was meant for BRA'HMA weighing *Vifhnu* and *Siva*, or *Sulramica*; the latter is heavieft. This alludes to the different fects, or followers of *Vifhnu* and *Siva*. Another figure alfo reprefented two perfons weighed in a balance, both equal, but the explanation of this I could not learn.

Second. Several people pulling at the head and tail of a great fnake, which
is

is twisted round a *Lingam*. This I had seen carved on the walls of the pagoda of *Wentigmetta*, near *Sidout*, in September 1792.

3d. Elephants treading a man under foot.

4th. A naked figure of a woman approaching the *Lingam*: in her left hand she holds the small pot used for ablution; in her right a string of beads *(Ingam valu)*: a hand appears issuing from the *Lingam*.

The *Bráhmens* explained the meaning of this sculpture, " ACUMA DEVI naked, approaching to worship " the *Lingam*; a hand appears suddenly from it, wav- " ing, and a voice is heard, forbidding her to approach " in that indecent situation." A maxim of decency, in the height of religious zeal is here inculcated.

5th. The story of MALLECARJEE and the sacred cow (the origin of the pagoda) is represented in two different places. The cow appears with its udder distended over the *Lingam*, which differs from the account of the *Bráhmens* in not being represented as a rough stone; a person near a tree is seen, as if looking on; a kind of division seems to separate these figures from a woman, in a sitting posture, with an umbrella held over her, to denote superior rank; on the right, behind a tree, is a figure very indistinct, probably intended to represent the herdsman: the trees are badly executed.

6th. Among the number of animals in the procession on the second and third row, two camels are represented with a person on each, beating the *nagra*, or great drum.

7th. In one compartment the figure of an alligator, or crocodile, with its scales and monstrous teeth is seen, running open mouthed, to devour a person lying before it; two women are standing near a third seated; they are looking on a child near them. I got no explanation of this.

8th. An elephant and tyger fighting.

The sculptures on the south and east sides are in good preservation; those on the west and north are more injured by the weather. The age of the first temple might perhaps be discovered from the inscriptions, if a translation of them could be obtained. I could gain no information on this head; but I suspect the building to be of higher antiquity than the knowledge, or, at least, than the use of gunpowder among these people; because among so great a variety of arms as are sculptured upon the walls, swords, bows, pikes, arrows, and shields of a round figure, the matchlock is not be found, though a weapon so much in use among the *poligars*. On enquiring of the *Brâhmens* the meaning of these carvings, one of them replied, " it was to shew how the Gods lived above;" but indeed they seem to have lost all traces of any knowledge they may have formerly possessed, and to be sunk into the profoundest state of ignorance.

XXI.

REMARKS ON THE PRINCIPAL ÆRAS AND DATES OF THE ANCIENT HINDUS.

BY MR. JOHN BENTLEY.

THE confusion and darkness that pervade and overspread, the *Hindu* chronology, I am inclined to think, proceed from two different causes: the one, owing to the fancy of their *Bráhmens* and poets, in disguising and embellishing their history with allegory and fiction; the other, to the ignorance of the modern *Hindus*, who, not able to discern the difference between the several æras and modes of dating, which were made use of by their ancient historians, *Bráhmens*, and poets, in recording past events, have blended the whole together, into one mass of absurdity and contradiction.

At this day, it is not easy to discover the meaning of all the different modes of dating formerly in use. It appears, however, from historical facts, that they were mostly, if not all *nominally* the same, but essentially different in other respects:—they all went under the appellation of *yugs*, divine ages, *Manwantaras*, &c. but the *yugs*, divine ages, *Manwantaras*, &c. of the astronomers were different in point of duration from those of the *Bráhmens* and poets, and those of the *Bráhmens* and poets were, in like manner, different from those of others: hence it becomes absolutely necessary that we know the difference between each, that is, the astronomic, the poetic, &c. &c. from each other before we can attempt to analyze the *Hindu* chronology on true principles. It is from this mode alone that we can discern truth though disguised by fiction; and, until the gordian knot, made fast by the hand of modern times, be untied, much will remain in obscurity.

The aftronomic *yugs*, divine ages, &c. are the only periods in which the real number of years meant, are not concealed: it may not therefore be improper before I proceed farther to ftate what thefe periods are, and their duration.

The *Calpa* is the greateft of all the aftronomical periods, and the duration of it is 4320000000 years. This period is compofed, or made up, of the leffer *yugs*, &c. in the following manner.

4 *Yugs*, viz. a *Satya*, a *Treta*, a *Dwapar*, and a *Cali yug*, make one divine age or *Maha yug*; 71 *Maha yugs* with a *Sandhi*, equal to a *Satya yug*, make 1 *Manwantara*; and 14 *Manwantaras* compofe a *Calpa*, at the commencement of which there is alfo a *Sandhi*, equal to a *Satya yug*. The duration of each period is as follows:

Sandhi at the beginning of the *Calpa*	1728000	
Satya yug -	728000	
Treta yug -	1296000	
Dwapar yug -	864000	
Cali yug -	432000	
One divine age or *Maha yug*	4320000	
71 *Maha yugs* -	306720000	
Add a *Sandhi* -	1728000	
A *Manwantara* -	308448000	
14 *Manwantaras* -		4318272000
A *Calpa*, or a grand period		4320000000

The *Calpa* is an anomaliftic period, at the end of which the *Hindu* aftronomers fay that the places of the planet's nodes and apfides will be precifely precisely the same as at the beginning of it; and the commencement of it was when the sun, moon, and all the planets, nodes and apsides, were in a line of conjunction, in the beginning of Aries, or 1955,884,897 years ago: therefore six *Manwantaras*, 23 *Maha yugs* of the seventh *Manwantara*, and as far as the 220897th year of the *Cali yug*, of the twenty-fourth *Maha yug*, are now (A° 1796) expired of the *Calpa*. The ancient astronomers, most probably, for the sake of convenience, made the present *Cali yug* of the *Hindus*, of which there are now 4897 years expired, to commence when just the first half, or 216000 years were elapsed of the above mentioned *Cali yug*, of the twenty-fourth *Maha yug*; and we are now only in the 4898th year of the second half of that period. I shall therefore by way of distinction, call the present *Cali yug* the " Astronomic Æra."

The *Bráhmens* and poets, in imitation of the astronomic periods above given, invented others for their history and poetry. These I shall distinguish by the name of " Poetic Ages," or æras, because they are embellished by fiction, and covered over with a mysterious veil: *nominally*, they appear the same as the astronomic periods, but historical facts prove them to be essentially different in point of duration; one astronomic year being equal to 1000 poetic ones: hence,

	Years	Real Years
A Poetic *Satya yug* of	1728000 is only	1728
Treta yug of	1296000	1296
Dwapar yug of	864000	864
Cali yug of	432000	432

The first of these Poetic Ages, or Satya yug, commenced at the creation and the rest in succession, agreeable to the following short chronological table, continued down to the present time.

CHRONOLOGICAL TABLE OF ANCIENT ÆRÅS, &c.

	Poetical Æras.	Year of the World.		Astronomic Æra	
Satya Yug, or Golden Age.	0	Adam	0	Cali Yug	0
	1		1	*	1
	130	Seth born	130		151
	905		905		751
	906		906		823
	1056	Noah born	1056		824
	1656	Flood	1656		882
	1728		1728	Pradyo-	
			1729	ta	1000
Treta Yug, or Silver Age.	1		1787	Budha I.	1002
	59	Nimrod	1905		1043
	177		1907		1101
	Icschwa-	Abraham	1948	Sisunga	1139
	chu and	Noah's death	2006	Nanda	1499
	Budhu		2014	Chandra-	
	179		2404	Gupta	1599
	220		2504	Pushpami-	
	278		2641	tra	1736
	316		2753	Vasude-	
	676		2758	va	1848
	776	Parasara	2825		1853
	913	Yudhishthir	2825		1920
	1025	Vyasa	2830		1920
	Rama 1030	Paricshit	2835		1925
	1097		2980		1930
	1097		3624		2075
	Val-				2119
	mic 1102				
	1107				
	1152				
	1296				

* The *Cali yug* commenced in February, in the 906th year of the world.

CHRO-

CHRONOLOGICAL TABLE OF ANCIENT ÆRAS, &c. continued.

	Poetical Æras.	Year of the World.	Astronomic Æra.
Dwapar Yug, or Brazen Age.	Cusha 1	3025	2120
	74	3098	Balin 2193
	530	3554	Chandrabija
	576	3600	2640
	676	3700	2695
	776	3800	2795
	864	3888	2895
		3889	2983
Cali Yug, or Iron Age.	1	3950	2984
	62	3983	Vicramaditya
	95	Christ 4007	3045
	119	4073	Devapala 3078
	185	4085	3102
	197	4088	Narayanpala
	200	4188	3168
	300	4320	Saca 3180
	432	4321	3183
		4505	3283
Satya Yug, or the IId Divine Age.	1	4520	3415
	185	4624	3416
	200	4720	Varaha 3600
	300	4920	3615
	400	5120	3715
	600	5320	3815
	800	5520	4015
	1000		4215
	1200		4415
			4615
	Curr. y. 1483	Curr. year 5803	Current year 4898

In the preceding table, I have placed the beginning of the astronomic æra of the *Cali yug*, of which 4897 years were expired in *April* last in the 906th year of the world; at which time 905 years were elapsed of the *Satya yug* of the Poets, reckoning from its commencement at the Creation: hence it is self-evident that the notion of the modern *Hindus*, who have confounded the fabulous or fictitious ages of their Poets with the astronomic periods merely from a similarity of names, are not only erroneous, but even quite opposite to the true intent and meaning of the ancient *Hindu* writers themselves; who, it may be proved, have sometimes adopted the astronomic æra of the *Cali yug*, during the periods of the *Treta* and *Dwapar yugs* of the Poets, and made use of either æra, (astronomic or poetic, and sometimes both), according as it suited their fancy, for recording not only past events in general, but even one and the same event.

The first instance I shall mention by way of proof is that of BUDHA the ancient MERCURY of the *Hindus*. The late Sir WILLIAM JONES, whose name can never be mentioned but with highest esteem, places the ancient BUDHA, or MERCURY who married ILA a daughter of NOAH about the beginning of the *Treta yug*; contemporary with JISCHWACU the son of NOAH. Now the *Hindus* in general, and the *Bhagawatamrita* in particular, say that " BUDHA became visible the 1002d year of the *Cali yug*" (astronomic æra): let us therefore examine this matter a little, and see whether this is not the same BUDHA who is recorded as living near the beginning of the *Treta yug* of the Poets; contemporary with the son of NOAH. First the 1002d year of the *Cali yug* was the 1907th from the Creation. Secondly, NOAH by the *Mosaick* account, did not die before the 2006th year from the Creation, or about 100 years after the appearance of BUDHA. Thirdly, and lastly, there was but one BUDHA in the time

time of NOAH; and he is said to have married ILA, the daughter of NOAH: hence we may safely infer, that the BUDHA, who appeared in the 1002d year of the Cali yug, or 1907 of the Creation, was the very same that married Noah's daughter, and is recorded as living near the beginning of the Treta yug of the Poets. Here we may plainly see, that the events, as well as the time, perfectly coincide; for the 1002d year of the Cali yug corresponds not only with the latter days of NOAH, but also with the 179th year of the Treta yug of the poets, as may be seen from the preceding table.

I shall now mention another instance, which, while it confirms what I have above said, respecting the ancient *Hindu* writers or historians, adopting the astronomic æra of the Cali yug, at different times during the periods of the Treta and Dwapar yugs of the Poets, will at the same time explain the cause of all the confusion and absurdities which at present appear in the ancient history and chronology of the *Hindus*.

VALMIC and VYASA were two ancient contemporary bards, whom the modern *Hindus* separate by no less a period than 864000 years, believing VALMIC to have lived near the close of the Treta yug, and VYASA near the close of the Dwapar yug; and though they cannot but admit that the two bards had frequently conversed together on the subject of their poems, yet they will rather account for it by supposing a miracle, than assign any real or probable cause for an absurdity, so contradictory, not only to nature, but to common sense.

VYASA was the son of PARASARA, an ancient astronomer, and PARASARA was the grandson of VASISHTHA, who was also an astronomer, and *piaboita* or family priest to RAMA, king of *Audhya* or *Oud*, who reigned,

reigned, according to the Hindu accounts near the close of the Treta yug of the Poets. PARASARA, the father of VYASA, was therefore about one or two generations after RAMA. But, from the observed places of the equinoxes and solstices in the year 3600 of the present Cali yug, by one VARAHA, an astronomer, and their places as mentioned by PARASARA, it would appear, that the observations of the latter must have been about 1680 years before VARAHA; which will therefore place PARASARA about the year 2825 of the world, corresponding to the 1097th of the Treta yug of the Poets; and as PARASARA may have been then between thirty and forty years old, we may place RAMA about the year 1030; and VALMIC and VYASA about the year 1102 of the Treta yug of the Poets, being the 2830th of the Creation. These years may not be the exact times in which they respectively lived; but, I believe, they do not vary from the truth above forty or fifty years either way, and nearer than this we cannot well expect to bring them.

By having thus obtained the respective times or years in which RAMA, PARASARA, VYASA, and VALMIC lived, we have ascertained a point of the utmost importance to the chronology of Hindus.

The war of MAHABARAT took place in the time of VYASA, in consequence of which he wrote his epic poem called the *Mahabarat*, and on the composition of which he consulted VALMIC. VYASA was therefore contemporary with CHRISHNA, ARJUN, ABHIMARIYIR, YUDHISHTHIR, PARICSHIT, and others engaged in that famous war.

Shortly after that war, and towards the close of the reign of PARICSHIT, the Hindu historians of that part of India, where PARICSHIT reigned, began

began to lay aside the the Poetic æras altogether, and to adopt the aftronomic æra of the *Cali yug*, of which near 2000 years were then expired.

This circumftance of laying afide the poetic æras, and adopting the aftronomic, it feems in the courfe of ten or twelve centuries after became either totally forgotten, or mifunderftood, fo much fo in fact that the very adoption of the aftronomic æra has been taken, by the modern *Hindus* for the actual beginning of the *Cali yug* itfelf. This erroneous notion, together with thofe which they entertained refpecting the duration of the different ages, the *Satya*, *Treta*, and *Dwapar yugs* of their poets, which they firmly believe to be the fame with the aftronomic periods of the fame name, and to have ended accordingly before the prefent *Cali yug* commenced, has been the caufe of all the confufion which appear in their ancient hiftory and chronology. For finding the immediate fucceffor of PARICSHIT mentioned in ancient hiftory as reigning in the *Cali yug*, they concluded, though erroneoufly, that PARICSHIT muft therefore have reigned at the clofe of the *Dwapar yug*; and from this circumftance, having removed PARICSHIT from the clofe of the *Treta yug* down to the clofe of the *Dwapar yug*, they were then obliged to place YUDHISHTHIR, ARJUN, CRISHNA, HABIMANYU, and VYASA, *at the clofe of the Dwaper yug* alfo; by which means they feparate VYASA, from VALMIC his contemporary and friend, and the reft who were engaged in the war of BHARAT from their proper places in hiftory by 864000 year of the poets.

It is owing to the fame erroneous notions repecting the *Cali yug*, that the modern *Hindus* have thrown the ancient hiftory and chronology of the kings of *Magadha* or *Bahar* into confufion. For having difcovered that SAHADEVA, the fon of JARASANDHA, was contemporary with YUDHISHTHIR, they concluded

that

that as they had already placed YUDHISHTHIR at the close of the Dwápar yug SAHADENA muſt be at the beginning of the Cali yug; and therefore, without further ceremony, not only removed SAHADEVA but his nineteen ſucceſſors, who fromed a dynaſty in the family of JARASÁNDHA from the proper period in hiſtory (between the years 1920 and 2193 of the Cali yug) and placed them immediately before PRADYOTA who began his reign in the 1000th year of the Cali yug. This removal was productive of two abſurdities at once, both of which are particularly noticed by the late Sir WILLIAM JONES in his chronology of the kings of *Magadha*. The one, that in conſequence of placing the names before PRADYOTA they were obliged to aſſert that the twenty princes reigned one thouſand years, that is from the beginning of the Cali yug in the year of 906 of the Creation down to the 1905th. ſo that they muſt have then reigned as well during the flood as before and after it. The other, that as a chaſm had been formed in that part of the hiſtory from which the twenty reigns were removed in order to make up that chaſm as well as they could, they were obliged to aſſert that a dynaſty of four princes of the *Canna* race, the firſt of whom (VASUDEVA) came to the throne in the year of the world 2753, or 1848 of the Cali yug, reigned no leſs than 345 years.

Now as YUDHISHTHIR was the uncle and immediate predeceſſor of PARICSHIT, and conſequently contemporary with PARASARA the father of VYASA; it is clear that both YUDHISHTHIR and SAHADEVA muſt have reigned about the year 2825 of the world: which is about ſeventy two years after the reign of the above VASUDEVA of the *Canna* race, and correſponding preciſely with the chaſm.

Innumerable other inſtances of the abſurdities of the modern HINDUS might be produced, but thoſe thofe, I have mentioned and explained, I think are fufficient. I fhall therefore conclude the fubject of the poetic æras with the following table, fhewing the moon's age and month, with the day of the week on which the Satya, Treta, Dwapar, and Cali yugs of the poets refpectively commenced; which will prove, beyond a probability of doubt, that they have no connection whatever with the aftronomical yugs of the fame name, belonging to the fyftem of MEYA explained at the beginning of this effay; for in the latter all the yugs, Manwantaras, &c. belonging to the fyftem begin unvariably, on the firft day of *Byfakh*, the moment the fun enters Aries in the *Hindu* fphere.

Poetic Æras.	Days of the Week.	Moon's Age and Month.
Satya yug	Sunday	3d titthee of the moon of *Byfakh*.
Treta do.	Monday	9th do. of do. *Cartic*.
Dwapar do.	Thurfday	28th do. of do. *Bhadro*.
Cali do.	Tuefday	15th do. of do. *Magh*.

Note. The lunar month takes its name from the folar month, in which the new moon happens to fall. 30 titthees make a lunation.

With refpect to the day of the week mentioned in preceding table fome of the *Hindu* accounts differ. The moon's age and month are extracted from the *Brohmo puran*, which agrees with the *Hindu* calendar, wherein the commencement of each yug is alfo recorded.

The following table of the dates of the ten *avatars* or incarnation of the deity, which took place in the above mention yugs, is extracted from an

augum

augum or *tontor* called "*Guhjateeguhja*" supposed to have been written by SEEB or SEEVA, a *Hindu* deity.

TABLE OF THE AVATARS.

Avatars.	Week Day.	Moon's Age and Month.	Nakshatra
1 Motchyo	Monday	1 titthee Chitro	Revati
2 Kurmo	Wednesday	2 Joist'ho	Rohini
3 Boraho	Sunday	7 Magho	Aswini
4 Nreesingho	Saturday	14 Bysakho	Swati
5 Bamono	Friday	12 Bhadro	Sravana
6 Porosuramo	Saturday	3 Bysakho	Rohini
7 Ramo	Monday	9 Chitro	Punaryobasee
8 Kreesno	Wednesday	23 Bhadro	Rohini
9 Boodho	Sunday	10 Asaro	Bysakha
10 Kolkee	Saturday	2 Agrahain	Purvasara

The 1st. 2nd. 3d. and 4th Avatars are supposed to have happened during the period of the Satya yug; the 5th. 6th and 7th. in the Treta yug; the 8th and 9th. in the Dwapar yug; and the 10th or last in the Cali yug of the Poets long since past.

Having then finished what I had to say respecting the poetic æras and the absurdities introduced into the history and chronology of the *Hindus*, by confounding them with the astronomic system of MEYA, I shall now proceed to a third system, wherein the Manwantaras appear to have been but of short duration, and to depend on the revolutions of either JUPITER or SATURN. This system, like that of the poetic æras, has been always confounded

confounded with that of MEYA's, and consequently the cause of much confusion in the records of ancient times. To distinguish it from MEYA's I shall call it the *Puranic* System, and, by way of introduction, give the following table of the dates, &c. of the fourteen puranic Manwantaras, as contained in a Hindu book entitled the *Uttara Chanda*, from which Captain FRANCIS WILFORD was so obliging as to favour me with an extract.

TABLE OF THE PURANIC MANWANTARAS.

Manwa	Day of the Week.	Moon's Age & Month	Nakshatra.
1	Began on *Sunday*.	9th titthee of *Aswin*.	*Sravana*.
2	—— *Thursday*.	12 —— *Cartic*.	*Utto Bhadropada*.
3	—— *Monday*.	3 —— *Chitr*.	*Critica*.
4	—— *Friday*.	3 —— *B.Jhar*.	*Hosta*.
5	—— *Tuesday*.	30 —— *Phalgun*.	*Solobhisa*.
6	—— *Saturday*.	11 —— *Pous*.	*Rhoini*.
7	—— *Friday*.	10 —— *Asar*.	*Swati*.
8	—— *Tuesday*.	7 —— *Magh*.	*Onurada*.[*]
9	—— *Sunday*.	23 —— *Srabon*.	*Rhonini*.
10	—— *Friday*.	15 —— *Ajar*.	*Uttora Sara*.
11	—— *Monday*.	15 —— *Cartic*.	*Critica*.
12	—— *Thursday*.	15 —— *Phalgun*.	*Uttora-Phalguni*.
13	—— *Wednesday*	15 —— *Chitr*.	*Chitra*.
14	—— *Wednesday*	15 —— *Yoishth*.	*Jeysta*.

[*] Onurada appears incorrect, as the moon of Magh must be 20 or 21 days old before it enters Onurada Nakshatr.

The order in which the above Manwantaras followed each other is not now known, but I have given them in the order in which they were written, in the memorial *ſloke* or verſe. However, as the firſt Manwantara commenced juſt when fifty years of Bra'hma's life (that is one half of the grand cycle of this ſyſtem) were expired it is eaſy to perceive that the 13th on the liſt muſt have been the firſt Manwantara; and I ſuſpect that the 10th was the ſecond, the 11th. the third, the 12th. the fourth and the 14th the fifth Manwantaras, all of which appear to have been computed according to mean motions only, the other nine having the appearance of being computed according to the true place of the planet, on which the regulation of the periods depended.

In this ſyſtem, which appears to have been in uſe before the time of Meya for yugs, viz. a Satya, Treta, Dwapar, and Cali yug formed a Maha yug; ſeventy-one Maha yugs with a Sandhi, equal to a Satya yug, formed a Manwantara; and fourteen of ſuch Manwantaras with a Sandhi, equal to a Satya yug, or 1000 Maha yugs, formed a *Calpa* or a day of Bra'hma, and his night was of the ſame length; 360 of ſuch days and nights form one of his years; and 100 of of ſuch years the period of his life or the grand *Puranic* cycle, in which all the planets with the nodes and apſides of their reſpective orbits were ſuppoſed to return to a line of conjunction in the beginning of aries the point they ſet out from at the commencement of the cycle.

From the apparent ſhortneſs of the *Puranic Manwantaras*, (which probably did not exceed 3 or 400 years at moſt) and conſequently of the Calpa, the cycle or term of Bra'hma's life above mentioned appears to have been abſolutely neceſſary in this ſyſtem to render is applicable to the purpoſe of aſtronomy.

nomy. But in the fyftem of MEYA *now in ufe* that cycle is now totally unneceffary, nor does it in fact belong to it, as the *Calpa* alone in the latter, contains all the leffer cycles of the revolutions of the planets, nodes, &c. within the period of its durations.

MEYA the fuppofed author of *Surya Sidhanta*, lived in the Satya yug of the 28th Maha yug, of the 7th Manwantara of the fifty-firft year of *Bráhma*'s life, and probably finding the *Puranic* fyftem either inconvenient, or not fufficiently correct, he invented the prefent one on a much larger fcale, extending the duration of a Manwantara to 308448000 years, and fimplified the fyftem by making the yugs, &c. to depend on folar motion alone; by which means, all the periods in his fyftem begin invariably on the firft day of *Byfakh*, the moment the fun enters Aries in the *Hindu* fphere, which circumftance alone, muft form a moft ftriking difference between it, and the *Puranic* fyftem.

In the *Surya Sidhanta*, MEYA has ftated the obliquity of the ecliptic in his time at 24°, from whence MR. S. DAVIS, a gentleman to whom the public is under very confiderable obligations, for his valuable paper on the aftronomical computations of the *Hindus*, publifhed in the *Afiatic Refearches*, computed that fuppofing the obliquity of the ecliptic to have been accurately obferved by the ancient *Hindus* as twenty-four degrees, and that its decreafe had been from that time half a fecond a year, the age or date of the *Surya Sidhanta* (in 1789) would be 3840 years; therefore MEYA muft have lived about the year 1956 of the creation.

The *Hindu* books place POROSU RAM one of the incarnate divinities in the 8th Manwantara of the *Puranic* fyftem, and fo they do VYASA, and OSOTHAMO, the

the son of DRON mentioned in the *Mahabharat*; and since the time of VYASA the remaining six Manwantaras have expired, as will appear from the following table of all the Patriarchs or *Munoos*, &c. from the time of SWOYOMBHOOBO or ADAM, who lived in the first Manwantara down to the end of the fourteenth, which I have extracted from the *Sreebhagobot*, and from which some rational idea may be formed respecting the duration of the *Puranic Manwantara* now generally confounded with the periods of the same name belonging to MEYA's system, in which we are now no further advanced than to the seventh Manwantara, and which was the same when he wrote long before the time of VYASA.

TABLE *of the* PATRIARCHS or MUNNOOS, *and others, during the fourteen Puranic Manwantaras.*

1st MANWANTARA.

SWOYOMBHOOBO, or ADAM. *Munoo.*
SOTOROOPA, his wife
PREEYOBROTO, his son
UTTANPADO, his second son
AKOOTEE SWOYOMBHOOS 1st daughter
DEBOOTE ditto, 2nd ditto
PROSOOTEE ditto, 3d ditto

ROOCHEE, the husband of AKOOTEE
KORDOM, ditto of DEBOOTEE
DOKSOPROJAPOOTEE, ditto of PROSOOTEE
TOOREETO
MOREECHEE
MEESRO
YOGO

2d MANWANTARA.

SWAROCHEESO. *Munoo*
RAJA DYUMOT his son
RAJA SUSENO ditto
RAJA ROCHLESMOT, ditto.

TOOREETO
URJOSTOMBHO
ROCHONO, & others.

3d MANWANTARA.

Uтомо. *Munoo*   Bedosuto
Pobono his son   Bhodro
Srinjoyo, ditto   Promodo
Jogotro, ditto   Sotyojeet, and many
Sotyo   others.

4th MANWANTARA.

Tamoso. *Munoo*   Beerso
Breesokhyatee his son   Bedhreetoyo
Norohketu, ditto   Joteerdma
Sotyokhoroyo   Treeseckhoisworo, and many others.

5th MANWANTARA.

Riboto. *Munoo*   Heronyoroma
Botee his son   Bedoseera
Beendho, ditto   Urdhobahoo
Bhootoroyo   Beebhoo, & many others.

6th MANWANTARA.

Chaksooso. *Munoo*   Apyo
Purru his son   Horyosmot
Purruso, ditto   Dweeroko
Sudyumno, ditto   Montrodrumo, and many
Prodyumno, ditto   others.

7th MANWANTARA.

Vavioswata, or Noah.   Preesodhro his 6th son
   Munoo   Nobhogo,   7th ditto
Icshwaku his 1st son   Kobee,   8th ditto
Nreego,   2nd ditto   Deesto,   9th ditto
Dreesto,   3d ditto   Baruno,   10th ditto
Soryati,   4th ditto   Adityo
Norisyanto, 5th ditto

7th MANWANTARA (continued.)

Bosu	Otri
Rudro	Bosisto
Biswedebo	Biswamitro
Morudgono	Goutomo
Osnikumar	Jomodognee
Ribhobo	Bhorodwajo
Kosyapo	Purondoro, & many others.

8th MANWANTARA.

Saborni *Manoo*.	Porosu Ram
Neermoko his son	Dipliman
Beerojoska ditto	Osotthamo son of Dron
Sutopa	Kreepo
Beeroja	Reesyosringo
Omreetoprobho	Vyasa or Byasa.
Gabolo	

9th MANWANTARA.

Doksosaborni *Manoo*	Ghorbo
Bootoketu his son	Paro
Diptiketu ditto	Dyutimot
Dreestoketu ditto	Sirutho and many others.
Morichi	

10th MANWANTARA.

Bromosabornee *Manoo*	Sukreeto
Bhurisin his son	Sotyo
Surasono	Joyo
Biridho	Murti
Hobisman	Sombhoo and many others.

11th MANWANTARA.

DHOMORSABORNEE *Munoo* NEERBANO
SOTYO DHORMO his fon ROOCHEE
BIHONGGONO ORUNO
KAMOGOMO BIDRETTO and many others.

12th MANWANTARA.

RUDROSABORNEE. *Munoo* TOPOMURTI
DEBOBAN his fon TOPOSEE
UPODEBO ditto OGNEEDROKO
DEBOSREESTO ditto GONDHODHAMA and many
HORITO others.

13th MANWANTARA.

DEBOSABORNEE. *Munoo* SUTRAMO
CHITROSENO his fon NEERMOKO
BICHITRO ditto DIBOSPOTEE and many
SUKORMÆ others.

14th MANWANTARA.

EENDROSOBORNI. *Munoo* OGNEE
URUNGGO his fon BAHOO
BHURU ditto SOOCHEE
BODHNO ditto SUDHO
POBETROO MAGODHO and many
CHAKSOOSO others.

NOTE. Several names in the foregoing table had the title of *Devtas, Reefhees*, &c. annexed to them, probably by way of diftinction or pre-eminence.

UTOMO, TOMOSO, and RIBOTO, the third, fourth, and fifth *Munoos*, were the grandfons of SWOYOMBHOOBO or ADAM; DOKSO SABORNEE, the

The 9th *Munoo* was the son of BARUNO or VARUNO, the tenth son of VAIVOSWATA: therefore it is easy to perceive that the *Puranic Manwantara*, which was considered in ancient times as the duration of the life of a *Munoo* or Patriarch could not be very long, and ought not to be confounded with the Manwantaras of the present system of MEYA, consisting of 308448000 years each.

A CHRONOLOGICAL TABLE

Of the solar and lunar line of princes, who are said to have reigned in the Cities of *Ayodhya* or *Audh* (now *Oud*), and *Pralishthana* or *Vitora*, otherwise *Hastinapoor* (now *Delhi*) respectively, from about the beginning of the Treta yug of the Poets, or 1002nd year of the astronomic Cali yug, down to the time the solar line of princes became extinct: when the country is supposed to have been conquered by some foreign power; probably ALEXANDER.

Poetic Æra.	Solar Line.	Year of the Wo.	Lunar Line.	Astr. Æra C. Yug
179	ICSWACHU	1907	BUDHA	1002
Treta Yug, or Silver Age.	VICUCSHI		PURURAVAS	
	CUCUSTA		AYUSH	
	ANENAS		NAHUSHA	
	PRITHU 5		YAYATI 5	
	VISWAGANDHI		PURU	
	CHANDRA		JANAMEJAYA	
	YUVANASWA		———	
	SRAVA		——— 10	
	VRIHADHASWA 10		———	
	DHUNDHUMARA			
	DRIDHASWA			

3d

Poetic Æra.	Solar Line.	Year of the Wo.	Lunar Line.	Astr. Æra C. Yug
Treta Yug, or Silver Age.	HERYASWA			
	NICUMBHA			
	CRISASWA 15			
	SENAJIT			
	YUVANASWA			
	MANDHATRI			
	PURUCUTSA		PRACHINWAT	
	TRASADASYU 20		PRAVIRA	
	ANARANYA		MENASYU	
	HERYASWA		CHARUPADA	
	PRARUNA		SUDYU	
	TRIVENDHANA		BAHUGAVA	
	SATYAVRATA 25		SANYATI	
	TRISANCU		AHANYATI	
	HARISCHANDRA		RAUDRASWA	
	RHOITA		RITEYUSH	
	HARITA		RAUTINAVA	
	CHAMPA 30		SUMATI	
	SUDEVA		AITI	
	VIJAYA		DUSHMANTA	
	BHARUCA		BHARATA	
	VRICA		VITATHA	
	BAHUCA 35		MANYU	
	SAGARA		VRIHATESHETRA	
	ASMANJAS			
	ANSUMAT		HASLIN	
	BHAGHIRATHA		AJAMEDHA	
			RICSHA	
	SRUTA 40		SAMWARANA	
	NABHA		CURU	

SIND-

Poetic Æras.	Solar Line.	Year of the Wo.	Lunar Line.	Aſtr. Æra C.Yug
	Sindhadwipa		Jahnu	
	Ayutayush		Suratha	
	Ritaperna		Viduratha	
	Saudasa 45		Sarvabhau-ma 45	
	Asmaca		Jayasinha	
	Mulaca		Radhica	
	Dasaratha		Ayutayush	
	Aidabidi		Acrodhana	
	Viswasaha 50		Devatithi 50	
	Chatawanga		Rusha	
	Derghabahu		Dillipa	
	Ragu		Pratipa	
	Aja		Santanu	
	Dasaratha 55		Vachytra-virya 55	
	Rama		Pandu	
1097	Vrihadbala	2825	Yudhishthi-ra	1920
1107	Vrihadrana	2835	Paricshit	1930
	*Urucrya		*Janamaja-ya	
	*Vatsavrid-ha 60		*Satanica 60	
	*Pratoyoma		*Sahasrina-ca	
	*Bhanu		*Aswamed-haja	
	*Devaca		*Asima-crishna	
	*Sahadeva		*Nemichac-ra	
	*Vira 65		*Upta 65	
1296	*Vridhaswa	3024	*Chitrara-ta	2119

Treta Yug, or Silver Age.

Dwapar

Poetic Æra.	Solar Line.	Year of the Wo.	Lunar Line.	Aftr. Æra C.Yug
1	Cusha	3025	*Suchiratha	2120
	Attithi		*Dhritimat	
	Nishadha		*Sushina"	
	Nabas 70		*Sunitha 70	
	Pundarica		*Nrichae-	
	Cshemad-		shuh	
	hanwas		*Suchinala	
	Devanica		*Pariplava	
	Ahsniagu		*Sunagar	
	Paripatra 75		*Medhavin	
	Ranachala		75	
	Vajranabha		*Nripanjava	
	Arca		*Derva	
	Sugana		*Trini	
	Vidhriti 80		*Vrihadra-	
	Hiranyana-		tha	
	bha		*Sudhasa 80	
	Pushya		*Satanica	
	Druvasand-		*Durmada-	
	hi		na	
	Sudersana		*Rahinara	
	Agniverna 85		*Dandapani	
	Sighira		*Nimi 85	
	Maru		*Cshimaca	
	Prasusruta		———	
	Sandhi		———	
	Amersana 90		———	
	Mahaswat		——— 90	
	Viswabhahu		———	
	Prasenhajit		———	
	Tacshaca		———	
	*Bannumat		———	
	95		——— 95	

Dwapar Yug, or Brazen Age.

Dwapar

Poetic Æra	Solar Line.	Year of the Wo.	Lunar Line.	Aſtr. Æra C.Yug
Dwapar Yug, or Brazen Age.	*Practicaswa		———	
	*Supratica		———	
	*Marudeva		———	
	*Sunaschatra		——— 100	
	*Pushcara		———	
	——— 100		———	
	*Antaricsha		———	
	*Sutapas		——— 105	
	*Amitrajit		———	
	*Vrihadraja		———	
	*Barhi 105		———	
	*Critanjaya		———	
	*Rananjaya		——— 110	
	*Slocya		———	
	*Sudhoda 110		———	
	*Langalada		———	
	*Prasenajit		———	
	*Csudraca		——— 115	
	*Sumitra		———	
	——— 115			
864	——— 117	3888	——— 117	2983

In the preceding table I have placed Yudhishthir in the year 2825 of the world corresponding to the 1097th of the Treta yug of the Poets, and to the 1020th of the aſtronomic Cali yug: that this is about the period in which Yudhishthir reigned I have not myſelf the ſmalleſt doubt, not only becauſe he muſt have been contemporary with Parasara the father

of

of VYASA, but also on account of the exact coincidence of that period with the chasm of the chronology of the kings of *Maghada*, which appears sufficiently evident to have been occasioned by the removal of the dynasty of SAHADEVA, who was contemporary with YUDHISHTHIR, from that period of history.

From the probabilities of the duration of life deduced from observations on bills of mortality, it appears, that the mean duration of human life, taking one man with another, does not exceed thirty-two or thirty-three years. Admitting, however, the mean duration of life to be thirty-three years of this we cannot allow more than a half, or seventeen years at the utmost, to each reign, in a long succession of princes. Therefore, as ICSHWACU the son of NOAH, began his reign near the beginning of the Treta yug, or in the year 179 of that period, if we divide the remaining years 1117 in the Treta yug by 17, we shall have about sixty-six reigns from ICSHWACU's time down to the end of the Treta yug; and this number of reigns is confirmed by the place of YUDHISHTHIR in the table, being the fifty-seventh reign, and at the same time about 200 years before the end of the Treta yug; so that in all probability, it would require at least nine or ten reigns more, from his time down to the end of that period. After the same manner, the number of computed reigns for the whole of the Dwapar yug or 864 years, would be fifty-one: which, with the former number, make altogether 117 computed reigns; and of this number, we find no more than 114 in the solar line of princes, and still considerably less in the lunar line.

In consequence of the ancient historians' adopting the astronomic æra of the Cali yug, at the close of PARICSHIT's reign, as already noticed, YUDHISHTHIR and PARICSHIT's in the lunar line, and with VRIHADBALA and VRIHADRANA, their contemporaries in the solar line were removed (with others) by the

the modern commentators from the close of the Treta
yug down to the close of the Dwapar yug of the Poets; therefore RAMA was supposed to have been the
last prince of the solar line who reigned in *Oud* at the
close of the Treta yug: and as they had placed the
immediate successors of PARICSHIT at the beginning
of the Cali yug; so, in like manner, the immediate
successors of VRIHADRANA may be supposed to have
been placed at the beginning of the Cali yug also:
hence the mode of correction required becomes obvious.

I have therefore restored VRIHADBALA and VRI-
HADRANA to their proper places in the Treta yug, as
contemporaries with YUDHISHTHIR and PARICSHIT;
and the remaining names down to the end of that period marked with a *, were their successors as placed
in the Cali yug.

The other names marked with a *, are the remaining princes mentioned in Sir WILLIAM JONES's
chronology as reigning in the Cali yug; all of whom,
however, if they reigned at all, must have reigned before the end of the Dwapar yug of the Poets; and
their being mentioned by ancient historians as reigning in the Cali yug, does not at all imply that they
reigned after the Dwapar yug, but only in the astronomical Cali yug, which commenced the 906th year
of the Satya yug of the Poets, and has been unfortunately confounded (by the modern Hindu commentators) with their Cali yug: with which however it has
no relation except in name: or to speak more correctly, they have confounded the fictitious ages of
the Poets with the real astronomic periods.

With respect to the chasm in the lunar line of
princes after JANANUJAYA the names that are missing
must either have been lost, or else, which is more
pro-

probable, mentioned by the ancient historians, as reigning in the Cali yug of the astronomical æra; and as JANANUJAYA is the first prince mentioned as reigning in the Cali yug, in the lunar line, it is very probable, he may be the same person recorded as reigning in the Treta yug; and if that should be the case, the eleven names that follow next to him, most likely will be those that should fill the chasms.

At what particular period of time, the solar line of princes became extinct, it is not easy to ascertain, by the table, it would appear, that it must have been fifty years before the year 3888 of the world; but as I allowed seventeen years to each reign, which is rather two much in a long succession of eldest sons, it is probable it must have ended about 100 years at least, earlier than given by the table; which will place the end of the last prince's reign, about the year 3788 of the world.

ALEXANDER the Great paid his visit to *India* about 200 years about the year 3888 of the world, or end of the Dwapar yug; but whether he was the cause of the solar line of princes becoming about that time extinct, or whether PRASENAJIT (the last prince but two mentioned in the table, and whose name might be pronounced, or corrupted into PORASNAJIT, PORUSNAJIT, or even PORUS itself, leaving out the termination NAJIT) was the prince named PORUS, whom ALEXANDER conquered and took prisoner, I will leave to others to decide.

A CHRONOLOGICAL TABLE

Of the king of *Magadha* or *Behar*, from the reign of PRADYOTA, in the year 1905 of the world, down to that of CHANDRABIJA in the year 3554 containing a period of 1649 years.

Anno

Anno Mundi		Cali Yug	Anno Mundi		Culi Yug
1905	Pradyota Palaca Visachayupa Rajaca Nandivirdana	1000		Sujyeshtha Vasumitra Abhadraca Pulinda Ghosha Vajramitra	
2044	Sisunga Cacaverna Cshemadherman Cshetrajirya	1139	2753	Bhagavata Devabuti Vasudeva Bhumitra Narayana Susarman	1848
	Vidisara Ajatasatru Darbaca Ajaya Nandeverdhana Mahanandi		2825	*Sahadeva *Marjari *Srutasrava *Ayutayush *Niramitra *Sunacshatra	1920
2404	Nanda	1499		*Vrishetsena	
2504	Chandragupta Varisara Asocaverdhana Suyasas Desaratha Sandgatha Salisuca Somasarman Satadhanwas Vriadratha	1599		*Carmajit *Srutanjaya *Vipra *Suchi *Cshema *Suvrata *Dhermasutra *Srama *Dridhasena	
2641	Pushpamitha Agnamitra	1736			

*Su-

no ndi		Cali Yug	Anno Mundi		Cali Yug

98	*Sumati
	*Subala
	*Sunita
	*Saytajit
	Balin
	Crishna
	Srisanta-
	  carna
	Paurnama-
	  sa
	Lambodara
	Vivilaca
	Meghaswata
	Vatamana.
	Talaca
		2193	3554	Sivaswati
				Purishabhe-
				  ru
				Sumandana
				Chacoraca
				Bataca
				Gomalin
				Purimat
				Medasiras
				Serascanda
				Yajnyasri
				Vijaya
				Chandra-
				  bija
					2649

The names with a * set before them, are those whom I mentioned in the foregoing remarks, to have been erroneously placed by the modern *Hindus* before Pradyota; for, Sahadeva, the first of the dynasty was contemporary with Yudhishthir, who reigned about the year 2825 of the world. I have therefore restored them again to their proper places in history, and by that means corrected the two absurdities pointed out by the late Sir William Jones, in the *Hindu* chronology of the kings of *Magadha* or *Behar*.

Calcutta, 2nd October, 1796.

XXII.

ON THE RELIGIOUS CEREMONIES OF THE HINDUS, AND OF THE BRA'HMENS ESPECIALLY.

BY H. T. COLEBROOKE, ESQ.

ESSAY I.

THE civil Law of the Hindus, containing frequent allusions to their religious rites, I was led, among other purfuits connected with a late undertaking, to peruse several treatises on this subject, and translate from the Sanscrit some entire tracts and parts of others. From these sources of information upon a subject on which the Hindus are by no means communicative, I intend to lay before the Society, in this and subsequent essays, an abridged explanation of the ceremonies, and verbal translations of the prayers used at rites, which a *Hindu* is bound constantly to perform. In other branches of this inquiry, the Society may expect valuable communications from our colleague Mr. W. C. BLAQUIERE, who is engaged in similar researches. That part of the subject to which I have confined my inquires will be also found to contain curious matter, which I shall now set forth without comment, reserving for a subsequent essay the observations which are suggested by a review of these religious practices.

A *Bráhmana* rising from sleep is enjoined under the penalty of losing the benefit of all rites performed by him, to rub his teeth with a proper withe, or a twig of the racemiferous fig tree, pronouncing to himself this prayer, " Attend, lord of the forest: SOMA, king of herbs and plants, has approached " thee:

"thee: mayest thou and he cleanse my mouth with glory and good auspices, that I may eat abundant food." The following prayer is also used upon this occasion, "Lord of the forest! grant me life, strength, glory, splendour, offspring, cattle, abundant wealth, virtue, knowledge, and intelligence." But if a proper withe cannot be found, or on certain days when the use of it is forbidden (that is, on the day of the conjunction and on the first, sixth, and ninth days of each lunar fortnight), he must rince his mouth twelves times with water.

Having carefully thrown away the twig, which has been used, in a place free from impurities, he should proceed to bathe, standing in a river or in other water. The duty of bathing in the morning and at noon, if the man be a householder, and in the evening also, if he belong to an order of devotion, is inculcated by pronouncing the strict observance of it in no less efficacious, than a rigid penance, in expiating sins, especially the early bath in the months of *Magha*, *Pholgina*, and *Cartica*: and the bath being particularly enjoined as a salutary ablution, he is permitted to bathe in his own house, but without prayers, if the weather, or his own infirmities prevent his going forth; or he may abridge the ceremonies and use fewer prayers, if a religious duty or urgent business require his early attendance. The regular bath consists of ablutions followed by worship and by the inaudable recitation of the *Gáyatri* with the names of the worlds. First sipping water, and sprinkling some before him, the priest recites the three subjoined prayers, while he performs an ablution by throwing water eight times on his head, or towards the sky, and concludes it by casting water on the ground to destroy the Demons, who wage war with the Gods. "1st. O waters! since ye afford delight, grant us present happiness, and the rapturous sight of the supreme God. 2d. Like tender Mothers make us here partakers of your most auspicious essence. 3d. We became contended with your

" your effence, with which ye fatisfy the univerfe.
" Waters! grant it unto us." For, as otherwife
" expounded, the third text may fignify, Eagerly do
" we approach your effence, which fupports the uni-
" verfal abode. Waters! grant it unto us." In the
Agni purána the ablution is otherwife directed:
" At twilight, let a man attentively recite the prayers
" addreffed to water, and perform an ablution by
" throwing water on the crown of his head, on the
" earth, towards the fky; again towards the fky, on
" the earth, on the crown of his head, on the earth,
" again on the crown of his head; and, laftly on the
" earth." Immediately after this ablution he fhould
" fip water without fwallowing it, filently praying in
thefe words, " Lord of facrifice! thy heart is in the
" midft of the waters of the ocean; may falutary herbs
" and waters pervade thee. With facrificial hymns
" and humble falutation we invite thy prefence: may
" this ablution be efficacious." Or he may fip water
while he utters inaudably the myfterious names of the
feven worlds. Thrice plunging into water he muft
each time repeat the expiatory text which recites the
creation; and having thus completed his ablution, he
puts on his mantle after wafhing it, and fits down to
worfhip the rifing fun.

This ceremony is begun by his tying the lock of
hair on the crown of his head, while he recites
the *Gáyatri*, holding much *cufa* grafs in his left, and
three blades of the fame grafs in his right hand;
or wearing a ring of grafs on the third finger of the
fame hand. Thrice fipping water with the fame text
preceded by the myfterious names of worlds, and
each time rubbing his hands as if wafhing them; and
finally, touching with his wet hand his feet, head,
breaft, eyes, ears, nofe, and navel, or his breaft,
navel, and both fhoulders, only (acording to another
rule) he fhould again fip water three times pronouncing to himfelf the expiatory text which recites
the creation. If he happen to fneeze, or fpit, he
muft

must not immediately sip water, but first touch his right ear in compliance with the maxim, "after sneezing, spitting, blowing his nose, sleeping, putting on apparel, or dropping tears, a man should not immediately sip water, but first touch his right ear." "Fire," says PARASARA, "water," the *védas*, "the "sun, moon, and air, all reside in the right ears of "*Bráhmanas. Ganga* is in their right ears, sacrificial "fire in their nostrils; at the moment when both are "touched, impurity vanishes." This, by the by, will explain the practice of suspending the end of the sacerdotal string over the right ear, to purify that string from the defilement which follows an evacuation of urine. The sipping of water is a requisite introduction of all rites; without it, says the *Samba purána*, all acts of religion are vain. Having therefore sipped water as above mentioned, and passed his hand filled with water briskly round his neck, while he recites this prayer: "May the waters pre- "serve me!" The priest closes his eyes, and meditates in silence, figuring to himself that BRA'HMA with fair faces, "and a red complexion, resides in his "navel; VISHNU with four arms and a black com- "plexion, in his heart; and SIVA with five faces and "a white complexion, in his forehead." The priest afterwards meditates the holiest of texts during three suppressions of breath. Closing the left nostril with the two longest fingers of his right hand, he draws his breath through the right nostril, and then closing that nostril likewise with his thumb, holds his breath while he meditates the text: he then raises both fingers off the left nostril, and emits the breath he had suppressed. While he holds his breath he must on this occasion repeat to himself the *Gáyatri* with the mysterious names of the worlds, the triliteral monosyllable, and the sacred text of BRA'HME. A suppression of breath so explained by the ancient legislator; YA'JNYAWALCYA consequently implies the following meditation, "Om! earth! sky! heaven! middle region! place of births! mansion of the blessed! abode of truth!" "We

" We meditate on the adorable light of the resplen-
" dent Generator which governs our intellects;
" which is water, lustre, favour, immortal faculty of
" thought, BRA'HME, earth, sky, and heaven."
According to the commentary, of which a copious
extract shall be subjoined, the text thus recited signifies, " That effulgent power which governs our in-
" tellects is the primitive element of water, the lus-
" tre of gems and other glittering substances, the favour
" of trees and herbs, the thinking soul of living be-
" ings ; it is the creator, preserver, and destroyer, the
" sun and every other deity and all which moves, or
" which is fixed in the three worlds, named, earth,
" sky, and heaven. The supreme BRA'HME, so ma-
" nifested, illumines the seven worlds ; may he unite
" my soul to his own radiance (that is to his own soul,
" which resides effulgent in the seventh world, or
" mansion of truth)." On another occasion, the concluding prayer, which is the *Gáyatri* of BRA'HME, is
omitted, and the names of the three lower worlds
only are premised : thus recited, the *Gáyatri* properly
so called, bears the following import : " On that
" effulgent power, which is BRA'HME himself, and is
" called the light of the radiant sun, do I meditate ;
" governed by the mysterious light which resides
" within me, for the purpose of thought ; that very
" light is the earth, the subtil ether, and all which ex-
" ists within the created sphere ; it is the threefold
" world, containing all which is fixed or moveable ; it
" exists internally in my heart, externally in the orb of
" the sun ; being one and the same with that efful-
" gent power. I myself am an irradiated manifestation
" of the supreme BRA'HME." With such reflections,
says the commentator, should the text be inaudibly
recited.

These expositions are justified by a very ample
commentary in which numerous authorities are cited ;
and to which the commentator has added many passages from ancient lawyers and from mythological
poems, showing the efficacy of these prayers in expiating

piating fin: as the foregoing explanations of the text are founded chiefly on the gloſs of an ancient philoſopher and legiſlator, *Yájnyawalcya*, the following extract will conſiſt of little more than a verbal tranſlation of his metrical gloſs:

" The parent of all beings produced all ſtates of exiſtence, for he generates and preſerves all creatures; therefore is he called the Generator. Becauſe he ſhines and ſports, becauſe he loves and irradiates, therefore is he called reſplendent or divine, and is praiſed by all deities. We meditate on the light which, exiſting in our minds, continually governs our intellects in the purſuits of virtue, wealth, love, and beatitude. Becauſe the being, who ſhines with ſeven rays, aſſuming the forms of time and of fire, matures productions. is reſplendent, illumines all, and finally deſtroys the univerſe, therefore, he who naturally ſhines with ſeven rays, is called Light, or the effulgent power. The firſt ſyllable denotes, that he illumines worlds; the ſecond conſonant implies, that he colours all creatures; the laſt ſyllable ſignifies, that he moves without ceaſing. From his cheriſhing all, he is called the irradiating Preſerver."

Although it appears, from the terms of the text, ("Light of the Generator or Sun,") that the ſun and the light ſpoken of are diſtant, yet, in meditating this ſublime text, they are undiſtinguiſhed; that light is the ſun and the ſun is light; they are identical. "The ſame effulgent and irradiating power which animates living beings, as their ſoul exiſts in the ſky, as the male being reſiding in the midſt of the ſun." There is conſequently no diſtinction; but that effulgence, which exiſts in the heart governing the intellects of animals, muſt alone be meditated as one and the ſame, however, with the luminous power reſiding in the orb of the ſun.

" That

"That which is in the fun and thus called light, or effulgent power, is adorable and muft be worfhipped by them who dread fucceffive births and deaths, and who eagerly defire beatitude. The being, who may be feen in the folar orb, muft be contemplated by the underftanding, to obtain exemption from fucceffive births and deaths and various pains."

The prayer is preceded by the names of the feven worlds, as epithets of it, to denote its efficacy; fignifying, 'that this light pervades and illumines the feven worlds, which, fituated one above the other, are the feven manfions of all beings: they are called the feven abodes, felf-exiftent, in a former period, renovated in this. Thefe feven myfterious words, are celebrated as the names of the feven worlds. The place where all beings, whether fixed or moveable, exift is called Earth, which is the firft world. That in which beings exift a fecond time, but without fenfation, again to become fenfible at the clofe of the period appointed for the duration of the prefent univerfe, is the world of re-exiftence. The abode of the good, where cold, heat, and light are perpetually produced, is named Heaven. The intermediate region, between the upper and lower worlds, is denominated the Middle World. The heaven where animals, deftroyed in a general conflagration at the clofe of the appointed period, are born again, is thence called the World of Births. That in which SANACA and other fons of BRA'HMA, juftified by auftere devotion, refide, exempt from all dominion, is thence named the Manfion of the Bleffed. Truth, the feventh world, and the abode of BRA'HME, is placed on the fummit above other worlds; it is attained by true knowledge, by the regular difcharge of duties, and by veracity: once attained, it is never loft. Truth is, indeed, the feventh world, therefore, called the Sublime Abode."

The names of the worlds are preceded by the triliteral monosyllable, to obviate the evil consequence announced by MENU, "A BRA'HMANA', beginning "and ending a lecture of the *véda*, (or the recital of "any holy strain,) must always pronounce to himself "the syllable *óm*: for unless the syllable *óm* precede, "his learning will slip away from him; and, unless "it follow, nothing will be long retained; or that syl- "lable is prefixed to the several names of worlds, de- "noting, that the seven worlds are manifestations of "the power signified by that syllable. As the leaf of "the *paláſá*," says YA'JNYAWALCYA, "is supported "by a single pedicle, so is this universe upheld by the "syllable *óm*, a symbol of the supreme BRA'HME." "All rites ordained in the *véda*, oblations to fire, and "solemn sacrifices, pass away, but that which passeth "not away," says MENU, is declared to be the sylla- "ble *óm*, then called *acſhara*, since it is a symbol of "GOD, the Lord of created beings."

"The concluding prayer is subjoined to teach the "various manifestations of that light, which is the Sun "himself. It is BRA'HME, the supreme soul. The "sun, says *Yájnyawalcya*, is BRA'HME; this is a "certain truth revealed in the sacred *upaniſhats*, and "in various *ſáchás* of the *védas*. So the *Bhaviſhya* "*purána*, speaking of the sun. Because there is none "greater than he, nor has been, nor will be, there- "fore he is celebrated as the supreme soul in all the "*védas*."

That greatest of lights, which exists in the sun, exists also as the principle of life in the hearts of all beings. It shines externally in the sky, internally in the heart; it is found in fire and in flame. This principle of life, which is acknowledged by the virtuous, as existing in the heart and in the sky, shines externally in the etherial region, manifested in the form of the sun. It is also
made

made apparent in the lustre of gems, stones, and metals, and in the taste of trees, plants, and herbs; that is, the irradiating being, who is a form of BRA'HME, is manifested in all moving beings (gods, demons, men, serpents, beasts, birds, insects, and the rest,) by their locomotion; and in some fixed substances, such as stones, gems, and metals, by their lustre; in others, such as trees, plants, and herbs, by their savour. Every thing, which moves, or which is fixed, is pervaded by that light, which, in all moving things, exists as the supreme soul, and as the immortal thinking faculty of beings, which have the power of motion. Thus, the venerable commentator says, " In the midst of the sun stands the " moon, in the midst of the moon is fire, in the midst " of light is truth, in the midst of truth is the unpe- " rishable being." And again, God is the unperishable " being, residing in the sacred abode; the thinking soul " is light alone; it shines with unborrowed splendour." This thinking soul, called the immortal " principle," is a manifestation of that irradiating power, who is the supreme soul.

This universe, consisting of three worlds, was produced from water. " He first, with a thought, created the waters, and placed in them a productive seed." *(Menu,* chap. i. v. 8.) Water which is the element, whence the three worlds proceeded, is that light, which is also the efficient cause of creation, duration, and destination, manifested with these powers, in the form of BRA'HMA, VISHNU, and RUDRA; to denote this, " earth, sky, and heaven," are subjoined as epithets of light. These terms bear allusion also to the three qualities of truth, passion, and darkness, corresponding with the three manifestations of power, as creator, preserver, and destroyer; hence it is also intimated, that the irradiating being is manifested as BRA'HMA, VISHNU, and RUDRA, who are respectively endued with the qualities of truth, passion, and darkness. The meaning is, that this irradiating being, who is the supreme
BRA'HME,

Brahme, manifested in three forms or powers, is the efficient cause of the creation of the universe, of its duration and destruction. So in the *Bhavishya purána*, Crishna says, "the sun is the god of per-"ception, the eye of the universe, the cause of day; "there is none greater than he among the immortal "powers. From him this universe proceeded, and in "him it will reach annihilation; he is time mea-"sured by instants, &c." Thus the universe, consist-ing of three worlds containing all which is fixed or moveable, is the irradiating being; and he is the cre-ator of that universe, the preserver and destroyer of it. Consequently nothing can exist, which is not that irradiating power.

These extracts from two very copious commentaries will sufficiently explain the texts, which are medi-tated while the breath is held as above mentioned. Immediately after these suppressions of breath, the priest should sip water reciting the following prayer, "May the sun sacrifice the regent of the firma-"ment and other deities who preside over sacrifice, "defend me from the sin arising from the imperfect "performance of a religious ceremony. Whatever "sin I have committed by night, in thought, word, "or deed, be that cancelled by day. Whatever sin be "in me, may that be far removed. I offer this water "to the sun, whose light irradiates my heart, who "sprung from the immortal essence. Be this obla-"tion efficacious." He should next make three ablu-tions with the prayers, "Waters! since ye afford de-light, &c." at the same time throwing water eight times on his head, or towards the sky, and once on the ground as before; and again make similar ablu-tions with the following prayer: "As a tired man "leaves drops of sweat at the foot of a tree; as "he who bathes is cleansed from all foulness; as "an oblation is sanctified by holy grass; so "may this water purify me from sin." And ano-ther ablution with the expiatory text, which re-hearses the creation. He should next fill the palm of his hand with water, and prefenting it to his nofe, inhale the fluid by one noftril, and, retaining it for a while, exhale it through the other, and throw away the water towards the north-eaft quarter. This is confidered as an internal ablution, which wafhes away fins. He concludes by fipping water with the following prayer, " Water ! thou doft penetrate all " beings ; thou doft reach the deep recelles of the " mountains ; thou art the mouth of the univerfe ; " thou art facrifice: thou art the myftick word *vafha*; " thou art light, tafte, and the immortal fluid."

After thefe ceremonies, he proceeds to worfhip the fun, ftanding on one foot, and refting the other againft his ankle or heel, looking towards the eaft, and holding his hands open before him in a hollow form. In this pofture he pronounces to himfelf the following prayers : 1ft, " The rays of light announce the " fplendid fiery fun, beautifully rifing to illumine " the univerfe." 2nd, " He rifes, wonderful, the " eye of the fun, of water, and of fire, collective power " of gods; he fills heaven, earth, and fky, with his " luminous net ; he is the foul of all which is fixed " or locomotive." 3d, " That eye, fupremely bene-" ficial, rifes pure from the eaft ; may we fee him " a hundred years ; may we live a hundred years ; " may we hear a hundred years." 4th, " May we, " preferved by the divine power, contemplating " heaven above the region of darknefs, approach the " deity, moft fplendid of luminaries." The following prayer may be alfo fubjoined, " Thou art felf-" exiftent, thou art the moft excellent ray ; thou " giveft effulgence : grant it unto me." This is explained as an allufion to the feven rays of the fun ; four of which are fuppofed to point towards the four quarters, one upwards, one downwards, and the feventh, which is centrical, is the moft excellent of all ; and is here addreffed, in a prayer, which is explained as fignifying, " May the fupreme ruler, who generates all things, whofe luminous ray is fel-

ex-

existent, who is the sublime cause of light, from whom worlds receive illumination, be favourable to us." After presenting an oblation to the sun, in the mode to be forthwith explained, the *Gáyatri* must be next invoked, in these words: " Thou art light; thou art seed; thou art immortal life; thou art effulgent: beloved by the gods, defamed by none, thou art the holiest sacrifice." And it should be afterwards recited measure by measure; then the two first measures as one hemistich, and the third measure as the other; and, lastly, the three measures without interruption. The same text is then invoked in these words: " Divine text, who dost grant our best wishes, whose name is trisyllable, whose import is the power of the Supreme Being; come thou mother of the *védas*, who didst spring from BRA'HME, be constant here." The *Gáyatri* is then pronounced inaudibly with the triliteral monosyllable, and the names of the three lower worlds, a hundred or a thousand times, or as often as may be practicable, counting the repetitions on a rosary of gems set in gold, or of wild grains. For this purpose, the seeds of the *putrajiva*, vulgarly named *pitonhia*, are declared preferable. The following prayers from the *Vishnu purána*, conclude these repetitions * : " Salutation to

* " I omit the very tedious detail respecting sins expiated by a set number of repetitions; but in one instance, as an atonement for unwarily eating or drinking what is forbidden, it is directed, that eight hundred repetitions of the *Gayatri* should be preceded by three suppressions of breath, touching water during the recital of the following text: ' The bull roars; he has four horns; three feet, two heads, seven hands, and is bound by a threefold ligature: he is the mighty resplendent being, and pervades mortal men.' The bull is justice personified. His four horns are the Brahma or superintending priest, the *Udgatri* or chanter of the *Samaveda*, the *Hotii* or render of the *Rigveda*, who performs the essential part of a religious ceremony, and *Adhwarin*, who fits in the sacred close and chants the *Yajurveda*. His three feet are the three *vedas*. Oblations and sacrifice are his two heads, roaring stupendously. His seven hands are the *Hotri*, *Mactravaruna*, *Brammanch bandafi*, *Gravattata*, *Adebhavac*, *Nishtri*, and *Potri*, names by which officiating priests are designed at certain solemn rites. The threefold ligature by which he is bound, is worshipped in the morning, at noon, and in the evening."

" the

" the sun; to that luminary, O BRA'HME, who is the
" light of the pervader, the " true generator of the uni-
" verse, the cause of efficacious rites." 2nd, " I bow to
" the great cause of day (whose emblem is a full blown
" flower of the *yava* tree) the mighty luminary sprung
" from CASYAPA, the foe of darkness, the de-
" stroyer of every sin:" or the priest walks a turn
through the south, rehearsing a short text, " I follow
" the course of the sun;" which is thus explained, " As
" the sun, in his course, moves round the world by
" the way of the south, so do I, following that lumi-
" nary, obtain the benefit arising from a journey round
" the earth, by the way of the south."

The oblation above mentioned, and which is called
Arg'há, consists of *tila*, flowers, barley, water, and
red sanders wood, in a clean copper vessel made in
the shape of a boat; this the priest places on his head,
and thus presents it with the following text, " He who
" travels the appointed path (namely the sun) is
" present in that pure orb of fire, and in the ethereal
" region, he is the sacrificer at religious rites, and he
" sits in the sacred close, never remaining a single day
" in the same spot, yet present in every house, in
" the heart of every human being, in the most holy
" mansion, in the subtle ether, produced in water, in
" earth, in the abode of truth, and in the stony moun-
" tains; he is that, which is both minute and vast."
This text is explained as signifying, that the sun
is a manifestation of the supreme being, present every
where, produced every where, pervading every place
and thing. The oblation is concluded by worshipping the sun with the subjoined text, " His rays, the
efficient causes of knowledge, irradiating worlds, appear like sacrificial fires."

Preparatory to any act of religion, ablutions must
be again performed in the form prescribed for
the mid-day bath; the practice of bathing at
noon

noon is likewife enjoined as requifite to cleanlinefs, conducive to health and efficacious in removing fpiritual as well as corporeal defilements: it muft neverthelefs be omitted by one who is afflicted with difeafe; and a healthy perfon is forbidden to bathe immediately after a meal, and without laying afide his jewels and other ornaments. If there be no impediment, fuch as thofe now mentioned or formerly noticed, in fpeaking of early ablutions he may bathe with water drawn from a well, from a fountain, or from a bafon of a cataract; but he fhould prefer water which lays above ground, choofing a ftream rather than ftagnant water, a river in preference to a fmall brook, a holy ftream before a vulgar river, and, above all, the water of the Ganges. In treating of the bath authors diftinguifh various ablutions, properly and improperly fo called, fuch as rubbing the body with afhes, which is named a bath facred to fire, plunging into water, a bath facred to the regent of this element: ablutions accompanied by the prayers, " O waters! fince ye afford delight, &c." which conftitute the holy bath: ftanding in duft raifed by the treading of cows, a bath denominated from wind or air; ftanding in the rain during daylight, a bath named from the fky or atmofphere. The ablution or bath properly fo called are performed with the following ceremonies.

After bathing and cleaning his perfon and pronouncing as a vow, " I will now perform ablutions," he who bathes fhould invoke the holy river; " O *Ganga, Yamuna, Sarafwati, Satadru, Marudvidha,* and *Jiyiciva!* hear my prayers; for my fake be included in this fmall quantity of water with the holy ftreams of *Paruflati Aficni,* and *Vitafta."* He fhould alfo utter the *radical prayer* confifting of the words " Salutation to *Narayana."* Upon this occafion a prayer extracted from the *Padma purána* is often ufed with this falutation called the *radical text;* and the ceremony is at once concluded by taking up the earth

and

and pronouncing the subjoined prayers: "Earth,
"supporter of all things, trampled by horses, tra-
"versed by cars, trodden by VISHNU! whatever sin
"has been committed by me, do thou, who art
"upheld by the hundred armed CRISHNA, incar-
"nate in the shape of a boar, ascend my limbs, and
"remove every such sin."

The text extracted from the *padma purána* follows:
"thou didst spring from the foot of VISHNU daughter
"of VISHNU, honoured by him; therefore pre-
"serve us from sin, protecting us from the day of
"our birth, even unto death. The regent of air has
"named thirty-five millions of holy places in the sky,
"on earth, and in the space between; they are all
"comprised in the daughter JAHNU. Thou art called
"she, who promotes growth, among the gods: thou
"art named the lotos; able, wife of PRITHU, bird,
"body of the universe, wife of SIVA, nectar, female
"cherisher of science, cheerful, favouring worlds; mer-
"ciful, daughter of JAHNU, consoler, giver of
"consolation. *Ganga*, who flows through the three
"worlds, will be near unto him, who pronounces these
"pure titles during his ablution."

When the ceremony is preferred in its full detail, the regular prayer is a text of the *véda*. "Thrice did
"VISHNU step, and at three strides traversed the uni-
"verse: happily was his foot placed on this dusty
"earth. Be this oblation efficacious!" By this prayer is meant, "May the earth, thus taken up, pu-
"rify me." Cow dung is next employed with a prayer importing, "Since I take up cow dung, invoking there-
"on the goddess of abundance, may I obtain pros-
"perity!" the literal sense is this: "I here invoke that
"goddess of abundance, who is the vehicle of smell,
"who is irresistible, ever white, present in this cow
"dung, mistress of all beings, greatest of ele-
"ments, ruling all the senses." Water is after-
"wards held up in the hollow of both hands
joined

joined, while the prayer denominated from the regent of water is pronounced: "Because VARUNA, king of waters, spread a road for the sun, therefore do I follow that route. Oh! he made that road in untrodden space, to receive the footsteps of the sun. It is he who restrains the heart-rending wicked." The sense is, "VARUNA, king of waters, who curbs the wicked, made an expanded road in the other real region to receive the rays of the sun; I therefore follow that route." Next, previous to swimming, a short prayer must be meditated: "Salutation to the regent of water! past are the fetters of VARUNA." This is explained as importing that the displeasure of VARUNA, at a man's traversing the waters which are his fetters, is averted by salutation: swimming is therefore preceded by this address. The priest should next recite the invocation of holy rivers, and thrice throw water on his head from the hollow of both hands joined, repeating three several texts: 1st. "Waters! remove this sin, whatever it be, which is "in me; whether I have done any thing malicious "towards others, or cursed them in my heart, or "spoken falsehoods." 2d. "Waters! mothers of "worlds! purify us; cleanse us by the sprinkled fluid "ye who purify through libations; for, ye, divine wa- "ters, do remove every sin." 3d. "As a tired man "leaves drops of sweat at the foot of a tree, &c." Again, swimming and making a circuit through the south, this prayer should be recited: "May divine "waters be auspicious to us for accumulation, for "gain, and for refreshing draughts: may they "listen to us, that we may be associate with good "auspices." Next reciting the following prayer the priest should thrice plunge into water: "O consum- "mation of solemn rites! who dost purify when per- "formed by the most greivous offenders; thou dost "invite the basest criminals to purification; thou "dost expiate the most heinous crimes. I atone "for sins towards the gods by gratifying them "with oblations and sacrifice; I expiate sins to- "wards mortals by employing mortal men to offici-
ate

" ate at sacraments. Therefore defend me from the
" pernicious sin of offending the gods."

Water must be next sipped with the prayer, " Lord
" of sacrifice, thy heart is in the midst of the waters
" of the ocean, &c." and the invocation of holy rivers
is again recited. The priest must thrice throw up water with the three prayers, " O waters since ye afford
" delight, &c." and again, with the three subjoined
prayers: 1st, " May the Lord of thought purify
" me with an uncut blade of *cusa* grass, and with the
" rays of the sun. Lord of purity, may I obtain that
" coveted innocence, which is the wish of thee, who
" is satisfied with this oblation of water and of me,
" who am purified by this holy grass." 2nd, " May
" the Lord of speech purify me, &c." 3d. " May
" the resplendent sun purify me, &c." Thrice plunging into water, the priest should as often repeat the
grand expiatory text, of which YAJNYAWALCY'A says,
" it comprises the principles of things, and the elements, the existence of the (chaotick) mass,
" the production and destruction of worlds." This
serves as a key to explain the meaning of the text,
which being considered as the essence of the *védas*,
is most mysterious. The author before me, seems to
undertake the explanation of it with great awe, and
intimates, that he has no other key to its meaning,
nor the aid of earlier commentaries. " The Supreme
" Being alone existed; afterwards there was universal
" darkness; next the watery ocean was produced,
" by the diffusion of virtue; then did the Creator,
" lord of the universe, rise out of the ocean, and successively frame the sun and moon, which govern
" day and night, whence proceeds the revolution of
" years; and after them he framed heaven and earth,
" the space between, and the celestial region." The
terms with which the text begins, both signify truth,
but here explained as denoting the supreme BRA'HME,
on the authority of a text quoted from the *véda*:

" BRA'HME

"Bra'hme is truth, the one immutable being. He is truth and everlasting knowledge." 'During the period of general annihilation, says the commentator, the Supreme Being alone existed. Afterwards, during that period, night was produced; in other words, there was universal darkness.' "This universe existed only in darkness, imperceptible, undefinable, undiscoverable by reason, and undiscovered by revelation as if it were wholly immersed in sleep." (Menu, ch. I. v. 5.) Next, when the creation began, the ocean was produced by an unseen power universally diffused; that is, the element of water was first reproduced, as the means of the creation: "He first, with a thought, created the waters, &c." (Menu, ch. I. v. 8.) Then did the Creator, when lord of the universe, rise out of the waters. 'The lord of the universe, annihilated by the general destruction, revived with his own creation of the three worlds.' Heaven is here explained the expanse of the sky above the region of the stars. The celestial region is the middle world and heavens above. The author before me, has added numerous quotations on the sublimity and efficacy of this text, which Menu compares with the sacrifice of a horse, in respect of its power to obliterate sins.

After bathing, while he repeats this prayer, the priest should again plunge into water, thrice repeating the text, "As a tired man leaves drops of sweat at the foot of a tree, &c." Afterwards, to atone for greater offences, he should meditate the *Gāyatrī*, &c. during three suppressions of breath. He must also recite it measure by measure, hemistich by hemistich; and, lastly, the entire text without any pause. As an expiation of the sin of eating with men of very low tribes, or of coveting or accepting what should not be received, a man should plunge into water, at the same time reciting a prayer which will be quoted on another occasion. One who has drunk spirituous liquors should
traverse

traverse water up to his throat, and drink as much expressed juice of the moon plant, as he can take up in the hollow of both hands, while he meditates the triliteral monosyllable, and then plunge into water, reciting the subjoined prayer, "O RUDRA! hurt "not our offspring and descendants; abridge not the "period of our lives; destroy not our cows; kill not "our horses; flay not our proud and irritable folks; "because, holding oblations, we always pray to "thee."

Having finished his ablutions, and coming out of the water, putting on his apparel after cleansing it, having washed his hands and feet, and having sipped water, the priest sits down to worship in the same mode, which was directed after the early bath: substituting, however, the following prayer, in lieu of that which begins with the words, "May the sun, sacrifice, &c." "May the waters purify the earth, "that she, being cleansed, may purify me: may the "lord of holy knowledge purify her, that she being "cleansed by holiness, may purify me: may the wa- "ters free me from every defilement, whatever be my "uncleanness, whether I have eaten prohibited food, "done forbidden acts, or accepted the gifts, of dis- "honest men." Another difference between worship at noon and in the morning, consists in standing before the sun with uplifted arms, instead of joining the hands in a hollow form. In all other respects the form of adoration is similar.

Having concluded this ceremony, and walked in a round beginning through the south, and saluted the sun, the priest may proceed to study a portion of the *véda*. Turning his face towards the east, with his right hand towards the south, and his left hand towards the north, sitting down with the *cusa* grass before him, holding two sacred blades of grass on the tips of his left fingers, and placing his right hand thereon, with the palm turned upwards, and having thus meditated the *Gáyatrí*, the priest should recite the proper text on commencing the lecture,

lecture, and read as much of the *védas* as may be practicable for him, continuing the practice daily until he have read the whole of the *védas*; and then recommencing the course.

Prayer on beginning a lecture of the *Rigveda*: " I praise the blazing fire, which is first placed at " religious rites, which effects the ceremony, for the " benefit of the votary, which performs the essential " part of the rite, which is the most liberal giver of " gems."

On beginning a lecture of the *Yajurveda*: " I ga- " ther thee, O branch of the *véda*, for the sake of rain ; " I pluck thee for the sake of strength. Calves! ye " are like unto air; (that is, as wind supplies the world " by means of rain, so do ye supply sacrifices by the " milking of cows). May the luminous generator of " worlds, make you attain success in the best of sa- " craments."

On the beginning a lecture of the *Samaveda*: " Re- " gent of fire, who dost effect all religious ceremo- " nies, approach to taste my offering ; thou who art " praised for the sake of oblations, sit down on this " grass."

The text which is repeated on commencing a lec- ture of the *Atharva véda* has been already quoted on another occasion : " May divine waters be auspi- " cious to us, &c."

In this manner should a lecture of the *védas*, or of the *védangas*, of the sacred poems and mytholo- gical history of law and other branches of sound literature be conducted. The priest should next proceed to offer barley, *tila* and water to the manes. Turning his face towards the east, wearing the sacrificial cord on his left shoulder, he should sit down and spread *cusa* grass before him
with

with the tips pointing towards the east. Taking grains of barley in his right hand, he should invoke the gods. "O assembled gods! hear my call, sit "down on this grass;" then throwing away some grains of barley, and putting one hand over the other, he should pray in these words: "Gods! who reside "in the ethereal region, in the world near us, and in "heaven above; ye whose tongues are flame, and "who save all them who duly perform the sacraments, "hear my call, sit down on this grass, and be cheer- "ful." Spreading the *cusa* grass, the tips of which must point towards the east, and placing his left hand thereon, and his right hand above the left, he must offer grains of barley and water from the tips of his fingers, (which are parts dedicated to the gods,) holding three straight blades of grass, so that the tips be towards his thumb, and repeating this prayer: "May the gods be satisfied; may the holy verses, "the scriptures, the devout sages, the sacred poems, "the teachers of them, and the celestial quiristers; "be satisfied; may other instructors, human beings, "minutes of time, moments, instants measured "by the twinkling of an eye, hours, days, fort- "nights, months, seasons, and years, with all their "component parts be satisfied herewith *." Next wearing the sacrificial thread round his neck, and turning towards the north, he should offer *tila*, or grains of barley with water, from the middle of his hand (which is a part dedicated to human be- ings), holding in it *cusa* grass, the middle of which must rest on the palm of his hand: this oblation he presents on grass, the tips of which are pointed towards the north; and with it he pronounces these words: "May SANACA be satisfied; may SAMAN- "DANA, SANATANA, CAPILA, ASURI, BODHU, "and PARCHASICHA, be satisfied herewith." Placing the thread, &c. on his right shoulder, and turning towards the south, he must offer *tila* and wa-

* The verb is repeated with each term, "May the holy verses "be satisfied; may the *vedas* be satisfied, &c."

ter from the root of his thumb (which is a part sacred to the progenitors of mankind) holding bent grass thereon; this oblation he should present upon a vessel of rhinoceros' horn placed on grass, the tips of which are pointed towards the south; and with it he says, "May fire, which receives oblations, presented to our forefather be satisfied herewith; may the moon, the judge of departed souls, the sun, the progenitors who are purified by fire, those who are named from their drinking the juice of the moon-plant, and those who are denominated from sitting on holy grass, be satisfied herewith!" He must then make a similar oblation, saying, "May NA'RA'-S'ARYA, PA'RA'S'ARYA, S'UCA, SA'CALYA, YAJ'-NYAWALCYA, JA'TUCARN'A, CA'TYA'YANA, APAS-TAMBA, BAUD'HA'YANA, VA'CHACUT'I', VACJAVA'-PI', HU'HU', LO'CA'CSHI', MAITRA'YAN'I', and AINDRA'YAN'I', be satisfied herewith." He afterwards offers three oblations of water mixed with *tila*, from the hollow of both hands joined, and this he repeats fourteen times with the different titles of YAMA, which are considered as fourteen distinct forms of the same deity. "Salutation to YAMA, salutation to DHERMARAJA, or the king of deities, to death, to ANTACA or the destroyer, to VAIVASWATA or the child of the sun, to time, to the slayer of all beings, to AUDHUMBARA or YAMA springing out of the racemiferous fig tree, to him who reduces all things to ashes, to the dark-blue deity, to him who resides in the supreme abode, to him whose belly is like that of a wolf, to the variegated being, to the wonderful inflictor of pains." Taking up grains of *tila*, and throwing them away while he pronounces this address to fire: "Eagerly we place and support thee; eagerly we give thee fuel; do thou fondly invite the progenitors, who love thee, to taste this pious oblation." Let him invoke the progenitors of mankind in these words: "May our progenitors, who are worthy of drinking the juice of the moon-plant, and they who are "purified

" purified by fire, approach us through the paths
" which are travelled by gods; and pleased with the
" food presented at the sacrament, may they ask for
" more, and preserve us from evil." He should
then offer a triple oblation of water with both
hands, reciting the following text, and saying, " I offer
" this *tila* and water to my father, such a one sprung
" from such a family." He must offer similar oblations to his paternal grandfather, great-grandfather;
and another set of similar oblations to his maternal
grandfather, and to the father and grandfather of that
ancestor; a similar oblation must be presented to
his mother, and single oblations to his paternal
grandmother and great-grandmother: three more oblations are presented, each to three persons, paternal
uncle, brother, son, grandsons, daughter's son, son-in-
law, maternal uncles, sister's son, father's sister's son,
mother's sister, and other relations. The text alluded
to bears this meaning: " Waters be the food of
" our progenitors; satisfy my parents, ye who con-
" vey nourishment, which is the drink of immortality,
" the fluid of libations, the milky liquor, the con-
" fined and promised food of the manes."

The ceremony may be concluded with three voluntary oblations; the first presented like the oblations to deities, looking towards the east, and with the
sacrificial cord placed on his left shoulder. The
second like that offered to progenitors, looking towards
the south, and with the string passed over his right
shoulder. The prayers which accompany these offerings are subjoined: 1st. " May the gods, demons,
" benevolent genii, huge serpents, heavenly quiristers,
" fierce giants, blood thirsty savages, unmelodious
" guadians of the celestial treasure, successful genii, spi-
" rits called *Cushmanda*, trees, and all animals, which move
" in air or in water, which live on earth, and feed abroad,
" may all these quickly obtain contentment, through
" the water presented by me." 2nd. " To satisfy
" them

"them who are detained in all the hells and places
"of torment, this water is prefented by me." 3d.
"May thofe, who are, and thofe who are not, of
"kin to me, and thofe who were allied to me in a
"former exiftence, and all who defire oblations of
"water from me obtain perfect contentment." The
firft text which is taken from the *Samaveda* differs a
little from the *Yajurveda:* "Gods, benevolent genii,
"huge ferpents, nymphs, demons, wicked beings,
"fnakes, birds of mighty wing, trees, giants; and
"all who traverfe the ethereal region, genii who che-
"rifh fcience, animals that live in water or traverfe
"the atmofphere, creatures that have no abode, and
"all living animals which exift in fin or in the prac-
"tice of virtue; to fatisfy them is this water prefented
"by me." Afterwards, the prieft fhould wring his
lower garment pronouncing this text: "May thofe
"who have been born in my family, and have died,
"leaving no fon nor kinfman, bearing the fame name,
"be contented with this water which I prefent by
"wringing it from my vefture." Then placing his
facrificial cord on his left fhoulder, fipping water,
and raifing up his arms, let him contemplate the fun,
reciting a prayer inferted above: "He who tra-
"vels the appointed path," &c. The prieft fhould
afterwards prefent an oblation of water to the fun pronouncing the text of the *Vifhnu purána* which has
been already cited, "Salutation to the fun," &c.
He then concludes the whole ceremony by worfhipping the fun with a prayer above quoted: "Thou
"art felf-exiftent," &c. by making a circuit through
the fouth while he pronounces, "I follow the courfe
"of the fun;" and by offering water from the hollow
of his hand while he falutes the regents of fpace
and other Deities. "Salutation to fpace; to the re-
"gents of fpace, to BRA'HMA, to the earth, to falu-
"tary herbs, to fire, to fpeech, to the lord of fpeech,
"to the pervader, and to the mighty Deity."

C. E. CAR-

C. E. CARRINGTON, ESQ.

Secretary to the Asiatick Society.

Sir,

THE sacrifice of human and other victims, and the sacrificial rites celebrated by the *Hindus*, having being represented to me as a subject of curious investigation, which, from a comparison with the ceremonies used on similar occasions, by other ancient nations, might perhaps be interesting, as well to the Society, as to the learned in *Europe*, I procured the *Calica Puran*, in which I was given to understand, I should meet with full information on the subject. To effect this purpose, I translated the *Rudhirádhyáyă* or sanguinary chapter, which treats of human, as well as of other sacrifices, in which blood is shed. I hope also in my next communication, to lay before the Society, a full account of the Goddess Cali, to whom these sacrifices are made, and of the *Bhairăvăs*, sons of Siva, to two of whom the chapter is addressed by Siva.

I am, &c. &c. &c.

W. C. Blaquiere.

Calcutta, August 15th, 1796.

XXIII.

THE RUDHIRÁDHYÁYÅ,

OR SANGUINARY CHAPTER;

TRANSLATED FROM THE CALICA PURAN.

BY W. C. BLAQUIERE, ESQ.

SALUTATION TO CALICA.

[*Shĭvă addreſses Betál, Bhairăva, and Bhairăvă.*]

I Will relate you, my fons, the ceremonies and rules to be obferved in facrifices, which being duly attended to are productive of the divine favour.

The forms laid down in the *vaiſhnăivi Tăntră*, are to be followed on all occafions, and may be obferved by facrificers to all Deities.

Birds, tortoifes, allegators, fiſh, nine fpecies of wild animals, buffaloes, bulls, he-goats, ichneumons, wild boars, rhinocerofes, antelopes, guanas, reindeer, lions, tygers, men, and blood drawn from the offerer's own body, are looked upon as proper oblations to the Goddefs *Chandica*, the *Bhairăvăs*, &c.

It is through facrifices that princes obtain blifs, heaven, and victory over their enemies.

The pleafure which the Goddefs receives from an oblation of the blood of fiſh and tortoifes tortoises is of one month's duration, and three from that of a crocodile. By the blood of the nine species of wild animals, the Goddess is satisfied nine months, and for that space of time continues propitious to the offerer's welfare. The blood of the wild bull and guana give pleasure for one year, and that of the antelope and wild boar for twelve years. The *Sărăbhă's* * blood satisfies the Goddess for twenty-five years, and buffalo's and rhinoceros's blood for a hundred, and that of the tyger an equal number. That of the lion, rein-deer, and the human species produces pleasure, which lasts a thousand years. The flesh of these, severally, gives the Goddess pleasure for the same duration of time as their blood. Now attend to the different fruits attending an offering of the flesh of a rhinoceros or antelope, as also of the fish called *rohita*.

The flesh of the antelope and rhinoceros pleases the Goddess five hundred years and the *rohita* fish and *Bardhrinasa* give my beloved (i. e. the Goddess CALI delight for three hundred years.)

A spotless goat, who drinks only twice in twenty-four hours, whose limbs are slender, and who is the prime among a herd, is called a *Bardhrinasa*, and is reckoned as the best of *Hăvyăs*, (i. e. offerings to the Deities); and *Căvyăs*, (i. e. offerings to deceased progenitors.)

The bird whose throat is blue and head red and legs black with white feathers, is called also *Bardhrinasi*, and is king of the birds, and the favorite of me and VISHNU.

By a human sacrifice attended by the forms laid down, DEVI is pleased one thousand years, and

* Sarabhas, an animal of a very fierce nature, said to have eight feet.

by a sacrifice of three men, one hundred thousand years. By human flesh, *Cámác'hyá*, *Chāndicá*, and *Bhairavī* who assumes my shape, are pleased one thousand years. An oblation of blood which has been rendered pure by holy texts, is equal to ambrosia; the head and flesh also afford much delight to the Goddess *Chāndicá*. Let therefore the learned, when paying adoration to the Goddess, offer blood and the head, and when performing the sacrifice to fire, make oblations of flesh.

Let the performer of the sacrifice be cautious never to offer bad flesh, as the head and blood are looked upon by themselves equal to ambrosia.

The gourd, sugar cane, spirituous liquors, and fermented liquors are looked upon as equivalent to other offerings, and please the Goddess for the same duration of time as the sacrifice of a goat.

The performance of the sacrifice, with a *Chāndrahāsā*, or *cātri* (two weapons of the ax kind) is reckoned the best mode, and with a hatchet or knife, or saw, or a *sangcul*, the second best, and the beheading with a hoe a *Bhāllāc* (an instrument of the spade kind), the inferior mode.

Exclusive of these weapons, no others of the spear or arrow kind ought ever to be used in performing a sacrifice, as the offering is not accepted by the Goddess, and the giver of it dies. He who, with his hands, tears off the head of the consecrated animal, or bird, shall be considered equally guilty with him who has slain a *Bráhmen*, and shall undergo great sufferings.

Let not the learned use the ax, before they have invoked it by holy texts, which have been mentioned heretofore, and framed by the learned

for

for the occasion; let those I now tell you, be joined to them and the ax invoked, and particularly so, where the sacrifice is to be made to the Goddesses *Durgá*, and *Cámác'hyá*.

Let the sacrificer repeat the word CA'LI twice, then the words *Devi Bajreswari*, then *Lawhā Dāndáyai, Namah!* which words may be rendered *Hail! Cali, Cali! Hail! Devi!* goddess of thunder, *Hail iron sceptered Goddess!* Let him then take the ax in his hand, and again invoke the same by the *Cálratriyá* text as follows.

Let the sacrificer say *Hrang Hring. Cali, Cali!* O horrid toothed Goddess; eat, cut, destroy all the malignant, cut with this ax; bind, bind; seize, seize; drink blood; spheng, spheng; secure, secure. Salutations to *Cali*. Thus ends the *Calratriyá Mántrā*.

The *Charga* (the ax) being invoked by this text called the *Cálratriyá Mántrā*, *Cálrátri* (the Goddess of darkness) herself presides over the ax uplifted for the destruction of the sacrificer's enemies.

The sacrificers must make use of all the texts directed previous to the sacrifice, and also of the following, addressing himself to the victim.

Beasts were created by the self-existing, himself to be immolated at sacrifices: I therefore immolate thee, without incurring any sin in depriving thee of life.

Let the sacrificer then name the Deity to whom the sacrifice is made, and the purpose for which it is performed; and by the above text immolate the victim

victim, whose face is to be towards the north, or else let the sacrificer turn his own face to the north, and the victim's to the east. Having immolated the victim, let him without fail mix salt, &c. as before mentioned with the blood.

The vessel in which the blood is to be presented, is to be according to the circumstances of the offerer, of gold, silver, copper, brass, or leaves sewed together, or of earth, or of tutenague, or of any of the species of wood used in sacrifices.

Let it not be presented in an iron vessel, nor in one made of the hide of an animal, or the bark of a tree; nor in a pewter, tin, or leaden vessel. Let not the blood be represented in the holy vessel named *srub* and *sruch,* nor on the ground. Let it not be presented in the *Ghătă* (i. e. an earthen jar always used in other religious ceremonies.) Let it not be presented by pouring it on the ground, or into any of the vessels used at other times for offering food to the Deity. Let not the good man who wishes for prosperity, offer the blood in any of these vessels. Human blood must always be presented in a metalic or earthen vessel; and never on any account in a vessel made of leaves, or similar substance.

The offering a horse, except at the *Aswamedha* sacrifice, is wrong, as also offering an elephant, except at the *Găjă Medha*; let therefore the ruler of men observe never to offer them except on those occasions. And on no account whatsoever let him offer them to the Goddess *Devi*, using the wild bull called *Chánrără* as a substitute for the horse, when the occasion requires one.

Let

Let not a *Bráhmen* ever offer a lion or a tyger, or his own blood, or spirituous liquors to the Goddess *Devi*. If a *Bráhmen* sacrifices either a lion, a tyger, or a man, he goes to hell, and passes but a short time in this world attended with misery and misfortune.

If a *Bráhmen* offers his own blood, his guilt is equal to that of the slayer of a *Bráhmen*; and if he offers spirituous liquors, he is no longer a Bráhmen.

Let not a *Cshectree* offer an antelope: if he does, he incurs the guilt of a Bráhmen slayer; where the sacrifice of lions, of tygers, or of the human species is required, let the three first classes act thus: having formed the image of the lion, tyger, or human shape with butter, paste, or barley meal, let them sacrifice the same as if a living victim, the ax being first invoked by the text *Němō*, &c.

Where the sacrifice of a number of animals is to take place it is sufficient to bring and present two or three to the Deity, which serves as a consecration of the whole. I have now related to you, O *Bhairává*, in general terms, the ceremonies and forms of sacrifices: attend now to the different texts to be used on the several different occasions.

When a buffalo is presented to *Devi*, *Bhairaree*, or *Bhairávi* let the sacrificer use the following Mántrá in invoking the victim.

" In the manner that thou destroyest horses, in the
" manner that thou carriest *Chándicá*, destroy my enemies, and bear prosperity to me, O buffalo!

" On

"O steed of death, of exquisite and unperishable form, produce me long life and fame. Salutation to thee, O buffalo!"

Let him then address the *Charga* (ax) calling it *Guhá Játă*, i. e. the cavern born, and besprinkle it with water, saying, "Thou art the instrument used in sacrifices to the gods and ancestors, O ax! of equal might with the wild rhinoceros, cut asunder my evils. O cavern-born! salutation to thee again and again."

At the sacrifice of an antelope, the following *Măntră* is to be used:

"O antelope! representative of BRA'HMA, the emblem of his glory, thou who art even as the foud *védas*, and learned, grant me extensive wisdom and celebrity."

At the sacrifice of a *Sărăbhă*, let the following *Măntră* be used: "O *eight*-footed animal! O sportful native of the *Chăndră Bhăgă* mountains! thou eight-formed long-armed animal*; thou who art called *Bhairăvă*: salutation to thee again and again! assume the terrifick form, under which thou destroyest the wild boar, and in the same manner destroy my enemies."

At the sacrifice of a lion: "O HERI, who, in the shape of a lion, bearest *Chăndicá*, bear my evils and avert my misfortunes. Thy shape, O lion! was assumed by HERI, to punish the wicked part of the human race, and under that form, by truth, the tyrant *Hirănyă Căsipu* was destroyed." I have now

---

* A mark of eminence.

related to thee, O *Bhairăvă*, who art void of ſin, the mode of paying adoration to the lion.

Now attend to the particulars relative to the offering of human blood.

Let a human victim be ſacrificed at a place of holy worſhip, or at a cemetery where dead bodies are buried. Let the oblation be performed in the part of the cemetery called *Heruca*, which has been already deſcribed, or at a temple of *Cămăc'hyá*, or on a mountain. Now attend to the mode.

The cemetery repreſents me, and is called *Bhairăvă*, it has alſo a part called *Tăntrăngă*; the cemetery muſt be divided into theſe two diviſions, and a third called *Heruca*.

The human victim is to be immolated in the eaſt diviſion, which is ſacred to *Bhairăvă*; the head is to be preſented in the ſouth diviſion, which is looked upon as the place of ſculls ſacred to *Bhairăví*, and the blood is to be preſented in the weſt diviſion, which is denominated *Heruca*.

Having immolated a human victim, with all the requiſite ceremonies at a cemetery or holy place, let the ſacrificer be cautious not to caſt eyes upon the victim.

On other occaſions alſo, let not the ſacrificer caſt eyes upon the victim immolated, but preſent the head with eyes averted.

The victim muſt be a perſon of good appearance, and be prepared by ablutions, and requiſite ceremonies, ſuch as eating conſecrated food the day before,

fore, and by abstinence from flesh and venery; and must be adorned with chaplets of flowers and besmeared with sandal wood.

Then causing the victim to face the north, let the sacrificer worship the several deities, presiding over the different parts of the victim's body: let the worship be then paid to the victim himself by his name.

Let him worship *Bráhma* in the victim's *Bráhma Rhandra*, i. e. cave of *Bráhma*, cavity in the skull, under the spot where the *saturæ coronalis* and *sagittalis* meet*. Let him worship the earth in his nose, saying, *Medinyaih nämäh*, and casting a flower; in his ears, *ácásä*, the subtil ether, saying, *ácásáyä nämäh*; in his tongue, *sarvata much'ha*, (i. e. *Bráhma Agni*, &c. the regents of speech, &c.) saying, *sarvata much'häya nämäh*; the different species of light in his eyes, and *Vishnu* in his mouth. Let him worship the moon on his forehead, and *Indra* on his right cheek. fire on his left cheek, death on his throat, at the tips of his hair the regent of the south-west quarter, and *Varuna* between the eye-brows; on the bridge of the nose let him pay adoration to wind, and on the shoulders to *Dhănêśwărä*, (i. e. god of riches,) then worshipping the *sărpă rájà*, (i. e. king of serpents,) on the stomach of the victim, let him pronounce the following *Mantrà*:

" O best of men! O most auspicious! O thou who
" art an assemblage of all the deities, and most exqui-
" site! bestow thy protection on me, save me, thy
" devoted, save my sons, my cattle, and kindred;
" preserve the state, the ministers belonging to
" it, and all friends, and as death is unavoida-
" ble, part with (thy organs of) life, doing an
" act of benevolence. Bestow upon me,

* This is done by casting a flower there, saying, *Brabmaye namah*; salutation to *Brahma*.

" O most

" O moſt auſpicious! the bliſs which is obtained by
" the moſt auſtere devotion, by acts of charity and
" performance of religious ceremonies; and at the ſame
" time, O moſt excellent! attain ſupreme bliſs thy-
" ſelf. May thy auſpices, O moſt auſpicious! keep
" me ſecure from *Rácſhaſas*, *Piſachos*, terrors, ſerpents,
" bad princes, enemies, and other evils; and death
" being inevitable, charm *Bhágavati* in thy laſt mo-
" ments by copious ſtreams of blood ſpouting from
" the arteries of thy fleſhy neck."

Thus let the ſacrificer worſhip the victim, adding whatever other texts are applicable to the occaſion,
and have been before mentioned.

When this has been done, O my children! the
victim is even as myſelf, and the guardian deities of
the ten quarters take place in him; then *Bráhma* and
all the other deities aſſemble in the victim, and be he
ever ſo great a ſinner, he becomes pure from ſin, and
when pure, his blood changes to ambroſia, and he
gains the love of *Me'hade'vi*, the Goddeſs of the *Yog
Niddrá*, (i. e. *the tranquil repoſe of the mind from an
abſtraction of ideas*;) who is the Goddeſs of the whole
univerſe, the very univerſe itſelf. He does not return
for a conſiderable length of time in the human form,
but becomes a ruler of the *Gănă Devătăs*, and is
much reſpected by me myſelf. The victim who is
impure from ſin or ordure and urine, *Cámác'hyá* will
not even hear named.

By the repetitions of the texts, and forms laid down
for the ſacrifice of buffalos, and other animals, their
bodies become pure and their blood acceptable to the
Goddeſs *Shivá*.

On

On occasions of sacrifices to other deities also, both the deities and victims must be worshipped, previous to the immolation.

The blind, the crippled, the aged, the sick, the afflicted with ulcers, the hermophradite, the imperfectly formed, the scarred, the timid, the leprous, the dwarfish, and the perpetrator of *méhá pataca*, (heinous offences, such as flaying a *Bráhmen*, drinking spirits, stealing gold, or defiling a spiritual teacher's bed,) one under twelve years of age, one who is impure from the death of a kinsman, &c. one who is impure from the death of *méhá guru*, (father and mother,) which impurity lasts one whole year: these severally are unfit subjects for immolation, even though rendered pure by sacred texts.

Let not the female, whether quadruped or bird, or a woman be ever sacrificed; the sacrificer of either will indubitably fall into hell, where the victim of either the beasts or birds creation, are very numerous, the immolation of a female is excuseable; but this rule does not hold good, as to the human species.

Let not a beast be offered under three months old, or a bird who is under three *pacsha* (forty-five days). Let not a beast or bird who is blind, deficient in a limb, or ill-formed, be offered to *Dévi*, nor one who is in any respect unfit, from the reasons which have been set forth, when speaking of the human race; let not animals and birds with mutilated tails, or ears, or broken teeth, or horns, be presented on any account.

Let not a *Bráhmen* or a *Chandala* be sacrificed; nor a prince; nor that which has been already presented to a *Bráhmen*, or a deity; nor the offspring of a prince, nor one who has conquered in battle; nor the offspring of a *Bráhmen*, or of a *Cſhettree*; nor a childleſs brother, nor a father, nor a learned perſon, nor one who is unwilling, nor the maternal uncle of the ſacrificer. Thoſe not here named, and animals, and birds of unknown ſpecies are unfit. If thoſe named are not forthcoming, let their place be ſupplied by a male aſs or camel. If other animals are forthcoming, the ſacrifice of a tyger, camel, or aſs muſt be avoided.

Having firſt worſhipped the victim, whether human, beaſt, or bird, as directed, let the ſacrificer, immolate him uttering the *Mántrā* directed for the occaſion, and addreſs the deity with the text laid down before.

Let the head and blood of a human victim be preſented on the right ſide of *Devi*, and the ſacrificer addreſs her ſtanding in front. Let the head and blood of a goat be preſented on the left, and the head and blood of a buffalo in front. Let the head and blood of birds be preſented on the left, and the blood of a perſon's own body in front. Let the ambroſia proceeding from the heads of carniverous animals and birds be preſented on the left hand, as alſo the blood of all aquatic animals.

Let the antelope's head and blood, and that of the tortoiſe, rhinoceros and hare and crocodile, and fiſh be preſented in front.

Let a lion's head and blood, be preſented on the right hand, and the rhinoceros's alſo; let not, on any account, the head or blood of a victim ever be preſented behind the Deity, but on the right, left, and in front.

Let

Let the confecrated lamp, be placed either on the right hand, or in front but on no account, on the left. Let incenfe be burnt on the left, and in front, but not on the right hand. Let perfumes, flowers, and ornaments, be prefented in front; with refpect to the different parts of the circle, where to prefent the offerings, the mode already laid down may be obferved. Let *Mădirá* (fpirituous liquor) be prefented behind other liquids on the left.

Where it is abfolutely neceffary to offer fpirits, let the three firft claffes of men fupply their place, by cocoanut juice in a brafs veffel, or honey in a copper one. Even in a time of calamity, let not a man of the three firft claffes, offer fpirituous liquor, except that made from flowers, or ftewed difhes. Let princes, minifters of ftate, counfellors, and venders of fpirituous liquors, make human facrifices, for the purpofe of attaining profperity and wealth.

If a human facrifice is performed, without the confent of the prince, the performer incurs fin. In cafes of imminent danger or war, facrifices may be performed at pleafure, by princes themfelves and their minifters, but by none elfe.

The day previous to a human facrifice, let the victim be prepared by the text *Mănastăc*, and three *Devi Gandhă Suctăhs*, and the texts *wădrăng*; and by touching his head with the ax, and befmearing the ax with fandal, &c. perfumes, and then taking fome of the fandal, &c. from off the ax, and befmearing the victim's neck therewith.

Then let the text *Ambĕ A'mbicĕ*, &c. and the *Rowdră* and *Bhairăvă* texts be ufed, and *Dévi* herfelf will guard the victim who, when thus purified, malady does not approach him, nor does his mind fuffer any derangement from grief and fimilar caufes, nor does the death or birth of a kinfman render him impure.

Now liften to the good and bad *omens*, to be drawn from the falling of the head, when fevered from the body.

If the head falls towards the north-eaft, or fouth-weft, the prince of the country and offerer of the facrifice will both perifh.

If the human head, when fevered from the body, falls in the following quarters, the following omens are to be drawn.

If in the eaft, wealth; if in the fouth-weft, power; if in the fouth, terror; if in the weft, profit; if in the north-weft, a fon; if in the north, riches.

Liften now to the omens to be drawn from the falling of the head of a buffalo, when fevered from the body.

If in the north, property; the north-eaft, lofs; in the eaft, dominion; fouth-eaft, wealth; the fouth, victory over enemies; if in the fouth-weft, fear; if in the weft, attainment of kingdom, if in the north-eaft, profperity: this rule, O *Bhirăvă!* holds good for all animals, but not for aquatick or oviparous creatures.

If the heads of birds, or fifhes, fall in the fouth, or fouth-eaft, quarter, it indicates fear, and if any of the other quarters profperity.

If

If a noife, proceeding from the chattering of the teeth of the victim's fevered head, or fnapping of the beak is perceptible, it indicates alarm. If tears proceed from the eyes of a human victim's fevered head it indicates deftruction to the prince.

If tears proceed from the fevered head of a buffalo at the time of prefenting it, it indicates that fome foreign inimical prince will die. If tears proceed from the eyes of other animals, they indicate alarm, or lofs of health.

If the fevered head of a human victim fmiles, it indicates increafe of profperity, and long life to the facrificer, without doubt; and if it fpeak, whatever it fays will come to pafs.

If the found *Hoonh* proceeds from the human victim's fevered head, it indicates that the prince will die, if phlegm, that the facrificer will die. If the head utters the name of a deity, it indicates wealth to the facrificer within fix months.

If at the time of prefenting the blood, the victim difcharge fæces or urine, or turns about, it indicates certain death to the facrificer; if the victim kicks with his left leg, it indicates evil, but a motion of his legs in any other mode, indicates profperity.

The facrificer muft take fome blood between his thumb and third finger, and difcharge it towards the fouth weft on the ground, as an offering to the deities, accompanied by the *Mehă Cawfici Măntră*.

Let the victim offered to DEVI, if a buffalo, be five years old, and if human twenty-five.

Let

Let the *Cawfici** Mantra* be uttered, and the sacrificer say *Efhā bāli Sevāhā*, "Mysterious praise to "this victim."

A prince *may sacrifice his enemy*, having first invoked the ax with holy texts, by substituting a buffalo or goat, calling the victim by the name of the enemy throughout the whole ceremony.

Having secured the victim with cords, and also with sacred texts, let him strike off the head, and present it to *Devi*, with all due care. Let him make these sacrifices in proportion to the increase or decrease of his enemies, lopping off the heads of victims for the purpose of bringing destruction on his foes, infusing, by holy texts, the soul of the enemy into the body of the victim, which will, when immolated, deprive the foe of life also.

Let him first say, "O Goddess of horrid form, O "*Chāndicā!* eat, devour, such a one, my enemy, " O consort of fire! Salutation to fire! This is the " enemy who has done me mischief, now personated " by an animal: destroy him, O *Mahamari!* Spheng! " Spheng! eat, devour." Let him then place flowers upon the victim's head. The victim's blood must be presented with the *Mantra* of two syllables.

If a sacrifice is performed in this manner on the *Mahānawani* (the ninth of the moon in the month of *Afjin,*) let the *homa,* (i. e. oblation to fire,) be performed with the flesh of the victim.

---

* The *Cawfici Mantra*: "Hail *Cawfici!* three-eyed Goddess; " of most terrifying appearance, around whose neck a string of " human skulls is pendant, who art the destroyer of evil spirits " who art armed with an ax, the foot of a bed and a spear, *Rbing* " *Cawfici*. Salutation to thee with this blood."

Using

Ufing the texts which are laid down in the *Durga Tantra* and purified fire, let the *Homa* be performed after the facrifice, and it will procure the death of foes.

Let not any one prefent blood drawn from any part of the body below the navel, or from the back. Let not blood drawn from the lips, or chin, or from any limb, be prefented. Blood drawn from any part of the body, between the neck and navel, may be prefented, but violent incifions for the purpofe of obtaining it, muft not be made.

Blood drawn from the cheeks, forehead, between the eye brows, from the tips of the ears, the arms, the breafts, and all parts between the neck and navel, as alfo from the fides, may be prefented.

Let not blood drawn from the ankles, or knees, or from parts of the body which branch out be prefented, nor blood which has not been drawn from the body for the exprefs purpofe of being offered.

The blood muft be drawn for the exprefs purpofe of an oblation, and from a man pure in body and mind, and free from fear: it muft be caught in the petal of a lotos, and prefented. It may be prefented in a gold, filver, brafs, or iron veffel, with the due from, and texts recited.

The blood, if drawn by an incifion made with a knife, ax, or *fangcul*, gives pleafure, in propotion to the fize of the weapon.

The facrificer may prefent one fourth of the quantity which a lotos petal will contian, but he muft not give more on any account; nor cut his body

more

more than is necessary. He who willingly offers the blood of his body and his own flesh, the size of a grain of linseed, *masha*, *tila*, or *mudga*, with zeal and fervency, obtains what he desires in the course of six months.

Now attend to the fruits obtained by offering *the burning wick* of a lamp placed upon the arms, ears, or breast, even for a single moment. He who applies the same obtains happiness and great possessions; and for three *Cälpăs* is even as the body of *Dévi* herself; after which he becomes a ruler of the universe.

He who, for a whole night, stands before the Goddess *Sivä*, holding the head of a sacrificed buffalo in his hands, with a burning lamp placed between the horns, obtains long life and supreme felicity in this world, and in the other resides in my mansion, holding the rank of a ruler in the *Ganadevatas*.

He who, for a single *cshana*, (a short space of time,) holds the blood which proceeds from a victim's head in his hands, standing before the Goddess in meditation, obtains all that he desires in this world, and supremacy in the *Dévi Loc*.

Let the learned, when he presents his own blood, use the following text followed by the *Mula Mänträ*, or principal text used in the worship of the Goddess *Dévi*, under the form which she is at that time addressed:

"Hail! supreme delusion! hail! Goddess of the "universe! Hail! thou who fulfillest the desires "of all. May I presume to offer thee, the "blood

"blood of my body; and wilt thou deign to accept
"it, and be propitious towards me."

Let the following text be used, when a person presents his own flesh:

"Grant me, O Goddess! bliss, in proportion to
"the fervency with which I present thee with my own
"flesh, invoking thee to be propitious to me. Salu-
"tation to thee again and again, under the mysterious
"syllables *hoong hoong*."

When the wick of a lamp is applied burning to the body, the following text is to be used:

"Hail! Goddess! Salutation to thee, under the
"syllables, *hōng hōng*. To thee I present this au-
"spicious luminary, fed with the flesh of my body,
"enlightening all around, and exposing to light also,
"the inward recesses of my soul."

On the autumnal *Meha Navami*, or when the moon is in the lunar mansion *Scanda* or *Bishácá*, let a figure be made, either of barley meal or earth, representing the person with whom the sacrificer is at variance, and the head of the figure be struck off: after the usual texts have been used, the following text is to be used in invoking an ax on the occasion:

"Effuse, effuse blood; be terrifick, be terrifick;
"seize, destroy, for the love of *Ambicá*, the head of
"this enemy."

Having struck off the head, let him present it, using the texts laid down hereafter for the occasion.

occasion, concluding with the word *phat*. Water must be sprinkled upon the meal, or earthen victim, which represents the sacrificer's enemy, using the text commencing with *răcta drăbaih*, (i. e. by streams of blood,) and marks must be made on the forehead with red sanders; garlands of red flowers must be put round the neck of the image, and it must be dressed in red garments, and tied with red cords, and girt with a red girdle. Then placing the head towards the north, let it be struck off with an ax, and presented, using the *Scănda* text. This is to be used at presenting the head, if the sacrifice is performed on the night of the *Scănda Năcshătra*, or lunar mansion *Scănda*. The *Vĭsăc'hă Măntră*, is to be used on the night the *Vĭsăc'hă* mansion. Let the sacrificer contemplate two attendants on the Goddess, as having fiery eyes, with yellow bodies, red faces, long ears, armed with tridents and axes in their two right hands, and holding human sculls and vases in their two left. Let them be considered as having three eyes and strings of human sculls, suspended round their necks, with long straggling frightful teeth.

In the month of *Chaitra*, on the day of the full moon, sacrifices of buffalos and goats give unto me of horrid form much pleasure; as do also honey and fish, " O my sons!"

Where a sacrifice is made to *Chăndĭcă*, the victim's head having been cut off, must be sprinkled with water, and afterwards presented with the texts laid down.

The sacrificer may draw an augury from the motions of the slain victim when near expiring, and for so doing he must first address the Goddess, considering the soul of the victim as taking its departure in a car, and his body as a holy spot, " O Goddess! make " known unto me, whether the omens are favourable " or not."

If

If the head of the flain victim, does not move fometime after this, the facrificer may look upon the circumftance as a good omen, and if the reverfe, as a bad one.

He who performs facrifices according to thefe rules, obtains his wifhes to the utmoft extent.

Thus are the rules and forms of facrifice, laid down and communicated by me to you. I will now inform you what other oblations may be made.

Thus ends the *Rudhirádhyáyă*.

XXIII.

XXIV.

AN ACCOUNT OF THE PEARL FISHERY IN THE GULPH OF MANAR,

IN MARCH AND APRIL 1797.

BY HENRY J. LE BECK, ESQ.

COMMUNICATED BY DOCTOR ROXBURG.

FROM the accounts of the former pearl fisheries at *Ceylon*, it will be found, that none have ever been so productive as this year's. It was generally supposed that the renter would be infallibly ruined, as the sum he paid for the present fishery was thought exorbitant when compared with what had been formerly given; but this conjecture in the event appeared ill founded, as it proved extremely profitable and lucrative.

The farmer this time was a *Tamul* merchant, who for the privilege of fishing with more than the usual number of donies or boats, paid between two and and three hundred thousand *Porto-novo* pagodas, a sum nearly double the usual rent.

These boats he farmed out again to individuals in the best manner he could, but for want of a sufficient number of divers some of them could not be employed.

The fishing, which commonly began about the middle of *Februrary*, if wind and weather allowed, was this year, for various reasons, delayed till the end of the month; yet so favourable was the weather, that the renter was able to take advantage of the permission granted by the agreement, to fish a little longer than the usual period of thirty days.

The fishery cannot well be continued after the setting in of the southern monsoon, which usually happens about the 15th of *April*, as, after that time, the boats would not be able to reach the pearl banks, and the water being then so troubled by heavy seas, diving would be impracticable; in addition to which, the sea-weed, a species of *fucus*, driven in by the southerly wind, and which spreads to a considerable distance from the shore, would be an impediment.

Many of the divers, being Roman Catholics, leave the fishery on *Sundays* to attend divine service in their church at *Aripoo*; but if either a *Mahomedan* or *Hindoo* festival happens during the fishing days, or if it is interrupted by stormy weather, or any other accident, this lost time is made up by obliging the Catholics to work on *Sundays*.

The fear of sharks, as we shall see hereafter, is also another cause of interruption. These, amongst some others, are the reasons that, out of two months, (from February till April,) seldom more than thirty days can be employed in the fishery.

As this time would be insufficient to fish all the banks (each of which has its appropriate name, both in Dutch and Tamul,) it is carried on for three or four successive years, and a new contract annually made till the whole banks have been fished, after which they are left to recover.

The length of time required for this purpose, or from one general fishing to another, has not yet been exactly determined: it was, therefore, a practice to depute some persons to visit the banks annually, and to give their opinion, whether a fishery might be undertaken with any degree of success [*]?

---

[*] A gentleman, who assisted at one of the last visits, being an engineer, drew a chart of the banks, by which their situation and size are now better known than formerly.

From

From various accounts, which I have collected from good authority, and the experience of those who assisted at such examinations, I conjecture, that every seven years such a general fishery could be attempted with advantage, as this interval seems sufficient for the pearl shells to attain their growth: I am also confirmed in this opinion, by a report made by a Dutch governor at *Jafnas* of all the fisheries that have been undertaken at *Ceylon* since 1722; a translation of which is to be found in Wolfe's Travels into *Ceylon*. But the ruinous condition in which the divers leave the pearl banks at each fishery, by attending only to the profit of individuals, and not to that of the public, is one great cause, that it requires twice the above mentioned space of time, and sometimes longer, for rendering the fishing productive. They do not pay the least attention, to spare the young and immature shells that contain no pearl; heaps of them are seen thrown out of the boats as useless, on the beach between *Manâr* * and *Aripoo*; if these had been suffered to remain in their native beds, they would, no doubt, have produced many fine pearls. It might, therefore, be adviseable, to oblige the boat people to throw them into the sea again, before the boats leave the bank. If this circumspection, in sparing the small pearl shells, to perpetuate the breed was always observed, succeeding fisheries might be expected sooner, and with still greater success: but the neglect of this simple precaution will, I fear, be attended with similar fatal consequences here, as have already happened to the pearl banks on the coast of *Persia*, *South America*, and *Sweden*, where the fisheries are by no means so profitable at present as they were formerly.

Another cause of the destruction of numbers of both old and young pearl shells, is the anchoring of so many boats on the banks, almost all of them used

---

* *Manara*, properly *Manar*, is a *Tamul* word, and signifies a sandy river, from the shallowness of the sea at that place.

differently formed, clumsy, heavy, wooden anchors, large stones, &c. &c. If this evil cannot be entirely prevented, it might, at least, be greatly lessened, by obliging them all to use anchors of a particular sort, and less destructive.

This season the *Seerwel* Bank only was fished, which lies above twenty miles to the westward of *Aripoo*, opposite to the fresh water rivers of *Moosalee Modragam* and *Pomparipoo*. It has been observed, that the pearls on the north-west part of this bank, which consists of rock, are of a clearer water than those found on the south-east, nearest the shore, growing on corals and sand.

Condatchey is situated in a bay, forming nearly a half moon, and is a waste, sandy district, with some miserable huts built on it. The water is bad and brackish, and the soil produces only a few, widely scattered, stunted trees and bushes. Those persons who remain here during the fishery are obliged to get their water for drinking from *Aripo*, a village with a small old fort, lying about four miles to the southward. Tigers, porcupines, wild hogs, pangolines, or the *Ceylon armadillos*, are, amongst other quadrupeds, here common. Of amphibia, there are tortoises, especially the *testudo geometrica* and various kinds of snakes. A conchologist meets here with a large field for his enquiries. The presents which I made to the people employed in the fishery, to encourage them to collect all sorts of shells which the divers bring on shore, produced but little effect; as they were too much taken up in searching after the mother of pearl shells to pay attention to any other object. However, my endeavours were not entirely useless; I will specify here a few of the number I collected during my stay: different kinds of *pectines**, *palium porphyreum*, *solen radiatus†*, *Venus castrensis*, *Linn*. ‡ *astrea hyotis* §, *ostr.*

* Scallops. † Radiated razor shell.
‡ Alpha cockle. § Double cocks-comb.

Forskolii.

Forskolii, oſtr. Malleus *, *mytilus hirundo Linn.* †, *spondilus crocius, pholas pusillus, Linn.* ‡, *mitra episcopalis, Linn., lepas striata Pennanti, (vide Zool. Brit.), patella tricarinata, Linn., bulla perfecta maculata* §, *harpa nobilis, porcellana salita, Rumph.* ‖, *strombus scorpio,* and other of inferior kinds. Amongst the *zoophytes,* many valuable species of *spongiæ, corallinæ, satulariæ,* &c. a great variety of sea stars, and other marine productions, that cannot be preserved in spirits, but should be described on the spot. These, as well as the description of the different animals inhabiting the shells, are the more worthy of our attention, and deserve farther investigation, as we are yet very deficient in this branch of natural history.

During the fishing season, the desert, barren place, *Condatchey,* offers to our view a scene equally novel and astonishing. A heterogeneous mixture of thousands of people of different colours, countries, casts, and occupations, the number of tents and huts, erected on the sea shore, with their shops or bazars before each of them; and the many boats returning on shore in the afternoon, generally richly laden; all together form a spectacle entirely new to an *European* eye. Each owner runs to his respective boat as soon as it reaches the shore, in hopes of finding it fraught with immense treasure, which is often much greater in imagination than in the shell; and though he is disappointed one day, he relies with greater certainty on the next, looking forward to the fortune promised him by his stars, as he thinks it impossible for the astrological predictions of his *Brâhmen* to err.

---

* Hammer oyster; these were pretty large, but many broken and some covered by a calcarious crust. It is very probable that, among those, there may be some precious *cubite* ones.
† Swallow muscle.   ‡ The wood piercer.
§ Diving snail, (Grew, Muſ.)   ‖ Salt-coury, Kl.

To prevent riot and disorder, an officer with a party of *Malays* is stationed here. They occupy a large square, where they have a field piece and a flag staff for signals.

Here and there you meet with brokers, jewellers, and merchants of all descriptions; also, suttlers offering provisions and other articles to gratify the sensual appetite and luxury. But by far the greater number are occupied with the pearls. Some are basely employed in assorting them; for which purpose they make use of small brass plates perforated with holes of different sizes; others are weighing and offering them to the purchaser; while others are drilling or boring them; which they perform for a trifle.

The instrument, these people carry about with them for this purpose, is of a very simple construction, but requires much skill and exercise to use it; it is made in the following manner: the principal part consists of a piece of soft wood, of an obtuse, inverted, conical shape, about six inches high and four in diameter in its plain surface; this is supported by three wooden feet, each of which is more than a foot in length. Upon the upper flat part of this machine are holes, or pits, for the larger pearls, and the smaller ones are beat in with a wooden hammer. On the right side of this stool, half a cocoa nut shell is fastened, which is filled with water. The drilling instruments are iron spindles, of various sizes, adapted to the different dimentions of the pearls, which are turned round in a wooden head by a bow. The pearls being placed on the flat surface of the inverted cone, as already mentioned, the operator sitting on a mat, presses on the wooden head of his instrument with the left hand, while, with his right, he moves the bow which turns round the moveable part of the drill; at the same time, he moistens the pearl, occasionally dipping

dipping the little finger of the fame hand into the water of the cocoa nut fhell, with a dexterity that can only be attained by conftant practice.

Amongft the crowd are found vagabonds of every defcription, fuch as *Pandarams*, *Andee*, or *Hindu* monks, fakirs, beggars, and the like, who are impertinently troublefome. Two of thefe wretches particularly attracted the attention of the mob, though their fuperftitious penance muft have difgufted a man of the leaft reflection: one had a gridiron, of one and a half foot long and the fame in breadth, faftened round his neck, with which he always walked about, nor did he take it off either when eating or fleeping; the other had faftened round that member, which decency forbids me to mention, a brafs ring, and fixed to it was a chain, of a fathom in length, trailing on the ground, the links of this chain were as thick as a man's finger, and the whole was exhibited in a moft fcandalous manner.

The peftilential fmell occafioned by the numbers of putrifying pearl fifhes, renders the atmofphere of *Condatchey* fo infufferably offenfive when the fouth-weft wind blows, that it fenfibly affects the olfactory nerves of any one unaccuftomed to fuch cadaverous fmells. This putrefaction generates immenfe numbers of worms, flies, mufkitoes, and other vermin; all together forming a fcene ftrongly difpleafing to the fenfes.

Thofe who are not provided with a fufficient ftock of money fuffer great hardfhips, as not only all kinds of provifions are very dear, but even every drop of good water muft be paid for. Thofe who drink the brackifh water of this place are often attacked by ficknefs. It may eafily be conceived what an effect the extreme heat of the day, the cold of the night, the heavy dews, and the putrid fmell, muft have on weak conftitutions. It is, therefore, no wonder that of those who fall sick many die, and many more return home with fevers, fluxes, or other equally fatal disorders.

The many disappointments, usually experienced by the lower classes of men in particular, make them often repent of their coming here. They are often ruined, as they risk all they are worth to purchase pearl shells; however, there are many instances of their making a fortune beyond all expectation. A particular circumstance of this kind fell within my own observation: a day labourer bought three oysters * for a copper fanam (about the value of two-pence) and was so fortunate as to find one of the largest pearls which the fishery produced this season.

The donies appointed for the fishery are not all procured at *Ceylon*; many came from the coasts of *Coromandel* and *Malabar*, each of which has its distinguishing number. About ten o'clock at night a gun is fired as a signal, when they sail from *Condatchey* with an easterly or land wind, under the direction of a pilot. If the wind continues fair, they reach the bank before day, and begin diving at sun rise, which they continue till the west or sea breeze sets in, with which they return. The moment they appear in sight, the colours are hoisted at the flag staff, and in the afternoon they come to an anchor, so that the owners of the boats are thereby enabled to get their cargoes out before night, which may amount to 30,000 oysters, if the divers have been active and successful.

Each boat carries twenty-one men and five heavy diving stones for the use of ten divers, who are called

---

* The *East India* pearl shell, is well known to be the *matrix perlarum* (mother of pearl) of RUMPHIUS, or the *Mytilus margaritiferus* of LINNÆUS; consequently the general term pearl oyster must be erroneous; however, as it has long been in common use, I hope to be excused for continuing it.

in *Tamul*, *kooly kárer*, the rest of the crew consists of a tandel, or head boatman, and ten rowers, who assist in lifting up the divers and their shells.

The diving stone is a piece of coarse granite, a foot long, six inches thick, and of a pyramidical shape, rounded at the top and bottom. A large hair rope is put through a hole in the top. Some of the divers use another kind of stone shaped like a half moon, to bind round their belly, so that their feet may be free. At present these are articles of trade at *Condatchey*. The most common, or pyramidical stone, generally weighs about thirty pounds. If a boat has more than five of them, the crew are either corporally punished or fined.

The diving, both at *Ceylon* and at *Tutucorin*, is not attended with so many difficulties as authors imagine. The divers, consisting of different casts and religions, (though chiefly of *Parrawer** and *Mussehmans*,) neither make their bodies smooth with oil, nor do they stop their ears, mouths, or noses with any thing, to prevent the entrance of salt water. They are ignorant of the utility of diving bells, bladders, and double flexible pipes. According to the injunctions of the shark conjurer they use no food while at work, nor till they return on shore, and have bathed themselves in fresh water. These *Indians*, accustomed to dive from their earliest infancy, fearlessly descend to the bottom in a depth of, from five to ten fathoms in search of treasures. By two cords a diving stone and a net are connected with the boat. The diver putting the toes of his right foot on the hair rope of the diving stone, and those of his left on the net, seizes the two cords with one hand, and shutting his nostrils with the other, plunges into the water. On reaching the bot-

* Fishermen of the Catholic religion.

tom, he hangs the net round his neck, and collects into it the pearl shells as fast as possible, during the time he finds himself able to remain under water, which usually is about two minutes. He then resumes his former posture, and making a signal, by pulling the cords, he is immediately lifted into the boat. On emerging from the sea, he discharges a quantity of water from his mouth and nose, and those who have not been long enured to diving frequently discharge some blood; but this does not prevent them from diving again in their turn. When the first five divers come up and are respiring the other five are going down with the same stones. Each brings up about one hundred oysters in his net, and if not interrupted by any accident, may make fifty trips in a forenoon. They and the boat's crew get generally from the owner, instead of money, a fourth of the quantity which they bring on shore; but some are paid in cash, according to agreement.

The most skilful divers come from *Collish*, on the coast of *Malabar*; some of them are so much exercised in the art, as to be able to perform it without the assistance of the usual weight; and for a handsome reward will remain under water for the space of seven minutes; this I saw performed by a *Caffry* boy, belonging to a citizen at *Karical*, who had often frequented the fisheries of these banks. Though Dr. HALLEY deems this impossible, daily experience convinces us, that by long practice any man may bring himself to remain under water above a couple of minutes. How much the inhabitants of the South Sea Islands distinguish themselves in diving we learn from several accounts: and who will not be surprised at the wonderful *Sicilian* diver NICHOLAS, surnamed the FISH*?

---

* According to KIRCHER, he fell a victim amongst the *Polypes* in the gulph of *Charybdis*, on his plunging, for the second time, in its dangerous whirlpool, both to satisfy the curiosity of his king, FREDERIC, and his inclination for wealth. I will not pretend to determine, how far this account has been exaggerated.

Every

Every one of the divers, and even the moſt expert, entertain a great dread of the ſharks, and will not, on any account, deſcend until the conjurer has performed his ceremonies. This prejudice is ſo deeply rooted in in their minds, that the government was obliged to keep two ſuch conjurers always in their pay, to remove the fears of their divers. Thirteen of theſe men were now at the fiſhery from *Ceylon* and the coaſt, to profit by the ſuperſtitious folly of theſe deluded people. They are called in *Tamul*, *Pillal Kadlär*, which ſigniſies one who binds the ſharks and prevents them from doing miſchief.

The manner of enchanting conſiſts in a number of prayers learned by heart, that nobody, probably not even the conjurer himſelf, underſtands, which he, ſtanding on the ſhore, continues muttering and grumbling from ſun riſe until the boats return; during this period, they are obliged to abſtain from food and ſleep, otherwiſe their prayers would have no avail, they are, however, allowed to drink, which privilege they indulge in a high degree, and are frequently ſo giddy, as to be rendered very unfit for devotion. Some of the conjurers accompany the divers in their boats, which pleaſes them very much, as they have their protectors near at hand. Nevertheleſs, I was told, that in one of the preceding fiſheries, a diver loſt his leg by a ſhark, and when the head conjurer was called to an account for the accident, he replied that an old witch had juſt come from the coaſt, who, from envy and malice, had cauſed this diſaſter, by a counter-conjuration, which made fruitleſs his ſkill, and of which he was informed too late; but he afterwards ſhewed his ſuperiority by enchanting the poor ſharks ſo effectually, that though they appeared in the midſt of the divers, they were unable to open their mouths. During my ſtay at *Condatchey*, no accident of this kind happened. If a ſhark is ſeen, the divers immediately make a ſignal, which, on perceiving, all the boats return inſtantly. A diver who trod upon a

hammer

hammer oyster, and was somewhat wounded, thought he was bit by a shark, consequently made the usual signal, which caused many boats to return; for which mistake he was afterwards punished.

The owners of the boats * sometimes sell their oysters, and at other times open them on their own account. In the latter case some put them on mats in a square, surrounded with a fence; others dig holes of almost a foot deep, and throw them in till the animal dies; after which they open the shells and take out the pearls with more ease. Even these squares and holes are sold by auction after the fishery is finished, as pearls often remain there, mixed with the sand.

In spite of every care, tricks in picking out the pearls from the oysters can hardly be prevented. In this the natives are extremely dexterous. The following is one mode they put in practice to effect their purpose: when a boat owner employs a number of hired people to collect pearls, he places over them an inspector of his own, in whom he can confide; these hirelings previously agree that one of them shall play the part of a thief, and bear the punishment, to give his comrades an opportunity of pilfering. If one of the gang happens to meet with a large pearl, he makes a sign to his accomplice, who instantly conveys away one of small value, purposely, in such a manner as to attract notice. On this the inspector and the rest of the men take the pearl from him: he is then punished and turned out of their company. In the mean time, while he is making a dreadful uproar, the real thief secures the valuable pearl, and afterwards the booty is shared with him who suffered for them all. Besides tricks like these the boat owners and pur-

---

* These are the individuals which farm one or more boats from the renter; and though they are in possession of them only during the fishery, they are commonly called the owners of the boats.

chafers often lose many of the best pearls, while the dony is returning from the bank; for, as long as the animal is alive and untouched, the shells are frequently open near an inch; and if any of them contain a large pearl, it is easily discovered and taken out by means of a small piece of stiff grass or bit of stick, without hurting the pearl fish. In this practice they are extremely expert. Some of them were discovered whilst I was there, and received their due punishment.

GMELIN asks if the animal of the *mytilus margaritiferus* is an *ascidia?* See LINN. Syst. Nat. tom. I. p. vi. 3350. This induces me to believe that it has never yet been accurately described: it does not resemble the *ascidia* of LINNÆUS, and may, perhaps, form a new genus. It is fastened to the upper and lower shells by two white flat pieces of muscular substance, which are called by *Houttuin* * *ears*, and extend about two inches from the thick part of the body, growing gradually thinner. The extremity of each *ear* lies loose, and is surrounded by a double brown fringed line. These lie almost the third of an inch from the outer part of the shell, and are continually moved by the animal. Next to these, above and below, are situated two other double fringed moveable substances, like the branchiæ of a fish. These *ears* and *fringes* are joined to a cylindrical piece of flesh, of the size of a man's thumb, which is harder and of a more muscular nature than the rest of the body. It lies about the centre of the shells, and is firmly attached to the middle of each. This, in fact, is that part of the pearl fish which serves to open and shut the shells. Where this column is fastened, we find on the flesh deep impressions, and on the shell various nodes of round or oblong forms, like imperfect pearls. Between this part, and the hinge *(cardo)*, lies the principal body of the animal, separated

---

* Vide Houtt. Nat. Hist. Vol. I. p. xv. p. 381, seq.

from the rest, and shaped like a bag. The mouth is near the hinge of the shell, enveloped in a veil, and has a double flap or lip on each side; from thence we observe the throat (œsophagus) descending like a thread to the stomach. Close to the mouth there is a carved brownish tongue, half an inch in length, with an obtuse point; on the concave side of this descends a furrow, which the animal opens and shuts, and probably uses to convey food to its mouth[*]. Near its middle are two bluish spots, which seem to be the eyes. In a pretty deep hole near the base of the tongue, lies the beard *(byssus)*, fastened by two fleshy roots, and consisting of almost one hundred fibres, each an inch long, of a dark green colour, with a metallic lustre; they are undivided, parallel, and flattened. In general the *byssus* is more than three quarters of an inch, without the cleft *(rima)*; but if the animal is disturbed, it contracts it considerably. The top of each of these threads terminates in a circular gland or head, like the *stygma* of many plants. With this *byssus* they fasten themselves to rocks, corals, and other solid bodies; by it the young pearl fish cling to the old ones, and with it the animal procures its food, by extending and contracting it at pleasure. Small shell fish, on which they partly live, are often found clinging to the former. The stomach lies close to the root of the beard, and has, on its lower side, a protracted obtuse point. Above the stomach are two small red bodies, like lungs; and from the stomach goes a long channel or gut, which takes a circuit

[*] The depth at which the pearl fish generally is to be found, hindered me from paying any attention to the locomotive power, which I have not the least doubt it possesses, using for this purpose its tongue. This conjecture is strengthened by the accurate observations made on *muscles* by the celebrated Reaumur, in which he found that this body serves them as a leg or arm, to move from one place to another. Though the divers are very ignorant with regard to the œconomy of the pearl fish, this changing of habitation has been long since observed by them. They alledge, that it alters its abode when disturbed by an enemy or in search of food. In the former case they say it commonly descends from the summit of the bank to its declivity.

round

round the muscular column above-mentioned, and ends in the anus, which lies opposite to the mouth, and is covered with a small thin leaf, like a flap. Though the natives pretend to distinguish the sexes, by the appearance of the shell, I could not find any genitalia. The large flat ones they call males, and those that are thick, concave, and vaulted, they call females, or *pedoo-chippy*; but, on a close inspection, I could not observe any visible sexual difference.

It is remarkable that some of these animals are as red as blood, and that the inside of the shell has the same colour, with the usual pearly lustre, though my servants found a redish pearl in an oyster of this colour; yet such an event is very rare. The divers attribute this redness to the sickness of the pearl fish; though it is most probable that they had it from their first existence. In the shade they will live twenty-four hours after being taken out of the water. This animal is eaten by the lower class of *Indians*, either fresh in their curries, or cured by drying; in which state they are exported to the coast; though I do not think them by any means palatable.

Within a mother of pearl shell I found thirteen *murices nudati* (vide CHEMNITZ's New System, Cabt. vol. XI. tab. 192, f. 1851 and 1852), the largest of which was three quarters of an inch long; but as many of them were putrid, and the pearl fish itself dead, I could not ascertain whether they had crept in as enemies, or were drawn in by the animal itself. At any rate turtles and crabs are inimical to the animals, and a small living crab was found in one of them.

The pearls are only in the softer part of the animal, and never in that firm muscular column above-mentioned. We find them in general near the earth, and on both sides of the mouth. The natives entertain the

same

same foolish opinion concerning the formation of the pearl which the ancients did. They suppose them formed from dew-drops in connection with sun-beams. A *Brâhmen* informed me that it was recorded in one of his *Sanscrit* books, that the pearls are formed in the month of May at the appearance of the *Sooatee* star (one of their twenty-seven constellations) when the oysters come up to the surface of the water, to catch the drops of rain. One of the most celebrated conchologists *, supposes that the pearl is formed by the oyster in order to defend itself from the attacks of the *pholades* and *boreworms*. But we may be assured that in this supposition he is mistaken, for although these animals often penetrate the outer layers of the pearl shell, and there occasion hollow nodes, yet, on examination, it will be found, that they are never able to pierce the firm layer, with which the inside of the shell is lined. How can the pearls be formed as a defence against exterior worms, when, even on shells that contain them, no worm-holes are to be seen? It is, therefore, more probable these worms take up their habitations in the nodes, in order to protect themselves from the attacks of an enemy, than that they are capable of preying on an animal, so well defended as the pearl-fish is. It is unnecessary to repeat the various opinions and hypotheses of other modern authors; it is much easier to criticise them, than to substitute in their place a more rational theory. That of REAUMUR, mentioned in the memoirs of the *French* Academy for 1712, is the most probable, viz. that the pearls are formed like bezoars and other stones in different animals, and are apparently the effects of a decease. In short it is very evident, that the pearl is formed by an extravasation of a glutinous juice either within the body, or on the surface of the animal: the former case is the most common. Between one and two hundred pearls have been found within one oyster. Such

* The Rev. Mr. CHEMNITZ at *Copenhagen*.

extravasations may be caused by heterogeneous bodies such as sand, coming in with the food, which the animal, to prevent disagreeable friction, covers with its glutinous matter, and which as it is successively secreted forms many regular lamellæ, in the manner of the coats of an onion, or like different strata of bezoars, only much thinner; this is probable, for if we cut through the centre of a pearl, we often find a foreign particle, which ought to be considered as the nucleus, or primary cause of its formation. The loose pearls, may originally have been produced within the body, and on their encrease may have separated and fallen into the cavity of the shell. Those compact ones, fixed to the shells seem to be produced by similar extravasation, occasioned by the friction of some roughness on the inside of the shell. These and the pearl-like nodes have a different aspect from the pearls, and are of a darker and bluer colour. In one of the former I found a pretty large, true oval pearl, of a very clear water; while the node itself was of a dark blueish colour. The yellow or gold coloured pearl, is the most esteemed by the natives; some have a bright, red, lustre; others are grey or blackish, without any shining appearance, and of no value. Sometimes when the grey lamella of a pearl is taken off, under it is found a beautiful genuine one, but it oftener happens that after having separated the first coat you find a worthless impure pearl. I tried several of them, taking one lamella off after another, and found clear and impure by turns, and in an impure pearl I met with one of a clear water, though in the centre of all I found a foreign particle. The largest and most perfect pearl which I saw during my stay at *Condatchey*, was about the size of a small pistol bullet, though I have been told since my departure, many others of the same size have been found. The spotted and irregular ones are sold cheap, and are chiefly used by the native physicians as an ingredient in their medicines.

We may judge with greater or lesser probability by the appearance of the pearl-shell, whether they contain pearls or not. Those that have a thick calcareous crust upon them, to which *serpulæ* (sea tubes) *Tubuli marini irregulariter intorti, Crista-gali Chamar lazuras, Lepas tintinabulum, Madreporee, Millipore, Cellipore, Gorgontæ, Spongiæ*, and other Zoophytes are fastened, have arrived at their full growth, and commonly contain the best pearls; but those that appear smooth, contain either none, or small ones only.

Were a naturalist to make an excursion for a few months to *Manár*, the small island near *Jafna* and the adjacent coast, he would discover many natural curiosities, still buried in obscurity, or that have never been accurately described.

Indeed no place in the *East Indies* abounds more with rare shells, than these: for there they remain undisturbed, by being sheltered from turbulent seas, and the fury of the surf. I will just name a few of them; viz. *Tellina foliaca* Lynn [*], *Tell, Spenglerii, Arca culculata* [†], *Arca Noæ, solen anatinus* Linn. *Ostrea Isognomum, Terebullum, albidum, striatum, Turbo scalaris* [‡] *Bula volva* Linn [||], *Vexillum ingritarum*, &c. Amongst the beautiful cone shells: *conus thalassiarchus Anglicanus cullatus* [§], *amadis thassiarchus, con. generaleis* Linn. *c. capitaneus* [**], *c. miles* [††], *c. stercus muscarum* [‡‡]. *c. retcaureum, c. glaucus* [||||]. *c. cereola, regia corona murus lapedius, canda erminea societas cordium*. There are many other besides those already mentioned, equally valuable and curious.

The great success of the Rev. Doctor John in conchology when at *Tutucorin* and assisted by G. An-

[*] The golden tong.   [†] Mounkscape.
[‡] Royal staircase.   [||] Weaver's shuttle.
[§] Red *English* admiral.   [**] Green stamper.
[††] Great sand stamper.   [||||] Capt. Gottw.

GELBECK

GELBECK, with a boat and divers: and the capital collections made by his agents, whom he afterwards sent there with the neceffary instructions and apparatus, may be seen in CHEMNITZ's elegant cabinet of shells in 4to (with illuminated plates), and how many new species of Zoophytes he discovered, we learn from another German work by ESPER at *Erlangen* the third volume of which is nearly finished.

XXV.

ASTRONOMICAL OBSERVATIONS MADE IN THE UPPER PROVINCES OF HINDUSTAN.

BY WILLIAM HUNTER, ESQ.

LATITUDES OBSERVED.

1795		Place.	Sun or Star.	Latitude.			Remarks.		Mean Latitude.		
				°	′	″			°	′	″
Feb.	23	Nawabgunge; Chubbooterah E.	☉ M.A.	27	26	46	clear,	moderate.			
	24	Alygunge; Mofque S. 66 E.	☉ M.A.	27	30	18	ditto.	ditto.			
	25	Doomree; Fort. S. 11 E. dift. 2.7. Fs.	☉ M.A.	27	33	13	ditto.	ditto.			
	26	Ejunpoor; N. 61.—89 W. 1.75. Fs.	☉ M.A.	27	41	12	ditto.	ditto.			
	27	Manhera; tents clofe to the town.	☉ M.A.	27	44	45	cloudy.	ditto.			
	28	Secundra; (named Raw.) N. 30. 72. E. 3 25. Fs.	☉ M.A.	27	41	29	ditto.	ditto.			
March	2	Mindoo; Mr. Orr's houfe. S. 34. E. 4. Fs.	☉ M.A.	27	37	56	clear.	ditto.			
	3	Ditto	☉ M.A.	27	38	17	cloudy.	ditto.	} 27	38	8	0
	4	Ditto	☉ M.A.	27	38	11	thin:flt clouds. do.				
	5	Coel; General Deboigne's houfe.	☉ M.A.	27	54	4	clear.	windy.			
	6	Ditto	☉ M.A.	27	54	8	ditto.	moderate.	} 27	54	6	0
	15	Jouar; dift. 2. 25. Fs.	☉ M.A.	27	36	42	ditto.	windy.			
	16	Hunfeali Gunge; dift. 3 Fs. mofque of Abd-ul-nubbec-Khan, at Matra. S. 26. W.	☉ M.A.	} 27	31	33 {	ditto.	moderate.			
	17	Matra; Litcha Bagh.	☉ M.A.	27	29	46	ditto.	ditto.			
	18	Areeng; ft. N. 71. E. 1. 5. Fs.	☉ M.A.	27	29	50	ditto.	ditto.			

[414]

1795	Place.	Sun or Star.	Latitude.	Remarks.	Mean Latitude.
			° ′ ″		° ′ ″ ″
March 19	Deeg; gate. N. 72. E. 3. 25. Fs.	☉ M. A.	27 29 6	clear.	windy.
20	Nugur; S. 83. E. 3. 7. Fs.	☉ M. A.	27 26 13	ditto.	moderate.
21	Alinagur; S. 30. 40. E. 1. M. 7. 3. Fs. Cohcry; Pahang. N. 2. W. 4. M. 2. 3. Fs.	☉ M. A.	27 31 58	ditto.	ditto.
30	Jablee, or Bijouly; Ft. S. 46. 67. W. 2. Fs.	β Urf. Maj.	27 22 1	ditto.	ditto.
31	Ditto	α Hydræ	27 24 8	brightnefs of the moon obfcrved the ftar.	} 27 23 4 5
April 7	Maat; S. 47. E. N. 49. E. 1. 75. Fs.	β Urf. Maj.	27 37 16	clear,	moderate.
8	Nop; Fort. N. 20. W.—N. 17 E. 2. Fs.	α Hydræ.	27 51 24	ditto.	ditto.
	Ditto	β Urf. Maj.	27 50 16	ditto.	ditto.
9	Tappei; Ft. N. 12.—62. W. 1. 4. Fs.	α Hydræ.	28 3 9	clear,	windy.
	Ditto	β Urf. Maj.	28 3 17	ditto.	moderate.
10	Ditto	β Urf. Maj.	28 3 1	ditto.	ditto.
11	Raghoopoor; N. 8. E.—N. 85. W. 0. 5. Fs.	α Hydræ.	28 14 46	ditto.	ditto.
12	Duncour; gate. S. 5. E.—3. 5. Fs.	α Hydræ.	28 21 31	ditto.	ditto.
13	Soorejpoore; S. 5. W.—S. 50. E. 1. 6. Fs.	α Hydræ.	28 31 10	ditto.	ditto.
14	Putpurgunge; S. 46.—81. E. 2. 3. Fs.	α Hydræ.	28 36 47	ditto.	ditto.
15	Dehly; garden of Shah Nizam-ud-deen.	α ʊp	28 38 55	ditto.	} 28 38 36 0
16	Ditto Ditto	α Draconis.	28 39 37		

1795	Place.	Sun or Star.	Latitude.	Remarks.	Mean Latitude.
			° ′ ″		° ′ ″
April 20	Ditto, palace of Sufder Jung.	α Hydrae.	28 40 47	clear, moderate.	} 28 40 12 5
		Aliath.	28 40 24		
June 15	Secundra; N. W. by N. 2. 3. Fs.	α ♍	26 40 2	thin clouds, móder.	
19	*Anoopſbeber*; Lieut. Chriſtie's bungalah.	α Draconis.	28 39 37	clear, calm.	
20	Ditto	α ♍	28 20 5	ditto.	
July 9	Camp, on bank of Neem-ca-nullah Bifwah. S. 40. W. 1. M 2. 2. Fs.	α Piſc. Auſt.	28 23 5	ditto. moderate.	
			28 23 5		
			27 49 59		
10	Kaſgunge; South-eaſt gate, N. 57. W. 5. 4. F.	Ditto.	27 48 37	ditto.	
1796	Amelia (village 1 mile from Choobepoor). N. 12. W. 1. 8. Fs.	⊙ M. A.	26 36 6	ditto.	
Feb. 13	Daipoor; camp cloſe to an old garden.	⊙ M. A.	26 58 25	ditto.	
19	Amirtgunge; gate. N. 60. W. 4. Fs.	⊙ M. A.	27 5 10	thin flitting cl. do.	
17	Dehliah; tent near the artillery ground, Cungalah. S, 66. E. one mile.	⊙ M. A.	27 21 48	clear, moderate.	} 27 21 51 0
27			27 21 54		
March 3	Ditto	⊙ M. A.	27 19 2	thin clouds, calm.	
4	Neemkarouly; gate. E. O. 8. F.	β Can. Maj.	27 18 58	clear, ditto.	} 27 18 58 5
	Ditto	Sirius.	27 18 54	ditto.	
	Ditto	δ Can. Maj.	27 19 00	clear,	} 27 19 58 5
	Ditto				

1796	Place.	Sun or Star.	Latitude.	Remarks.	Mean Latitude.
March 5	Agut-ke-feray; N. 23.—60. E. 2. Fs.	☉ M. A.	27 20 53	thin clouds, moder.	
	Ditto	β Can. Maj.	27 21 5	clear,	
	Ditto	Sirius.	27 21 1	calm.	27 21 12 57
	Ditto	δ Can. Maj.	27 21 52	clear,	
6	Aleepoor-R,hera; S. 25.—62. E. 1. F.	☉ M. A.	27 19 31	windy.	
	Ditto	♌	27 20 2	ditto.	
	Ditto	ν Urſ. Min.	27 19 35	moderate.	27 19 39 0
	Ditto	β ♌	27 19 27		
7	Beechnar; N. 37.—77. E. 1. F.	ε Draconis.	27 20 31	ditto.	
		α ♌	27 20 5		27 20 18 0
		β Urſ. Min.	27 19 57		
8	Jumlapoor; N. 20.—39. E. 1. 6. F.	☉ M. A.	27 25 31	ditto.	
	Ditto	β Can. Maj.	27 25 5	ditto.	27 25 11 0
	Ditto	Sirius.	27 24 54		
9	Sukeet; Fort. S.—S. 51. E. 1. F.	δ Can. Maj.	27 25 15	ditto.	
	Ditto	α Draconis.	27 26 39	ditto.	
	Ditto	♌	27 25 24	do. do. alt.fufpect-edtoogreat	
	Ditto	β Urſ. Min.	27 27 5	ditto.	27 26 20 0
	Ditto	3 ♌	27 25 50	ditto.	
10	Ditto	☉ M. A.	27 26 42	windy.	
	Ditto	β Urſ. Min.	27 26 42	calm.	
	Ditto	β ♌	27 25 57		

[417]

1790	Place.	Sun or Star.	Latitude.	Remarks.	Mean Latitude.
			° ′ ″		° ′ ″
11	Etap; S. 33. E.—S. 12. W. South gate, S. 7. F. 2. 1. F.	☉ M. A.	27 34 18	clear,	27 34 15 0
	Ditto	β Can. Maj.	27 33 29		
	Ditto	Sirius.	27 34 1	windy.	
	Ditto	δ Can. Maj.	27 35 4		
	Ditto	β Urf. Min.	27 34 12		
	Ditto	β ♎	27 34 27		
12	Nadowly; Ft. S. 76. E.—N. 88. E. 3. 5. Fs.	☉ M. A.	27 34 55	clear,	27 34 42 0
	Ditto	Sirius.	27 34 16		
	Ditto	δ Can. Maj.	27 34 45	windy.	
	Ditto	? Urf. Min.	27 35 5		
	Ditto	δ ♎	27 34 27	ditto.	
13	Secundra (Raw); S. 74. E. N. 35. W. clofe.	☉ M. A.	27 41 33	ditto.	27 42 27 0
14	Mulloy, Mr. Stewart's houfe.	☉ M. A.	27 42 45	ditto.	
	Ditto	α Draconis.	27 42 34		
	Ditto	π ♎	27 42 18	ditto.	
	Ditto	β Urf. Min.	27 42 12	calm.	
	Ditto	α ♎	27 42 23		
15	Jelaly; Mr Longcroft's houfe; N. E. 3. 5. Fs.	β Urf. Min.	27 51 56		27 52 10 0
	Ditto	β ♎	27 52 6	ditto.	
	Ditto	β ♎	27 52 28	ditto.	

[419]

1796	Place.	Sun or Star.	Latitude.	Remarks.	Mean Latitude.
			° ′ ″		° ′ ″
March 16	Bellah, Mr. Lenham's houfe; S. 85. E. 4. 7. Fs.	γ Draconis.	27 55 2		
	Ditto	α ♎	27 54 48	ditto.	
	Ditto	ξ Urf. Min.	27 55 13	ditto.	27 54 53 0
	Ditto	α ♎	27 54 28		
17	Atrawley, North gate; S. 16. W. 2. 7. Fs.	δ Can. Maj.	28 3 16		
	Ditto	α Draconis.	28 2 2		
	Ditto	α ♎	28 1 27	thin clouds, moder.	28 2 14 0
	Ditto	β Urf. Min.	28 2 5		
	Ditto	β ♎	28 2 21		
18	Debay; S. 2. E.—S. 13. W. North gate; S. 6. W. 7. 2. Fs.	☉ M. A.	28 14 1	clear, moderate.	
20	Anoopſhehbr; Col. Wares bungalow.	☉ M. A.	28 23 6	clear, windy.	
21	Ditto	☉ M. A.	28 23 21	ditto.	
22	Ditto	α ♎	28 22 49	clear, calm, ſtars rather obſcured by the brightneſs of the moon.	28 23 7 0
	Ditto	β ♎	28 23 14		
24	Atrawly; South gate, diſt. 4. 6. F.	ι Can. Maj.	28 1 31	clear, calm.	
	Ditto	ν Can. Maj.	28 1 43		
	Ditto	σ Navis.	28 2 36		28 1 54 0
	Ditto	α Hydrae.	28 1 49		

[419]

1796	Place.	Sun or Star.	Latitude.	Remarks.	Mean Latitude.
			° ′ ″		° ′ ″
March 29	Aly gunge; E. gate, dift. 1. 3. Fs.	☉ Navis.	27 30 27		
	Ditto	α Hydrae.	27 29 54	clear, windy.	27 29 38 0
	Ditto	β Urſ. Maj.	27 29 9		
	Ditto	β Urſ. Maj.	27 29 3		
May 30	Betourah; N. 62. E. 1 mile, right hand bank of Ganges.	α ♍	26 2 52		
		α Draconis.	26 1 23	ditto. ditto.	26 1 54 0
		α ♎	26 1 29		
		β Urſ. Min.	26 1 51		
31	Yacoot gunge; (ſmall village left hand bank of Ganges); Sharadpoor; S. 22. W. about 2 miles.	α ♍	25 40 2	clear, moderate.	25 25 21 0
June 1	*Allahabad*; Ft. S. E. angle.	Aliath.	25 24 54		
		α ♍	25 25 54	hazy, calm.	
		α ♎	25 25 14		
2	Mudura, near Litchageer.	Aliath.	25 17 47		25 17 1 0
		♍	25 17 31		
		α Draconis.	25 16 6		
3	Mirzapoor; E. ½ mile.	π Draconis.	25 16 42		
		α ♎	25 9 6	clear, moderate.	25 9 43 0
		α ♎	25 10 20		
		β Urſ. Min.	25 9 43		

[420]

Eclipses of Jupiter's Satellites observed with Dollond's Achromatic Telescope magnifying 80 Times.

Apparent Time.	Sat.	I/Em	Place of Observation.	Longit.	Weather.	Remarks.
1701 D. H. M. S.				° ′ ″		
Jan. 24 17 28 44	1	Im	Tundah.	82 11 0	a little hazy, mod.	
March 4 15 54 8	1	Im	Lucknou (Mr. Orr's house).	80 39 15	clear, calm.	The brightness of Jupiter made the satellite indistinct.
21 14 59 15	2	Im	Acinpoory.	78 30 15	ditto, windy.	
April 29 12 41 40	1	Im	Pruttegurgh.	79 18 0	ditto, moderate.	
May 2 14 44 57	2	Im	Ditto	79 16 15	ditto. ditto.	
18 10 30 10	1	Im	Ditto	79 18 30	ditto, windy.	
June 3 11 19 21	2	Im	Kankpoor (Mr. Yeld's bungalah).	79 55 0	ditto, moderate.	
1702						
March 23 17 0 31	1	Im	Camp near Alinagar.	76 51 15	ditto. ditto.	The planet was clouded, a few seconds, about the time of immersion.
May 1 15 41 42	1	Im	Denaxy, Sufden Jung's house.	76 42 0	thin clouds, calm.	
3 16 13 43	2	Im	Ditto	76 48 45	clear, moderate.	The satellite is certainly visible till this time; as the sky was not very clear, the immersion may have been some seconds later. As the telescope was shaken by the wind, the emersion was probably a little earlier.
17 13 58 6	1	Im	Ditto	76 48 15	ditto.	
27 14 29 15	3	Em	Ditto	78 2 45	clear, windy.	
28 12 18 41	2	Im	Ditto	76 43 15	ditto, clear.	
June 4 15 55 00	2	Im	Anoopsheher.	77 8 45	ditto. ditto.	
22 10 22 51	2	Im	Ditto	77 48 45	ditto. ditto.	
July 11 10 36 40	1	Im	Erjunpoor.	76 34 45	ditto, moderate.	The observation very distinct; but there is some uncertainty in the time, from an irregularity in the watch this day.
Nov. 13 6 42 30	2	Em	Futtegurgh.	79 49 15	ditto, calm.	
21 7 23 22	1	Em	Ditto	80 2 45	ditto.	
Dec. 14 7 29 12	1	Em	Ditto	79 49 15	ditto.	

It had been losing at the rate of 56 seconds a day, mean time; but between the 4th, and 7 minutes and a quarter, and the 5th, at the same hour, lost 2 minutes 59 seconds, from being wound up five hours later than usual, i. e. at 5 P. M. on the 4th instead of noon. I observed again at a quarter after four P. M. and found the loss, in 9 hours apparent time, to be 40 seconds. Allowing this rate from 4 A. M. to 7 and a quarter, and the loss in that time will be 16 seconds, giving watch flow for apparent time, 2 hours, 18 minutes, 30 seconds, at the time of observation, and this is the quantity here allowed. Planet rather near the horizon.

The Variation of the Compass, observed by the Sun's Azimuth. N.B. Both the Altitudes and Azimuth were taken with the Theodolite.

1792		Place.	A.orP.M	Altitude.	Azimuth.	Variation.	Mean.
Feb.	23	Baad	P	22 39 0	116 2 0E	1 8 0E	
May	1	Oujein	A	11 25 53	78 8 0	0 2 0E	0 19 30W
1796	2	Ditto	A	14 4 45	79 34 0	0 41 0W	
April	9	Futtchgurgh	P	1 20 0	82 20 0	1 37 0E	
	12	Ditto	A	22 30 57	90 19 0		1 42 13 E
				23 20 57	89 52 0	1 47 27E	
				23 54 0	89 33 0		

1796, April 15, at Futtchgurgh; observed the following distances of the Moon from Aldebaran and Spica.

Time by Watch.	Distant Moon & Aldebaran, nearest Limb.	Time by Watch.	Distant Moon & Spica, farthest Limb.
H. M. S.	° ′ ″	H. M. S.	° ′ ″
6 43 22	61 10 51	8 1 58	72 54 30
50 20	13 0	5 10	52 15
57 5	15 15	8 46	51 15
7 3 45	18 0	12 2	49 45
9 5	19 45	15 49	47 30
6 56 43	61 15 15	8 8 45	72 51 3

Also the following Altitudes for rectifying the Watch.

Time by Watch.	Altitude Aldebaran	Time by Watch.	Altitude Spica
7 36 58	24 39 45 doubleangle	7 46 4	64 40 0 doubleangle
		48 33	64 36 30
		51 9	65 34 15

Error of the Sextant 2' 15" subtractive.

Results

Watch slow by Aldebaran
    by Spica

  H. M. S.
  46 49
  42
  46
  47

  46 46

Mean slow for Apparent Time

	Apparent Time.	Apparent Altitude.		True distance: centre Moon & Star.	Longitude.
		Moon.	Star.		
	H. M. S.				
1st set Alde.	7 43 29	78 49 41	21 7 9	61 38 36	79 41 45
2d set Spica	8 55 31	64 20 48	35 54 52	72 14 54	80 7 45

Longitude of Futteghur by mean of both sets 79 54 45

NOTE

Respecting the Insect described in Page 213.

THIS insect is the *Meloë Chihorri* of LINNÆUS. The following extract from a late publication will shew how much the gentlemen of the faculty are indebted to Captain HARDWICKE for having pointed out to them so valuable an addition to their *Materia Medica* in this country.

"I shall only observe, that the Papilio, &c. are
"here extremely common, as is likewise the *Meloë*
"*Cichorii* Lin. towards which Doctor MANNI has en-
"deavoured to direct the attention of his countrymen.
"It remains from *May* to *August*, and especially during
"*June* and *July*, in astonishing quantities, not only upon
"the *cichoreum* but also upon the *cerealis carduus* and
"*cynora cardunculus*. The common people have long
"used the liquor that distils from the insect, when the
"head is torn off. for the purpose of extirpating
"warts; and Mr. CASIMIR SANSO has often employed
"it in lieu of the common blistering drug: but to
"render it more generally useful Doctor MANNI has
"made a variety of experiments, and found that forty-
"five grains of the MELOE, and fifteen grains of *Eu-*
"*phorbium* fermented with flour and common vinegar,
"and well mixed up, made a most excellent blistering
"plaister. The proportions must be increased, or di-
"minished, according to the age, sex and constitution
"of the person, but the above mentioned quantity
"usually produces a proper effect in thirteen or four-
"teen hours. These insects are collected morning
"and evening, and put into a covered vessel, when
"they are kept until they are dead, when they are
"sprinkled with strong vinegar, and exposed to the
"hot sun, until they become perfectly dry; after
                                            "which

"they are put into glass bottles and carefully kept from humidity."

Travels to Naples by CHARLES ULYSSES, of SALIS MORSCHLINS.—*translated from the* GERMAN by ANTHONY AUFRERE, Esq. London, 1795, p. 148.

NOTE

Referring to Page 204 of this Volume.

HAVING lately passed *Benares*. I took that opportunity of again examining the observatory, and ascertained the circle which stands on the elevated terrace to the East (respecting the position of which I formerly spoke with some degree of hesitation) to be situated in a plane parallel to the Equator.

W. HUNTER.

Sept. 28 1797.

CONTENTS

OF THE FIFTH VOLUME.

	Page
I. Historical Remarks on the Coast of Malabar, with some Description of its Inhabitants	1
II. An Account of two Fakeers, with their Portraits	37
III. Enumeration of Indian Classes	53
IV. Some Account of the Sculptures at Mahabalipoorum, usually called the Seven Pagodas	69
V. Account of the Hindustanee Horometry	81
VI. On Indian Weights and Measures	91
VII. On the City of Pegue, and the Temple of Shoemadoo Praw	111
VIII. Description of a Tree called by the Burmas Launzan	123
IX. Specimen of the Language of the People inhabiting the Hills in the Vicinity of Bhaugulpore	127
X. An Account of the Discovery of two Urns in the Vicinity of Benares	131
XI. Account of some ancient Inscriptions	135
XII. Observations on the Alphabetical System of the Language of Awa and Rac'hain	143
XIII. Some Account of the Elastic Gum-vine of Prince of Wales's Island, and of Experiments made on the milky juice which it produces; with hints respecting the useful Purposes to which it may be applied	157
XIV. A Botanical Description the Urceola Elastica or Caout Chouc Vine of Sumatra and Pulo-Penang	167
XV. Some Account of the Astronomical Labours of Jayasinha, Rajah of Ambhere, or Jayanagar	177

Vol. V.   D d   XVI. Descrip-

		Page
XVI.	Defcription of a Species of Meloë an Infect of the 1ft or Coleopterous Order in the Linnean Syftem, found in all Parts of Bengal, Behar, and Oude ; and poffefling all the properties of the Spanifh bliftering Fly or Meloë Veficatorius	213
XVII.	A Comparative Vocabulary of fome of the Languages fpoken in the Burma Empire	225
XVIII.	On the Chronology of the Hindus	241
XIX.	Remarks on the Names of the Cabirian Deities, and on fome Words ufed in the Myfteries of Eleufis	297
XX.	Account of a Pagoda at Perwuttum	303
XXI.	Remarks on the principal Æras and Dates of the Ancient Hindus	315
XXII.	On the Religious Ceremonies of the Hindus and of the Bráhmens efpecially	345
XXIII.	The Rudhirádhyáyă, or Sanguinary Chapter, tranflated from the Calica puran	371
XXIV.	An Account of the Pearl Fifhery in the Gulph of Manar in March and April 1797	391
XXV.	Aftronomical Obfervations made in the upper Provinces of Hinduftan	413

MEMBERS OF THE ASIATIC SOCIETY.

1797.

PATRONS.

The Honourable Sir JOHN SHORE, Baronet, Governor General, &c. &c. &c.

Sir Alured Clarke, K. B. Com. in Chief, &c.
Peter Speke, Efq.
William Cowper, Efq.
} *Members of the Supreme Council.*

PRESIDENT, Sir JOHN SHORE, Baronet.

1ft. Vice Prefident, John Fleming, Efq.

2d. Vice Prefident John Herbert Harrington, Efq.

William Roxburgh, M. D.
James Dinwiddie, LL. D.
Francis Horfley, Efq.
William Coates Blaquiere, Efq.
William Hunter, Efq.
} *Committee of Papers with the Prefident, Vice Prefidents, and Secretary.*

Treafurer, Henry Trail, Efq.

Secretary, Codrington Edmund Carrington, Efq.

Dr. James Anderfon.
David Anderfon, Efq.
Lieut. Anderfon.
Capt. Limington Baillie.
William Baillie, Efq.
Francis Balfour, M. D.
George Hilaro Barlow, Efq.
Stephen Bayard, Efq.
John Bebb, Efq.
Rev. Dr. J. Bell.
John Belli, Efq.
John Bentley, Efq.
Andrew Berry, M. D.
Robert Biddulph, Efq.
Robert Blake, Efq.
Sir Charles Wm. Blunt, Bart.
Lieut. Blunt.
R. H. Boddam, Efq.
Charles Boddam, Efq.
George Boyd, Efq.
John Briftow, Efq.
Ralph Broome, Efq.
Rev. D. Brown.

Francis Buchanan, M. D.
William Burroughs, Efq.
Adam Burt, Efq.
Capt. W. Burton.
Alexander Campbell, M. D.
General John Carnac.
Sir Robert Chambers, Knt.
Charles Chapman, Efq.
George F. Cherry, Efq.
Hon. John Cochrane.
Henry Colebrooke, Efq.
Capt. Robert Colebrooke.
Lieut. Col. John Collins.
Capt. Hiram Cox.
Burrifh Crifp, Efq.
John Crifp, Efq.
Thomas Daniell, Efq.
Samuel Davis, Efq.
William A. Devis, Efq.
John Dickens, Efq.
George Dowdifwell, Efq.
Hon. Jonathan Duncan.
N. B. Edmonftone, Efq.

[428]

John Eliot, Esq.
John Farquhar, Esq.
William Farquharson, Esq.
Nicholas Fontana, Esq.
H. P. Forster, Esq.
Francis Fowke, Esq.
Capt. William Francklin.
Capt. Charles Fraser.
Major Gen. John Fullarton.
John Gilchrist, Esq.
Francis Gladwin, Esq.
J. Goldingham, Esq.
Thomas Graham, Esq.
Charles Grant, Esq.
James Grant, Esq.
Lieut. Col. Christ. Green.
Major Henry Haldane.
Alexander Hamilton, Esq.
James Hare M. D.
Capt. John Hardwicke.
Herbert Harris, Esq.
Warren Hastings, Esq.
Edward Hay, Esq.
Benjamin Heyne, M. D.
W. N. W. Hewett, Esq.
Lieut. J. G. Hoare.
Robert Horne, Esq.
James Howison, Esq.
Capt. Isaac Humphries.
Osias Humphreys, Esq.
Richard Johnson, Esq.
Ralph Irving, Esq.
Sir John Kennaway, Bart.
Richard Kennaway, Esq.
Major William Kirkpatrick.
Lieut. Col. Alex. Kyd.
Anthony Lambert, Esq.
Thomas Law, Esq.
Major Herbert Lloyd.
Capt. Colin Macaulay.
Lieut. Alexander Macdonald.
Capt. Robert Macgregor.
Capt. Colin Mackenzie.
Francis Macnaghten, Esq.
Col. Allen Macpherson.
Sir Charles Ware Malet, Bart.
William Marsden, Esq.

Bartholomew Marsh, Esq.
Charles Fuller Martyn, Esq.
G. Mercer ————, Esq.
Nathaniel Middleton, Esq.
Edmund Morris, Esq.
Sir John Murray, Bart.
Gore Ousley, Esq.
Lieut. Col. William Palmer.
John David Paterson, Esq.
George Perry, Esq.
John Rawlins, Esq.
Capt. David Richardson.
Henry Richardson, Esq.
Lieut. Col. R. E. Roberts.
James Robertson, M. D.
Capt. G. Robertson.
Charles Rothman, Esq.
Hon. Mr. Justice Royds.
Alexander Russel, Esq.
Robert Saunders, Esq.
Lieut. Col. William Scott.
Major John Scott.
Helenus Scott, M. D.
Lieut. Col. Richard Scott.
John Shoolbred, Esq.
Sir Robert Sloper, K. B.
Courtney Smith, Esq.
James Stuart, Esq.
Capt. Michael Symes.
John Taylor, Esq.
Isaac Titsingh, Esq.
Henry St. George Tucker, Esq.
Capt. Sam. Turner.
John Peter Wade, Esq.
Capt. Francis Wilford.
Charles, Wilkins, Esq.
John Lloyd Williams, Esq.
John Zoffany, Esq.

HONORARY MEMBERS.

M. Carpentier de Cossigny.
M. Le Gentil.
Rev. Dr. John.
M. Henry J. Le Beck.
Rev. Thomas Maurice.
M. Volney.

Directions to the Binder for Placing the Plates, &c.

To face Page

Portrait of Praun Poory Oordhbahu - 37

Portrait of Purrum Soatuntre Purkafanund Brehmchary - - - - - 49

Hindooſtance Horal Diagram - - 81

Cancel the Leaves of White Paper after Pages 132 and 140, and inſert Pages of Wood Cuts 133 and 141, (Octavo Edit.)

Two Plates of the Alphabetical Syſtem of the Language of Awa and Rac'hain 143

Urceola Elaſtica - - - - 167

Broadſide Genealogical Table - - 241

The Half Sheet Sig. L with a Star to come before the whole Sheet Sig. L.

The Pages 133 and 141 Wood Cuts (in the the Quarto Edition) muſt be folded in, to prevent their Work being cut into.

In Page 215 mention is made of a Drawing accompanying the Deſcription of the Meloë Inſect, to which References are made in Page 217; but there does not appear to have been any Plate engraved from the Drawing, as there is none in the Calcutta Edition, from which this was Printed.

www.ingramcontent.com/pod-product-compliance
Lightning Source LLC
Chambersburg PA
CBHW031959300426
44117CB00008B/833